Pastor

6 - 14 - 08

Errors of Pretribulation
RAPTURE THEORY

Exposing False Teachings Concerning the Second Coming

Errors of Pretribulation
RAPTURE THEORY

Exposing False Teachings Concerning the Second Coming

PASTOR FELTON SHOULTS

ACW Press
Eugene, Oregon 97405

Scripture quotations are taken from the King James Version of the Bible.

Errors of Pretribulation Rapture Theory
Copyright ©2003 Felton Shoults
All rights reserved

Cover Design by Alpha Advertising
Interior design by Pine Hill Graphics

Packaged by ACW Press
85334 Lorane Hwy
Eugene, Oregon 97405
www.acwpress.com
The views expressed or implied in this work do not necessarily reflect those of ACW Press.
Ultimate design, content, and editorial accuracy of this work is the responsibility of the
author(s).

Library of Congress Cataloging-in-Publication Data
(Provided by Quality Books Inc.)

Shoults, Felton.
    Errors of pretribulation rapture theory : exposing
false prophecies concerning the second coming / Felton
Shoults.
    p. cm.
    Includes bibliographical references.
    ISBN 1-932124-10-1

    1. Rapture (Christian eschatology) I. Title.

BT887.S56 2003   236'.9
                    QBI03-200218

Printed in the United States of America.

Table of Contents

Author's Preface

This book has taken many hours of study, research, prayer, and work. There is now a peace and joy in the hope that this work will be used in bringing the Church into unity concerning the second advent, and related doctrines.

My great concern was to write truth backed up by historical and biblical truths in order to help college professors, pastors, evangelists, teachers, and laymen fulfill the five-fold ministry in Ephesians 4:11-16. It is my firm conviction that this work is needed to dispel false doctrine concerning the pretribulation rapture theory and related doctrines.

I wish I could have exposed errors without naming anyone, but it would be close to impossible to make corrections without naming the source of error. I do not believe any of the dispensationalists I name in this book set out to deceive, but they let their own interpretation of dispensations take them away from what the Bible teaches concerning the second advent. I pray that this book will give enough light on the subject that the Church can begin to speak the same thing as Paul advised, *Now I beseech you, brethren, by the name of our Lord Jesus Christ, that ye all speak the same thing, and that there be no division among you; but that ye be perfectly joined toether in the same mind and in the same judgment* (I Corinthians 1:10).

God's people are going to need truth and faith in order to keep themselves strong in the faith as we see the world enter the most troublesome time in the history of man.

I want to thank family and friends who prayed for me while working on the book, and also those who proofread. I also want to thank my friends who helped me out of many hair-pulling episodes on the computer.

Biblical and Historical Solutions for Error

First of all I want to thank God for the grace that He has given me through our Lord Jesus Christ. I realize it is the grace of God that has allowed me to write this book about the coming of the Lord. It is complex, sorting out all the different teachings and doctrines, but when we take away all the doctrines of men, the truth is so simple to see. I could not have separated truth from error as I have done in this book without God's help, but it is still subject to the Word and holy men of God. It is the work of the Holy Spirit that brings to our hearts and minds what is desired by the Holy Spirit. I am humbled as I think of what Paul wrote to the Corinthian church concerning our calling, and I realize our calling is far above our capabilities: *For ye see your calling, brethren, how that not many wise men after the flesh, not many mighty, not many noble, are called: 27 But God hath chosen the foolish things of the world to confound the wise; and God hath chosen the weak things of the world to confound the things which are mighty; 28 And base things of the world, and things which are despised, hath God chosen, yea, and things which are not, to bring to nought things that are: 29 That no flesh should glory in his presence* (I Corinthians 1:26-29).

God's people have strayed a long way from what Jesus, the apostles, and our forefathers believed and taught concerning the time element of the rapture of the Church. This book is not to bring more division in doctrine concerning the Lord's coming, but to bring about unity by truth into the body of Christ after a critical examination. I pray this book will bring our churches, colleges, evangelists, pastors, teachers, and laymen back to a true theology concerning the Lord's coming.

This book will show the issue is not whether the pretribulation rapture theory was taught before John Darby began to systemize dispensationalism and teach a pretribulation rapture of the Church in 1830, but will show how the pretribulation rapture theory can only survive by dispensationalism, which John Darby and Dr. C. I. Scofield developed.

This book attacks the very heart of the pretribulation rapture theory. It shows where the error was made, and gives scriptural proof of correction. It will show what Jesus taught about His second coming, and how His teachings are for the Church. The Church is built upon the foundation of the apostles and prophets with Jesus Christ Himself being the chief cornerstone. Dispensationalists separated from the Church the very foundation of pure doctrine concerning the coming of the Lord by declaring that the Law extends through the Gospels to the second chapter of Acts, and saying the Gospels do not apply to the Church. Through this teaching the pretribulation rapture was birthed. I will expose this great error in theology in which dispensationalists say that what Jesus taught in the Gospels about His coming applies to the Jew only, and not the Church. Paul let us know that through this teaching the very foundation of the Church was being destroyed (Ephesians 2:18-20). I will show that the prophets and Jesus did not teach a different coming of the Lord than Paul taught in the epistles.

This book provides the key to unlock the door to error of the pretribulation rapture theory. You will be able to look into every aspect of the error dispensationalists made that lead to the pretribulation rapture. You will be able to see when and why the authors of the pretribulation rapture theory made void the Gospels for the Church. When God's people understand the Gospels are for the Church, it opens to them a new enlightenment that makes the words of Jesus in the Gospels a personal message. The Gospels are the very foundation of the Church and give us the time element of the Lord's coming. When Jesus talks about His coming in Matthew 24, He is not talking to the Jews only, but also to the Church. I will show how the pretribulation rapture theory was developed, and will prove it to be a false teaching.

I believe this book will breathe new life into the Church because some important doctrines have been put aside. It will show why the kingdom of heaven, the kingdom of God, and the kingdom of Israel were given a wrong interpretation. It will also show why the interpretation of these three kingdoms was made to be in error because of dispensational teachings. This book will be a springboard for God's people to bring these important doctrines back with purity into the Church.

Books dealing with the pretribulation rapture theory are bestsellers in the Christian realm. Books such as *Left Behind, Apocalypse, Beginning of the End,* and many others on Revelation and the end time are written by pretribulationists. Most of these books tell Christians what is going to happen in the tribulation period after the Church is raptured. The time will come when events unfold that Christians were taught would happen only after the rapture, and will leave them disillusioned, skeptical about God, their faith, and the Bible. The correction must be made before those days come because God's people can deal with truth better than deception.

A number of books have been written concerning the untruths of the pretribulation rapture theory, but for the most part, very few readers have changed their belief concerning the error. Either those who could have brought change did not read the books, or else no one has yet written a book that reveals and lays bare the errors of the pretribulation rapture theory. This book shows how the pretribulation rapture could only ride on the back of dispensational teachings that discounted the Gospels and part of the Revelation for the Church. By God's grace, this book will expose the untruths of this theory that has deceived the Body of Christ for many years. I believe God's people will see how the founders of the pretribulation rapture theory built a doctrine upon sand that has no foundation when tried by the Word.

Imagine the pretribulation rapture theory being brought to trial by two plaintiffs—the first plaintiffs being Christian Jews who have grown weary of preachers and teachers telling the whole world that the Jewish people will suffer the wrath of God during the tribulation period. God said a remnant will be grafted into the Body of Christ before the rapture of the Church. The second plaintiff would be those Christians who have become heartsick over those who continue to spread the error of a pretribulation rapture taking place in Revelation 4:1. The words of the prophets, Jesus, Paul, and John will bring condemning evidence of error, and leave pretribulationists arguing their defense with the false doctrine of dispensationalism, which separated the Gospels and part of Revelation from the Church. Pretribulationists would be found guilty of teaching false doctrine, built on theory and not fact.

This book will act as the prosecuting attorney. It will bring evidence against this terrible doctrine that is based on a theory of theology. The Word of God will be used as a defense against those who made proselytes by unfounded doctrines of dispensationalism. I believe the trial Judge (the Word) will pronounce a death sentence to this false doctrine of a pretribulation rapture. This book will examine how this doctrine had its beginning, and distinguishes between the word *tribulation* and the word *wrath*. This book answers questions such as, "Are the Gospels for the Jew, or are they for the Church also?"

I developed a time-line chart to insert at the end of the chapters, "The Seventy Weeks of Daniel," and "Nineteen Hundred Years of Church History Restored." These time lines show the Old Covenant vanishing away, and how the new dispensation begins with Jesus and the Gospels. It will show the Church age and the gap between the week sixty-nine and seventy of Daniel. It shows God's plan for the New Jerusalem, and the beginning of eternity. Some Bible charts have masterful design, but offer little proof of the time element of events, especially the Lord's coming. I will offer less design, but more scriptural proof of last day events and bring this chart into conformity with the Word of God.

One reason people do not see truth is because it is natural for people to accept what their college or church has taught them. Once a person believes a certain doctrine, it is hard to change that person's belief. I ask pretribulationists to search this book and compare it with Scripture, just as the early church did. In the book of Acts they searched the Word daily to see if what they were taught was true. If God's people would do the same, there would not be so many denominations or false doctrines. You will see how the same spirit of the founders of the pretribulation rapture has been passed on to our colleges and churches.

Most pretribulationists preach and teach the pretribulation rapture theory because they believe their doctrine is true. For the most part, pretribulationists do not know all facts concerning the theory's origin, but this book will bring to light the errors; therefore they will be without excuse after reading this book. I believe every sincere Christian will admit error, as Paul did before he came to truth; therefore God will show mercy, because they do it ignorantly: *Who was before a blasphemer, and a persecutor, and injurious: but I obtained mercy, because I did it ignorantly in unbelief* (I Timothy 1:13).

This book is long overdue for the Church. I believe it will breathe a new fervency in preaching the Gospels, the Epistles, and the book of Revelation. Think of all the books that have been written and all the messages that have been preached in the last 170 years that have been in error concerning the pretribulation rapture of the Church. This has been to no avail in giving the Church truth. Hosea said it best: *My people are destroyed for lack of knowledge: because thou hast rejected knowledge, I will also reject thee, that thou shalt be no priest to me: seeing thou hast forgotten the law of thy God, I will also forget thy children* (Hosea 4:6).

This generation more than any other generation should see the mistakes that have been made in doctrine, the coming of the Lord, and prophecy because this is the generation that will see the fulfillment of all things. It will be false teaching and preaching in these last days that will lead to the apostasy and spiritual famine that is to come.

If I am correct, and I believe that I am, and if truths which I present in this book do not bring about a change to these most important doctrines, God help us! The future will hold many disappointments because pretribulationists rejected great truths which God gave to the Church in the Gospels.

Since I started writing this book, the Y2K scare has come and gone, along with the scare which self-proclaimed prophets frightened millions throughout the world with their messages of disaster and the apocalyptic Second Coming. On September 11, 2001 we saw terrorists attack the twin towers of the World Trade Center and the Pentagon. The twin towers collapsed before the eyes of millions, and the Pentagon was badly damaged. This horrific tragedy will be burned into the minds of people forever. America can no longer sit in her pride and say, "God will never let us suffer the wrath of man." These events are only a small portion of those prophesied in Matthew 24:7-14 and I Timothy 3:1-5. We will see many pretribulation prophesies fail in these last days, and persecutions and tribulations will increase. Let sound doctrine be restored to the Church in the beginning of this twenty-first century.

You may disagree with some point of doctrine in this book or my phraseology, but the one area in which we should not disagree is the error made by John Darby and Dr. C. I. Scofield concerning the pretribulation rapture. If you disagree in some point, check all the evidence I have given before making final judgment. Remember, the main focus of this book is to expose the great error of the pretribulation rapture theory. We are standing on the threshold of end time prophecy being fulfilled. The Church will need truth, not theory. There will be pretribulationists who will say before they read the book, "You can go through the tribulation period if you want too, but I am not." This book is not about the question of whether or not we want to go through the tribulation period—it is a question of what the Bible teaches.

I wrote over one hundred pages on the seven seals and the seven trumpet judgments. I realized the book would be too lengthy to cover all of Revelation, and that the errors of the pretribulation rapture theory need to be exposed and corrected first. God's people should see how important the Gospels and all the book of Revelation are to the Church. The Church should know how the seven seals and the seventh trumpet judgments will affect the Church, and need to be in the light concerning the coming of the Lord (I Thessalonians 5:4-6).

To the best of my ability, I have not added or taken anything away from the Bible. I desire truth, and I pray this book will be a blessing to the Church. My whole desire is to bring God's people back to truth concerning the coming of the Lord and connected doctrines. I have tried to back up everything by the Word. Now it's time for God's people to try my spirit by the Word, and see if my spirit is in line with God's Spirit and the Word.

All Scriptures in this book are the King James Version, and all headings are followed by supporting Scriptures. They show and provide to the reader what Scriptures are used to form every doctrine. I not only give my words, but I give the Word of God to form the base of every doctrine. I pray you will see the difference between this book and all else you have read and heard concerning the posttribulation rapture and coming of the Lord. I challenge each of you who believe in a pretribulation rapture of the Church to read every page of this book, and see it is not a book about the philosophies of men.

Origin of Pretribulation Rapture Errors

I was in my twenties when I began to see some of the errors made concerning the coming of the Lord and the pretribulation rapture of the Church. I listened to pretribulationists teach and preach the pretribulation rapture of the Church, but did not see them lay a foundation on which to build their doctrine. I began to see that dispensationalists had no foundation in what Jesus said in the Gospels about the rapture of the Church, because they believed what Jesus said in the Gospels was for the Jew only. Over forty years have passed since those early days, and I now realize Jesus always used a foundation of the Old Testament for His ministry recorded in the Gospels. I believe any doctrine taught today without a foundation built on what Jesus taught in the Gospels is a false doctrine, and I will put the pretribulation rapture theory at the top of the list.

Jesus taught His disciples how to carry on the work which He commanded them. This command was to go to the Gentile as well as the Jew: *Go ye therefore, and teach all nations, baptizing them in the name of the Father, and of the Son, and of the Holy Ghost: 20 Teaching them to observe all things whatsoever I have commanded you: and, lo, I am with you alway, even unto the end of the world. Amen* (Matthew 28:19-20). The disciples had been under the teaching of Jesus so they would be able to carry on the ministry after His departure. The Gospels, Epistles, and Revelation had not yet been given, therefore all they had was the Old Testament, the teachings of Jesus, and their witness to the death, burial, and resurrection of the Lord. This was all the early Church had until the rest of the New Testament was given. This early teaching was called the apostles' doctrine in Acts 2:42, 28:23. The apostles were steadfast in teaching the people after Pentecost. This early teaching was pure in the early Church concerning the coming of the Lord. There was no teaching of the postmilleniumism, pretribulation, or midtribulation coming of the Lord. The purity of the posttribulation coming of the Lord was the same message that Jesus had preached in Matthew 24, and had taught them. Jesus warned them that false Christs and false prophets would arise, and fool the very elect if it were possible. It did not take long for this prophecy to become a reality. After Paul had established the church at Thessalonica, false teachers came to corrupt the doctrine concerning the coming of the Lord.

Thessalonians was probably the first epistle Paul wrote to the churches. Paul did not write to establish a new doctrine concerning a pretribulation rapture theory as many teach today. Paul's letter did not reveal anything different from what Jesus had already taught the disciples in the Gospels. The second letter Paul wrote proves that he preached the same message that Jesus had preached. Paul said in his second letter that Jesus would not return until there comes a falling away first and the man of sin is revealed. Paul's letter was a letter to correct false teaching in the church, not to establish a new doctrine.

John wrote to the seven churches of Asia in approximately A.D. 95. False teachings and corruption of doctrine had already taken root in these churches from the time of their inception, continuing until the time John wrote to them. John had a message to them from the Lord: *As many as I love. I rebuke and chasten: be zealous therefore, and repent* (Revelation 3:19). It's time today's Church listens to what John said. If there is no repentance and correction, judgment will follow. I write this book to ask our churches and our pastors to correct the errors that have infiltrated most Protestant, denominational, and independent churches concerning the coming of the Lord.

Before the pretribulation rapture theory was birthed, there were only two main teachings concerning the coming of the Lord: postmillennialism and premillennialism. Philip Schaff tells us in his *Religious Encyclopaedia* that premillennialism appeared shortly after the reformation of the sixteenth century and this belief was held by most Protestants after the Reformation when they separated themselves from the Catholic Church. The same message that Jesus and the early Church preached was being preached again. (Premillennialists believed Jesus would come before the millennium, but before the wrath of God.) Most of the great saints of our past held this view, as well as most of those who were in the time of the great revivals. Schaff points out how the Jesuit Lucanza and Pere Lambert changed from the view of postmillennialism to the pretribulation rapture theory in the early 1800s when Lucanza wrote a book that supported the creation of the pretribulation rapture theory. Schaff also points out how some followers of Edward Irving in Scotland and many disciples of Mr. W. Miller in America were led astray by Irving and his calculation of the time of the second advent. It was in those days that the pretribulation rapture took hold.

Amillennialism is a doctrine similar to postmillennialism. It shows no distinction between the rapture and the second coming, holding that the kingdom is present in the Church age and precedes the second coming of Christ. Amillennialists, look for the Church to conquer the world and offer up the kingdom to Christ. Amillennialism and postmillenialism are taught in Catholic doctrine, but others believe that when the Jews rejected Jesus as their Messiah, God established the Church, and the Church is the spiritual Israel. They believe the nation of Israel, which was founded in 1948, is just another nation in the world and has no bearing on prophecy in these last days. Some believe that most of Revelation has already been fulfilled in the ancient past. With such a wide array of beliefs today, it is impossible to go into every detail. I do know that God's people should seek for truth in these last days.

Pre-Wrath is yet another belief concerning the rapture of the Church. This name was coined by Marvin Rosenthal and Robert Van Kampen. Both have written books about the Pre-Wrath rapture question. They believe the rapture takes place between the sixth and seventh seals, and the same day the rapture takes place, the wrath of God begins. They believe that the 144,000 of the children of Israel are not of the Church, but are saved and sealed after the rapture for their protection against the wrath of God which is to soon follow.

I do not hold to the Pre-Wrath view about the rapture of the Church taking place in the sixth seal. There is not one word about the rapture and resurrection occurring in that portion of Scripture. The great multitude of saints that stand before the throne in Revelation 7:9 are the saints who come out of great tribulation because of the persecution of the antichrist (Rev. 7:14). The saints standing before the throne with white robes in Revelation 7:9 do not have resurrected bodies any more than the saints who are standing before the throne in white robes in Revelation 4:4, or the saints in white robes who were told to rest a little season until their fellow servants and brethren should be killed as they were (Rev. 6:11). Paul implies that the saints who die in the Lord will be given a temporary body and clothing until their resurrection (II Cor 5:1-9). The saints who had died and did not defile their garments in the church of Sardis were presently walking with the Lord in white when the Lord gave the Revelation to John; (Rev. 3:4-5). These Scriptures let us know that all saints who have died in Christ are dressed in white and are before the throne of God, waiting to come back with the Lord to receive their resurrected bodies. The 144,000 of Israel who are sealed in the seventh chapter of Revelation are a remnant of Israel grafted back into the body of Christ. They are part of the Church because the rapture takes place at the last trumpet in Revelation 11:15, and the 144,000 are standing before the throne of the Lord without fault in the heavenly Mount Zion (Rev. 14:1-5). If the 144,000 were not of the church and missed the rapture, how could they appear in heaven before the throne of God? I do not believe the rapture takes place in the sixth seal.

The tribulation period, and Daniel's week 70 has not been fulfilled as some preterists teach (Daniel 9:27). The rapture and resurrection can only take place in Daniel's week 70 (Daniel 12:1-13). God gives a dividing line between the fall of Jerusalem in A.D. 70 and the Lord's coming again in Matthew 24:13-44, Mark 13:14-37, Luke 21:25-36. This book will show that Daniel's week 70, and the tribulation period are yet to be fulfilled.

For the most part, professing Evangelical and Fundamental Christians are either pretribulationist or posttribulationist, with Pre-Wrath and amillennialism making some inroads. Pretribulationists believe the Lord will come for the rapture of the Church before the tribulation period begins, based primarily upon the dispensational teaching of John Darby and later C. I. Scofield. Most Fundamentalists and Evangelicals have gradually accepted this theory. Posttribulationists of today base their doctrine on the words of Jesus in the Gospels, and on II Thessalonians 2:1-5, that there will come a falling away first and the man of sin will be revealed before the Lord will come. For the most part the old premillennialists and the posttribulationists of today are of the same doctrine; only the terms have changed since the pretribulation rapture theory was birthed. Posttribulationists differ much from the pretribulationists, as you will see in this book.

I believe in a posttribulation coming of the Lord, and believe that the Lord will come at the end of the tribulation period to rapture the Church as taught in Matthew 24:29-31 and II Thessalonians 2:1-3. But before God pours out His wrath upon the unbelieving world. I believe this is what Jesus and the apostles taught the Church.

The pretribulation rapture theory was all I knew in my early years of serving the Lord. It has been over forty years since I first suspected something was wrong with the pretribulation rapture theory. In those passing years, I heard pretribulationists preach and teach a doctrine I felt was in error. I did not know a church or pastor who taught a post-tribulation rapture of the Church; therefore, I sought diligently for truth by prayer and searching the Word because I did not want to mislead myself, or anyone else, in a false doctrine. I now feel convinced that I am making a correct interpretation of the Word of God. After searching the Bible, Bible encyclopedias, and books, I have come to the conclusion that a great error has been made with the pretribulation rapture theory. By God's grace, I will untangle the root cause of such a deceiving and untrue doctrine.

God's people need to know how a split theory of the coming of Christ originated. This theory states that the rapture of the church is to take place secretly before the tribulation period, and then at the end of the tribulation, the Lord will come back with his saints, called the Revelation of Christ, when every eye will see him. The teaching of a pretribulation rapture in church creeds or writers is seldom found before the 1800s. J. N. Darby developed dispensationalism, and accepted a futurist belief for the interpretation of Revelation. This approach allowed the pretribulation rapture theory to be accepted by many.

Revelation: Four Views, edited by Steve Gregg gives four interpretations and how they tie in with what is taught today: "A preterist is one who believes that most of the prophecies of the Apocalypse have been fulfilled in the past. The historist (or presentist) considers the events of the Revelation are now in the process of fulfillment, while the futurist believes that the bulk of book refers to the events to come. The idealist (herein labeled the spiritual approach) views the Revelation as a great drama involving transcendent truths such as the conflict between right-eousness and unrighteousness or the victory over Satan."

After the Reformation most Reformers were historists, who believed the "beast" was the papacy. The futurist view was developed to counteract the Reformer's view concerning the papacy. Greg gives this account:

"Some critics object to futurism on the basis of its ori-gins. Francisco Ribeira, a Spanish Jesuit, is known to have originated this approach to Revelation in 1585 for the pur-pose of refuting the historicist view, and the Reformers' insistence that the 'beast' was the papacy. Ribeira taught that the 'Antichrist' had not yet come and would be an indi-vidual arising 'in the last days.' Protestants rejected this view for over 200 years, but it was finally introduced in Protestant circles by Samuel Maitland in 1827 and popular-ized in the works of J. N. Darby, the founder of dispensa-tionalism, beginning in 1830. Protestant interpreters sometimes still look upon this approach with suspicion because of these roots."

We know that the "Antichrist" has not appeared, but we should not replace one wrong with another error of dispensationalism and the pretribulation rapture theory.

He continues with the development of dispensationalism:

"Until the nineteenth century most premillennialists used the historicist method of interpretation, while today the usual premillennial emphasis is futurist. The historist movement was largely replaced in the nineteenth century through the development of dispensationalism. John Nelson Darby, an early Plymouth Brethren leader, articulated the dispensationalists understanding of prophesy, and his ideas became popular in the English-speaking world."

Darby became a futurist who believed that the rapture takes place in Revelation 4:1, and from that point in Revelation until the beginning of the millennium is fulfilled in seven years. Gregg tells about the rise of the futurist movement, and how Darby incorporated the futurist belief into his dispensational theology:

> "For approximately two centuries, Protestants had regarded *futurism* as a product of the papacy's self-defense against the claims of the Reformers. Non-Catholics had generally shunned it, though a form of futurism was adopted by the Fifth Monarchy Men in the seventeenth century. Their excesses brought it into dispute, but it was renewed in the nineteenth century by the early teachings of the Plymouth Brethren and by the Bible Conference movement in the nineteenth and twentieth centuries. The official entrance of the *Futurist* approach to Revelation into Protestant circles came through Samuel R. Maitland, librarian to the archbishop of Canterbury, around 1827. The Plymouth Brethren leader, John Nelson Darby, then incorporated it into his dispensational theology, for which he is most remembered."

Greg gave the account of the futurists' origin, and how Darby's teaching ties in with it, and now in this twenty-first century, the futurist approach to Revelation has become the dominant teaching. I believe this came about because truths, which I make known in this book about dispensationalism and the birth of the pretribulation rapture, were not made known to God's people.

I show how Scofield ties into the doctrines that the Brethren and Darby taught, and how dispensationalism and the pretribulation rapture got into our colleges and churches. David Dunlap wrote an article that appeared in *Uplook* magazine. He gives a good description of Scofield from his birth to the printing of the Scofield Reference Bible in his article, "Origins of the Scofield Bible." His sources of information came from Arno C Gaebelein, *The History of the Scofield Bible*, Living Words Foundation, WA, 1991; Sea Cliff Gospel Chapel 1889-1989, *A Century of Proclaming God's Word*, Sea Cliff, NY, 1989. Scofield was born on August 19, 1843. He served in the Civil War as a Confederate soldier. After the war, he studied law in St. Louis, and later he was admitted to the Kansas bar. He was converted to Christ in 1879 by Thomas McPheeters, and not long after his conversion, made acquaintance with James H. Brookes. It was Brookes who helped him study the Bible, and introduced him to dispensational teaching. Scofield became a popular speaker while serving in a Congregational Church in Dallas, TX.

There are other men who greatly influenced Scofield: Arno C. Gaebelein gave much encouragement in his work, along with Alwyn Ball, Jr., John T. Pirie, and Francis E. Fitch, who organized the Sea Cliff Bible Conference in Sea Cliff, NY. These men belonged to Brethren assemblies, and played a big part in the publishing of the Scofield Reference Bible. Fitch owned a printing company and was the publisher of the Scofield Bible Course in its first years. Pirie, and Ball financially supported Scofield's work. There were other Bible conferences held at Parie Green between 1901 to 1906, where Richard Hill, John Hill, Arno Gaebelein, C. I. Scofield, and William Isaac were conference speakers, and it was in Scofield's home where the Sea Cliff assembly began.

In the introduction of his Scofield Reference Bible, Scofield made notes which laid the groundwork for a division to be made between what Jesus said in the Gospels about His coming, and what Paul said in the Epistles. Scofield states:

> "The Acts of the Apostles record the descent of the
> Holy Spirit, and the beginning of a new thing in human his-
> tory, the Church. The division of the race now becomes
> threefold—the Jew, the Gentile, and the Church of God.
> Just as Israel is in the foreground from the call of Abram to
> the resurrection of Christ, so now the Church fills the scene
> from the second chapter of Acts to the fourth chapter of
> the Revelation."

This paragraph brought about the great distinction between the Gospels and the Epistles, between what Jesus said in the Gospels about

His coming, and what Paul said in the Epistles. Dispensationalists claim what Jesus taught about His coming in the Gospels was for the Jew only, and will take place at the end of the tribulation period, and believe what Paul taught in the Epistles about the Church rapture takes place before the tribulation begins. Scofield said in his notes that the mission of Jesus was primarily for the Jews, and the doctrines of grace are to be sought in the Epistles, not in the Gospels. He went on to state that much in the Gospels belongs in strictness of interpretation to the Jews or the kingdom.

This book shows that the Gospels are for the Church, as well as for the Jew, and that Jesus did not postpone the kingdom of heaven, nor the kingdom of Israel. Dispensationalists believe that the first advent of Jesus offered an earthly kingdom to the Jews, but when they rejected Jesus and his kingdom, Plan B went into effect. It was then Jesus went to the cross and initiated the dispensation of grace and the Church age. They believe that the Church and the dispensation of grace started in Acts 2, and will end with the rapture of the Church in Revelation 4:1. This book will show there was never a Plan B in the mind of God.

Jesus never offered the Jews an earthly kingdom in the first advent, but offered them a New Covenant of Salvation, which would be sealed by his own blood, as a Lamb slain before the foundation of the world. I will show that salvation for the Jew is no different than salvation for the Gentiles; both are by faith. The book of Hebrews makes this plain. By one offering Jesus died for all, and by one offering He perfected forever those who are sanctified. The covenant of salvation has already been given to both Jew and Gentile, and both have a responsibility to the Lord under this New Covenant, (Hebrews 10:1-25). Before Jesus ever started His ministry, John the Baptist had already told the Jewish nation what they must do in order for God to raise up children unto Abraham. Some believed and became the first members of the New Covenant and the Church, but some of the Pharisees and Sadducees rejected his message in unbelief and were hewn down: *Then went out to him Jerusalem, and all Judaea, and all the region round about Jordan, 6 And were baptized of him in Jordan, confessing their sins. 7 But when he saw many of the Pharisees and Sadducees come to his baptism, he said unto them, O generation of vipers, who hath warned you to flee from the wrath to come? 8 Bring forth therefore fruits meet for repentance: 9 And think not to say within yourselves, We have Abraham to our father: for I say unto you, that God is able of these stones to raise up children unto Abraham. 10 And now also the ax is laid unto the root of the trees: therefore every tree which bringeth not forth good fruit is hewn down, and cast into the fire* (Matthew 3:5-10).

God has one eternal purpose for both Jew and Gentile—that both will be made one in Christ (Eph. 2:11-16). There will be one fold, and one shepherd (John 10:16). Jesus must fulfill this because the Law makes nothing perfect (Heb. 7:19). Jesus is surety of a better Testament (Heb. 7:22). The promise God made to Abraham in Genesis 22:17-18, is fulfilled in Christ (Gal. 3:6-9; Heb. 11:8-19). The Law was just a shadow of the good things to come (Heb. 10:1).

Some pretribulation rapture writers tell their readers that the Epistles teach a pretribulation rapture of the Church. They also say that the early Church writers wrote about the imminent return of Christ and a pretribulation rapture of the Church. I have seen no early Church writings from which modern-day pretribulationists could have gotten their doctrine. I gave how others influenced Darby in the formation of dispensationalism and the pretribulation rapture theory, and I believe the pretribulation rapture for the most part is the direct result of the theology that was developed, systematized, and promoted by Darby and then Scofield. Darby and Scofield for the most part are responsible for the pretribulation rapture theory known today. The survival of the pretribulation rapture theory lies at the feet of dispensational teachings that arose out of the early 1800s. Men like Pierre Poiret, John Edwards, Isaac Watts, and others may have had a form of dispensational teaching, but it was Darby and the Plymouth Brethren that systemized dispensationalism and promoted it into a well-established doctrine.

Dispensational Teaching

I began to see the main problem with the pretribulation rapture theory—it was buried in dispensationalism. God's people must understand the meaning of terms that lay buried in these doctrines when the pretribulation rapture theory was birthed. Most Christians today that believe in the pretribulation rapture theory have no idea of all the ramifications of dispensationalism established by Darby and then Dr. Scofield. I believe when you finish this book you will be able to discuss the subject objectively with anyone.

Many pastors and Christians have no idea how pretribulation rapture started. Many think that pretribulation rapture has always been true church doctrine concerning the second advent. They began to read into the Word what they had been taught. There is not one word in the Bible concerning a pretribulation rapture for the Church. As you will read this book concerning the errors of pretribulation rapture, you will gain a good understanding of how the Church has been deceived.

I have already given how Scofield was converted, and how the Plymouth Brethren influenced his doctrinal beliefs concerning dispensationalism and the pretribulation rapture of the Church, which he believed would take place before the tribulation. He then developed his own style of dispensationalism, and put the very foundation of the pretribulation rapture theory in his notes in the Scofield Reference Bible. On page VI he states, "Just as Israel is in the foreground from the call of

Abram to the resurrection of Christ, so now the Church fills the scene from the second chapter of Acts to the fourth chapter of Revelation."

Scofield discounted the Gospels, first chapter of Acts, and the chapters following the third chapter of Revelation for the Church. He said the Gospels and the chapters after Revelation 4:1 were for the Jew only, because they were under the dispensation of the Law and not under the dispensation of grace. Countless numbers of Scofield's teachings were printed along with the Scofield Reference Bible. Even today the Scofield Reference Bible is still a big-seller. He has influenced theology in America more than any other man concerning dispensational teaching and the pretribulation rapture theory. Theologians, professors, pastors, and layman incorporated many of his teachings into their doctrines, especially the pretribulation rapture of the Church. He put Jesus and His ministry under the dispensation of Law. Jesus was born under the Law, but his life and ministry were not an extension of the Law.

Most college professors, church pastors, evangelists, and laymen who believe in the pretribulation rapture theory have overlooked one of the most important points concerning dispensationalism by putting the Gospels under the dispensation of the Law. This is the beginning of their whole problem. If there was ever a dividing line of a new dispensation, it would be the ministry of Jesus in the Gospels. Jesus was born under the Law, but His ministry was to choose twelve disciples to carry on the work that He started. Luke let it be known that the law and the prophets were until John: since that time the kingdom of God is preached (Luke 16:16). Luke let it be known that when Jesus began to preach, a new dispensation had begun of the kingdom of God. He let it be known that the kingdom of God is within the believer: *And when he was demanded of the Pharisees, when the kingdom of God should come, he answered them and said, The kingdom of God cometh not with observation: 21 Neither shall they say, Lo here! or, lo there! for, behold, the kingdom of God is within you* (Luke 17:20-21). John made it plain that Jesus was the beginning of a new dispensation of grace and truth, not Law: *For the law was given by Moses, but grace and truth came by Jesus Christ* (John 1:17). This new dispensation takes the Gospels out from the dispensation of Law, and puts them under a new beginning of grace and truth by Jesus Christ. He gives salvation to all mankind, both Jew and Gentile: *But as many as received him, to them gave he power to become the sons of God, even to them that believe on his name* (John 1:12). This makes what Jesus taught in the Gospels about salvation and His coming the same doctrine as what Paul taught in the Epistles.

If dispensationalists could give just one scriptural proof that the Gospels are not for the Church, and of the rapture taking place in Revelation 4:1, it would give some credence to their doctrine, but there is none. Their whole doctrine is built on the theology of dispensationalism. When you tear this away, there is not one Scripture they can give that would support a pretribulation rapture of the Church. I give Scripture after Scripture and proof after proof in this book that Jesus tells in the Gospels about the only rapture, and His coming again. There is no split coming of Jesus. God gave us his HOLY INSPIRED WORD for our doctrine, to reprove, and it corrects us of error. By God's grace his Holy WORD will bring the correction: *All scripture is given by inspiration of God, and is profitable for doctrine, for reproof, for correction, for instruction in righteousness: 17 That the man of God may be perfect, thoroughly furnished unto all good works* (II Timothy 3:16-17).

The word *dispensation* according to Webster means: 1 a: a general state or ordering of things; *specif*: a system of revealed commands and promises regulating human affairs b: a particular arrangement or provision esp. of providence or nature.

Scofield listed the seven dispensations in the Scofield Reference Bible; 1- Innocence, 2-Conscience, 3- Human Government, 4-Promise, 5- Law, 6-Grace, 7- Kingdom. He said a dispensation is a period of time during which man is tested in respect to some specific revelation of the will of God. A system regulating human affairs. I want to examine Law, Grace, and Kingdom. These last three deal with the very foundation of our faith in Christ and the Bible. Scofield states that the Dispensation of Law starts with Moses and goes through the Gospels, to Acts chapter 2, and starts again for the Jew after the Church is raptured in Revelation chapter 4. This teaching makes void the Gospels for the Church.

There are only four places in the Bible where the word *dispensation* is used, and all four are in Paul's writings. Dispensation signified primarily a stewardship, and management or disposition of the affairs that God had entrusted to Paul. Paul had an order from God to preach in the dispensation of the gospel (I Cor. 9:17). God's plan was in the dispensation of the fullness of time to gather together in one all things in

Christ, which were in heaven and in earth (Eph.1:10). The commission, or dispensation, of the grace of God was given unto Paul (Eph. 3:2), and Paul was made a minister according to the commission, or dispensation, of God, to fulfill the word of God (Col. 1:25). Other than these references concerning dispensations, it had never been a popular subject until Darby popularized it around 1830 in England. Dispensational teaching opened the door to the pretribulation rapture theory. After Scofield was converted in America, and developed his own dispensational teaching, it grew to be the dominant teaching, especially the pretribulation rapture of the Church.

I believe that Darby and Scofield's understanding and explanation of the dispensation of the Law do not come into conformity with the Word of God or the historical teachings of the Gospels. Their explanation of the dispensation of Law, and its extension through the Gospels and the second chapter of Acts, has led many of God's people astray. To put the Law of Moses, the ministry of Jesus, His death, burial, resurrection, and the Gospels in the same dispensation has done much damage to Church doctrines. It made Darby and Scofield err concerning the Gospels being for the Church, the coming of the Lord, the kingdom of heaven, the kingdom of God, and the kingdom of Israel. When man takes God's Word by dispensationalism and promotes a theory that does not conform to what is taught in the Old and New Testaments, it brings into question those individuals' concept of rightly dividing the Word of truth. Man's concept of dispensation must be brought into conformity to God's Word. Man's every word and doctrine must be in conformity with the foundation that was laid for the Church by the apostles and prophets, Jesus Christ himself being the chief cornerstone: *And are built upon the foundation of the apostles and prophets, Jesus Christ himself being the chief corner stone* (Eph. 2:20).

The theme of the Bible is Jesus, and all dispensations, from the time of the fall of Adam and Eve, pointed to Jesus. Genesis 3:15 gives the first promise of a Savior. Christ was the "seed" of the woman, not of man, and He suffered the Devil's wrath in the crucifixion. Satan is yet to have his head bruised, but Paul said it would come shortly (Rom. 16:20). Satan will be bound one thousand years at the end of the battle of Armageddon (Rev. 20:2), but will be cast in the Lake of fire when he makes war with God's people for the last time (Rev. 20:10). The

Noaichal dispensation, like the *Adamical*, required repentance of sin, faith in God's mercy, and hope in the promised Saviour represented by offering sacrifices. Under the *Abrahamic* covenant, the promise was made that in his seed all nations would be blessed (Gen 22:18). Abraham had two sons, which stood for two covenants, one of the bondmaid Hagar, which stood for the Law and the earthly Jerusalem; (Gal 4:22-25). Isaac was the promised son, and stood for the Jerusalem above, which is free. He was born of promise, not of the flesh. The bondwoman was to be cast out and not be made heir with the free-woman (Gal. 4:26-31). The covenant of the bondwoman was the dispensation of the Law. Jesus was the Promised One who would redeem His people from the curse of the Law, in order that the blessings of Abraham might come on both Jews and Gentiles through Jesus Christ (Gal. 3:13-14).

When you take all the above Scriptures concerning the two covenants, you cannot take Jesus, the Gospels, and all His teachings of the New Covenant and put them under the dispensation of Law and the Old Covenant. Moses and the Law cannot be under the same covenant as Jesus and the New Covenant. Jesus and the Gospels are the fulfillment of all the plans of God from the beginning, to gather together in one all things in Christ, which were in heaven and in earth (Eph. 1:10). The Gospels, which record the birth, life, and ministry of our Lord Jesus Christ must not be put under the dispensation of the Law, because it is an offense to everything God planned down through the annals of time.

Those who developed dispensationalism as we know it today made a determination that extends the Law through the Gospels unto Acts. This determination in reality would nullify why Jesus came into the world to seek and to save that which was lost. Jesus was born under the Law, but when the fulness of time came, God sent forth His Son to redeem both Jew and Gentile as adopted Sons: *But when the fulness of the time was come, God sent forth his Son, made of a woman, made under the law, 5 To redeem them that were under the law, that we might receive the adoption of sons* (Galations 4:4-5). The Law was intended to drive sinners to Christ for salvation. The dispensation of law ended when John prepared the way of the Lord in John 1:6-14, 29-34, and pointed to Jesus as the Messiah. After John was put in prison, Jesus began preaching the

Gospel: *And saying, The time is fulfilled, and the kingdom of God is at hand: repent ye, and believe the gospel* (Mark 1:15). The kingdom of God comes into being when God takes residence within us (Luke 17:20-21) and is the beginning of a new dispensation. The one verse following is enough evidence to show dispensationalists have erred in doctrine: *The law and the prophets were until John: since that time the kingdom of God is preached, and every man presseth into it* (Luke 16:16). John bore witness of the One which dealt with man in a way that man had never known before, and a new dispensation began: *John bare witness of him, and cried, saying, This was he of whom I spake, He that cometh after me is preferred before me: for he was before me. 16 And of his fulness have all we received, and grace for grace. 17 For the law was given by Moses, but grace and truth came by Jesus Christ* (John 1:15-17).

Jesus had a mission for the salvation of the whole world. He trained the twelve disciples to carry out this mission after His departure. Jesus commanded the disciples to go into all the world and make disciples, teaching them to observe all things whatsoever He had commanded them (Matt. 28:16-20). Jesus never intended for a barrier to be put up between the Gospels and the Church. The book of Acts is not a dividing line between the Law and the Church. The Acts of the Apostles were authored by the apostle Luke. The very first verse of Acts shows there is a continuation of all that Jesus began to do and teach: *The former treatise have I made, O Theophilus, of all that Jesus began both to do and teach* (Acts 1:1). Luke is letting Theophilus know that Acts is a continuation of the account he had given in the Gospel of Luke. If the book of Acts is a continuation of all that Jesus began both to do and teach, man has no right to separate the Gospels from the Church by a theory of dispensationalism. What Jesus taught in the Gospels about His return in the clouds, when every eye will see Him, as recorded in Luke 21:25-28, is the same event as when the Church will see Jesus coming in the clouds in Acts 1:11 or I Thess. 4:17.

Jesus was the beginning of a new dispensation, and never intended for the Church to have a doctrine that Luke 21:25-28 or Matthew 24:29-31 is for the Jews only. The disciples, who were early Church members, came to Jesus when He was departing from the temple to show Him the buildings of the temple. Jesus then told them that the temple would be destroyed, (which took place in A.D. 70 in the Church age, and His coming will also take place in the Church age.) Jesus then went to the Mount of Olives where *the disciples came unto him privately, saying, Tell us, when shall these things be? and what shall be the sign of thy coming, and of the end of the world?* (Matthew 24:1-3). The answer Jesus gave in Matthew 24 regarding the destruction of the temple and His return had its root in the Old Testament, and would be the foundation for the Epistles and Revelation. Jesus told them of the persecution that would follow, and how the gospel must be preached to all the world before He would come again. There is only one true gospel, not two, as dispensationalists teach. Jesus gave the disciples signs that would appear before He came again, and Paul also referred to these signs in I Thessalonians 5:1-6. The third verse has nothing to do with the coming of the Lord only for the Jews. The Jewish disciples were the first members of the Church, and what Jesus said to them about His coming is for the Church, the same as when Jesus said to them in Matthew 28:19-20: *Go ye therefore, and teach all nations, baptizing them in the name of the Father, and of the Son, and of the Holy Ghost: 20 Teaching them to observe all things whatsoever I have commanded you: and, lo, I am with you alway, even unto the end of the world. Amen.* Jesus was talking to the disciples about the great commission, telling them to teach all nations to observe all things whatsoever He had commanded them. It is wrong for dispensationalists to take what Jesus said about His coming and say it is for the Jew only, then take what He said in Matthew 28 about the great commission and say it is for the Church. If the great commission applies to the Church, then His answer to the disciples about His coming also applies to the Church. There is no distinction.

Charles C. Ryrie in his book *Dispensationalism Today* charts the beliefs of Pierre Poiret, John Edwards, Isaac Watts, J. N. Darby, James H. Brookes, James M. Gray, and C.I. Scofield concerning dispensationalism. These men all have a different view of the dispensations from Adam to the millenium. If each of these men has a different view concerning dispensationalism, then it is certain that Darby and Scofield made mistakes concerning the dispensation of the Law when they said it extended through the Gospels to the second chapter of Acts. There is not one Scripture that verifies or justifies such a doctrine. When the dispensation of Law stops with John and the dispensation of Grace and Truth starts with Jesus, it makes void the argument that Jesus taught a different coming than Paul (John 1:17). The Church needs to listen to what Jesus said about His coming instead of the theology of man. Jesus taught the Church, both Jew and Gentiles, when He would come again. Let us believe Jesus, which dismantles the pretribulation rapture theory espoused by Darby and Scofield.

Ryrie points out how others before Darby wrote about dispensations, and said neither Darby nor the Brethren originated the concepts. He said Scofield's teaching on dispensationalism follows more in line with Isaac Watts' dispensational teaching than Darby's. It may be true that Scofield was influenced by Watts, but others also influenced him. We know for sure that contact between Darby, MacDonald, and Irving is fact, and that Darby developed, systemized, and promoted dispensational teachings, along with the pretribulation rapture theory. Darby came to America six times and established his doctrines of dispensationalism and the pretribulation rapture. After Scofield was saved, he first received Bible teaching by the Brethren. This and his research in the writings of the Brethren and Darby most influenced the Scofield Reference Bible, then Scofield and his Reference Bible influenced many colleges and churches in America.

If God ordained dispensations in dealing with mankind, then those dispensations should be interpreted according to the Word, and not according to the theology of man. If the message of John the Baptist and all the words which Jesus spoke in the Gospels, including His death, burial, and resurrection, are put under the dispensation of Law, it is a most serious mistake. This is similar to calling " light," "darkness." If there was ever a dispensation where God dealt with mankind in a certain way, it was under the new dispensation of the New Covenant of Jesus and the Gospels. We can separate Moses and the Law from the New Covenant, but not Jesus and the Gospels from the Church.

If people would only stop and think, they would know that Jesus and His teachings in the Gospels were not the same as Moses taught under the Law. Moses established the Old Covenant, and Jesus established the New. If there has ever been a distinction in dispensations in which God is dealing with man, it is between the Law of Moses and the Gospels. The Law came by Moses, but grace and truth came by Jesus Christ. Two verses shoot an arrow to the very heart of dispensationalism as taught by Darby and Scofield: *And the Word was made flesh, and dwelt among us, (and we beheld his glory, the glory as of the only begotten of the Father,) full of grace and truth. 17 For the law was given by Moses, but grace and truth came by Jesus Christ* (John 1:14,17).

Dispensationalists have made more errors than putting Jesus and the Gospels under the dispensation of Law. They also teach that when Jesus came in the first advent, He offered the Jews an earthly kingdom, but was rejected, therefore the kingdom of heaven was postponed until the millennium. The kingdom of heaven was not postponed by His rejection and crucifixion, but were in God's plan for the salvation of both Jews and Gentiles (Rom. 11:11-12). Dispensationalists changed the true meaning of the kingdom of heaven. Jesus let Pilate know that His kingdom was not of this world, or else His servants would come and fight, and He would not be delivered to the Jews (John 18:33-36). Jesus was talking about the kingdom of heaven that He would establish.

Jesus received all power in heaven and earth to reign over his Church from heaven (Matthew 28:18). God never instituted Plan B, nor was the Church age an afterthought of God. Everything happened just as God foreknew, and the prophets had prophesied. John the Baptist and Jesus let the disciples know that the kingdom of heaven was at hand (the Church age), Matt.3:2 and 4:17, and after Jesus arose and before He ascended into heaven He let His disciples know that the kingdom of Israel would come in God's timing, but first the Church age, and the Holy Spirit would be poured out upon all flesh for power to witness: *When they therefore were come together, they asked of him, saying, Lord, wilt thou at this time restore again the kingdom to Israel? 7 And he said unto them, It is not for you to know the times or the seasons, which the Father hath put in his own power. 8 But ye shall receive power, after that the Holy Ghost is come upon you: and ye shall be witnesses unto me both in Jerusalem, and in all Judaea, and in Samaria, and unto the uttermost part of the earth* (Acts 1:6-8).

Darby and Scofield, who started the dispensational teaching of the pretribulation rapture as we know it today, put a division between the Church and Israel. Their teaching does not allow for the grafting of Israel into the Church and the Body of Christ before the coming of the Lord. They say that the Church will be raptured before the tribulation period, but the Jews will go through the tribulation period, which they call the wrath of God. Their doctrine teaches that when the Jews rejected Jesus as their Messiah and Savior, God delayed their kingdom until after the rapture of the Church. Therefore, they believe Israel and the Church cannot be brought into one body.

Jesus laid the foundation in the Gospels to bring both Jew and Gentiles to God through the blood of Christ. It was once Gentiles who were aliens from the commonwealth of Israel, and strangers from the covenants of promise. God's desire was to make both one in Christ. If God has promised to reconcile the Jews and graft them back into the Body of Christ, then it will be done according to promise. If God broke them off from the Church, He is able to graft them in again. Paul tells the Church of Ephesus how both would be made one in Christ: *Wherefore remember, that ye being in time past Gentiles in the flesh, who are called Uncircumcision by that which is called the Circumcision in the flesh made by hands; 12 That at that time ye were without Christ, being aliens from the commonwealth of Israel, and strangers from the covenants of promise, having no hope, and without God in the world: 13 But now in Christ Jesus ye who sometimes were far off are made nigh by the blood of Christ. 14 For he is our peace, who hath made both one, and hath broken down the middle wall of partition between us; 15 Having abolished in his flesh the enmity, even the law of commandments contained in ordinances; for to make in himself of twain one new man, so making peace; 16 And that he might reconcile both unto God in one body by the cross, having slain the enmity thereby* (Ephesians 2:11-16).

Pretribulationists teach that the Church must be raptured before Daniel's seventieth week can begin. This is what makes their doctrine have a split coming of Jesus: One for the secret rapture of the Church, and then another seven years later for the revelation when every eye will see Jesus, after which He will set up His kingdom on earth. They teach that Matthew 24 and the verses after Revelation 4:1 are for the Jew only, while I Thessalonians 4:13-18 is for the Church concerning the secret rapture before the tribulation period starts. This might sound good in dispensational teaching, but there is not one word in I Thessalonians, or the Bible that tells us that the Church will have a pretribulation rapture. There is not one word in Revelation 4:1 concerning the rapture of the Church in the manner pretribulationists teach.

Christian writers say that posttribulationists do not consider the writings of Christians before Darby and Scofield who taught the imminent return of Christ. Grant Jeffrey's book *Apocalypse* quotes some of these writings, misrepresenting them in trying to prove the pretribulation rapture theory by some of the early Church fathers:

> A Church manual from approximately A.D. 110, called the Didache, confirms the belief of these Christians in the imminent return of Christ for believers. This was written

less than fifteen years after John wrote the Revelation.

In the Didache 16, we find the following instructions. "1. Be watchful for your life! Let not your lamps be extinguished nor your loins ungirded, but be ye ready! For ye know not the hour in which the Lord cometh. 2. Assemble yourselves frequently, seeking what is fitting for your souls. For the whole time of your faith will not be profitable to you, if you are not made perfect in the last time... then the world deceiver shall appear as a son of god and shall work signs and wonders...6. And then shall the signs of the truth appear, first the sign of a rift in heaven, then the sign of the sound of the trumpet, and thirdly, a resurrection of the dead. 7. But not of all, but as it was said, "The Lord will come and all His saints with him.' 8 Then shall the world see the Lord coming on the clouds of heaven."

In this short passage we see a strong belief in the imminent return of Christ: "Be ye ready! For ye know not the hour in which your Lord cometh."

We can see Grant Jeffrey is not interpreting what the Didache said correctly. The Didache is not talking about a pretribulation rapture but a posttribulation coming. The manual said to watch. You can find it in Matthew 24:42, and Revelation 22:7. These Scriptures are telling the Church that the man of sin will appear before the trumpet sounds and the resurrection comes. This manual is teaching the same message that Jesus, the apostles, and Irenaeus taught. This is the same message that Paul warned the Thessalonian Church about, saying the apostasy would come first and the man of sin be revealed before the saints would be gathered to the Lord (I Thess. 2:1-5). The Bible tells every generation to be ready and looking for the coming of the Lord, although it has been two thousand years since He ascended to heaven. God wants every generation to be ready for Jesus to come. The Bible can talk of the imminent return of Christ because in God's timing a thousand years is as one day.

Grant Jeffrey also quotes from Hippolytus Treatise on Christ and the Antichrist. Hippolytus lived from A.D. 170 to 236. Hippolytus quoted I Thessalonians 4:17: "Then we which are alive and remain shall be caught up together with them in the clouds to meet the Lord in the air; and so shall we ever be with the Lord." Grant Jeffrey comments on this. "He reminds his readers of the hope of Christ's imminent return. He wrote that we should be 'looking for that blessed hope and appearing of our God and Savior.' The Bible tells us in the Gospels, Epistles and Revelation, that we are to watch and be ready for we know not the hour of His coming. To say this Scripture is teaching a pretribulation rapture of the Church is misleading. Just because Hippolytus quotes I Thessalonians 4:17 does not mean Hippolytus is teaching a pretribulation rapture.

There are other books and magazine articles that give the names of people who taught a pretribulation rapture before 1830. One thing they all have in common is that they misinterpret what saints were truly saying, or, in the case of the Jesuits after the Reformation, they were only trying to get off their backs those Christians who were critical to the Catholic Church. Those Jesuits gave no scriptural proof of the correctness of the pretribulation rapture but were trying to mislead the critics by implying the rapture would take place before the man of sin was revealed. True doctrine is not established by the words of man. It is established by comparing scripture with scripture (I Cor. 2:13, II Tim. 3:15-16). Incorrect dispensationalism does not make the pretribulation rapture theory right.

Irenaeus, who lived in the second century, shows the development of the authoritative canon of the New Testament. He frequently mentions the rule of truth. He also advanced the claim that the consensus of all the bishops of the churches of admitted and continuous apostolic foundation provided the sole safe guide to the interpretation of Scripture. He speaks of a posttribulation coming of the Lord. Tertullian, who was born after Irenaeus, makes references concerning the posttribulation coming of the Lord taking place after the oppression of the antichrist. All of these early church writers believed in a premillennium (posttribulation) coming of the Lord: Didache, Barnabas, Justin Martyr, Irenaeus, The Shepherd of Hermas, Tertullian, Hippolytus, Cyprian, Victorinus. Many of them warned how the antichrist would arise and the Church would have tribulation before the Lord comes.

What pretribulationists call rightly dividing the Word of truth is only a division of dispensationalism which divides the Gospel and Revelation from the Epistles and the Church. The Gospels must not be kept under the Law, but put back under grace as it was before Darby's form of dispensationalism arrived. The Old Testament, the Gospels, the Epistles, and Revelation must be put back into unity as God intended.

FOUNDING OF
THE PRETRIBULATION
RAPTURE

In 1812, Jesuit Manuel Lacunza wrote *The Coming Messiah in Glory and Majesty*. He taught that there are different stages in the resurrection. *The Cyclopedia of Religious Knowledge* gives this account of Lucunza's work. In 1825, Scottish preacher Edward Irving translated a Spanish book by Juan Josafat Ben Ezra, *The Coming Messiah in Glory and Majesty*, which was, in reality, the composition of Lacunza. We do know that shortly after Irving published the book in English, he began preaching that Christ would first come for his saints in a secret rapture. Then after a period of seven years of tribulation, He would come with His saints to destroy the antichrist and reign on earth. Irving said he heard a voice from heaven, and began to preach a pretribulation rapture of the Church. Irving was arraigned before the Presbytery of London in 1830, convicted of heresy, ejected from his new church in Regent's Square in 1832, and finally deposed in 1833 by the presbytery of Annan, which had licensed him. However the majority of his congregation adhered to him, and gradually a new form of Christianity developed, commonly known as Irvingism, though Irving had very little to do with its development. His health failed, then he went to Scotland and died there in 1834. This account confirms the one given by Schaff, the Church historian.

Dave MacPherson details in his book *The Incredible Cover-up*, how Edward Irving and the founders of the Catholic Apostolic Church believed God would restore the gifts of the Spirit, including prophecy, and the ministries of the apostles and prophets. Irving and his church set out to accomplish this. It was reported that J.B. Cardal's wife, a leader in the church, was at a prayer meeting in a private home in London when she began to speak in tongues and prophesy, "The Lord hasteneth his coming, The Lord cometh." This is the first known case of speaking in tongues in London. Tongues and related prophecies concerning the Lord's coming were soon heard regularly in the Regent Square church.

Dave MacPherson located a rare book by Dr. R. Norton in which Norton gives details of how Margaret MacDonald's brothers and sisters got saved, and how they attended Rev. Irving's and Campbell's churches. Norton stated that McDonald's brothers, James and George, probably had a great influence on their young sister Margaret, who was an invalid. They found lodging for their sister in Roe, where Rev. John McLeod Campbell was preaching to great crowds in his church. McDonald was soon saved and healed. She had a vision of a two-stage coming of the Lord. She said this vision of the new revelation needed to be revealed to others concerning a partial rapture of those who were filled with the Spirit. In the vision she said only they who were Spirit-filled would be caught up with the Lord in the rapture for the marriage of the Lamb. She prophesied and saw a series of raptures, but the first would remove some of the believers from the earth before the antichrist was revealed. Irving visited MacDonald to investigate her vision and prophecies. Darby of the Brethren also heard about the unusual goings on in Scotland, and decided to see for himself what was going on. Darby knew of Irving's work and McDonald's visions and began to develop his dispensational system of prophetic interpretation of the pretribulation rapture theory.

CLARENCE Larkin had a book published in 1918 entitled *Dispensational Truth*. He was a dispensationalist, and his writings confirm the correctness of what I have written about the origin of the pretribulation rapture theory. The following paragraph appears on page 5 of his book:

"The 'Futurist School' interprets the language of the Apocalypse 'literally,' except such symbols as are named as such, and holds that the whole of the book, from the end of the third chapter, is yet 'Future' and unfilled, and that the greater part of the book, from the beginning of chapter six to the end of chapter nineteen, describes what shall come to pass during the last week of 'Daniel's Seventy Weeks.' This view, while it dates in modern times only from the close of the Sixteenth Century, is really the most ancient of the three. It was held in many of its prominent features by the primitive Fathers of the Church, and is one of the early interpretations of scripture truth that sunk into oblivion with the growth of Papacy, and that has been restored to the Church in these last times. In its present form it may be said to have originated at the end of the Sixteenth Century, with the Jesuit Ribera, who, actuated by the same motive as the Jesuit Alcazar, sought to rid the Papacy of the stigma of being called the 'Antichrist,' and so referred the prophecies of the Apocalypse to the distant future. This view was accepted by the Roman Catholic Church and was for a long time confined to it, but, strange to say, it has wonderfully revived since the beginning of the Nineteenth Century, and that most Protestants. It is the most largely accepted of the three views. It has been charged with ignoring the Papal and Mohammedan systems, but this is far from truth, for it looks upon them as foreshadowed in the scriptures, and sees in them the 'Type' of those great 'Anti-Types' yet future, the 'Beast' and the 'False Prophet.' The 'Futurist' interpretation of scripture is the one employed in this book."

Larkin's confirms that the "Futurist School" had its origin in modern times by Jesuits out of the Catholic Church. They wanted to rid the claim of how the antichrist would come through the "Papal Church." Jesuit Lacunza authored his book, and Irving's book was a composition of it. After hearing a voice from heaven, he began teaching the pretribulation rapture. The Jesuit's teachings, the prophecies in Irving's church, or MacDonald's vision alone could not have established the pretribulation rapture without future generations trying these prophecies and visions by the Word and finding error. When Darby believed the futurist view of interpretation, which discounts the Gospels and the verses following the fourth chapter of Revelation for the Church, it gave the methodology for the pretribulation rapture theory to survive. It can only survive by riding on the back of dispensationalism.

Jesus warned the Church about false prophets who would arise and show great signs and wonders. The Church should take heed to what Jesus said: *For there shall arise false Christs, and false prophets, and shall show great signs and wonders; insomuch that, if it were possible, they shall deceive the very elect.25 Behold, I have told you before* (Matthew 24:24-25).

The exercise of spiritual gifts, tongues, and visions was common in Irving's church and MacDonald's home. However the gift of discerning of spirits was not in operation or else they would have seen the errors made by the Jesuits, and themselves (I Cor:12:10). Paul told the church of Corinth that when prophecy was given, it must be judged by others (I Cor. 14:29). Paul said the spirit of the prophet is subject to the prophets in I Corinthians 14:32. There is no place where the prophecies given in Irving's church or by MacDonald were tried by the Word.

Charles Finney said, "When we use the Word without the Spirit, or the Spirit without the Word it will create wildfire." This is how wildfire got into the doctrine concerning the Lord's return. The pretribulation rapture theory perverts the gospel of Christ because it preaches another gospel than what Jesus taught in the Gospels, or what was taught in the Epistles, or Revelation. Paul told the Galatian church that if even an angel preached another gospel than what was preached they were not to believe it. Irving and his church members did not follow what Paul said, nor did Darby in his research, or his visit to MacDonalds, nor did Scofield concerning the doctrine of the return of the Lord. We can be just as guilty of untruth by saying that what Jesus taught concerning His coming again in the Gospels does not apply to the Church, but only to the Jew. Paul said we are not to pervert the gospel of Christ: *I marvel that ye are so soon removed from him that called you into the grace of Christ unto another gospel: 7 Which is not another; but there be some that trouble you, and would pervert the gospel of Christ. 8 But though we, or an angel from heaven, preach any other gospel unto you than that which we have preached unto you, let him be accursed. 9 As we said before, so say I now again, If any man preach any other gospel unto you than that ye have received, let him be accursed. 10 For do I now persuade men, or God? or do I seek to please men?*

40

for if I yet pleased men, I should not be the servant of Christ. 11 But I certify you, brethren, that the gospel which was preached of me is not after man. 12 For I neither received it of man, neither was I taught it, but by the revelation of Jesus Christ (Galatians 1:6-12).

Schaff and other writers give us information about the formation of the Brethren and how Darby became a dominant personality in the movement after he joined them. Darby had a great interest in Bible prophecy, and introduced the pretribulation rapture theory in a Prophetic Conference in 1833. The Plymouth Brethren spread in the nineteenth century to the British Dominions and the United States. They were known as Brethren, or Darbyites, but among themselves they were called simply Brethren. Darby carried the doctrines of dispensationalism and the pretribulation rapture theory to France, Switzerland, Germany, and America. Between the years of 1833 to 1859, by Darby's leadership, the dispensational doctrine of the pretribulation rapture theory became well established.

In the chapter "Is the Coming of Christ for His Saints the Proper Hope of the Church" from *The Collected Writings of J. N. Darby*, Doctrinal No 3, volume 10, Darby argues between the hope of the Church, which he believes is the rapture before the tribulation period, and the Lord's coming back to earth with His saints at the end of the tribulation period. Darby put a great distinction between Paul's writings in the Epistles and the Lord's teachings in the Gospels. He believed Paul was speaking to the Church, while Jesus was speaking to the Jews only. Darby believed the warnings Jesus gave in the Gospels were only for the Jews and not the Church, and that Matthew 24 was speaking to the Jewish remnant and had nothing to do with the Christian dispensation of the Church. He stated that Paul alone teaches the Church about the rapture.

In his synopsis of I and II Thessalonians, *Synopsis of the Books of the Bible from Colossians to Revelation, Vol. No 5*, Darby tells us again that the Lord's coming for his saints in the Thessalonians is different than what Jesus taught in the Gospels. Yet, what Paul taught in the Epistles was not a different doctrine about the Lord's coming than what Jesus taught in the Gospels. The Gospels are for the Church.

As the Prophetic and Bible Conference movement began, many were attracted to Darby and his teachings concerning dispensationalism and the pretribulation rapture theory. The Brethren and their teachings were well established when Scofield got saved. George Eldon Ladd gives details in his book, *The Blessed Hope*, about these conferences. One was held in 1878 in the Holy Trinity (Episcopal) church. Another series of meetings of greater importance were held at Niagara on Lake Ontario from 1883-1897. Ladd gives many names of those who attended these conferences. After these conferences were discontinued, a new conference at Seacliff, Long Island, was opened in 1901. It was at these conferences where the plan for the Scofield Reference Bible, which embodied the dispensational system of interpretation, occurred.

Drafts for the Scofield Reference Bible were completed in the home of John Pirie in Long Island, NY. He enlisted the help of Emily Farmer for proofreading. She was well-versed in dispensational doctrines, and made sure his notes matched the doctrines on dispensationalism. The Scofield Reference Bible was influenced by his early teachings from Brookes and other Brethren. His visits to Oxford, England from 1902-1909 were greatly influenced by the writings of the Brethren while researching material. The Reference Bible would reflect the dispensational distinctives, prophetic highlights, and doctrines which Darby and the Brethren taught. It would also include the pretribulation rapture theory. The Scofield Reference Bible was published by the Oxford Press in 1909. In the chapter, "What does dispensational teaching mean," Scofield took some of the early teachings of the Brethren and incorporated them into The Scofield Reference Bible. He separated the Gospels and the verses after the fourth chapter of Revelation from the Church in forming his dispensational teachings.

It is not known for certain whether the writings of men such as Isaac Watts had some influence on Scofield, but we do know that Darby and his writings, along with his acquaintance with the Brethren, had a great influence on him concerning the doctrine of the pretribulation rapture and dispensational teaching. It is a mystery why this doctrine, which is being taught in our colleges and churches today, is not being questioned by more of God's people. George Muller, the great man of God, broke away from Darby because of his doctrinal teachings, but Scofield, who developed his own style of dispensational teachings along with the pretribulation rapture theory, never saw the errors that had been made.

Men such as W. J. Erdman, Robert Cameron, and Henry W. Frost, who attended the Bible Conferences when dispensational teachings and the pretribulation rapture theory was in its infancy in America, turned away from these teachings because what was taught did not come into agreement with the Bible. Ladd gives us some details about Erdman, pastor of the Moody Church in Chicago when Darby visited, who at first accepted Darby's pretribulation, any-moment view of Christ's return. Upon further searching of the Scriptures, however Erdman decided that this view was not taught in the Word, and felt he could no longer support a view for which he could not find scriptural warrant. He then wrote the tract, "A Theory Reviewed," in which he questioned the any-moment theory, concluding with these words: "Should any deplore the adoption of the belief that the Lord will come any moment, as if it would take away all joy and comfort, it is enough to answer in the words of another, 'Better the disappointment to truth than the fair but false promises of error.' The time has come for the whole Church to wake up and search for and believe truth."

After searching the Word in the early years of Moody Bible Church, men such as Erdman opposed the teachings of Darby, but in later years pastors adopted the pretribulation rapture theory. H. A. Ironside became a "Brethren worker," and became the pastor of Moody Bible Church. His labors with the Brethren influenced his belief in the pretribulation rapture theory. He also authored books on the subject, playing a big part in the furtherance of the pretribulation rapture, and acknowledged that it was at the Power Court Meetings in London in 1833 where the pretribulation rapture of the Church was brought to light. Moody Bible Institute is still producing Christian workers and preachers that teach and preach a pretribulation rapture.

Scofield died on July 24, 1921. The First Congregational Church that Scofield had pastored in Dallas was renamed Scofield Memorial under the leadership of Dr. Lewis Sperry Chafer. Chafer, with the boards of Scofield Memorial and First Presbyterian of Dallas, formed Evangelical Theological College, later named Dallas Theological Seminary. It became the dispensational theological graduate school of America, and has been the foremost proponent of pretribulation rapture teaching. John F. Walvoord, who became president of the college, pushed the pretribulation rapture in his books on theology. J. Dwight

Pentecost has many books dealing with prophetic subjects and the pretribulation rapture. Hal Lindsey, another graduate of Dallas Theological Seminary, has popularized the pretribulation rapture in his teachings and books. The leadership of the Christian Colleges of America was influenced by dispensational teachings that produced the pretribulation rapture theory, and the graduates of these colleges cover America with their unfounded doctrine. Most of these men are honest, sincere men, and believe what they preach about the coming of the Lord to be true, but the time has come when God's people must take a second look at the evidence given concerning the error of the pretribulation rapture.

We live in a generation when the pretribulation rapture theory has crossed the boundaries of most major Protestant denominations. The Assemblies of God teach the pretribulation rapture. Graduates of Dallas Theological Seminary, Moody Bible Institute, and many Baptist colleges accept the teachings of Scofield. Denominational, Pentecostal, Independent, Bible, and Baptist churches are filled with the teachings of a pretribulation rapture. Pretribulation rapture teachers and pastors explain away truths that prevailed before the early 1800s of great premillinnial preachers, and instituted a futurist view of unproven dispensationalism concerning the pretribulation rapture theory. Some say this teaching was just neglected for many centuries, and was revived, but I have found no evidence it ever existed as a proven doctrine of the Church. The pretribulation rapture theory almost succeeded in replacing what Jesus, the apostles, and the early Church taught about the Lord's coming, but God has been gracious in letting the truth of his Word survive. It reminds me of what Jesus said to the church of Sardis in Revelation 3:2-4, 6: *Be watchful, and strengthen the things which remain, that are ready to die: for I have not found thy works perfect before God. 3 Remember therefore how thou hast received and heard, and hold fast, and repent. If therefore thou shalt not watch, I will come on thee as a thief, and thou shalt not know what hour I will come upon thee. 4 Thou hast a few names even in Sardis which have not defiled their garments; and they shall walk with me in white: for they are worthy.6 He that hath an ear, let him hear what the Spirit saith unto the churches.*

I say with sadness that the Prophetic Conferences of today have very few differences from the pretribulation rapture birthed at the Power Court Meeting in London in 1833. They are still preaching the same doctrine with a little more refinement since the doctrine was birthed.

Pretribulationists are still preaching the Lord's imminent coming. Today's conference speakers will sometimes quote the signs of Jesus' coming that are recorded in the Gospels, but disregard what Jesus said about His coming as applicable to the Church. Jesus told us we would see the signs of His coming immediately after the tribulation in Matthew 24:29-31. Pretribulationists who disregard what Jesus taught are disregarding the very words of the One who is coming for the Church.

I often wonder if churches are becoming like the church of Laodicea, a lukewarm church seeking more for material prosperity than holiness or truth. The Church of today only wants to hear what seems and sounds good, and tickles its ears (II Tim. 4:3-4). I do not see a church that is ready for the tough decisions that will have to be made in the tribulation period about which Jesus warned us. The pretribulation rapture theory continues to exist because teachers are taking an untrue doctrine and fitting the Word to the doctrine. God's people should take the Word and fit true doctrine to it.

One of the major reasons why the pretribulation rapture theory is so popular and attractive to those who hear it is that they are promised they will not suffer any tribulation or go through the tribulation period. This promise appeals to most people, but this promise is not according to the Scriptures. God did not promise His Church that they would not have tribulation, but He did promise his Church that they would not suffer His wrath. I pray every pretribulationist will find truth and will see what lies ahead for the Church. Time proves all truth or error, but when the tribulation period comes upon the Church, and there has been no rapture, the teachers of the pretribulation rapture theory will be just as disillusioned as those whom they taught. The Church must not wait until that hour comes which will try every person's faith.

Oswald J. Smith was taught pretribulation rapture by W. E. Blackstone in his book *Jesus Is Coming*. The Scofield Reference Bible was used. Prophetic Conferences were attended. He began to search the Scriptures for facts and proofs of what he had been taught, and found there was no proof of a pretribulation rapture that he and others had been taught.

The Tribulation People by Arthur Kallerjohn with Mark Fackler, gives this account of Smith. In the pamphlet "Tribulation or Rapture – Which?" Smith tells the story of his "first awakening" to the posttribulation view at a time when he fully believed that Christ would rapture the Church before the tribulation. Smith was preaching a prophetic series during the early 1920s, and had taken his congregation through the teachings in Daniel. But, as he reports,

> "No sooner had I started on Matthew 24 than I got into trouble…I was in a maze, for I was perplexed…If the rapture was before the Tribulation, the Lord Jesus Christ would certainly have given some hint of it at least. It is unthinkable that He would have spoken so minutely of the Tribulation without stating that the Church would escape. Instead, he purposely led His hearers to the belief that His followers would be in it. Hence, I staggered, nor could I honestly defend my previous position."

That experience led him to a long and thorough reexamination. Smith concluded:

> "When I began to search the Scriptures for myself I discovered that there is not a single verse in the Bible that upholds the pretribulation theory, but that the uniform teaching of the Word of God is of a postribulation rapture."

Smith began to search for truth and found it. He found the Bible did not teach a pretribulation rapture for the saints, or a secret rapture where those left on earth would not know where the Church went. He found out the Church would endure the wrath of the antichrist in the tribulation period, but would not suffer the wrath of God, when God judges the world for their sins and rebellion. There are many great men of our past who did not teach pretribulation rapture, but a posttribulation rapture. We should not overlook this fact. Here are a few post tribulationists: John Bunyan, Jonathan Edwards, Charles Finney, John Fox, Matthew Henry, John Huss, John Knox, David Livingstone, George Muller, Isaac Newton, Polycarp, Leonard Ravenhill, Savonarole, Oswald J. Smith, Charles Spurgeon, William Tyndale, Charles and John Wesley, John Wycliffe, and George Whitefield. The list could go on and on of great men who did not believe in a pretribulation rapture.

Dr. Paul N. Benware, a pretribulationist, authored *Understanding End Times Prophecy*. He said that Darby did not originate the pretribulation theory. The following is Benware's account:

> "Peter Jurieu in his book *Approaching Deliverance of the Church* (1687) taught that Christ would come in the air to rapture the saints and return to heaven before the battle of Armageddon. He spoke of a secret Rapture prior to His coming in glory and judgment at Armageddon. Philip Doddridge's commentary on the New Testament (1738) and John Gill's Commentary on the New Testament (1748) both used the term *"rapture"* and speak of it as imminent. It is clear that these men believed that His coming will precede Christ's descent to the earth and the time of judgment. The purpose was to preserve believers from the time of judgment. James MacKnight (1763) and Thomas Scott (1792) taught that the righteous will be carried into heaven, where they will be secure until the time of judgment is over. A detailed chronology is not given by these writers, but it is evident that they did see a distinction between the rapture and the second Coming and see believers removed from the earth before the judgment. Why did these and other writers begin to speak of a Rapture that is distinct from the second Coming and see the believers removed from the earth prior to the judgments?"

We must remember that pretribulation rapture is a new term, and before that term was coined there were premillennialists and postmillennialists. I do not have these books Benware is quoting, but from the impression he gives me in his quotes, they are only teaching the rapture of the Church takes place before the judgment of God. It appears these men are not teaching anything different than what Jesus taught in the Gospels, or the disciples taught in the Apostles' Doctrine, or the Reformers taught concerning the coming of the Lord. These men are only teaching that the Church will be raptured before the wrath of God. This is in accordance with I Thessalonians 4:13-18; II Thessalonians 2:1-5; Matthew 24:40-42, and I Corinthians 15:51-53. The rapture will take place, and the Saints will be safe in the Lord's chambers. Then He and His angels, who are the reapers, will come back to earth for the reaping, and the battle of Armageddon (Matthew 13:39; Revelation 11:18; 16:1-21). Benware admits there is not a detailed chronology given by these men, but only a distinction between the second coming, the rapture, and that these precede the time of judgment. I do not find fault with that, but I do find great fault with the pretribulation rapture theory.

The early Berean church in Acts 17:10-11, searched the Scriptures daily to see if that which they were taught be true or not. It's time God's people search for themselves for the truth, and realize have they accepted a spirit that needed to be tried concerning the pretribulation rapture. John tells us the solution: *Beloved, believe not every spirit, but try the spirits whether they are of God: because many false prophets are gone out into the world* (I John 4:1).

High Cost of Doctrinal Error

We always pay a high price when we come against an accepted doctrine such as the pretribulation rapture. For over forty years I have been ridiculed and scorned because of my opposition. Now I can look back with great joy in seeing the walls of dispensationalism is being questioned because it was built on a foundation of unproven doctrines. Every doctrine must have a historical and scriptural foundation. It makes us wonder how this doctrine could escape so many learned men without being detected. When we look back on Church history, we realize Paul had to deal with the same issue in the early Church as we are dealing with today.

Paul wrote the first epistle to the Thessalonians in A.D. 54. The second letter shows that the doctrine concerning the resurrection and the coming of the Lord had already been corrupted by false teachers. It took less than seventy years in the book of Revelation for six of the seven churches of Asia to be corrupted. Many Church doctrines were subsequently corrupted by the Catholic Church down through the centuries, which brought on the Reformation. The Catholic Church has changed very little since the charges were made against her in the Reformation. Many of her daughters have corrupted themselves just as badly. In these last four hundred years we have seen all kinds of cults and churches arise. Many call themselves the true church, yet are so far from true. I believe the tribulation period will be a time which God has chosen as His last effort to bring a worldly and backslidden Church to repentance and correction. He has told us that the apostasy and the man of sin will be revealed before He comes again (II Thess. 2:1-3). There will come the time when God begins separating light from darkness and the chaff from the wheat. It will be a time when doctrines of men will be tried and found wanting.

I have learned over the years how important it is for every professing Christian to try the spirit of every doctrine to see if what they believe is in conformity with what God has said. Let me give an illustration. There was once a young man who married a lady who was a Jehovah's Witness. He did not want to change; therefore she left with the children and broke all ties. He had no contact with them for over fifty years. Then one day, contact was made again after this long period of time. I was fortunate to meet the father's children, great-grandchildren, and great, great-grandchildren. There was not one of the whole family who had not become devout Jehovah's Witnesses. The beliefs of these children and grandchildren will be hard to change to what other family members on the father's side believed, because the children were brought up by the mother to have the same spirit that Charles Taze Russell had, who founded the organization.

I knew another family in which one of the sons married a girl who belonged to an Apostolic Church. Before long he was converted to their teaching. Now his children and grandchildren have the same belief. They feel very confident that their church is the true church, and have the right doctrine with no need to change anything. Each one in this family took on the same spirit held by his wife's family.

Another family to whom I had witnessed for many years rejected God's plan of salvation. They said they did not have time to go to church, because they were too busy. He and his wife had a large family, and now most every one of his children and grandchildren have no church, or ever were saved. Each one in the family took on the same spirit of unbelief that the father and mother had. When the father and mother rejected truth that day it affected them, their children, and their grandchildren.

I give these three instances to show how easy it is to influence others. The sad fact is that many people who are in error never change, and hold doctrines which are not in conformity to the Word of God. Most religions and denominations feel they are right, but most of those who believe in an untrue doctrine will never try their belief by the Word to see if what they believe is true or not. This is because they believe they are right, and all others are in error. I believe those who believe in a pretribulation rapture are just as entrenched in a doctrine that is false, and it will be hard for them to let go because they believe they have truth. When a young person goes to college or to a church that teaches a pretribulation rapture theory, they are likely to believe the things they are taught, and take to themselves the same spirit that Darby and Scofield had concerning the pretribulation rapture theory.

Now it becomes your turn to try the doctrine of the pretribulation rapture and see if you come to the same conclusion as men like George Muller, Oswald J. Smith, W. J. Eedman, Robert Cameron, and Henry W. Frost. They tried the spirit of the pretribulation rapture theory, and found that it did not conform to the Word of God.

The great cry of churches today is to put away doctrines because they divide. This is the way to their own destruction, because they will put away truth along with the false. Can you imagine where we would be today if the Reformers had done this? They could not put away what they knew was truth. People need to emulate the early Church of Acts 17:11, where they searched the Word daily to see if what they were taught be true or not. There needs to be a new beginning where God's people ferret out false doctrine that has gotten into the churches. Jesus said we are sanctified by truth.

The oneness that Jesus talked about in John 17:21-23 is not found in church unity where the truth of God's Word is being cast aside. If God's Word never changes, why are the King James Bible and the *Textus Receptus* manuscript being cast aside by God's people? This Bible has stood the test of time through the Reformation and every revival since that time. The choice of manuscripts today for modern translations of the Bible are the Westcott and Hort Greek. Translations from these manuscripts make a big change in wording. There are places where the meaning of verses has been changed, and other places where whole and half verses are left out. Were great revivalists such as Wesley and Finney using the wrong Bible, or is it today's Church leaders who are being led astray by the spirit of ecumenicalism?

We know there will be a one-world church in the last days, but God's people should have no part of it. You cannot unite darkness with light, or truth with untruth. You cannot unite those who on one side believe in a salvation by works, and the other on a salvation by faith. Oneness with God cannot be achieved by throwing away pure doctrine and replacing it with doctrines of men. Oneness can only come about in believing the truth: *And for their sakes I sanctify myself, that they also might be sanctified through the truth. 20 Neither pray I for these alone, but for them also which shall believe on me through their word; 21 That they all may be one; as thou, Father, art in me, and I in thee, that they also may be one in us: that the world may believe that thou hast sent me. 22 And the glory which thou gavest me I have given them; that they may be one, even as we are one: 23 I in them, and thou in me, that they may be made perfect in one; and that the world may know that thou hast sent me, and hast loved them, as thou hast loved me* (John 17:19-23).

There are those who have religious leaders who will not seek for truth. They will keep their people under bondage, and will not turn them loose, as Jesus said in Matthew 23:15: *Woe unto you, scribes and Pharisees, hypocrites! for ye compass sea and land to make one proselyte, and when he is made, ye make him twofold more the child of hell than yourselves.* It's time the wise began to disperse knowledge, and fulfill Proverbs 15:7: *The lips of the wise disperse knowledge: but the heart of the foolish doeth not so.* Those who will not be corrected fulfill Proverbs 15:10-12: *Correction is grievous unto him that forsaketh the way: and he that hateth reproof shall die. 11 Hell and destruction are before the LORD: how much more then the hearts of the children of men?12 A scorner loveth not one that reproveth him: neither will he go unto the wise.*

Those who are of the world will never be in unity with Christ, but will perish at the Lord's coming unless converted. The Lord will keep His own, because the Lord has given them His Word. The world always hates the Word, because they are of darkness, and not of light. I pray we let truth become our sanctification concerning the coming of the Lord and connecting doctrines. When pretribulationists believe what Jesus said in Matthew 24, they will no longer be pretribulationists. John said it is truth that sanctifies: *And now I am no more in the world, but these are in the world, and I come to thee. Holy Father, keep through thine own name those whom thou hast given me, that they may be one, as we are. 12 While I was with them in the world, I kept them in thy name: those that thou gavest me I have kept, and none of them is lost, but the son of perdition; that the scripture might be fulfilled. 13 And now come I to thee; and these things I speak in the world, that they might have my joy fulfilled in themselves. 14 I have given them thy word; and the world hath hated them, because they are not of the world, even as I am not of the world. 15 I pray not that thou shouldest take them out of the world, but that thou shouldest keep them from the evil. 16 They are not of the world, even as I am not of the world. 17 Sanctify them through thy truth: thy word is truth* (John 17:11-17).

God's people have a vital task in preaching the truth concerning when Jesus is coming again. The marriage is not too far in the future. The Lord's bride should be ready. The sad part is those who hear the gospel, and turn a deaf ear to it, will be cast into outer darkness, because they were never clothed with the robe of Christ's righteousness. Those who are cast out are trying to get to heaven by their own righteousness, and not His. Many will be called but few will be chosen because they would not believe truth. Jesus said there will be weeping and gnashing of teeth by those who are cast into outer darkness: *Go ye therefore into the highways, and as many as ye shall find, bid to the marriage. 10 So those servants went out into the highways, and gathered together all as many as they found, both bad and good: and the wedding was furnished with guests. 11 And when the king came in to see the guests, he saw there a man which had not on a wedding garment: 12 And he saith unto him, Friend, how camest thou in hither not having a wedding garment? And he was speechless. 13 Then said the king to the servants, Bind him hand and foot, and take him away, and cast him into outer darkness; there shall be weeping and gnashing of teeth. 14 For many are called, but few are chosen* (Matthew 22:9-14).

It is often hard for those who are in denominations to change because they take on the same spirit. It will also be hard for those who are in churches that teach a pretribulation rapture to change, but God is able to open eyes for each to see truth concerning the Lord's coming. I do not claim to be a theologian, or know all the answers, but I do know there has been a mistake made concerning the pretribulation rapture theory that affects millions of people whom I love. I do know that if it is not corrected it will mislead and destroy the faith of many in coming years when their teachings fail.

WHERE DARBY
AND SCOFIELD
WENT WRONG

I realize how fallible mankind really is when I see learned men with college degrees make bad doctrinal decisions, while we see other great men like George Muller pushed aside when he challenged Darby and the pretribulation rapture theory. I pray this generation will humble themselves and admit that mistakes were made concerning the pretribulation rapture theory and correct it.

Darby went wrong when he believed the writings of the Jesuit Manuel Lacunza, and maybe others of whom we have no records, but we do know after visiting McDonald he became convinced there was going to be a pretribulation rapture for the Church. This could only come about if he separated the Church and Israel by the dispensational teaching he developed. He should have tried the spirit of Manuel Lacunza and Margaret McDonald by the Word, and found the error, but he did not. Scofield went wrong as a young man by the early influence of the Brethren concerning dispensationalism. He became convinced that their doctrine was right and took on the same spirit as he was taught. Scofield also had a responsibility to try the spirit of dispensationalism and see if it was in line with the Word. Both Darby and Scofield should have followed the advice of I John 4:1: *Beloved, believe not every spirit, but try the spirits whether they are of God: because many false prophets are gone out into the world.*

Darby went wrong in doctrines when he changed from a historist to a futurist method of interpretation of Revelation. This method of dispensationalism places the rapture in Revelation 4:1, and from that point the seven-year tribulation would start. As a futurist he believed that the bulk of Revelation would be fulfilled after the rapture of the Church. The tragedy is that this method of interpretation become the dominant interpretation of Revelation, and can be easily traced from Darby to Scofield, and to men such as, W. E. Blackstone, G. Campbell Morgan, H. A. Ironside, A. C. Gaebelein, and to pretribulationists today. When a person takes away the dispensationalist's view that the rapture of the Church takes place in Revelation 4:1, and understands that the angel was talking to John, not the Church, to come up hither, it changes the whole meaning of Revelation concerning the Church and Israel. When we read the fourth chapter, we immediately see a throne was set in heaven, and the early Church Saints around the throne who had died, or were killed before A.D. 95. The fourth chapter is not about the tribulation period. Darby went wrong when he took a futurist view of interpretation of the Revelation, and millions of others have followed his doctrine.

False doctrines concerning the coming of the Lord and the tribulation period began in Paul's day in the Thessalonian Church, and took another twist when Darby and Scofield developed dispensationalism. Paul had to correct the false prophets who had gotten into the Thessalonian church and were teaching that the tribulation period was already in progress. Paul let them know in his second letter that this was false teaching, and that the Lord would not gather His saints unto Himself until the apostasy comes first and the man of sin be revealed (I Thessalonians 2:1-3). The mistake that was made concerning dispensationalism and the pretribulation rapture is just as serious today as the false prophets were in the Thessalonian church—both bring confusion and apostasy. When the man of sin is revealed and tells the saints that he is god, and that they should worship him, it will overthrow the faith of many because the rapture has not taken place. Many will believe the false prophet and the man of sin, fulfilling what Jesus said concerning the apostasy (Matthew 24:9-12, 48-51). The teachings of dispensationalism and the pretribulation rapture as taught by Darby and Scofield will be a greater problem in these last days to the Church than the false teachers in the Thessalonian church.

You can find the beginning of Scofield's error in the introduction to his Scofield Reference Bible: "Just as Israel is in the foreground from the call of Abraham to the resurrection of Christ, so now the Church fills the scene from the second chapter of Acts to the fourth chapter of Revelation." Dispensationalists believe that the dispensation of Law starts with Moses and goes through the Gospels to Acts chapter 2 and starts again for the Jew after the Church is raptured in Revelation the fourth chapter. They call the rapture of the Church, where no one will see it take place, the secret coming of the Lord, and then seven years later every eye will see Him coming in the revelation. There is no secret coming before the tribulation period. The entire Church rapture theory is built on the assumption that the Gospels are not for the Church.

John the Baptist proved this to be wrong, and showed that Jesus was the beginning of a new dispensation, and prepared the way of the Lord. John pointed out that all men, Jew and Gentile, were under a new dispensation when he said in John 1:12: *But as many as received him, to them gave he power to become the sons of God, even to them that believe on his name.* John let the people know that God's grace was passing from Moses and the Law unto the grace and truth of Jesus Christ. Jesus starts a new dispensation in the Gospels, not Acts the chapter 2. *John bare witness of him, and cried, saying, This was he of whom I spake, He that cometh after me is preferred before me: for he was before me. 16 And of his fulness have all we received, and grace for grace. 17 For the law was given by Moses, but grace and truth came by Jesus Christ* (John 1:15-17).

God has always been a God of grace. John is letting all people know that God is shifting grace from the Law of Moses and the Old Covenant to the grace of salvation by faith in Jesus Christ. John lets us know that a new dispensation starts with Jesus; therefore what Jesus said in Matthew 24 about His coming applies to the Church, and not to the Jew only.

I wanted to test the teaching of Darby and Scofield concerning the coming of the Lord and see if dispensational teaching had remained the same, so I contacted a friend who belonged to the Plymouth Brethren. I told him that I believed Darby and Scofield had made a mistake concerning the pretribulation rapture of the Church and the coming of the Lord. I told him, I believe the Gospels, I Thessalonians 4, II Thessalonians 2, and Revelation teach only one coming, which is posttribulation. He said, "No! no! that can not be so, because the Gospels belong under the dispensation of law, not grace. Therefore the Lord's coming in the Gospels is speaking only to the Jew and not the Church." His analysis will hold true to dispensationalists of today.

The first six chapters of this book reveal why and how the pretribulation rapture theory had its beginning. The teaching of a pretribulation rapture of the Church has caused many pastors, teachers, and laymen to receive a doctrine not based upon facts, but upon dispensational teaching. There are many pastors who teach and preach a pretribulation rapture because they have never been taught the truth concerning the coming of the Lord, or how the doctrine got started. Many of these pastors would never teach their members that the Gospels are not for the Church because they know that would be error, yet they continue to teach a pretribulation rapture. Truth should be taught about the origin of the pretribulation rapture so pastors can know what Jesus taught about His coming is for the Church, and teach truth concerning the Lord's coming. Paul did not change the Lord's doctrine that is recorded in the Gospels. When truth is made known, the words of Jesus in the Gospels take on a new meaning, and the walls built by misinterpretation of dispensationalism come tumbling down.

Many Churches of today, along with pastors and teachers, are equally blind to the facts concerning the Lord's coming as the Jews were in realizing that Jesus was the Messiah. The Jews had the word of the Old Testament, but could not see its true meaning, just as today we have the Old and New Testaments, yet Bible teachers and preachers explain away the truth concerning the Lord's coming. Scofield and Darby went wrong in their development of dispensational teachings and doctrines that do not hold true to the Word. Out of this, the pretribulation rapture theory was developed. They accepted the spirit of error, and passed this spirit on to the Church.

Many dispensationalists say the prophetic time clock stopped concerning Israel with the birth of the Church and will start again at the Church rapture, but before the seven year tribulation period. God's prophetic time clock never stops for the Jews or Gentiles until all of the Old and New Testaments are fulfilled. God did not cast away all His people, and abandon them to wrath and ruin until the rapture, but saved those who believed according to the election of grace. In Elijah's time there was a chosen remnant saved according to the election of grace, just as in the early Church there was a much larger remnant of

Jews saved. Paul makes it plain that the clock did not stop for the Jew when the Church began: *I say then, Hath God cast away his people? God forbid. For I also am an Israelite, of the seed of Abraham, of the tribe of Benjamin. 2 God hath not cast away his people which he foreknew. Wot ye not what the scripture saith of Elias? how he maketh intercession to God against Israel, saying, 3 Lord, they have killed thy prophets, and digged down thine altars; and I am left alone, and they seek my life. 4 But what saith the answer of God unto him? I have reserved to myself seven thousand men, who have not bowed the knee to the image of Baal. 5 Even so then at this present time also there is a remnant according to the election of grace. 6 And if by grace, then is it no more of works: otherwise grace is no more grace. But if it be of works, then is it no more grace: otherwise work is no more work* (Romans 11:1-6).

Israel did not obtain that which they sought for, but the election hath obtained and the rest were blinded. It was through their fall that salvation came unto the Gentiles, to provoke them to jealousy. If the fall of them be the riches of the world, how much more shall they be a blessing to the Church when they are grafted back into the Church (Rom. 11:7-15). The conversion of the Jews which had been broken off because of unbelief will bring great joy to the Church. The early Jewish believers were the olive tree and the Gentiles were a wild olive branch that was grafted in. The branches that were broken off will be much easier to graft into the olive tree (verse 17). God could not graft the Jews back into the olive tree if the Church is raptured as pretribulationists teach.

The time clock did not stop for Israel at the end of Daniel's sixty-ninth week. After the Messiah's death Jerusalem was destroyed, and the Jews were scattered throughout the whole world as Daniel had prophesied, but the prophetic time clock did not stop for Israel. It continued to run even in their dispersion: *And after threescore and two weeks shall Messiah be cut off, but not for himself: and the people of the prince that shall come shall destroy the city and the sanctuary; and the end thereof shall be with a flood, and unto the end of the war desolations are determined* (Daniel 9:26). Just because there is a gap between the sixty-ninth and seventieth weeks does not mean the time clock stopped for Israel. The dispersion of the Jews to the four corners of the earth in A.D. 70 took place over forty years after the Messiah was crucified. If God's time clock had stopped for the Jew, they would not have been brought back to their own land in 1948 before the rapture of the Church. If the Gentiles, being a wild olive tree were grafted in, surely God is able to graft the natural branches in again to fulfill Romans 11:14-32. Blindness is only in part to Israel until the Gentiles come in. Daniel's seventieth week will begin before the rapture of the Church because of the election of grace. The early Church had a remnant of Jews saved, and Jews have been saved down through Church history; thousands are saved every year. There will be at least 144,000 of the children of Israel saved in the tribulation period before the rapture of the Church because Revelation pictures the 144,000 standing before the throne of God in heaven (Rev. 14:1:4). When God says a remnant will be saved and grafted into the olive tree, it will be accomplished, regardless of errors made by dispensationalists.

The time clock did not stop for Israel because there are many prophecies that Isaiah made concerning Israel and the Church that must be fulfilled in the Church age. Isaiah 53 deals with the death of Jesus. In chapter 54 is a song that accompanies salvation. Israel had been a barren wife, but the Gentiles would bring forth children because God is a God of the whole earth, redeeming both Jew and Gentile in verse 5. Chapter 55 calls for a global salvation for every one that is thirsty, and they are asked to come and drink of the waters of salvation. In chapter 56, verses 7-8 deal with the salvation of Jews and Gentiles, fulfilled in what Jesus said in John 10:16. Jesus used the Old Testament prophets as a foundation of His ministry, and often quoted them. Paul also used the prophets and Moses as a foundation of his ministry. When he stood before King Agrippa, he told him that he had said none other thing than what the prophets and Moses did say should come, and that Jesus would suffer and die, and be a light unto the people, and the Gentiles (Acts 26:19-23). You cannot take the root of Old Testament prophecies and the Gospels and cut them off from the Church. The following Scripture could not have been fulfilled concerning the Jews and Gentiles if the time clock had stopped for Israel when the Church had its beginning: *The Lord GOD which gathereth the outcasts of Israel saith, Yet will I gather others to him, beside those that are gathered unto him* (Isaiah 56:8). God's time clock will only stop when the last enemy is destroyed which is death, and the Lord delivers the kingdom of God unto the Father (I Corinthians 15:20-28).

This chapter shows where Darby and Scofield went wrong in doctrine concerning dispensationalism and the pretribulation rapture theory. The next two chapters concerning the Babylonian captivity for the Jews and Daniel's seventy weeks help us to understand the New Covenant recorded in the Gospels, and will show that the Gospels were given to both Jew and Gentile. It will show how important the Gospels and Revelation are for the Church. Daniel's sixty-ninth week and the Law ended with John the Baptist, and a new dispensation of grace and truth began with Jesus. Jesus gave salvation to all that believed (John 1:11-17). I will show in these next two chapters that Jesus, His ministry, and what He taught about His coming again applies to the Church, and must not be discounted by dispensationalism.

THE BABYLONIAN CAPTIVITY FOR JUDAH

For many years I have seen graphs and charts which were contrary to the Word and history. It is very important that our graphs and time lines line up with the Word first, and also with history. I searched the Word and books for correct historical dates in acquiring information for this and the next chapter. It is very important that we have accurate dates for the beginning and end of Daniel's sixty-nine weeks. You will see proof in these two chapters that John the Baptist brought an end to the dispensation of Law, and a new dispensation had its beginning. The chart at the end of the next chapter will correct much misunderstanding.

Nebuchadnezzar's first attack on Jerusalem was in 598 B.C. He took Ezekiel and other captives to Babylon, and while there Ezekiel was called to be a prophet. In 587 B.C. the Babylonian army began the siege of Jerusalem, and it fell to Nebuchadnezzar in August 586 B.C. The walls were broken down, the temple destroyed, and the furnishings of the temple were taken to Babylon for the fulfillment of seventy years of serving the king of Babylon (Jeremiah 25:11-12). Perhaps 50,000 Jews were transported to Babylon in the two deportations of Nebuchadnezzar. Daniel, Hananiah, Mishael, Asariah, and Zedekiah were only a small number of those taken. They took the best of the people from Judah to Babylon: *Children in whom was no blemish, but well favoured, and skilful in all wisdom, and cunning in knowledge, and understanding science, and such as had ability in them to stand in the king's palace, and whom they might teach the learning and the tongue of the Chaldeans* (Daniel 1:4).

While Daniel was in Babylon he interpreted the dream of Nebuchadnezzar concerning the great image which he had seen (Daniel 2:31-45). The head of gold on the image represented the Babylonian Empire, his breast and arms of silver represented the kingdom that followed, which was the Medes and Persians empire (538-333 B.C.). The belly and the thighs of brass stood for Alexander the Great and the Greek Empire, which became the third empire after the fall of Media and Persian Empire. The legs of iron were the fourth kingdom, which was the Roman Empire that would break in pieces and subdue all things. The feet and toes of the image, which were part iron and part miry clay, will be the last Gentile ruling world power (Daniel 11:36-45; 12:1-13). The Lord will destroy the Antichrist and the last Gentile world power at his coming (Daniel 2:41-45). Daniel was shown all the world empires that would affect the children of Israel during the fulfillment of Daniel's seventy weeks.

Belshazzar the king made a great feast for a thousand of his lords and drank wine out of the golden and silver vessels that his father Nebuchadnezar had taken from the temple in Jerusalem. They drank wine and praised the gods of gold and silver, of brass, of iron, of wood, and of stone. The same hour came forth fingers of a man's hand writing on the plaster of the wall of the king's palace. The king's wise men could not read the writing, nor make known to the king the interpretation. When Daniel was brought before the king, he interpreted the writing. Daniel told Belshazzar that God had numbered his kingdom, and finished it; he was weighed in the balances, and found wanting. Daniel let him know that his kingdom would be given to the Medes and Persians (Daniel 5:1-28). That same night Belshazzar was slain, and Darius the Mede took the kingdom of Babylon in 539 B.C. (Daniel 5:30-31).

Cyrus the Great founded the ancient Persian Empire and was king of Media and Persia. In 539 B.C. during the first year of his reign, he issued a decree that the temple in Jerusalem be rebuilt, and the gold and silver which Nebuchadnezzar had taken from the temple be restored (Ezra 1:1-11). Darius, who had conquered Babylon, became king of the Medean and Persian Empire, and searched to find the decree made by Cyrus. Darius authorized the Jews to resume the work that had been hindered and finish the temple at Jerusalem, in accordance with the earlier decree of Cyrus. This was completed in 516 B.C., the sixth year of Darius (Ezra 6:15). This fulfilled the seventy years of desolation (II Chronicles 36:20-21). Darius made a decree, after God delivered Daniel from the lion's den, that every dominion of his kingdom tremble and fear before the God of Daniel. Daniel prospered in the reigns of Cyrus and Darius (Daniel 6:25-28). After the reign of Darius, his son Xerxes 1 took the throne in 485 B.C. The younger son of Xerxes 1, Artaxarxes 1, became king. He reigned from 465 to 424 B.C. In the seventh year of Artaxerxes, he made a decree that allowed Ezra the priest to rebuild the city of Jerusalem. Nehemiah, his cupbearer, was appointed as governor of Judaea in 445 B.C. The decree permitted all the people of Israel, including the priests and Levites in his realm, to go up to Jerusalem with Ezra (Ezra 7:1, 6-28). The Encyclopedia Britannica states the decree was made in 458 B.C. There were eighty years between the decree made by Cyrus and the decree made by Artaxerxes that all the Jews could go back to their own land.

From the time Babylon conquered Jerusalem in 598 B.C., it took three decrees before all the Jews could return to their homeland. It took 140 years since Jerusalem fell until Artaxarxes gave the decree that Ezra and all the children of Israel could go back to Jerusalem in 458 B.C. Jeremiah's prophecy said that the land would be a desolation and the Jews will serve the king of Babylon for 70 years, and God would punish the king of Babylon for his iniquity, and would visit His people, causing them to return to their land (Jeremiah 25:11-12; 29:10). In the first year of the reign of Darius, Daniel understood by the books the number of years whereof the word of the LORD came to Jeremiah the prophet, that he would accomplish seventy years in the desolation of Jerusalem (Daniel 9:1-2). While Daniel was in prayer, the man Gabriel came to him and gave him skill and understanding concerning seventy weeks that were to be upon his people, and upon Jerusalem.

THE SEVENTY
WEEKS OF DANIEL

The Babylonian captivity was the turning point in the history of the Jews. From that point forward until 1948, the Jews have been under the domination of other nations. They have one more domination to endure before the Lord delivers them and judges the Gentile nations. While Daniel was in captivity in Babylon, he was praying and acknowledging the sins of his people and how they had departed from God's precepts and judgments. This took place in the first year Darius was made king over the realm of the Chaldeans. While Daniel was speaking and praying, Gabriel, whom he had seen in the vision at the beginning, informed him that he had come to give him skill and understanding of the vision concerning the seventy weeks upon his people and upon the holy city of Jerusalem. Gabriel told Daniel that he was greatly beloved, therefore he would give him understanding of the matter, and consider the vision: *Seventy weeks are determined upon thy people and upon thy holy city, to finish the transgression, and to make an end of sins, and to make reconciliation for iniquity, and to bring in everlasting righteousness, and to seal up the vision and prophecy, and to anoint the most Holy. 25 Know therefore and understand, that from the going forth of the commandment to restore and to build Jerusalem unto the Messiah the Prince shall be seven weeks, and threescore and two weeks: the street shall be built again, and the wall, even in troublous times. 26 And after threescore and two weeks shall Messiah be cut off, but not for himself: and the people of the prince that shall come shall destroy the city and the sanctuary; and the end thereof shall be with a flood, and unto the end of the war desolations are determined. 27 And he shall confirm the covenant with many for one week: and in the midst of the week he shall cause the sacrifice and the oblation to cease, and for the overspreading of abominations he shall make it desolate, even until the consummation, and that determined shall be poured upon the desolate* (Daniel 9:24-27).

Moses had given the children of Israel warning of the punishment that results from sin: *But if ye will not hearken unto me, and will not do all these commandments;15 And if ye shall despise my statutes, or if your soul abhor my judgments, so that ye will not do all my commandments, but that ye break my covenant:16 I also will do this unto you; I will even appoint over you terror, consumption, and the burning ague, that shall consume the eyes, and cause sorrow of heart: and ye shall sow your seed in vain, for your enemies shall eat it.17 And I will set my face against you, and ye shall be slain before your enemies: they that hate you shall reign over you; and ye shall flee when none pursueth you.18 And if ye will not yet for all this hearken unto me, then I will punish you seven times more for your sins. 21 And if ye walk contrary unto me, and will not hearken unto me; I will bring seven times more plagues upon you according to your sins. 24 Then will I also walk contrary unto you, and will punish you yet seven times for your sins. 28 Then I will walk contrary unto you also in fury; and I, even I, will chastise you seven times for your sins. 33 And I will scatter you among the heathen, and will draw out a sword after you: and your land shall be desolate, and your cities waste.34 Then shall the land enjoy her sabbaths, as long as it lieth desolate, and ye be in your enemies' land; even then shall the land rest, and enjoy her sabbaths* (Lev. 26:14-34). God would punish Israel for their sins according to His Word given by the prophets. God knew the future of Israel, and gave Daniel the interpretation of the seventy weeks concerning His people, and the holy city Jerusalem.

The Hebrews had weeks of years, which were reckoned from one sabbatical year to another, and consisted of seven times seven years, and "the space of seven sabbaths of years shall be unto the forty and nine years" (Lev. 24:8). Laban used this method when he told Jacob to fulfill Rachel's week of seven years before she could be his wife (Gen. 29:26-28). After the Egyptian bondage, God spoke to Moses concerning the judgment of the children of Israel because of the sin of unbelief in possessing the promised land: God established a day for a year in *Numbers 14:32:24: But as for you, your carcases, they shall fall in this wilderness. 33 And your children* shall wander in the wilderness forty years, and bear your whoredoms, until your carcases be wasted in the wilderness. 34 After the number of the days in which ye searched the land, even forty days, each day for a year, shall ye bear your iniquities, even forty years, and ye shall know my breach of promise (Num. 14:11-45). Ezekiel was taken captive to Babylon with Daniel. God spoke to Ezekiel concerning Israel and Judah. His prophecy used the same method in counting a day for a year concerning Israel and Judah (Ezek. 4:1-6). Judah was aware of the method of counting a day for a year in Daniel's time.

The seventy weeks of Daniel represent each week as seven years, therefore seventy weeks is 70 X 7 = 490 years before the vision is fulfilled. Daniel 9:25 says that from the going forth of the commandment to restore and to build Jerusalem unto the Messiah would be seven weeks, (49 years,) and threescore and two weeks, (434 years). Both of these added together make a total of 483 years. We must take special notice of verse 25 because it does not say that the sixty-nine weeks start with the rebuilding of the temple, but start when the commandment is given to restore and to build again, and the wall, even in troublous times. Daniel 9:26 tells us that after the sixty-two weeks the Messiah would be cut off, and the city destroyed, and the desolation of Israel would follow. The desolation lasted until 1948 when the Lord brought his people back to their own land as He promised in Ezekiel 36 and 37. There are seven remaining years to be fulfilled.

Before the Babylonian exile, months were commonly designated by number in the Jewish calendar, but during the exile the Jews adopted the Babylonian names of the months. These names spread to Palestine, where Nisan, Sivan, Elul, Kislev, Tebet, Shebat, and Adar are used in the Bible. The fact that months and years cannot be divided exactly by days, and years cannot be divided exactly by months, leads to different calculations in figuring years. The Hebrew year is based on the moon, and normally consists of twelve months. You cannot take a 360-day Hebrew year in calculating the 483 years of Daniel's sixty-nine weeks without adding the extra days that they allowed in order to make their lunar years correct over a period of time. I believe the only adjustment that needs to be made in counting the years is the error that was made concerning the date of the birth of Christ.

There must be an accounting of the sixty-nine weeks or 483 years in Daniel 9:25. The *Dictionary of the Bible, Britannica, Columbia,* and

World Book Encyclopedias give much information about the dates of the subsequent events and dates after the fall of Babylon in 539 B.C., but the Bible is the final authority. Cyrus made a proclamation that the God of heaven charged him to build Him a house in Jerusalem. Zerubbabel acted as governor, and 49,867 Jews returned to Jerusalem to begin the work of rebuilding the temple (Ezra 2:64-65). This decree took place in 538 B.C. The work on the temple was hindered until Darius was made king of Persia in 521 B.C. In the first year of his reign he searched and found the decree made by Cyrus, and decreed that the proclamation made by Cyrus must be fulfilled (Ezra 6:3). In the second year of the reign of Darius, work resumed on the temple (Ezra 4:24). The temple was finished and dedicated in the sixth year of his reign, 516 B.C. (Ezra 6:1-17). There are some years of silence until Artaxerxes comes to power. He made a decree in the seventh year of his reign that Ezra, all priests, Levites, and Jews could return to Jerusalem (Ezra 7:1-28), and this took place in 458 B.C. Several years passed before Nehemiah was appointed governor by Artaxerxes in 445 B.C. (Neh. 5:14). Nehemiah was given permission to take a larger group to Palestine to build the walls and restore Jerusalem in the twelfth year of the reign of Artaxerxes (Nehemiah 2:1-20). The walls were finished in seventy days (Nch. 6:15-16). There was an eighty-year span between the decree made by Cyrus to rebuild the temple and the decree made by Artaxerxes that all Jews could go to Jerusalem.

We cannot start the fulfillment of the sixty-nine weeks when Cyrus made the decree in 538 B.C. because it was in the first year of Darius that Gabriel revealed the secret to Daniel. The fulfillment of the sixty-nine weeks could not start in that year because the 483 years would be fulfilled 50 years before the birth of Jesus. The fulfillment of the 69 weeks cannot start when Darius authorized the Jews to honor the decree made by Cyrus concerning rebuilding the temple, either. Daniel said the time would start when the commandment was given to restore and to build Jerusalem unto the Messiah (Daniel 9:25). Darius made this decree in 519 B.C., and this would make the fulfillment of the 483 years fall 31 years before Jesus was born. There can only be one place where the fulfillment of the 483 years of Daniel's sixty-nine weeks can start, and it is when King Artaxerxes made the decree in 458 B.C. that all the people of Israel could go back to Jerusalem. This makes the time element concur with Scripture. We must first make a correction in the calendar concerning the birth of Jesus. Herod died in 4 B.C., and we know that Jesus was born before his death. Joseph and Mary fled to Egypt until the death of Herod (Matthew 2:1, 19-20). The *Dictionary of the Bible*, edited by James Hastings, and many other references set the date when Jesus was born as being 5 B.C. If Jesus was born in 5 B.C. and His ministry began at age 30, that would make His ministry begin in A.D. 25, and His crucifixion take place in A.D. 28. If the sixty-nine weeks of Daniel, or the 483 years, is to be fulfilled from the going forth of the commandment to restore and to build Jerusalem by Artaxerxes unto the Messiah the Prince in Daniel 9:25, we must deduct 5 years from 458 B.C., which would be 453 years unto the time Jesus was born, in order to account for Jesus being born in 5 B.C. Then there must be another 30 years in order to fulfill the 483 years of Daniel's sixty-nine weeks unto the Messiah. When you take the going forth of the decree by Artaxerxes in 458 B.C. until the end of the ministry of John the Baptist, the beginning of the ministry of Jesus at age 30 is 483 years. This makes the fulfillment of Daniel's sixty-nine weeks.

The date for the closing of the sixty-nine weeks was when John the Baptist ended his ministry. He prepared the way of the Lord, and quoted Isaiah the prophet in Matthew 3:3: *For this is he that was spoken of by the prophet Esaias, saying, The voice of one crying in the wilderness, Prepare ye the way of the Lord, make his paths straight.* His message was, "Repent, for the kingdom of Heaven is at Hand," not the millennial kingdom, but the rule of the Lord in His spiritual kingdom. Jesus began the fulfillment of this Scripture when He called His disciples, and they were the first members of the called-out assembly, the Church. James made it plain in the book of Acts that the prophets said both Jews and Gentiles would be part of the called-out assembly (Acts 15; 13-18). John let the Jews know that the ax was laid to the root of the Jewish nation, and every tree which did not bring forth fruit would be hewn down as prophesied in Daniel 9:26. He let them know that Jesus would baptize with the Holy Ghost and with fire (Matt. 3:10-11). John was ending the dispensation of Law, and introducing them to a new dispensation of salvation. John pronounced judgment on their nation (Matthew 3:7-10), and prepared them for a new dispensation of the Lord in order to fulfill what the prophet Isaiah had prophesied (Matt. 3:1-3; Mark 3:1-6; John 1:15-17). Jesus let all know that the Law and the prophets were until John, and a new dispensation had begun: *The law and the prophets were until John: since that time the king-dom of God is preached, and every man presseth into it* (Luke 16:16). God's kingdom is within us, and is given unto us at the time of our salvation: *And when he was demanded of the Pharisees, when the kingdom of God should come, he answered them and said, The kingdom of God cometh not with obser-vation: 21 Neither shall they say, Lo here! or, lo there! for, behold, the kingdom of God is within you* (Luke 17:20-21). John the Baptist makes it plain that Jesus was the beginning of a new dispensation from the grace of God under the Law of Moses unto the grace of God that is in Christ Jesus who gives salvation to all. The Law was given by Moses, but grace and truth came by Jesus Christ: *John bare witness of him, and cried, saying, This was he of whom I spake, He that cometh after me is preferred before me: for he was before me. 16 And of his fulness have all we received, and grace for grace. 17 For the law was given by Moses, but grace and truth came by Jesus Christ* (John 1:15-17). All was under sin until Jesus came, and the Law was our schoolmaster to bring us unto Christ, so we could be justified by faith (Gal. 3:22-26).

The dispensation of Law does not end in the second chapter of Acts, as dispensationalists teach, but ends with John the Baptist when the sixty-nine weeks of Daniel were fulfilled. Jesus is the beginning of a new dispensation. Paul tells us the reason Jesus came into the world: *This is a faithful saying, and worthy of all acceptation, that Christ Jesus came into the world to save sinners; of whom I am chief. 16 Howbeit for this cause I obtained mercy, that in me first Jesus Christ might show forth all longsuffering, for a pattern to them which should hereafter believe on him to life everlasting. 17 Now unto the King eternal, immortal, invisible, the only wise God, be hon-our and glory for ever and ever. Amen* (I Timothy 1:15-17). John the Baptist tells us why Jesus came into the world: *The next day John seeth Jesus coming unto him, and saith, Behold the Lamb of God, which taketh away the sin of the world* (John 1:29).

The Scriptures above make it plain that the prophets and the Law were in effect until John the Baptist. He prepared the way of the Lord, which was the beginning of a new dispensation. Jesus came as a Lamb slain before the foundation of the world for the salvation of both Jews and Gentiles. John the Baptist closes the sixty-nine weeks, or 483 years, of *Daniel 9:25*. He brings to a close the dispensation of Law, but the Jews continued to use the temple and offer sacrifices until it was destroyed (Luke 16:16). Judgment was announced on the Jewish nation because they had brought forth no fruit in the 483 years since leaving Babylon (Matthew 3:7-10). Jesus began His ministry after John was cast into prison. His own people did not receive Him, but He offered salvation to all who would believe: *But as many as received him, to them gave he power to become the sons of God, even to them that believe on his name* (John 1:11-12). Jesus asked the twelve disciples to go to the lost sheep of the house of Israel first, because they were God's chosen people (Matthew 10:5-8). Jesus did not announce immediate judgment, but first called the Jewish nation to repentance and salvation. There was only a remnant who believed and were saved. Jesus spoke a parable concerning His ministry to the Jewish nation. If it did not bear fruit in three years it was to be cut down: *He spake also this parable; A certain man had a fig tree planted in his vineyard; and he came and sought fruit thereon, and found none. 7 Then said he unto the dresser of his vineyard, Behold, these three years I come seeking fruit on this fig tree, and find none: cut it down; why cumbereth it the ground? 8 And he answering said unto him, Lord, let it alone this year also, till I shall dig about it, and dung it* (Luke 13:6-9). After three years Jesus was rejected and crucified, fulfilling Daniel 9:26. Three thousand were saved on the day of Pentecost, and many others were saved in the early Church. Others were blinded because God had given them ample time to repent and believe on Jesus as the Messiah. Paul went to the Jewish synagogues first, but they also rejected him: *It was necessary that the word of God should first have been spoken to you: but seeing ye put it from you, and judge yourselves unworthy of everlasting life, lo, we turn to the Gentiles* (Acts 13:46). The Jewish nation was now sealed for judgment.

Jesus was the beginning of a new dispensation of grace and truth for the salvation of all people. If the Law and the prophets were until John, when a new dispensation started, it must be reconciled with the end of Daniel's sixty-nine weeks: *And after threescore and two weeks shall Messiah be cut off, but not for himself: and the people of the prince that shall come shall destroy the city and the sanctuary; and the end thereof shall be with a flood, and unto the end of the war desolations are determined. 27 And he shall confirm the covenant with many for one week: and in the midst of the week he shall cause the sacrifice and the oblation to cease, and for the overspreading of abominations he shall make it desolate, even until the consummation, and that determined shall be poured upon the desolate* (Daniel 9:26-27). Verse 26 tells us after sixty-two weeks the Messiah will be cut off, or crucified. This took place three years after the ministry of John the Baptist ended, and the ministry of Jesus was completed (John 17:1-18). After the cross, the city of Jerusalem was destroyed in A.D. 70. Daniel said at the end of the war the desolation of Jerusalem would follow. The dispersion of the Jews lasted until 1948 when Israel became a nation again. The seventieth week of Daniel is yet to be fulfilled. The twelfth chapter of Daniel lets us know about the great tribulation period and the fulfillment of the seventieth week. The resurrection takes place at the end of the seventieth week (Daniel 12:1-3), and will include both Jews and Gentiles. The resurrection recorded in Daniel 12:1-3 and Revelation 20:4-6 is the same resurrection that takes place before the wrath of God is poured out on the wicked in the Epistles. Paul did not teach a different resurrection for the righteous than Daniel or Jesus taught, but taught the same resurrection for the saints in I Thessalonians 4:13-17. This chapter gives insight concerning the seventy weeks of Daniel, and how the ministry of Jesus and His great salvation fit into the gap between the sixty-ninth and the end of the seventieth week of Daniel. This book will show how important the Gospels and the book of Revelation is to the Church.

Just because the Jews are God's chosen people and God gave them the first opportunity for salvation does not mean that the Gospels are not equally important to the Gentiles. John marks the end of the old dispensation of the Law and the sixty-nine weeks. Jesus begins the new dispensation for the salvation of both Jews and Gentiles. Paul makes this plain in Romans 1:13-17: *Now I would not have you ignorant, brethren, that oftentimes I purposed to come unto you, (but was let hitherto,) that I might have some fruit among you also, even as among other Gentiles. 14 I am debtor both to the Greeks, and to the Barbarians; both to the wise, and to the unwise. 15 So, as much as in me is, I am ready to preach the gospel to you that are at Rome also. 16 For I am not ashamed of the gospel of Christ: for it is the power of God unto salvation to every one that believeth; to the Jew first, and also to the Greek. 17 For therein is the righteousness of God revealed from faith to faith: as it is written, The just shall live by faith.*

The Church must not accept forms of dispensationalism that are contrary to the Word of God. Darby and Scofield were wrong when they extended the dispensation of Law to the second chapter of Acts. By this method of dispensationalism, they voided what Jesus said about His coming again applying to the Church. Thus, the pretribulation rapture was made believable and brought us where we are today.

The Church should also reject a form of dispensationalism that teaches that Israel and the law extends through Acts. They believe the dispensation of grace begins with Paul in Romans and extends to Philemon, where the rapture takes place. They also believe the gospel of the kingdom begins in Hebrews and extends through Revelation. This is another form of dispensationalism which does not conform to the Word. God's paople should be careful in accepting every wind of doctrine in these last days (Ephesians 4:13-16).

When Jesus called His disciples and they believed He was the Messiah and followed Him, this began the New Testament Church and the beginning of the fulfillment of the gap between the sixty-ninth and seventieth weeks of Daniel. The ministry and resurrection of Jesus took place after the sixty-ninth week ended, and these facts make the Gospels, the death and resurrection, and the covenant of salvation apply to all people and not to the Jew only. This time-line chart gives scriptural proof of when the dispensation of Law ended and began to vanish away.

THE 70 WEEKS OF DANIEL

(I) Daniel had a vision while in captivity in Babylon concerning the sins and transgressions of his people, and the future of Jerusalem. Gabriel gave him understanding concerning the vision, and the seventy weeks of years (Daniel 9:20-27).

The sixty-nine weeks of Daniel started when King Artaxerxes made a decree that all the people of Israel could go back to Jerusalem in 458 B.C. (Ezra 7:12-13), and it stops at the end of John's ministry, which make's 483 years.

Jesus was born before Herod died in 4 B.C., therefore He was born about 5 B.C. He began His ministry at age 30 (Luke 3:23). Therefore, it is not accurate to say Jesus began His ministry in A.D. 30, and crucified in A.D. 33. If you start year one at the birth of Jesus in 5 B.C., and add 30 years to the beginning of His ministry, it would be about A.D. 26, and would make our present calendar off by about 4 years.

THE END OF 69 WEEKS

(II) Jesus was born under the Law, to redeem those who were under the Law (Gal. 4:4-5). John and his ministry were under the law and brought to an end the 69 weeks of Daniel, and the dispensation of Law (Luke 16:16). John said he was not the"Christ, but was sent before Him, and that Jesus must increase, but he would decrease (John 3:28-30).

The Messiah would be crucified after the sixty-nine weeks were fulfilled. Desolation would follow, and there would be a gap between the sixty-ninth and seventieth week (Daniel 9:26).

Jesus was the beginning of a new dispensation for the salvation of all people. This new covenant was a covenant of faith in Jesus Christ (the Messiah) for salvation (John 1:11-12, 3:16). The Law was a shadow of good things to come (Heb. 10:1), and was a schoolmaster to bring them to Christ (Gal 3:19:24). The priesthood of Jesus was superior to the Aaronic priesthood, and there"is made of necessity a change also of the Law (Heb. 7:11-12).

(III) When Jesus said, "It is finished," the atonement was made so that all people could be saved, both Jew and Gentile. Jesus fulfilled all the requirements of the Law, and sealed the New Covenant with His blood. The temple veil, which divided between the holy place and the most holy place, was rent in twain from the top to the bottom (Matt. 27:51). This showed that all people could come freely to God without an intermediary and He would put the Law in their heart and mind under the New Covenant of Salvation (Heb.10:1-23). The Old Covenant was made old by the New, and began to decay and vanish away (Heb. 8:13).

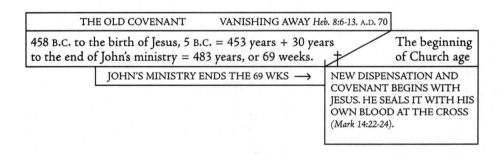

The New Covenant Promised

Some may wonder what the New Covenant has to do with the coming of the Lord. I give this information because dispensationalists discounted the Gospel's application to the Church. Yet the New Covenant was given to the Church (Jew and Gentile). When Jesus was talking in the Gospels about His coming again, He was addressing the first members of the New Testament Church, under the New Covenant that had been promised by the prophets.

Most pretribulationists give the same Scripture in attempting to prove a pretribulation rapture. Much of their problem is a lack of understanding the New Covenant given to the Church. Pretribulationists give I Thessalonians 4:16-17, and *I Corinthians 15:51-52* as the rapture of the Church. There is no error with these Two Scriptures concerning the rapture of the Church. The error is when Scriptures such as Matthew 24: 44—*Therefore be ye also ready: for in such an hour as ye think not the Son of man cometh*—are used as part of the proof concerning a pretribulation rapture. When pretribulationists use only one Scripture in the Gospels to support their belief in a pretribulation rapture, they are taking the Scripture out of context by their own teaching.

Pretribulationists go back to the Gospels and pull out a few verses to prove a pretribulation rapture, which breaks their own doctrine that the Gospels are not for the Church. If pretribulationists use one Scripture in the Gospels trying to prove their doctrine, then they should agree with what Jesus said about the timing of His coming, and the time is after the tribulation, just as Jesus said: *Immediately after the tribulation of those days shall the sun be darkened, and the moon shall not give her light, and the stars shall fall from heaven, and the powers of the heavens shall be shaken: 30 And then shall appear the sign of the Son of man in heaven: and then shall all the tribes of the earth mourn, and they shall see the Son of man coming in the clouds of heaven with power and great glory* (Matthew 24: 29-30).

God's people the Church need to come into agreement with the same oneness as the Father and the Son are in oneness—oneness concerning all truth, purpose and action. There needs to be a oneness in what the Bible teaches concerning the Jew and the Gentile (the Church). Look at a few differences between what the pretribulationists and posttribulationists believe:

- Pretribulationists believe that the Gospels are only for the Jew, and not the Church.
- Pretribulationists believe in a pretribulation rapture, and say Matt. 24 is not for the Church.
- Pretribulationists believe I Thessalonians 4:13-17 is the pretribulation rapture.
- Pretribulationists believe that when the Jews rejected Christ, the Lord delayed the kingdom of heaven for the Jews until the millennium.
- Pretribulationists believe the New Covenant spoken of in Jeremiah and Ezekiel will be fulfilled after the Church rapture for the Jews.

Pretribulationists should go back and search for truths taught by God's people before Darby and Scofield brought erroneous dispensational teaching into the Church concerning the coming of the Lord and connecting doctrines.

- Posttribulationists believe that the Gospels are for the Church, and the New Covenant of salvation had its beginning in the Gospels. Just because some Jews rejected Jesus as savior did not change God's plan of salvation for those who would receive Jesus: *He came unto his own, and his own received him not.12 But as many as receive him, to them gave he power to become sons of God, even to them that believe on his name* (John I:11-12). When the Gospels are discounted for the Church, the New Covenant is also discounted.

+ Posttribulationists believe that the second advent is for the rapture and resurrection at the end of the tribulation, and not before. There is no "split" or "secret" coming. The wrath of God and the judgment follows the rapture. The second coming in the Gospels and the Epistles are the same coming.

+ Posttribulationists do not believe that the kingdom of heaven was set aside, but is in effect now, and His Church is ruled by the Lord Himself from heaven. The Jews were broken off, and a remnant will be grafted back into the Body of Christ again before the rapture. The kingdom of Israel is not the kingdom of heaven. The kingdom of Israel will be set up in the millenium for those not raptured, but who survived the judgment of God. Those who are left on earth will not have resurrected bodies, and will be the fulfillment of Acts 1:6-7.

Many dispensationalists get so bogged down in keeping a division between the Church and Israel that they overlook God's promises. I realize God gave the covenants to Israel (Romans 9:4), and the Gentiles were aliens from the commonwealth of Israel, and strangers from the covenants of promise, but it was Christ who made Gentiles nigh unto God by his own blood (Eph. 2:11-13). Jesus abolished in His (own crucified) flesh the enmity that was caused by the Law, and made a new man, reconciling both Jew and Gentile into one body (Eph. 2:14-16). God gave to the Jew, His covenant people, and to the Gentiles, who were made heirs of Abraham by faith in Jesus, the New Covenant of salvation (Rom. 4:9-25; Gal, 3:6:9,13-14, 22-29; Eph. 3:2-6). God broke off Israel because of unbelief, but His new covenant grafts them back into the Body of Christ again (Rom. 11:20-27). If you take away the Gospels and what Jesus taught from the Church, the foundation of the New Covenant is destroyed. We must not explain away the Gospels and what Jesus meant for the Church by erroneous interpretation of dispensationalism, because God is over all whom He called, both Jew and Gentile (Rom. 9:5, 24).

Dispensationalism, which keeps Jesus and the Gospels under the dispensation of the Law, also keeps God's people in darkness concerning many great truths and the coming of the Lord. Jesus began His ministry by saying, *Repent, for the kingdom of heaven is at hand*. It was the beginning of a new dispensation (Matt. 1:17). The Law was given by Moses, but grace and truth were given by Jesus Christ. A new dispensation began with Jesus and the Gospels for the salvation of the whole world (John 1:15-17, 29). It is Jesus that takes away the sin of the whole world, something no animal sacrifice could ever accomplish in the Old Covenant. There has always been only one way of salvation, and that way is faith. The New Covenant was ratified by the blood of Jesus, but this did not stop the disciples from getting saved by faith in Jesus before He went to the cross. Jesus was the beginning of a new dispensation, and God would deal with man in a way that would bring man out of the Old Covenant and give them all the blessings of the New Covenant. Pretribulationists think they already have the truth, and there is no need to change. They are the Pharisees of our day in believing they have all truth, but yet are so far from it. The Pharisees would not listen to Jesus, the disciples, or the Word of God under the new dispensation of Jesus. They thought they were right, but perished because they refused truth.

J. Dwight Pentecost in his book *Things to Come* quotes Darby concerning the New Covenant:

> "He presented the view that there was one and only one New Covenant in Scripture, made with the house of Israel and Judah and to be realized at a future time, to which the Church bears no relationship whatsoever. This covenant of the letter is made with Israel, not with us; but we get the benefit of it…Israel not accepting the blessing, God brought out the Church, and the Mediator of the covenant went on high. We are associated with the Mediator. It will be made good to Israel by-and-by." He goes on to say, "The gospel is not a covenant, but the revelation of the salvation of God. It proclaims the great salvation. We enjoy indeed all the essential privileges of the new covenant, its foundation being laid on God's part in the blood of Christ, but we do so in spirit, not according to the letter. The New Covenant will be established formally with Israel in the millennium."

Just because some of the Jews rejected Jesus as the Messiah does not mean that God did not establish the New Covenant with those who believed in Jesus, Jew or Gentile. The New Covenant, which gives every one who believes a new mind and a new heart, went into effect for all that believed: *He came unto his own, and his own received him not.12 But as many as received him, to them gave he power to become the sons of God, even to them that believe on his name:13 Which were born, not of blood, nor of the will of the flesh, nor of the will of man, but of God* (John 1:11-13). The New Covenant will be completed to the Jew in Ezekiel 36:24-27 when the Jews who were broken off are grafted back into the Body of Christ. I pray God's people will see what dispensationalism has done in saying the Gospels are not for the Church, but for the Jew only. There would probably be no pretribulation rapture theory if it were not for the mistake Darby and Scofield made concerning dispensationalism.

The beginning of the ministry of Jesus was the beginning of the New Covenant of Salvation for all people. This new dispensation started in the Gospels, not in the book of Acts. The book of Acts was a continuation of the Gospels (Acts 1:1) and the beginning of the New Covenant of salvation for all people. John the Baptist was the beginning of the end for the works of the law of Moses, and the beginning of a salvation by faith in Jesus: *The law and the prophets were until John: since that time the kingdom of God is preached, and every man presseth into it* (Luke 16:16). Jesus began to call the disciples unto Himself, and told them He would make them fishers of men. Paul preached the gospel which Jesus established, and was not ashamed of it, because it was the power of God unto salvation to everyone that believeth; to the Jew first, and also to the Greek. John the Baptist was the beginning of the end of the Old Covenant of Moses, and Jesus was the beginning of a new dispensation of the New Covenant. Paul showed us that it is the gospel of Christ that saves, and reveals the righteousness of God, from faith to faith (Romans 1:16-17).

A covenant is an agreement between two or more parties about things that are in their own power to come into agreement. The New Covenant was given by the Lord and He is the mediator of it. He sealed it with His own blood, and He secures to every believer the blessings of salvation and eternal life. The Second Covenant, or New Covenant, would be a better covenant than the old. Hebrews shows us the difference between the two covenants, and how the New Covenant by means of the death of Christ would secure salvation for those under the Old

Covenant, and everyone thereafter who believed in Christ. This New Covenant would be the Last Will and Testament between the Lord and His Church, the Body of Christ. When the veil was rent in twain, it opened up and secured the right for every believer, (Jew or Gentile) to become a son of God by faith in Jesus Christ: *The Holy Ghost this signifying, that the way into the holiest of all was not yet made manifest, while as the first tabernacle was yet standing: 9 Which was a figure for the time then present, in which were offered both gifts and sacrifices, that could not make him that did the service perfect, as pertaining to the conscience; 10 Which stood only in meats and drinks, and divers washings, and carnal ordinances, imposed on them until the time of reformation. 11 But Christ being come an high priest of good things to come, by a greater and more perfect tabernacle, not made with hands, that is to say, not of this building; 12 Neither by the blood of goats and calves, but by his own blood he entered in once into the holy place, having obtained eternal redemption for us. 13 For if the blood of bulls and of goats, and the ashes of an heifer sprinkling the unclean, sanctifieth to the purifying of the flesh: 14 How much more shall the blood of Christ, who through the eternal Spirit offered himself without spot to God, purge your conscience from dead works to serve the living God? 15 And for this cause he is the mediator of the new testament, that by means of death, for the redemption of the transgressions that were under the first testament, they which are called might receive the promise of eternal inheritance* (Hebrews 9:8-15). This portion of Scripture settles the argument. Jesus and the Gospel were the transition from the Old Covenant to the New for the salvation of both Jews and Gentiles.

If a person is writing a Last Will and Testament, the heirs of the will are heirs before the death of the testator. The heirship does not change after the testator dies. If the Jews and Gentiles (the Church) were heirs of the Last Will and Testament after the death of Christ, then the Last Will and Testament is for both, as found in the Gospels. If the Church is an heir, then Jesus was talking to the Church about His coming in Matthew 24. If John 1:12 or 3:16 is for the Church, so is Matthew 24.

Simeon prophesied concerning Jesus on the days of His purification according to the Law. He foresaw how the Jews and Gentiles, would be under the New Covenant of the Lord. He saw how the Gentiles would come to the light. He foresaw the crucifixion and resurrection of Jesus. Pretribulationists try to separate the Gentile Church from this Covenant of salvation for Jew and Gentile although there is not a different covenant in the Gospels for the salvation of Gentiles: *And, behold, there was a man in Jerusalem, whose name was Simeon; and the same man was just and devout, waiting for the consolation of Israel: and the Holy Ghost was upon him. 26 And it was revealed unto him by the Holy Ghost, that he should not see death, before he had seen the Lord's Christ. 27 And he came by the Spirit into the temple: and when the parents brought in the child Jesus, to do for him after the custom of the law,28 Then took he him up in his arms, and blessed God, and said, 29 Lord, now lettest thou thy servant depart in peace, according to thy word: 30 For mine eyes have seen thy salvation, 31 Which thou hast prepared before the face of all people; 32 A light to lighten the Gentiles, and the glory of thy people Israel. 33 And Joseph and his mother marvelled at those things which were spoken of him. 34 And Simeon blessed them, and said unto Mary his mother, Behold, this child is set for the fall and rising again of many in Israel; and for a sign which shall be spoken against; 35 (Yea, a sword shall pierce through thy own soul also,) that the thoughts of many hearts may be revealed* (Luke 2:25-35).

Simeon knew what the prophets had prophesied concerning Jesus. He knew that Jesus would be a covenant of all the people and a light unto the Gentiles. Simeon knew Jesus' name would be great among the Gentiles. Any doctrine that cuts the Church off from Jesus, the Gospels, and His words is in error. The basis of what Simeon saw has its root in the Old Testament: *I the LORD have called thee in righteousness, and will hold thine hand, and will keep thee, and give thee for a covenant of the people, for a light of the Gentiles* (Isaiah 42: 6). *For from the rising of the sun even unto the going down of the same my name shall be great among the Gentiles; and in every place incense shall be offered unto my name, and a pure offering: for my name shall be great among the heathen, saith the LORD of hosts* (Malachi 1:11).

The woman who was at the well in Samaria drank living water that Jesus gave her before His resurrection. The hour had already come when the worshipper could worship God in spirit and truth: *But the hour cometh, and now is, when the true worshippers shall worship the Father in spirit and in truth: for the Father seeketh such to worship him* (John 4:23). She went into her city and brought conversion to many. They were heirs of the New Covenant as much as were the disciples, and Jewish believers according to the Word. The Gentiles (the Church) did not have to wait until after the death of Jesus to become heirs of the New Covenant.

Merrill C. Tenney gives a good explanation of the meaning of the word *New Testament* in his *New Testament Survey*. The name *New Testament*, given to the second half of the English Bible, comes from the Latin Novum Testamentum, which is itself a translation of the Greek, *He Kaine Diatheke*, which means "a last will, or testament."

The New Covenant consists of twenty-seven books, the four Gospels, the book of Acts, the Epistles, and Revelation. The Gospels give us the genealogy of the birth of Jesus, showing Jew and Gentile that Jesus is the promised Messiah. The miracles proved his Messiahship. He and His teachings would be the very foundation of the New Covenant for the Church. All Church doctrine has roots extending forth from the Gospels. The Gospels give an eye-witness account of the death, burial, and resurrection of the Lord, and gives an account of all that was prophesied of Him.

Passover was celebrated in the Old Testament. A Passover lamb was needed in commemoration of the children of Israel's deliverance from Egypt. The blood on the doorposts and lintel acted as a mark of salvation and pointed to the Lord's blood, which atoned for all our sins (Exod. 12:1-36). The blood of the lamb slain in Egypt for the Passover was a type of Jesus, the Lamb of God slain before the foundation of the world. Forgiveness and deliverance from the bondage of sin came through Jesus (I Peter 1:18-23). The ministry of Jesus was the beginning of a new dispensation of grace and truth. Luke gives us the events of the Passover. The feast of unleavened bread was called the Passover. On the day of unleavened bread, the Passover must be killed (Luke 22:1, 7). Jesus sent Peter and John to prepare the Passover, and when the hour was come, Jesus sat down with the twelve: *And he took the cup, and gave thanks, and said, Take this, and divide it among yourselves: 18 For I say unto you, I will not drink of the fruit of the vine, until the kingdom of God shall come. 19 And he took bread, and gave thanks, and brake it, and gave unto them, saying, This is my body which is given for you: this do in remembrance of me. 20 Likewise also the cup after supper, saying, This cup is the new testament in my blood, which is shed for you* (Luke 22:17-20).

The Passover in which Jesus was crucified was the fulfillment of all the types and shadows made under the Law, and when Jesus said, "It is finished," He had fulfilled all righteousness the Law required, and the ceremonial Law, and nailed it to the cross (Col. 2:14). The Church was built upon the foundation that Jesus laid (I Cor. 3:10-11, Eph. 2:20). When dispensationalists separated the last Passover that Jesus and His disciples celebrated and put it under Law, and then put the observing of the Lord's supper recorded in I Corinthians 11:23-32 under the dispensation of grace, they destroyed the very foundation Jesus laid for the Church. These two events cannot be separated by dispensationalism. When Jesus fulfilled all the requirements for salvation at Calvary, He instructed His disciples to tarry in Jerusalem until they be endued with power from on High. The fifty days between the Passover and Pentecost acted as the transfer of allegiance from Moses, the giving of the Law, and feast of weeks in the Old Covenant to the New Covenant sealed by the blood of Christ. Both are under the dispensation of the grace and truth of Jesus.

The feast of unleavened bread opened the ripening season, and lasted forty-nine days, a week of weeks. On the fiftieth day, the feast of Pentecost took place. Pentecost commemorated the giving of the Law on Sinai. Leviticus gives us the events that took place between the Passover and Pentecost. Leviticus 23:4-8 is the Passover and feast of unleavened bread, verses 9-14 talk about the offering of the first fruits, and verses 15-22 tell about the wave loaves and Pentecost. Pentecost took place at the end of the reaping season, when all the wheat and barley had been cut and gathered, and marked especially the termination of the wheat harvest. Before Jesus was taken up into heaven, He instructed His disciples about the necessity of the cross and the great commission, and told them to tarry at Jerusalem until they were endued with power from on High (Luke 24:36-53). The feast of weeks pointed to the day of Pentecost when the Holy Spirit was poured out for the power needed to preach the gospel to the ends of the earth (Acts 2:1-4, 37-40, Rom. 1:16-17). On the day of Pentecost, the Holy Spirit was poured out on the twelve disciples, and the 120 in the upper room. Three thousand were saved when Peter preached with power (Acts 2:38-41). The outpouring of the Holy Spirit gave the Church the power need to preach the gospel to all the earth under the New Covenant (Luke 24:46-49, Acts 1:8).The New Covenant was established upon better promises than the Old (Heb. 8:6-13).

The New Covenant was a covenant of salvation for all mankind. Jesus engaged the disciples first into the work. Then he called the apostle

Paul to carry the message to the Gentiles (Acts 26:14-18). The Gentile Church then became a great instrument in God's hand to carry out the great commission, which the Lord had given in Matthew 28:19-20. The Jew and Gentile Church was to teach what the Lord taught His disciples. The New Covenant was sealed by the blood of Christ and was to be celebrated by all believers. Every time the Church celebrates the Lord's supper the Church is renewing its remembrance of the body that was broken and the blood that sealed the New Covenant. There is no way God intended to cut this New Covenant in half, giving the Gospels to the second chapter of Acts and then after the fourth chapter of Revelation for the Jew only, while giving from the second chapter of Acts to Revelation 4:1 for the Church. This kind of doctrine that cuts the New Covenant in two did not come from the Lord, or the Word. It came from men out of the misinterpretation of dispensationalism. One of the greatest problems with dispensationalism is it doesn't accept the New Covenant as the covenant that was promised.

This New Covenant means an arrangement made by one party which may be accepted or rejected by another party, but the second party cannot alter it. When accepted, it binds both parties by its terms. Tenney contrasts this with the meaning of the word *Covenant* as used in Exodus 24:1-8, which describes the acceptance of the Law by the people of Israel at Mt. Sinai, to the New Covenant which Jesus made with His disciples at the Last Supper.

The communion service is one of the best examples in showing that the Gospels are for the Church. Jesus showed us the Gospels are for the Church when He celebrated the Last Supper with his disciples in Mark 14:22-25. This service did not change for the Gentile Church, but is still celebrated: *And when the hour was come, he sat down, and the twelve apostles with him. 15 And he said unto them, With desire I have desired to eat this passover with you before I suffer: 16 For I say unto you, I will not any more eat thereof, until it be fulfilled in the kingdom of God. 17 And he took the cup, and gave thanks, and said, Take this, and divide it among yourselves: 18 For I say unto you, I will not drink of the fruit of the vine, until the kingdom of God shall come. 19 And he took bread, and gave thanks, and brake it, and gave unto them, saying, This is my body which is given for you: this do in remembrance of me. 20 Likewise also the cup after supper, saying, This cup is the new testament in my blood, which is shed for you* (Luke 22:14-20).

Jesus said the kingdom of God would not come visibly to be seen with the eye, but would be a spiritual kingdom where God takes up residence in the heart of every believer: *And when he was demanded of the Pharisees, when the kingdom of God should come, he answered them and said, The kingdom of God cometh not with observation: 21 Neither shall they say, Lo here! or, lo there! for, behold, the kingdom of God is within you* (Luke 17:20-21). Paul gives us the definition of the kingdom of God, and shows the Church that it is a spiritual kingdom inside the believer by the work of the Holy Spirit: *For the kingdom of God is not meat and drink; but righteousness, and peace, and joy in the Holy Ghost* (Romans 14:17).

In Acts, Peter and the disciples were carrying out the great commission, which Jesus commanded them in the Gospels. They drank and ate with Jesus after His resurrection, fulfilling what He had promised. It is impossible to take away the commands of Jesus and the Gospels from the Church to satisfy dispensationalists, and have true doctrine at the same time: *And he commanded us to preach unto the people, and to testify that it is he which was ordained of God to be the Judge of quick and dead. 43 To him give all the prophets witness, that through his name whosoever believeth in him shall receive remission of sins* (Acts 10:42-43).

The time has come for the walls built by dispensationalists to be broken down. Paul celebrated the same communion service with the Corinthians as Jesus celebrated with the disciples. Paul also taught the same second coming as Jesus. There is only one Body of Christ, not two. If the cup is the New Testament in His blood, the Gospels are for the Church also: *For I have received of the Lord that which also I delivered unto you, That the Lord Jesus the same night in which he was betrayed took bread: 24 And when he had given thanks, he brake it, and said, Take, eat: this is my body, which is broken for you: this do in remembrance of me. 25 After the same manner also he took the cup, when he had supped, saying, This cup is the new testament in my blood: this do ye, as oft as ye drink it, in remembrance of me. 26 For as often as ye eat this bread, and drink this cup, ye do show the Lord's death till he come* (I Corinthians 11:23-26).

To cut off the Church from the Gospels through dispensational teaching is to cut off the blood of the everlasting covenant from the Church. Most all who believe in a pretribulation rapture theory will say, "Well I don't cut the blood of the everlasting covenant from the Church. I believe in the blood." The question then becomes, "Why don't you believe what Jesus said about His coming again if He's the author of the New Covenant." It was through the blood of the everlasting covenant that God raised up Jesus from the dead: *Now the God of peace, that brought again from the dead our Lord Jesus, that great shepherd of the sheep, through the blood of the everlasting covenant, 21 Make you perfect in every good work to do his will, working in you that which is wellpleasing in his sight, through Jesus Christ; to whom be glory for ever and ever. Amen* (Hebrews 13:20).

When dispensationalists say the Gospels are not for the Church, it is like telling an adopted son that the will his father left did not cover him because he was an adopted son. This is what Darby and Scofield are saying when they say the Gospels are not for the Church, but for the Jew only. By this same reasoning they say Matthew 24 is not for the Church because Jesus was talking only to the Jews. However, Jesus was answering the disciples' question about His coming, and the disciples were the first members of the New Testament Church; therefore Jesus was talking to the Church. The testator died and sprinkled His blood into the Holy Place for us: therefore we have rights to all of His Last Will and Testament, as recorded in the Gospels.

Matthew Henry wrote about the following verses:

> "In these verses the apostle considers the gospel under
> the notion of a Will or Testament, the New or Last Will
> and Testament of Christ. It shows the necessity and efficacy
> of the blood of Christ to make this Testament valid and
> effectual. The Gospel is here considered as a Testament, the
> New and Last Will and Testament of our Lord and Savior
> Jesus Christ. It is observable that solemn transactions that
> pass between God and man are sometimes called a
> covenant, here a Testament. A covenant is a written agree-
> ment, or promise between two or more parties about things
> that are in their own power, or may be so, for the perform-
> ance of some action. This last will has a mediator which is
> Jesus Christ, the head of the Church. This agreement was
> taught to his disciples while he was living. A last will and
> testament is a voluntary act and deed of a single person, duly
> executed and witnessed, bestowing what was promised upon
> the heirs as is described and characterized by the testator in

his last Will and Testament. Its promises will take effect upon all heirs at the time of the death of the testator until its benefits are distributed to all heirs. This Last Will and Testament secures a home in heaven for all the heirs secured by the blood of Christ."

This description is a far cry from what Darby and Scofield said about the New Covenant.

The writer of Hebrews lets us know that the New Covenant came into full force immediately after the death of Christ, and before the Epistles were written. The New Covenant was not a delayed covenant for the Jew only, but to all that believe in the blood of Christ for salvation, Jew and Gentile: *For where a testament is, there must also of necessity be the death of the testator. 17 For a testament is of force after men are dead: otherwise it is of no strength at all while the testator liveth. 18 Whereupon neither the first testament was dedicated without blood. 19 For when Moses had spoken every precept to all the people according to the law, he took the blood of calves and of goats, with water, and scarlet wool, and hyssop, and sprinkled both the book, and all the people, 20 Saying, This is the blood of the testament which God hath enjoined unto you. 21 Moreover he sprinkled with blood both the tabernacle, and all the vessels of the ministry. 22 And almost all things are by the law purged with blood; and without shedding of blood is no remission. 23 It was therefore necessary that the patterns of things in the heavens should be purified with these; but the heavenly things themselves with better sacrifices than these. 24 For Christ is not entered into the holy places made with hands, which are the figures of the true; but into heaven itself, now to appear in the presence of God for us* (Hebrews 9:16-24).

Just because the New Covenant did not come into full force until after the death of Christ (the testator) does not mean that Jesus' words of His Last Will and Testament were not for the Church. The Law was given by Moses, but the time for the New Covenant had come for the salvation of all mankind. The covenant of grace and truth was being formed by Jesus (John 1:17). Jesus did not come to represent the son of Abraham that was of the bondwoman, but of the freewoman through the promised son, Isaac. Jesus came to cast out the bondwoman (the Law) and raise up children unto God through Abraham's seed, which was through Jesus. The Church represents the children of the freewoman, not the bondwoman. Jesus did not come to extend the Law of the bondwoman, but gave a New Covenant to the freewoman, therefore the Gospels are for Jew and Gentile (the Church), who are the seed of the freewoman: *For it is written, that Abraham had two sons, the one by a bondmaid, the other by a freewoman. 23 But he who was of the bondwoman was born after the flesh; but he of the freewoman was by promise. 24 Which things are an allegory: for these are the two covenants; the one from the Mount Sinai, which gendereth to bondage, which is Agar. 25 For this Agar is mount Sinai in Arabia, and answereth to Jerusalem which now is, and is in bondage with her children. 26 But Jerusalem which is above is free, which is the mother of us all. 27 For it is written, Rejoice, thou barren that bearest not; break forth and cry, thou that travailest not: for the desolate hath many more children than she which hath an husband. 28 Now we, brethren, as Isaac was, are the children of promise. 29 But as then he that was born after the flesh persecuted him that was born after the Spirit, even so it is now. 30 Nevertheless what saith the scripture? Cast out the bondwoman and her son: for the son of the bondwoman shall not be heir with the son of the freewoman. 31 So then, brethren, we are not children of the bondwoman, but of the free* (Galatians 4:22-31).

When the Church of Galatia was struggling to free itself from Judaizers, Paul taught them that the Law was no longer binding to the believer under the New Covenant. Justification by faith was set in motion by the Lord, and became the new theology of the Church under Paul. The covenant Jesus gave set them free from the bondage of the bondwoman. It exposed the Judaistic error and defended the doctrine of justification by faith. This New Covenant of the Lord sets all believers free; therefore they are not to be entangled in the yoke of bondage again: *Stand fast therefore in the liberty wherewith Christ hath made us free, and be not entangled again with the yoke of bondage. 4 Christ is become of no effect unto you, whosoever of you are justified by the law; ye are fallen from grace. 5 For we through the Spirit wait for the hope of righteousness by faith* (Galatians 5:1, 4-5).

It does not seem possible to have a theology that would deny the Gospels to a son of Abraham through Jesus Christ. If the Gentiles became sons of God by adoption, then they have the same rights as a natural-born son through the Last Will and Testament of Jesus. Those who are the heirs of the New Covenant (the Church) should not be told that the testator was not talking to them in the Last Will and

Testament of the Lord, but only to the Jew. This is a great error, because the saints are joint heirs with Jesus Christ. It is a terrible thing to have to argue the point that the Gospels are for the Church. When I got saved I became heir to the covenant Jesus gave me. The great Scriptures below show our heirship. How could the Church preach the gospel if the Gospels are not for the Church: *That the Gentiles should be fellowheirs, and of the same body, and partakers of his promise in Christ by the gospel* (Ephesians 3:6). *And if ye be Christ's, then are ye Abraham's seed, and heirs according to the promise* (Galatians 3:29). *For the promise, that he should be the heir of the world, was not to Abraham, or to his seed, through the law, but through the righteousness of faith. 17 (As it is written, I have made thee a father of many nations,) before him whom he believed, even God, who quickeneth the dead, and calleth those things which be not as though they were. 18 Who against hope believed in hope, that he might become the father of many nations, according to that which was spoken, So shall thy seed be* (Romans 4:13, 17-18).

If the Jews had repented and turned to Jesus for their salvation, at that time God would have honored His promise that He had made to them in Ezekiel. God promised them that He would give them a new heart, and a new spirit, as found in Ezekiel 18:30-32. Only the apostles and a small remnant received this promise and came under the New Covenant by faith. John let them know that *when Jesus came unto his own, and his own received him not*, their eyes would be closed in part until the Gentiles come in (Rom. 11:25). When the Jews refused to accept Jesus as their Messiah and savior, it did not prevent the New Covenant from coming into force to all those who believed. Those who believed in Jesus, both Jew and Gentile, became sons of God. These believers received a new heart and a new mind, which God had promised. Through the law of the Spirit, Christ would make them free from the law of sin and death (Romans 8:3-4). The saved were to put off the old man, become renewed in the spirit of their mind, and put on the new man which was created in righteousness and true holiness (Ephesians 4:22-24). Both Jew and Gentiles who believe in Him would become sons of God. The New Covenant was instituted for the salvation of all who will believe that Jesus is the Son of God, and that He is full of grace and truth. This is the theme of the New Covenant: *He came unto his own, and his own received him not. 12 But as many as received him, to them gave he power to become the sons of God, even to them that believe on his name:*

13 Which were born, not of blood, nor of the will of the flesh, nor of the will of man, but of God. 14 And the Word was made flesh, and dwelt among us, (and we beheld his glory, the glory as of the only begotten of the Father,) full of grace and truth (John 1:11-14).

This covenant of salvation is offered to all because of God's great love for the whole world: *That whosoever believeth in him should not perish, but have eternal life. 16 For God so loved the world, that he gave his only begotten Son, that whosoever believeth in him should not perish, but have everlasting life. 17 For God sent not his Son into the world to condemn the world; but that the world through him might be saved. 18 He that believeth on him is not condemned: but he that believeth not is condemned already, because he hath not believed in the name of the only begotten Son of God* (John 3:15-18).

God knew His only begotten Son would be rejected in order to fulfill what was written of Him. John preached a message of repentance saying: *In those days came John the Baptist, preaching in the wilderness of Judaea, 2 And saying, Repent ye: for the kingdom of heaven is at hand. 3 For this is he that was spoken of by the prophet Isaiah, saying, The voice of one crying in the wilderness, Prepare ye the way of the Lord, make his paths straight* (Matthew 3:1-3).

God wanted children brought up unto Abraham through Israel. The gospel went forth first by the Jew and for the Jew because salvation was of the Jew (John 4:22). When the Jew rejected the gospel, Paul said in Acts 13: 46: *Then Paul and Barnabas waxed bold, and said, It was necessary that the word of God should first have been spoken to you: but seeing ye put it from you, and judge yourselves unworthy of everlasting life, lo, we turn to the Gentiles.* Only a remnant believed and were saved. The eyes of the rest were blinded waiting for the judgment, which happened in A.D. 70. These words were spoken by John before Jesus started His ministry, and nothing took the Lord by surprise. We can look at the first message of John the Baptist, and see the warning God was giving to the unbelieving Jews that their nation would soon be destroyed: *And think not to say within yourselves, We have Abraham to our father: for I say unto you, that God is able of these stones to raise up children unto Abraham. 10 And now also the ax is laid unto the root of the trees: therefore every tree which bringeth not forth good fruit is hewn down, and cast into the fire* (Matthew 3:9-10).

In Ezekiel 18, the call for repentance was given so iniquity would not be their ruin. God promised to give them a new heart and new mind. This promise would be fulfilled in the New Covenant, but the Jews rejected the Messiah when He came unto them (John 1:11). The offer was given unto them, *But as many as receive him, to them gave ye power to become sons of God, even to them that believe on his name* (John 1:12). God, knowing the future, knew the Jews would reject the Messiah, and their nation would be destroyed as prophesied in Daniel 9:26. God took no joy in judging the Jewish nation to fulfill what was prophesied by Ezekiel. The disciples and all the Jews who did accept Jesus as the Messiah and their savior did receive the New Covenant promises of salvation. Those who rejected the New Covenant were not given a new mind or a new heart because of unbelief. The Lord will deal with the Jewish nation once again in Ezekiel 36:24-27, fulfilling the covenant promise. John the Baptist was giving them a warning, the same as Ezekiel: *Therefore I will judge you, O house of Israel, every one according to his ways, saith the Lord GOD. Repent, and turn yourselves from all your transgressions; so iniquity shall not be your ruin. 31 Cast away from you all your transgressions, whereby ye have transgressed; and make you a new heart, and a new spirit: for why will ye die, O house of Israel? 32 For I have no pleasure in the death of him that dieth, saith the Lord GOD: wherefore turn yourselves, and live ye* (Ezekiel 18:30-32).

Although the Jews were scattered throughout the world, yet God brought them back to their own land in 1948. In Ezekiel 37, God says their dry bones would take on life. God will graft them back into the Body of Christ, fulfilling the promise He made to them in Ezekiel. They will receive a new heart and new spirit because God's Spirit will live within them. This prophecy could not be fulfilled if God took the Holy Spirit out of the earth before the tribulation period, as pretribulationists teach. The Holy Spirit is not going to be taken out of the earth, nor is there going to be a pretribulation rapture. These Jews will receive the same Holy Spirit, and the same salvation, that the disciples and the early church received. There is no difference. The Jews which were broken off will be grafted back into the Body of Christ. Ezekiel was looking forward to the time after God gathered them again from all the countries which they had been scattered: *For I will take you from among the heathen, and gather you out of all countries, and will bring you into your own land. 25 Then will I sprinkle clean water upon you, and ye shall be clean: from all your filthiness, and from all your idols, will I cleanse you. 26 A new heart also will I give you, and a new spirit will I put within you: and I will take away the stony heart out of your flesh, and I will give you an heart of flesh. 27 And I will put my spirit within you, and cause you to walk in my statutes, and ye shall keep my judgments, and do them* (Ezekiel 36:24-27).

Jesus does not have two kinds of salvation, one for the Jews and another for the Gentiles, neither does He have two covenants of salvation. The one covenant of salvation, which Jesus purchased with His own blood, is the only covenant for salvation. Ezekiel is only telling the time element of how God will deal with the Jews who were broken off in the last days. The covenant in Hebrews below is not talking about a different covenant.

Hebrews speaks of how Jesus is a mediator of a better covenant than the old. This New Covenant of salvation and forgiveness of sin gives all who believe a new heart and a new spirit. The foundation of this New Covenant was laid in the Old Testament. The New Covenant was given and preached by Jesus in the Gospels, confirmed in the Epistles, and stands strong for all Jew or Gentile believers forever. We can see in Hebrews 8:13 that the Old Covenant has already vanished away, because God let the temple be destroyed and the Jews be scattered throughout the earth before the sacrifices and the ceremonial laws would cease. All believers could then seek the benefits of the New Covenant. In verse 6, the New Covenant has already been established. God's people do not have to wait for the millennium to enjoy the New Covenant blessings. Verse 6 lets us know that the New Covenant is past tense, not future: *But now hath he obtained a more excellent ministry, by how much also he is the mediator of a better covenant, which was established upon better promises. 7 For if that first covenant had been faultless, then should no place have been sought for the second. 8 For finding fault with them, he saith, Behold, the days come, saith the Lord, when I will make a new covenant with the house of Israel and with the house of Judah: 9 Not according to the covenant that I made with their fathers in the day when I took them by the hand to lead them out of the land of Egypt; because they continued not in my covenant, and I regarded them not, saith the Lord. 10 For this is the covenant that I will make with the house of Israel after those days, saith the Lord; I will put my laws into their mind, and write them in their hearts: and I will be to them a God, and they shall be to me a people: 12 For I will be merciful to their unrighteousness, and their sins and their iniquities will I remember no more. 13 In that he saith, A new covenant, he hath made the* first old. Now that which decayeth and waxeth old is ready to vanish away (Hebrews 8:6-10, 12-13). Hebrews was written about A.D. 64, and the temple would be destroyed in A.D. 70. When Jerusalem was conquered and the temple destroyed, sacrifices ceased and the Jews were scattered throughout the earth, but the New Covenant will stay in force until all have had the opportunity for salvation, Jew and Gentile.

The New Covenant was already in effect, but Israel as a nation refused the salvation of the Lord. Paul said God will deal with the Jews as a nation once again and graft them back into the Body of Christ. This Scripture cannot be fulfilled after the Church rapture, because these Jews will be grafted back into the Body of Christ, just as were the Gentiles. The two must become one body in Christ before the rapture. Only those Jews who do not come under the New Covenant before the Lord comes will be left behind to go through the wrath of God and the battle of Armageddon. They will mourn when they see that Jesus was the Messiah and that they refused him (Zechariah 12:10-14). The Scripture below shows us the Jews will be grafted back into the Body of Christ, fulfilling the covenant promises: And they also, if they abide not still in unbelief, shall be grafted in: for God is able to graft them in again. 24 For if thou wert cut out of the olive tree which is wild by nature, and wert grafted contrary to nature into a good olive tree: how much more shall these, which be the natural branches, be grafted into their own olive tree? 25 For I would not, brethren, that ye should be ignorant of this mystery, lest ye should be wise in your own conceits; that blindness in part is happened to Israel, until the fulness of the Gentiles be come in. 26 And so all Israel shall be saved: as it is written, There shall come out of Zion the Deliverer, and shall turn away ungodliness from Jacob: 27 For this is my covenant unto them, when I shall take away their sins. 28 As concerning the gospel, they are enemies for your sakes: but as touching the election, they are beloved for the fathers' sakes. 29 For the gifts and calling of God are without repentance (Romans 11:23-29).

Jesus offered a sacrifice for sin forever, and ascended to the right hand of the Father until His enemies be made His footstool. The sacrifice has already been offered, and the covenant given, and by one offering He hath perfected forever them that are sanctified: But this man, after he had offered one sacrifice for sins for ever, sat down on the right hand of God; 13 From henceforth expecting till his enemies be made his footstool. 14 For by one offering he hath perfected for ever them that are sanctified (Hebrews 10:12-14).

Hebrews gives us the New Covenant. It is sealed with the blood of Christ for the redemption of all, Jew and Gentile. The Lord gave this covenant to the Church. Part of Joel's prophecy was fulfilled at Pentecost, and the New Covenant promise by Jeremiah and Ezekiel was in force. All believers would be given a new mind and a new spirit. The Spirit of God would live within them, and the Laws of God would be placed in their minds and hearts. The sinner is washed by the blood of Christ. Jesus made one offering for sin, and the New Covenant is in force: *This is the covenant that I will make with them after those days, saith the Lord, I will put my laws into their hearts, and in their minds will I write them; 17 And their sins and iniquities will I remember no more. 18 Now where remission of these is, there is no more offering for sin* (Hebrews 10:16-18).

This covenant is for the Church, Jew and Gentile, and it offers a new and living way. We can draw near to God with a true heart in full assurance of our faith. God's people are to hold fast their profession of faith in Christ. It would be well for all who believe to obey the following word of God: *Having therefore, brethren, boldness to enter into the holiest by the blood of Jesus, 20 By a new and living way, which he hath consecrated for us, through the veil, that is to say, his flesh; 21 And having an high priest over the house of God; 22 Let us draw near with a true heart in full assurance of faith, having our hearts sprinkled from an evil conscience, and our bodies washed with pure water. 23 Let us hold fast the profession of our faith without wavering; (for he is faithful that promised;) 24 And let us consider one another to provoke unto love and to good works: 25 Not forsaking the assembling of ourselves together, as the manner of some is; but exhorting one another: and so much the more, as ye see the day approaching* (Hebrews 10:19-25).

The Word proves the New Covenant is in force for the Church, Jew and Gentile, and is sealed by the blood of Christ. This is more evidence that the death sentence should be pronounced on the pretribulation rapture theory.

One Body
of Christ

It was very important to understand that the Body of Christ is the Church, and the Lord is not going to divide Himself into two bodies, one for the Jew, and another for the Gentile. Dispensationalists have put such a gulf between Israel and the Church that it totally destroys God's purpose in these last days for the Church and the Jews.

Jesus came to reconcile both Jew and Gentile into the one body, because it is only through Jesus we both have access by one Spirit unto the Father. The Gentiles are fellow citizens with the saints of Israel. The Church was built upon the foundation of the apostles and prophets, *Jesus Christ himself being the chief corner stone.* This Scripture shows you cannot make void the Gospels to the Church as dispensationalists has done. Jesus gives the time element of His coming in the Gospels. You cannot destroy the time element unless you leave the Church in darkness concerning the coming of the Lord. Dispensationalists are in error when they disqualify the Gospels for the Church, because Paul said the Church is built upon the foundation of the apostles and prophets, Jesus Christ himself being the chief cornerstone. The Church has its foundation in the Gospels; therefore the pretribulation rapture is in error. The coming of the Lord in the Gospels is the same coming that Old Testament prophets taught, Paul taught in the Epistles, and John taught in Revelation. These Scriptures let the Church know that its foundation started with the prophets and apostles, and not in the book of Acts. The Church can be assured that Jesus knew more about His coming than a theologian who explains away the truth concerning Jesus coming: *And that he might reconcile both unto God in one body by the cross, having slain the enmity thereby: 17 And came and preached peace to you which were afar off, and to them that were nigh. 18 For through him we both have access by one Spirit unto the Father. 19 Now therefore ye are no more strangers and foreigners, but fellow citizens with the saints, and of the household of God; 20 And are built upon the foundation of the apostles and prophets, Jesus Christ himself being the chief corner stone; 21 In whom all the building fitly framed together groweth unto an holy temple in the Lord* (Ephesians 2:16-21:).

There are not separate places for the Church saints and for the Jews saved during the tribulation period. Jews will be grafted back into the Body of Christ, so there will be only one body. There is only one heaven for all saints. *In the dispensation of the fulness of times, God will gather together in one all things in Christ, both which are in heaven, and which are on earth; even in Him* (Ephesians 1:10).There is only one Body of Christ. The following Scriptures show this.

Ephesians 4:4-6:
There is one body, and one Spirit, even as ye are called in one hope of your calling; 5 One Lord, one faith, one baptism, 6 One God and Father of all, who is above all, and through all, and in you all.

Romans 12:4:
For as we have many members in one body, and all members have not the same office:

I Corinthians 12:13:
For by one Spirit are we all baptized into one body, whether we be Jews or Gentiles, whether we be bond or free; and have been all made to drink into one Spirit.

I Corinthians 12:25-27:
That there should be no schism in the body; but that the members should have the same care one for another. 26 And whether

one member suffer, all the members suffer with it; or one member
be honoured, all the members rejoice with it. 27 Now ye are the
body of Christ, and members in particular.

Dispensationalism has put such a distinction between Israel and the Church that it has caused many people to overlook what Paul wrote in the book of Romans concerning the salvation of both Jew and Gentile in the Church age. Paul's desire was that all Israel be saved, because many in Israel were blind to the righteousness that comes by faith in Jesus Christ. He gave the plan of salvation for both Jew and Gentile in chapter 10 of Romans. In Romans 10:16, Paul verified the fulfillment of Isaiah 53 that Jesus the Messiah that was to come, had come. Paul told in Romans 10:19-21 how the Gentiles would provoke Israel to jealousy, and that some would be saved by faith in the Lord. Paul quoted another prophecy in Romans 10:20 concerning the Gentiles coming to Jesus for salvation, thus fulfilling Isaiah 65:1. Paul let the Church know in Romans 11 that God did not cast away His people whom He foreknew, because Paul was an Israelite himself. God did not completely reject Israel; there would be a remnant saved because of the election of grace (Rom. 11:1-6). The rest of Israel would be hardened because of unbelief, but it was through Israel's hardness that the conversion of the Gentiles took place. Down through Church history there has been a remnant of Jews saved as individuals; both Jew and Gentile can believe or reject the gospel, and it is conditional. The rejection of the Messiah by the Jews was partial, not total, and the restoration of the Jews is an event that God has determined to bring about fulfilling (Rom. 11:23-29). God concluded all in unbelief, that he might have mercy on all (Rom. 11:32).

There will be only a remnant of Israel grafted back into the Body of Christ in these last days before the rapture of the Church (Rom. 11:23); however, there will be many in Israel who will not accept Jesus as savior in the latter rain (Zech. 10:1). Those Jews who miss the rapture will see the Lord when He comes for the Church. They will look upon the nail prints in the hands of Him whom they pierced and realize Jesus was the Messiah, and they will mourn for Him as one mourneth for his only son (Zech. 12:10-1; 13:6-7). The Lord will save Judah first, and then seek to destroy all nations that come against Jerusalem (Zech. 12:7-9). The Lord will bring a third part of Israel through the seven last vials, the battle of Armageddon, and the Day of the Lord. Those Jews who are left and were not in the rapture will go into the millennium with a fleshly body (Zech. 13:9). Everyone else left of all the nations that came against Jerusalem will go up from year to year to worship the King, the Lord of Hosts (Zech. 14:16-17). Those in the millennium with fleshly bodies are not part of the Church. There is only one body, both Jew and Gentile (the Church), and they will be in the rapture and safe in the Lord's chambers when the wrath of God is poured out.

The Church and the Gospels

We should rejoice in knowing that what Jesus said is for the Church (Jew and Gentile). I emphasize that the Gospels are for the Church because the whole of the pretribulation rapture theory hinges on dispensationalist teachings that say the Gospels are not for the Church, but for the Jew only. Scofield's foundational error is in his introduction, "Just as Israel is in the foreground from the call of Adam to the resurrection of Christ, so now the Church fills the scene from the second chapter of Acts to the fourth chapter of Revelation." Jesus founded the New Testament Church, and is its head. How could Jesus be the head of the Church, and not say one word to the Church in the Gospels about a pretribulation rapture? When pretribulationists realize that the Gospels are for the Church, and Jesus and the Gospels are its foundation, they will believe what Jesus said about His coming, and see the time element in the Gospels is very important to the Church. Jesus said to look for the signs of His coming in the clouds immediately after the tribulation.

Establishing the Church was not an afterthought of God. When Jesus heard John was in prison, He immediately began to fulfilled what was prophesied of Him by Isaiah concerning the preaching of the Gospel that would be preached to both Jew and Gentile (Matt. 4:12-17). Jesus gave a direct prophecy of the Church. He asked His disciples to give their opinion as to who He was. Peter answered, "Thou art the

Christ, the Son of the living God" (Matt. 16:16). Jesus replied, "Thou art Peter, and upon this rock I will build My Church; and the gates of hell shall not prevail against it" (v18). This verse tells us that Jesus is the rock on which the Church is built. The Church is His work, and He said, "I will build." The Church was to be a progressive work, and Jesus would give stability to it. He said, "The gates of hell shall not prevail against it." Dispensationalists must cease from putting the Gospels under the dispensation of Law because it goes against everything Jesus taught. Jesus established the Church and died for it.

I know of no Fundamental preacher who would not be very upset if someone came into their church and began to preach that Jesus gave the great commission to the Jew only. That preacher would leave by the way of the back door faster than he came through the front. Yet every week in America and around the world Fundamentalist preachers preach that what Jesus said in the Gospels about His coming does not apply to the Church, but to the Jew only. If the great commission is for the Church, so is Matthew 24. I believe it's time preachers see the double standard allowed behind their pulpits, and see it was after the Scofield Reference Bible was published that most Fundamental and Evangelical colleges and churches changed from a posttribulation to a pretribulation coming of the Lord. This was great error.

There are Fundamentalists today who believe the Church started in the Gospels, and not in the book of Acts. I agree 100 percent. The Church was built upon the foundation of the apostles and prophets, Jesus Christ himself being the chief cornerstone (Ephesians 2:20). You cannot separate the apostles, prophets, and the Gospels from the Church, and be true in doctrine. The apostles, prophets, Jesus, and the Gospels are the very foundation of the Church. If a college student or church member has never been taught the whole truth concerning the pretribulation rapture theory they will not see the error, and will teach and preach only what they have been taught. If a student of the Word believes the Gospels were for the Church, then they also should believe the time element Jesus gave concerning His coming in Matthew 24 is for the Church. Matthew 24 is as much for the Church as any other part of the Gospels.

Pretribulationists who think the Gospels are not for the Church need to answer two questions. How can anyone preach the Gospels to the Church if the Gospels are not for the Church? And how could the Apostles preach and teach the Apostles' Doctrine in Acts 2:42 if the Gospels were not for them? There were a number of years when all the Apostles had was the Old Testament, the words which Jesus taught in the Gospels, and the message of His death, burial, and resurrection. The Gospel of Matthew was written about A.D. 37. Paul's first epistle was probably I Thessalonians, and it was written about A.D. 52. Revelation was written by John about A.D. 95. There were a number of years when the Church did not have the complete Bible as we know it today. They depended on the Apostles' Doctrine until the New Testament was completed. Irenaeus was one of the first to make use of the completed New Testament. There were many years between the death of Christ and the completion of the New Testament. For someone to come up with a doctrine, and say the Gospels are not for the Church, is to deny what the apostles preached and taught to the early Church. I believe pretribulationists and truth are about 1800 years apart.

The apostles and the Apostles' Doctrine were a most important part of the early Church and the fivefold ministry that the Lord gave to the Church as recorded in Ephesians 4:11-14. The apostles established the truth, and the doctrines that Jesus had taught them. The apostles were the first ones to carry out the great commission that Jesus had commanded in Matthew 28:19-20. The prophets that the Lord gave to the Church were to proclaim truth to the Church, not error. The apostles' ministry was handed down to our evangelists, pastors, and teachers of today, but dispensationalists changed it. Their doctrine of dispensationalism denies the Church the Gospels, the Apostles' Doctrine, and the truth concerning the coming of the Lord.

Jesus gave these ministries to the Church for the perfecting and building up of the Body of Christ, until all come into the unity of the faith and of the knowledge of the Son of God. If dispensationalists are allowed to take away the Gospels and the Apostles' Doctrine from the Church, the Church cannot be brought to its perfection. God's people should let the Word correct the terrible error that has been made so we are no longer tossed to and fro and carried about with every wind of doctrine by the trickery of men. Let the Church rise up to her duty and bring correction of doctrine and edification to the Church: *And he gave some, apostles; and some, prophets; and some, evangelists; and some, pastors and teachers; 12 For the perfecting of the saints, for the work of the ministry, for the edifying of the body of Christ: 13 Till we all come in the unity of the faith, and of the knowledge of the Son of God, unto a perfect man, unto the measure of the stature of the fulness of Christ: 14 That we henceforth be no more children, tossed to and fro, and carried about with every wind of doctrine, by the sleight of men, and cunning craftiness, whereby they lie in wait to deceive* (Ephesians 4:11-14).

The meaning of the word *gospel* comes from the Anglo-Saxon "god-spell," "good tidings." This is the English equivalent of the Greek *euaggelion*, which signifies "glad" or "good tidings." This term was used to designate the four biographies of our Lord by Matthew, Mark, Luke, and John. These four Gospels contain the good news that the savior (the Messiah) had come into the world. This good news gives a history of Jesus from His birth to His resurrection and the great commission. The Gospels also give an account of Jesus fulfilling all that was prophesied of Him, and His teachings. He commanded us to observe all things, which He had commanded His disciples to observe. The Gospels record the finished work of Jesus on the cross for the redemption of all mankind. The word *gospel* is used about 85 times between the book of Acts and Revelation. How could the doctrines of man separate the gospel from the Gospels and say they are rightly dividing the Word of truth? The words of Jesus, including what He said about His second coming, were preached in the early Church. Paul was not ashamed to preach the gospel of Christ, to the Jew first and then to the Gentiles: *For I am not ashamed of the gospel of Christ: for it is the power of God unto salvation to every one that believeth; to the Jew first, and also to the Greek* (Romans 1:16).

Schaff wrote in the *History of the Christian Church*, volume 1, page 70, a far different explanation concerning the Law and the Gospels than what dispensationalists teach regarding the difference between the Church and the Gospels. He shows that the Church started in the Gospels, and that the disciples were the first members:

"Immediately before the advent of the Messiah the whole Old Testament, the Law and the prophets, Moses and Isaiah together, reappeared for a short season embodied in John the Baptist, and then in unrivalled humility disappeared as the red dawn in the splendor of the rising sun of the new covenant. This remarkable man, earnestly preaching repentance in the wilderness and laying the axe at the root of the tree, and at the same time comforting with prophecy and pointing to the atoning Lamb of God, was indeed, as the immediate forerunner of the New Testament economy, and the personal friend of the heavenly Bridegroom, the greatest of them that were born of woman; yet in his official character as the representative of the ancient preparatory economy he stands lower than the least in that kingdom of Christ, which is infinitely more glorious than all its types and shadows in the past."

"This is the Jewish religion, as it flowed from the fountain of divine revelation and lived in the true Israel, the spiritual children of Abraham, in John the Baptist, his parents, and disciples, in the mother of Jesus, her kindred and friends, in the venerable Simeon, and prophetess Anna, in Lazarus and his pious sisters, in the apostles and the first disciples, who embraced Jesus of Nazareth as the fulfiller of the law and the prophets, the Son of God and the Savior of the world, and who were the first fruits of the Christian Church."

Schaff did not believe the Gospels were in the dispensation of the Law. He was correct in his assessment of Jesus and the New Covenant. Jesus was the beginning of the new dispensation for which God's people had waited. Schaff pointed out how the Church started in the Gospels, which are for the Church and not under the dispensation of the Law. Mark makes it plain about the mission of John the Baptist. The message of baptism was not taught under the dispensation of Law. The following Scripture corrects the falsehood of Darby and Scofield's dispensational teaching concerning the Gospels: *The beginning of the gospel of Jesus Christ, the Son of God; 2 As it is written in the prophets, Behold, I send my messenger before thy face, which shall prepare thy way before thee. 3 The voice of one crying in the wilderness, Prepare ye the way of the Lord, make his paths straight. 4 John did baptize in the wilderness, and preach the baptism of repentance for the remission of sins (Mark 1:1-4).*

John the Baptist began to preach how Jesus would baptize them with the Holy Ghost. He prepared the way of the Lord: *And preached, saying, There cometh one mightier than I after me, the latchet of whose shoes I am not worthy to stoop down and unloose. 8 I indeed have baptized you with water: but he shall baptize you with the Holy Ghost* (Mark 1:7-8). Jesus fulfilled all righteousness, and was baptized in the river of Jordan by John. The doctrine of baptism would follow the Church down through the Church age. Jesus set the example for the Church to be baptized and be filled with the Holy Spirit: *And it came to pass in those days, that Jesus came from Nazareth of Galilee, and was baptized of John in Jordan. 10 And straightway coming up out of the water, he saw the heavens opened, and the Spirit like a dove descending upon him: 11 And there came a voice from heaven, saying, Thou art my beloved Son, in whom I am well pleased* (Mark 1:9-11). When John was put in prison, Jesus began to preach the gospel of the kingdom saying, "*The time is fulfilled. The kingdom of God is at hand.*" This message had nothing to do with a millennial kingdom, which dispensationalists said was postponed. Jesus was talking about salvation by faith in Jesus Christ, and setting up His rule within, every person who believes on Jesus as savior. There is only one true Gospel: *Now after that John was put in prison, Jesus came into Galilee, preaching the gospel of the kingdom of God, 15 And saying, The time is fulfilled, and the kingdom of God is at hand: repent ye, and believe the gospel* (Mark 1:14-15).

Jesus made it plain that the kingdom of God was a spiritual kingdom where He would rule His Church from heaven. Man cannot see the Holy Spirit when He takes up residence in the believer, because the Spirit of God sets up God's rule within the heart of man. Jesus said the kingdom of God is within us: *And when he was demanded of the Pharisees, when the kingdom of God should come, he answered them and said, The kingdom of God cometh not with observation:21 Neither shall they say, Lo here! or, lo there! for, behold, the kingdom of God is within you* (Luke 17:20-21).

Jesus called Simon and Andrew, his brother, to make them soul-winners. They would now catch men, not fish. Simon and Andrew had become believers in Christ at this point. This new dispensation had already begun when Jesus began to call the first New Testament believers; therefore dispensationalism is in error by teaching that the Church started at Pentecost. Jesus began calling the first members of the Church in Mark 1:16-18, 20: *Now as he walked by the sea of Galilee, he saw Simon and Andrew his brother casting a net into the sea: for they were fishers.17 And Jesus said unto them, Come ye after me, and I will make you to become fishers of men. 18 And straightway they forsook their nets, and followed him. 20 And straightway he called them: and they left their father Zebedee in the ship with the hired servants, and went after him.*

Jesus' dealings with the disciples about their belief in Him proves that salvation, and the Church, began in the Gospels. The Father gave the disciples salvation the moment they believed Jesus was the promised Messiah. There is a big difference between salvation and the beginning of the New Testament Church, and the fullness of power, which took place on the day of Pentecost. The disciples, and all who believed Jesus was the Messiah, were saved when they believed. They did not have to wait until Pentecost. When Jesus called the disciples and they followed Him by faith, that was the beginning of their salvation and the New Testament Church. John came to prepare the way of the Lord, or the Messiah. He came for a witness of the Light, that all men might believe (John 1:6-7). Just because some of the Jews rejected Jesus as the Messiah did not hinder those who believed from being saved: *He came unto his own, and his own received him not. 12 But as many as received him, to them gave he power to become the sons of God, even to them that believe on his name* (John 1:11-12). When Jesus asked the disciples, Whom do men say that I the Son of man am? They answered him, and then Jesus asked them this question: *He saith unto them, But whom say ye that I am? 16 And Simon Peter answered and said, Thou art the Christ, the Son of the living God* (Matthew 16:15-16). Peter's answer confirmed that he believed in a salvation by faith through belief that Jesus was the promised Messiah. Christ means "Messiah," or "anointed." John gives the confirmation of the time of salvation in I John 5:1: *Whosoever believeth that Jesus is the Christ is born of God: and every one that loveth him that begat loveth him also that is begotten of him.*

The Scriptures above have nothing to do with the extension of the Law through the Gospels, but show the beginning of the New Testament Church. Dispensationalists doctrines say the Gospels are not for the Church, and out of this, the pretribulation rapture theory was developed, which does not stand true when tested by the Word.

The following Scripture shows those who believed in Jesus were given eternal life, and were the beginning of the called-out assembly (the Church). Only those who did not believe Jesus was the Messiah turned back, and followed Him no more: *But there are some of you that believe not. For Jesus knew from the beginning who they were that believed not, and who should betray him. 65 And he said, Therefore said I unto you, that no man can come unto me, except it were given unto him of my Father. 66 From that time many of his disciples went back, and walked no more with him. 67 Then said Jesus unto the twelve, Will ye also go away? 68 Then Simon Peter answered him, Lord, to whom shall we go? thou hast the words of eternal life. 69 And we believe and are sure that thou art that Christ, the Son of the living God. 71 He spake of Judas Iscariot the son of Simon: for he it was that should betray him, being one of the twelve* (John 6:64-71).

Darby and Scofield developed the erroneous dispensational teachings that the Gospels were not for the Church. They believe the Gospels up to Acts 2 are under the dispensation of the Law; therefore they say you cannot apply the Gospels to the Church. I show when Jesus was talking about His coming again, He was not talking to the Jews alone but to the Church, also. There is no reference that Jesus was talking to the Jews alone in Matthew 24. Jesus is talking to the Church, Jew and Gentile, when He said in John 14:3: *And if I go and prepare a place for you, I will come again, and receive you unto myself; that where I am, there ye may be also.* Jesus was not talking about setting up a kingdom on earth for Israel, but a place for the saints in heaven. Therefore Jesus is talking as much to the Church in Matthew 24 as He is in John 14:3.

Many pretribulationists say, "I am not teaching what Darby or Scofield taught." Many say, "I know nothing about what they taught," and, "I only teach what the Bible says." Pretribulationists may think this, not realizing that the doctrine which they believe has been passed on to them through colleges, churches, and by other preachers, teachers, and believers. The root of what they believe can be traced back to Scofield, and then to Darby, who developed dispensational teaching and the pretribulation rapture theory.

The Gospels establish the New Covenant. If a person discounts Jesus' words in the Gospels for the Church, there would be no covenant between the Lord and His Church. We must remember in these last days that God spoke to us through His only begotten Son in the

Gospels, Epistles, and Revelation: *God, who at sundry times and in divers manners spake in time past unto the fathers by the prophets, 2 Hath in these last days spoken unto us by his Son, whom he hath appointed heir of all things, by whom also he made the worlds; 3 Who being the brightness of his glory, and the express image of his person, and upholding all things by the word of his power, when he had by himself purged our sins, sat down on the right hand of the Majesty on high* (Hebrews 1: 1-3).

John bore record of the Word of God, and the teachings of Jesus. This record is given in the Gospels and confirmed in Revelation. The words of Jesus in Revelation would be meaningless from chapters 1-22 without the Gospels. The Gospels, the Epistles, and Revelation must be dovetailed together concerning Jesus' coming. God gave all of Revelation to the Church, not just the first three chapters. His servants are the Church: *The Revelation of Jesus Christ, which God gave unto him, to show unto his servants things which must shortly come to pass; and he sent and signified it by his angel unto his servant John: 2 Who bare record of the word of God, and of the testimony of Jesus Christ, and of all things that he saw. 3 Blessed is he that readeth, and they that hear the words of this prophecy, and keep those things which are written therein: for the time is at hand* (Revelation 1:1-3).

Jeremiah spoke about the New Covenant. There are not two covenants of salvation, one for the Jews and another for the Gentiles. This New Covenant is a covenant for both Jew and Gentile in Jeremiah 31:31-34. The Gospels establish the New Covenant. When Jesus' words in the Gospels are discounted for the Church, the covenant between the Lord and His Church becomes nonexistent. The title of the New Testament was the New Law, or New Covenant, or New Testament. The testator of the New Testament had to die before the New Will and Testament would come into full force (Hebrews 9:15-17). This New Covenant was established in the Gospels. This New Covenant would make the first covenant old (Hebrews 8:13). The death of Jesus, the mediator of the New Testament, would secure the redemption of the transgressions that were under the first testament, that they might receive the promise of eternal inheritance (Hebrews 9:15). By the death of Jesus, His blood paved the way for the saints to enter into the Holy Place behind the veil. This offered a new and living way for God's children (Hebrews 10:19-20).

The Word does not say that no one could get saved under the Old Covenant. They could be saved by faith just as they are under the New Covenant, but those under the Old Covenant offered sacrifices for sin once a year. When Jesus called the disciples to follow Him, they accepted Him as the Messiah and savior, and Jesus began to establish the New Covenant. Jesus fulfilled all that was written of Him, and fulfilled all the ceremonial law, and was the mediator of a better covenant, which was established upon better promises. Under the New Covenant, Jesus' blood was the atonement for sins once and for all, and the yearly sacrifice for sin would soon cease. Jesus entered once into the Holy Place with His own blood, and this offering and atonement for sin is eternal. The Law under the Old Covenant was only a shadow of good things to come, but the New Covenant would offer a new and living way. Those who accepted Jesus could draw near to God in full assurance of salvation.

The Gospels and this New Covenant were not under the dispensation of Law for the Jews alone, but were under the beginning of the New Covenant of salvation for all that believed. There were four hundred years since the last prophet until John, and he was the end of the Old Covenant. The virgin birth proved Jesus was the Messiah, and John prepared the way of the Lord and the New Covenant. Jesus had taught the disciples to carry on the ministry after His death and gave the Church four Gospels that contained His Last Will and Testament. This New Testament came into full force after the death of Jesus. The ceremonial law was abolished by the death of the testator, and this New Testament was for the Church, not for the Jews under the dispensation of Law. At the death of Jesus, the ceremonial laws were fulfilled and nailed to the cross: *And you, being dead in your sins and the uncircumcision of your flesh, hath he quickened together with him, having forgiven you all trespasses; 14 Blotting out the handwriting of ordinances that was against us, which was contrary to us, and took it out of the way, nailing it to his cross; 15 And having spoiled principalities and powers, he made a show of them openly, triumphing over them in it* (Colossians 2:13-15).

Jesus showed the termination of the Old Covenant and the installation of the New with the Last Supper. Jesus had given the Church the New Covenant in the Gospels. Therefore, I defend the fact that the Gospels were given to the Church, Jew and Gentile, and when we realize that the Gospels are for the Church, the pretribulation rapture theory is made void. Jesus is signifying the New Covenant is in force by celebrating the Lord's supper with the first members of the Church. If the disciples were not saved, nor belonged to the Church, why were they baptized and taking the Lord's Supper? The baptism of Jesus and the Lord's supper continue to be celebrated throughout all the Church age. Dispensationalists who say the Gospels are not for the Church concerning the Lord's coming continue to read Scriptures in the Gospels before a communion service without giving thought of their error: *And as they did eat, Jesus took bread, and blessed, and brake it, and gave to them, and said, Take, eat: this is my body. 23 And he took the cup, and when he had given thanks, he gave it to them: and they all drank of it. 24 And he said unto them, This is my blood of the new testament, which is shed for many* (Mark 14:22-24).

By God's providence, the division of the old ceremonial law and the New Covenant was clearly given to all by the destruction of the temple and the cessation of its service. The Jews were dispersed to the four corners of the earth in A.D. 70. The Jews could no longer offer sacrifices in the temple or keep the ceremonial law. God was showing that the New Covenant was in force, and that it provided a salvation for all by faith in the Lamb of God (Jesus Christ), God's only begotten Son. The New Testament would be divided into four parts, the Gospels, the Acts of the Apostles, the Epistles, and Revelation. The collection of the teachings of Jesus in the Gospels has been taught since the early church, and it brings dishonor to Christ and His church to say the Gospels are not for the Church.

If the Gospels are not for the Church, why did Jesus say in John 10:16 that He had other sheep that were not of this fold and they would hear His voice, and that there would only be one fold, and one shepherd? How can anyone say the Gentiles are not to hear the voice of the Lord in the Gospels if they are of the same fold? Jesus went on to say in John 10:27-29: *My sheep hear my voice, and I know them, and they follow me: 28 And I give unto them eternal life; and they shall never perish, neither shall any man pluck them out of my hand 29 My Father, which gave them me, is greater than all; and no man is able to pluck them out of my Father's hand.* Is not the Church those sheep who hear the voice of the Lord in the Gospels? This is the covenant promise to the sheep.

John the Baptist qualified his ministry by what was written of him by the prophets, and Jesus also qualified His ministry by what was written of Him by the prophets. Jesus always went back to Isaiah and Moses and quoted them, because there had to be a foundation built to show He was the Messiah and the only Begotten Son of God. The Gospels are the very foundation of Jesus' ministry and the Church. How can anyone possibly read the Gospels of Jesus Christ and apply them only to the Jew, and not the Church! The very foundation of our faith in Jesus Christ is built upon the apostles, the prophets, and Jesus Christ Himself being the chief cornerstone.

Many Scriptures prove the Gospels are for the Church and not for the Jew only. I do not give all these Scriptures to be repetitive, but to convince and convict God's people that the pretribulation rapture is in error; therefore, every error must be dealt with thoroughly. The whole pretribulation rapture theory collapses when proven by the Word that Matthew 24, Mark 13, and Luke 21 are not for the Jew only, but for the Church, concerning the Lord's coming. The Gospels plainly tell the Church the Lord's coming will be after the tribulation. When God's people see this truth, the pretribulation rapture theory dies because it has no foundation.

When Jesus began to preach in Matthew 4:17, *Repent for the kingdom of heaven is at hand*, the new message of the gospel of the kingdom had begun. Up until Jesus was thirty years of age the Jews did not hear the gospel. Jesus had a new message for the salvation for all, not for the Jew only. The new message of grace and truth began at that point: *From that time Jesus began to preach, and to say, Repent: for the kingdom of heaven is at hand* (Mathew 4: 17).

Through the foreknowledge of God, John knew Jesus had to go to the cross and die for man's sins before the kingdom of Israel was to be set up. Isaiah 53 had to be fulfilled by Jesus first. The Church age would require this gospel to be preached to all the world before Jesus would set up the kingdom of Israel. Jesus told His disciples this before He ascended in Acts 1:6-8. (This subject is covered under the heading of the kingdom of Israel later in the book.) John the Baptist knew this through the Holy Spirit, which was working in him when he told Israel the ax is laid unto the root of the trees (Israel's destruction). This prophecy was made before Jesus started His ministry, and was fulfilled in A.D. 70 by Titus. Therefore, Jesus did not come to set up an earthly kingdom. He came to establish the kingdom of God and the kingdom of heaven, which Jesus tells us in the Gospels. Pretribulationists must change their doctrine to fit the Word: *But when he saw many of the Pharisees and Sadducees come to his baptism, he said unto them, O generation of vipers, who hath warned you to flee from the wrath to come? 8 Bring forth therefore fruits meet for repentance: 9 And think not to say within yourselves, We have Abraham to our father: for I say unto you, that God is able of these stones to raise up children unto Abraham. 10 And now also the ax is laid unto the root of the trees: therefore every tree which bringeth not forth good fruit is hewn down, and cast into the fire* (Matthew 3:7-10).

Some Fundamental pastors who were brought up under the teachings of the Scofield Bible will say that Scofield was wrong when he said the Church had its beginning at Pentecost, and not when Jesus called His disciples. Those that see this error should also see what Jesus said in the Gospels about His coming is for the Church, and not for the Jew only. Its hard to understand how a person can believe that the Church had its beginning when Jesus called His disciples, without believing what Jesus said to His disciples about His second coming is for the Church. If a person believes the Gospels are for the Church, that person should also believe what Jesus said about the time element of His coming: *Immediately after the tribulation of those days shall the sun be darkened, and the moon shall not give her light, and the stars shall fall from heaven, and the powers of the heavens shall be shaken: 30 And then shall appear the sign of the Son of man in heaven: and then shall all the tribes of the earth mourn, and they shall see the Son of man coming in the clouds of heaven with power and great glory* (Matthew 24:29-30). The signs of Jesus coming in the clouds are immediately after the tribulation. Therefore you cannot believe the Gospels are for the Church without believing Jesus comes immediately after the tribulation. The rapture takes place at the same time in I Thessalonians 4:13-17 as it does in Matthew 24:31, 40-42: *And he shall send his angels with a great sound of a trumpet, and they shall gather together his elect from the four winds, from one end of heaven to the other. 40 Then shall two be in the field; the one shall be taken, and the other left. 41 Two women shall be grinding at the mill; the one shall be taken, and the other left. 42 Watch therefore: for ye know not what hour your Lord doth come.* Paul is talking about the same rapture in I Thessalonians 4:15-17 as Jesus was in Matthew 24:31, 40-42.

Jesus gave the Church similar Scriptures about His second coming in Mark 13:24-27, and Luke 21:25-28 as He does in Matthew 24. Jesus gives signs of His coming in all three. Jesus said He would come in the clouds in the Gospels just as Paul said in I Thessalonians 4:17. Jesus and Paul are not talking about two different comings. It's time the Church realizes that Jesus and Paul were talking about the same event. The apostasy and the man of sin must be revealed before we are gathered unto the Lord: *Now we beseech you, brethren, by the coming of our Lord Jesus Christ, and by our gathering together unto him, 2 That ye be not soon shaken in mind, or be troubled, neither by spirit, nor by word, nor by letter as from us, as that the day of Christ is at hand. 3 Let no man deceive you by any means: for that day shall not come, except there come a falling away first, and that man of sin be revealed, the son of perdition; 4 Who opposeth and exalteth himself above all that is called God, or that is worshipped; so that he as God sitteth in the temple of God, showing himself that he is God. 5 Remember ye not, that, when I was yet with you, I told you these things?* (II Thessalonians 2:1-5)

There is not one Scripture to substantiate a pretribulation rapture. Pretribulationists can offer only words of theology without scriptural proof, and if there is not a change in Church doctrine concerning the Church and the tribulation period, many will be left in darkness about the Lord's second coming just as the Pharisees were concerning His first coming.

The Gospel and the Gospels Are for Both Jew and Gentile

I came to realize how wrong dispensationalists were in separating the Gospels from the Church by dispensationalism. Jesus was the beginning of a new dispensation of grace and truth, and the disciples were the first members of the Church. This made me see that the gospel and the Gospels were equally for both Jew and Gentile. Paul gives reference that the gospel goes back to Moses. It should grieve every member of the Body of Christ when dispensationalists teach that the Gospels are not for the Church, but for the Jew only.

The gospel was preached by Moses to Israel concerning the Messiah, but it did not profit them because they did not accept His promises, His power, or His salvation by faith (Deu. 18:15-19, Heb. 3:5-19, 4:2). This prophet and savior, Jesus, came into the world born of a virgin, and was the fulfillment of Moses' prophecies. Many of the Jews rejected him as the Messiah. They rejected the One that was the Gospel and preached the Gospel. Paul let King Agrippa know that he had not preached any other gospel than that which the prophets and Moses preached concerning the death and resurrection of Jesus, and that Jesus is a light unto the Gentiles: *Whereupon, O king Agrippa, I was not disobedient unto the heavenly vision: 20 But showed first unto them of Damascus, and at Jerusalem, and throughout all the coasts of Judaea, and then to the Gentiles, that they should repent and turn to God, and do works meet for repentance. 21 For these causes the Jews caught me in the temple, and went about to kill me. 22 Having therefore obtained help of God, I continue unto this day, witnessing both to small and great, saying none other things than those which the prophets and Moses did say should come: 23 That Christ should suffer, and that he should be the first that should rise from the dead, and should show light unto the people, and to the Gentiles* (Acts 26:19-23).

Jesus appeared to Peter and Cleopas on the road to Emmaus and corrected them about their wrong conception concerning His coming to set up an earthly kingdom of Israel. He let them know that the prophets had prophesied all things concerning His death, resurrection, and how these things must take place before He entered into His glory. Jesus did not come to set up an earthly kingdom before all that was prophesied of Him was fulfilled. All New Testament teachings have their root in the Old Testament. Jesus made this plain when He used the prophets as a root of all His teachings. Dispensationalists should take special note of these Scriptures: *And he said unto them, What things? And they said unto him, Concerning Jesus of Nazareth, which was a prophet mighty in deed and word before God and all the people: 20 And how the chief priests and our rulers delivered him to be condemned to death, and have crucified him. 21 But we trusted that it had been he which should have redeemed Israel: and beside all this, to day is the third day since these things were done. 22 Yea, and certain women also of our company made us astonished, which were early at the sepulchre; 23 And when they found not his body, they came, saying, that they had also seen a vision of angels, which said that he was alive. 24 And certain of them which were with us went to the sepulchre, and found it even so as the women had said: but him they saw not. 25 Then he said unto them, O fools, and slow of heart to believe all that the prophets have spoken: 26 Ought not Christ to have suffered these things, and to enter into his glory? 27 And beginning at Moses and all the prophets, he expounded unto them in all the scriptures the things concerning himself* (Luke 24:19-27).

For those who are critical of using the root of Old Testament prophecies concerning the coming of the Lord, I remind you that Jesus referred to the Old Testament prophets in founding the Church, and Paul also used them in his ministry. Dispensationalists made a mistake when they separated Old Testament prophecies and the Gospels from the Church concerning the coming of the Lord, the rapture, and the resurrection. If Paul used the law of Moses and the prophets concerning the kingdom of God, for the salvation of all man, we can also use them as the root of all our doctrines: *And when they had appointed him a day, there came many to him into his lodging; to whom he expounded and testified the kingdom of God, persuading them concerning Jesus, both out of the law of Moses, and out of the prophets, from morning till evening. 24 And some believed the things which were spoken, and some believed not* (Acts 28:23-24). The kingdom of God is within us (Luke 17:20-21).

Isaiah also prophesied that Jesus would be born out of the stem of Jesse and would sit on David's throne (Isaiah 11:1-5). He told of the Church age and how the Gentiles would seek him in verse 10: *And in that day there shall be a root of Jesse, which shall stand for an ensign of the people; to it shall the Gentiles seek: and his rest shall be glorious.* He told how the Lord would gather Israel the second time from the four corners of the earth in verses 11-12. He said they would be saved with an everlasting salvation (Isa. 45:17). Chapter 26 of Isaiah tells about Israel being in pain, as a woman with child in the tribulation period. Then he promises them the resurrection of the dead, and that the Lord would hide them in His chambers until the indignation, or the judgment of nations is over (Isaiah 26:17-21). In the chapter 61, Isaiah told how the Spirit of the LORD would be upon Jesus to preach the gospel. Moses and Isaiah preached the gospel about Jesus, both Moses and Isaiah understanding how Jesus would preach the gospel about His death, burial, and resurrection. All three understood that the rejection of the Lord by Israel would come before the Gentiles would seek the Lord (the Church age). When John the Baptist said the ax is laid to the root in Matthew 3:1-3, 7-10, he was telling the Jews that their nation would be destroyed. Jesus preached the same message in Matthew 4:12-17. The source of their message goes back to Isaiah, and even further to Moses. There is only one true Gospel, neither Jesus nor Paul preached a different gospel.

The disciples had followed Jesus for three years, and it was getting close to the end of the Lord's ministry when the disciples came to Him to show Him the temple. Jesus then told them about the destruction of the temple. The following question was asked: *And as he sat upon the mount of Olives, the disciples came unto him privately, saying, Tell us, when shall these things be? and what shall be the sign of thy coming, and of the end of the world?* (Matthew 24:3). At this point, the question the disciples asked Jesus about His coming again has nothing to do with the Jews only, because the disciples were the first members of the Church. Dispensational teachers tell the Church that the Gospels are not for them, but for the Jew only, under the dispensation of the law. This makes the words of Jesus about His coming again void to the Church. The message which dispensationalists preach and teach is untrue when they say that what Jesus taught in the Gospels about His coming again is for the Jew only, and not for the Church. The Word of God shows that Paul taught about the Lord's second coming is no different than what Jesus taught. Jesus said to look for His coming immediately after the tribulation, not before. The One who brought the four Gospels to the Jew first brought the same message to the Gentiles. The disciples and many other Jews of the early Church believed the gospel of Jesus, and entered into His rest. The Gentiles enter into the same rest as the Jews. There are not two gospels, nor are there two rests, one for the Jew and another for the Gentile. We also enter into His rest when we believe the Gospels are for the Church: *For unto us was the gospel preached, as well as unto them: but the word preached did not profit them, not being mixed with faith in them that heard it. 3 For we which have believed do enter into rest, as he said, As I have sworn in my wrath, if they shall enter into my rest: although the works were finished from the foundation of the world* (Hebrews 4:2-3).

John the Baptist and Jesus preached the same message: "Repent, the kingdom of heaven is at hand." This heavenly rule from heaven would become a reality after the cross and Jesus' ascension to the right hand of the Father to rule in the kingdom the Father had given Him. Jesus promised that after He ascended to heaven, He would send back the Holy Spirit to dwell in all believers.

God choose the Jews to be His chosen people; therefore the disciples and Paul always went to the Jew first to preach the gospel. Jesus instructed the disciples to go to the Jew and not to the Gentiles because the Jews were to have the first opportunity to receive the gospel. When the Jews rejected the gospel, they also rejected Jesus as the Messiah. Paul told them after they rejected his message, "Lo, we turn to the Gentiles." *And the next sabbath day came almost the whole city together to hear the word of God. 45 But when the Jews saw the multitudes, they were filled with envy, and spake against those things which were spoken by Paul, contradicting and blaspheming. 46 Then Paul and Barnabas waxed bold, and said, It was necessary that the word of God should first have been spoken to you: but seeing ye put it from you, and judge yourselves unworthy of everlasting life, lo, we turn to the Gentiles. 47 For so hath the Lord commanded us, saying, I have set thee to be a light of the Gentiles, that thou shouldest be for salvation unto the ends of the earth. 48 And when the Gentiles heard this, they were glad, and glorified the word of the Lord: and as many as were ordained to eternal life believed. 49 And the word of the Lord was published throughout all the region (Acts 13:44-49).*

- The Gospel according to Matthew presents Jesus as the King of Kings.
- The Gospel according to Mark presents Jesus as the Servant of Jehovah.
- The Gospel according to Luke presents Jesus as the Son of man.
- The Gospel according to John presents Jesus as the Christ, the Son of God.

We can see the Gospels and how each presents Christ in a very special way. The Gospels are the backbone of our preaching and teaching about Jesus. All great preachers used the Gospels in a most powerful way in their preaching. If the Gospels were not for the Church, it would be foolish to preach something that was not meant for them.

I am trying to close all the loopholes that dispensational teachers have made for over 150 years concerning a pretribulation rapture theory. They have done to the Gospels concerning the coming of the Lord what adulterers would do in justifying their sin. They would simply say, "The Commandments were given by Moses to the children of Israel under the dispensation of the law; therefore it does not apply to me." This is the same reasoning that the dispensationalists use concerning Matthew 24. They cast it aside, saying this Scripture is for the Jews and not for the Church. Most of our preachers, evangelists, and college professors preach a pretribulation rapture theory and call it rightly dividing the Word of Truth. God's Word calls it deception and false doctrine.

Jesus commands us to preach the gospel to all the world. The interpretation of Matthew 24:14 is wrong in Scofield's notes. He states the gospel here relates to the end-time prophecy concerning the Jewish remnant preaching the gospel of the kingdom during the tribulation period. It is a shame for someone to twist the Word to fit their own doctrine and say this is a different gospel than He commanded us to preach to all the world. There is only one true gospel, not two or three.

Dispensationalists have spent over 150 years in preaching error to the Church. The time has come for all to see that the Gospels are for the Church and to see His teachings about His coming again are for the Church, both Jews and Gentiles. Let the same gospel the early Church preached be preached until this witness has been preached to all nations. The gospel of the kingdom Jesus preached, is the same gospel Paul preached: *And this gospel of the kingdom shall be preached in all the world for a witness unto all nations; and then shall the end come* (Matthew 24:14).

The word *Church* means "called-out assembly." Most dispensational teachers teach that the Church started on the day of Pentecost. Scofield asserts in his notes in the Scofield Bible that the Church spans the second Chapter of Acts to the fourth chapter of Revelation, as stated earlier. Therefore, he taught the rapture had to be in Revelation 4:1, and the rest of Revelation was dealing with the Jews and not the Church, because the Church was not mentioned again in the book of Revelation. This is foolishness.

In his Scofield Reference Bible, Scofield says that the doctrine of grace is to be sought in the Epistles, and not the Gospels. When the Church follows this line of thinking, of course the Church will come up with the same doctrines as Scofield, when he discounted the Gospels for the Church. This is the reason why there is a pretribulation rapture theory today. Jesus was full of grace from the beginning, He did not have to wait until the Epistles to show He was the God of all grace, and the Messiah, savior of the world.

Jesus did not alter His plans because the Jews rejected Him. Jesus knew that within a few days He would be killed. He knew He would break off the Jew and graft the Gentile into His body, thus raising Himself up a Church fulfilling Psalms 118:21-24. He became the salvation for both the Jew and Gentile. He become the corner, and top stone of the Church. All power and judgment was given Him in heaven. Those that stumbled at the stone would be broken and ground to powder whether they be Jew or Gentile. Scripture shows the Lord's intention concerning the kingdom of heaven where He would rule over His Church after His crucifixion: *Then said the lord of the vineyard, What shall I do? I will send my beloved son: it may be they will reverence him when they see him. 14 But when the husbandmen saw him, they reasoned among themselves, saying, This is the heir: come, let us kill him, that the inheritance may be ours. 15 So they cast him out of the vineyard, and killed him. What therefore shall the lord of the vineyard do unto them? 16 He shall come and destroy these husbandmen, and shall give the vineyard to others. And when they heard it, they said, God forbid. 17 And he beheld them, and said, What is this then that is written, The stone which the builders rejected, the same is become the head of the corner? 18 Whosoever shall fall upon that stone shall be broken; but on whomsoever it shall fall, it will grind him to powder* (Luke 20:13-18).

The Gentiles were once without Christ, and aliens from the commonwealth of Israel. They were strangers from the covenants of promise, but were made fellow heirs of the same body by the blood of Christ. The covenant of promise that gives salvation to all begins in the Gospels, not the book of Acts. The verses below prove you cannot divide the Gospels and Jesus from the Church by dispensational theology, as Darby and Scofield have done. Believing Gentiles were made fellow heirs of the same body with believing Jews, and partakers of God's promises. The kingdom of Israel will be set up in the Millennium, and God never intended it before: *Wherefore remember, that ye being in time past Gentiles in the flesh, who are called Uncircumcision by that which is called the Circumcision in the flesh made by hands; 12 That at that time ye were without Christ, being aliens from the commonwealth of Israel, and strangers from the covenants of promise, having no hope, and without God in the world: 13 But now in Christ Jesus ye who sometimes were far off are made nigh by the blood of Christ. 14 For he is our peace, who hath made both one, and hath broken down the middle wall of partition between us; 3:5- 6: Which in other ages was not made known unto the sons of men, as it is now revealed unto his holy apostles and prophets by the Spirit; 6 That the Gentiles should be fellowheirs, and of the same body, and partakers of his promise in Christ by the gospel* (Ephesians 2:11-14).

The Bible does not say the Church started in the book of Acts. The New Testament Church started in the Gospels, as I have already stated. I will give enough evidence to destroy the untruths of dispensationalism. I attended the late Dr. Jack Hyles Pastors' School and respect him highly for the great work he has done. He believed in the pretribulation rapture of the Church, yet in his book *The Church*, he states, "The Church was probably started in Matthew chapter ten when Jesus called his disciples to a mountainside and named them as his disciples. For the first time there was a called out assembly."

I concur because the beginning of the called-out assembly of the New Testament was when Jesus began to call His disciples unto Himself in order to carry on the work after His death. Jesus was the beginning of a new dispensation of the grace of God for the salvation of all who would believe, both Jew and Gentile. The Church was not an afterthought of God, but was planed from eternity. When Jesus began calling His disciples He said, "Repent: for the kingdom of heaven is at hand," and He called Simon Peter and Andrew his brother. "Follow me, and I will make you fishers of Men." Jesus then called James and John (Matthew 4:17-22). His disciples believed He was the Messiah (John 1:41). Jesus said, "Upon this rock I will build my Church, and the gates of Hell shall not prevail against it" (Matthew 16:13-19). If the Church started at this point in the book of Matthew, then the Gospels are for the Church. This makes the pretribulation theory an error, because Jesus told us when he would return in Matthew 24. If the disciples were of the Church, then the Gospels are for the Church also. Jesus began to call His own unto Him: *And when he had called unto him his twelve disciples, he gave them power against unclean spirits, to cast them out, and to heal all manner of sickness and all manner of disease. 2 Now the names of the twelve apostles are these; The first, Simon, who is called Peter, and Andrew his brother; James the son of Zebedee, and John his brother; 3 Philip, and Bartholomew; Thomas, and Matthew the publican; James the son of Alphaeus, and Lebbaeus, whose surname was Thaddaeus; 4 Simon the Canaanite, and Judas Iscariot, who also betrayed him. 5 These twelve Jesus sent forth, and commanded them, saying, Go not into the way of the Gentiles, and into any city of the Samaritans enter ye not: 6 But go rather to the lost sheep of the house of Israel. 7 And as ye go, preach, saying, The kingdom of heaven is at hand. 8 Heal the sick, cleanse the lepers, raise the dead, cast out devils: freely ye have received, freely give* (Matthew 10:1-8). God's plan was that the gospel would be preached to the Jews first and then to the Gentiles.

Many disciples did not believe Jesus was the Messiah and subsequently turned back from following the Lord, but Simon Peter let it be known to the Lord that they believed He was the Christ, the Son of the Living God, and that He alone had the words of life: *Then said Jesus unto the twelve, Will ye also go away? 68 Then Simon Peter answered him, Lord, to whom shall we go? thou hast the words of eternal life. 69 And we believe and are sure that thou art that Christ, the Son of the living God* (John 6:67-69). By faith they were saved, and became members of the called-out assembly before the day of Pentecost.

Salvation and justification has always been by faith. Those who believed that Jesus was the Messiah in the Gospels were saved and justified the same as were Abel, Enoch, Noah, Abraham, Isaac, Jacob, Joseph, Moses, and Rahab in Hebrews 11:7-31. The Gospel of John proves the Church started in the Gospels, and not the book of Acts. The following Scriptures give the account of the disciples, priest, chief rulers, and many others including Samaritans, who believed Jesus was the Messiah, and were saved: John 2:11,22-23; 4:6-42, 53; 10:41-42; 11:41-45; 12:42; and 17:1-9. Those who believed on Jesus and were saved needed to be endued with power from on high, and were told to tarry at Jerusalem until they received the power that was needed to carry the gospel to all nations (Luke 24:49; Acts 1:8). The called-out assembly started in the Gospels when they believed on Jesus, and the three thousand who were saved on the day of Pentecost were added to the Church: *Then they that gladly received his word were baptized: and the same day there were added unto them about three thousand souls* (Acts 2:41). The disciples were endued with power on the day of Pentecost, but they did not get saved or baptized again because they were already saved. Dwight L. Moody, Charles G. Finney, and many other saints down through the Church age received the same enduement of power after their salvation.

Jesus sent the disciples first to the Jews because they were His chosen people. They were given the first opportunity for salvation, but when the Jews refused to believe in Jesus, Paul turned to the Gentiles in Acts 13:46. The book of Romans helps us to understand why God dealt with the Jew first: *For I am not ashamed of the gospel of Christ: for it is the power of God unto salvation to every one that believeth; to the Jew first, and also to the Greek* (Romans 1:16). *Tribulation and anguish, upon every soul of man that doeth evil, of the Jew first, and also of the Gentile; 10 But glory, honour, and peace, to every man that worketh good, to the Jew first, and also to the Gentile* (Romans 2:9-10). *Then Paul and Barnabas waxed bold, and said, It was necessary that the word of God should first have been spoken to you: but seeing ye put it from you, and judge yourselves unworthy of everlasting life, lo, we turn to the Gentiles* (Acts 13:46).

Multitudes were following Jesus in Mark 8:1. Jesus had fed the four thousand and healed the blind man near Bethsaida. Jesus then went out and asked His disciples, "Whom do men say that I am?" Then He asked them, "Whom say ye that I am." Peter's answer shows he believed that Jesus was the Messiah and put faith in Him. This is salvation by faith, undeniably making the Gospels for the Church: *And Jesus went out, and his disciples, into the towns of Caesarea Philippi: and by the way he asked his disciples, saying unto them, Whom do men say that I am? 28 And they answered, John the Baptist: but some say, Elias; and others, One of the prophets. 29 And he saith unto them, But whom say ye that I am? And Peter answereth and saith unto him, Thou art the Christ* (Mark 8:27-29).

Immediately after the day of Pentecost, Peter preached. Peter wanted the whole House of Israel to know who Jesus was just as he had already acknowledged in Mark 8:29. Therefore, Peter was preaching to them what he had received under the ministry of Jesus in the Gospels: *Therefore let all the house of Israel know assuredly, that God hath made that same Jesus, whom ye have crucified, both Lord and Christ* (Acts 2:36).

The following is the same question about which Jesus dealt with the disciples. The Jews heard Peter and they wanted the same salvation as Peter, and he told them what they must do to get saved. If you take away the Gospels from the Church, then you are throwing away the disciples' training under Jesus. Jesus and the disciples established the New Testament Church in the Gospels: *Now when they heard this, they were pricked in their heart, and said unto Peter and to the rest of the apostles, Men and brethren, what shall we do? 38 Then Peter said unto them, Repent, and be baptized every one of you in the name of Jesus Christ for the remission of sins, and ye shall receive the gift of the Holy Ghost. 39 For the promise is unto you, and to your children, and to all that are afar off, even as many as the Lord our God shall call. 40 And with many other words did he testify and exhort, saying, Save yourselves from this untoward generation. 41: Then they that gladly received his word were baptized: and the same day there were added unto them about three thousand souls* (Acts 2:37-41).

Jesus came to the Jews in the Gospels and offered them salvation. Many of the Jews did not believe Jesus was the Messiah, but a remnant was saved. Jesus came to offer salvation to all in the Gospels: *He came unto his own, and his own received him not. 12 But as many as received him, to them gave he power to become the sons of God, even to them that believe on his name* (John 1:11-12).

Jesus was the seed of Abraham, so all the earth might be blessed through Him. The purpose of Jesus was to save and turn every one from their iniquity, the Jew first, and then the Gentile: *Ye are the children of the prophets, and of the covenant which God made with our fathers, saying unto Abraham, And in thy seed shall all the kindreds of the earth be blessed. 26 Unto you first God, having raised up his Son Jesus, sent him to bless you, in turning away every one of you from his iniquities* (Acts 3:25-26).

If Abraham rejoiced to see the day of Jesus, it is an insult to the Gospels and to Jesus to let dispensational doctrines say that the Gospels are not for the Church, especially when this is what Abraham saw, as Jesus quotes: *Your father Abraham rejoiced to see my day: and he saw it, and was glad* (John 8:56). Abraham did not rejoice to see Jesus come and set up an earthly kingdom, but he rejoiced when he saw the salvation of the Lord, and that through his seed the whole world would be blessed in the Church age through Jesus the Messiah. He saw a small glimpse of salvation that would come to the Jews and Gentiles through faith in the Son of God. John the Baptist knew and prophesied Israel would be destroyed, and he declared how God was able to raise up children unto Abraham in: *And think not to say within yourselves, We have Abraham to our father: for I say unto you, that God is able of these stones to raise up children unto Abraham. 10 And now also the ax is laid unto the root of the trees: therefore every tree which bringeth not forth good fruit is hewn down, and cast into the fire* (Matt. 3:9-10).

I have not found one verse of Scripture where Jesus said He came to set up an earthly kingdom of Israel before the cross, but I do find the Lord's intention to bring up children unto Abraham. When we place the Gospels and Galatians side by side we can see the Lord's intention to save those who were under the law that they might become children of Abraham by faith: *Know ye therefore that they which are of faith, the same are the children of Abraham 8 And the scripture, foreseeing that God would justify the heathen through faith, preached before the gospel unto Abraham, saying, In thee shall all nations be blessed. 9 So then they which be of faith are blessed with faithful Abraham. 10 For as many as are of the works of the law are under the curse: for it is written, Cursed is every one that continueth not in all things which are written in the book of the law to do them* (Galatians 3:7-10).

Jesus came to redeem Israel from the curse of the Law, so that the blessings of Abraham might be on the Jew and Gentile. Both could receive the promise of the Spirit through faith: *Christ hath redeemed us from the curse of the law, being made a curse for us: for it is written, Cursed is every one that hangeth on a tree: 14 That the blessing of Abraham might come on the Gentiles through Jesus Christ; that we might receive the promise of the Spirit through faith* (Galatians 3:13-14).

I believe it is an offence to God to say that the Gospels are under the dispensation of the Law and are for the Jew only, and not for the Church. God called both Jew and Gentile and made them seed unto Abraham: *Brethren, I speak after the manner of men; Though it be but a man's covenant, yet if it be confirmed, no man disannulleth, or addeth thereto. 16 Now to Abraham and his seed were the promises made. He saith not, And to seeds, as of many; but as of one, And to thy seed, which is Christ. 17 And this I say, that the covenant, that was confirmed before of God in Christ, the law, which was four hundred and thirty years after, cannot disannul, that it should make the promise of none effect. 18 For if the inheritance be of the law, it is no more of promise: but God gave it to Abraham by promise* (Galatians 3:15-18).

The pretribulation rapture theory can only be propped up by the doctrines of men. The Law was given as a schoolmaster to bring both Jew and Gentile to Christ. Don't put the Gospels under the dispensation of the law: *But the scripture hath concluded all under sin, that the promise by faith of Jesus Christ might be given to them that believe. 23 But before faith came, we were kept under the law, shut up unto the faith which should afterwards be revealed. 24 Wherefore the law was our schoolmaster to bring us unto Christ, that we might be justified by faith* (Galatians 3:22-24).

When the disciples believed in the Lord and followed Jesus, they were on longer under the Law, but under the grace of God by faith. All who accepted Jesus throughout the Gospels became the children of Abraham immediately. They did not have to wait until Acts 2 to be saved and become the children of Abraham. There is no record that the disciples made a profession of salvation again, or were baptized a second time after Jesus baptized them. It was those who were baptized unto John's baptism who were baptized again: *But after that faith is come, we are no longer under a schoolmaster. 26 For ye are all the children of God by faith in Christ Jesus. 27 For as many of you as have been baptized into Christ have put on Christ. 28 There is neither Jew nor Greek, there is neither bond nor free, there is neither male nor female: for ye are all one in Christ Jesus. 29 And if ye be Christ's, then are ye Abraham's seed, and heirs according to the promise* (Galatians 3:25-29).

When God's timing was come, God sent forth His Son to redeem those bound under the Law, so they could be adopted as sons, and Jesus came to save them that were under the Law. Paul is telling the Galatian Church that the ministry of Jesus was for the redemption of the Jews by faith, and not the law: *But when the fulness of the time was come, God sent forth his Son, made of a woman, made under the law, 5 To redeem them that were under the law, that we might receive the adoption of sons* (Galatians 4:4-5).

The Gospels are not about the covenant of Sinai and the Law, which keep her children in bondage. The Gospels are about the Jerusalem above, which is free to all who will come to Jesus by faith: *For this Hagar is mount Sinai in Arabia, and answereth to Jerusalem which now is, and is in bondage with her children. 26 But Jerusalem which is above is free, which is the mother of us all* (Galatians 4:25-26).

Abraham saw afar off how Jew and Gentile would be united into one body in Christ (the Church). Faith in Christ unites us into one family of God, (Jew and Gentile). Christ redeemed both from the curse of the Law, which makes both children of Abraham by faith in Christ. The inheritance did not come by Law, but was given to Abraham by promise. God included all under sin, that the promise by faith of Jesus Christ could be given to all those who believed. The Law was given to bring all to Christ so they could be justified by faith. God's purpose was to make Jew and Gentile one in Christ. Where God unites both Israel and the Church together, let it be according to the Word. Let us unite the two where God unites, and let us divide the two where God divides. God never intended for anyone to separate the Gospels from the Church merely to satisfy a dispensational doctrine. Theologians can use their formulas, but if their formula is in error, then what they teach is also in error. The Gospels are the foundation of the Church to bring Jew and Gentile into one body in Christ. Paul compared a loving husband and wife relationship to Jesus and the Church (Ephesians 5:21-33). The Law was powerless to bring about a loving relationship as Jesus and His grace produced. We can glory in the cross of Christ, which produced love for Christ and one-another. In Christ both Jew and Gentile are one new creation: *But God forbid that I should glory, save in the cross of our Lord Jesus Christ, by whom the world is crucified unto me, and I unto the world. 15 For in Christ Jesus neither circumcision availeth any thing, nor uncircumcision, but a new creature. 16 And as many as walk according to this rule, peace be on them, and mercy, and upon the Israel of God* (Galatians 6:14-16).

We should understand how foolish it would be to say that Isaiah 53 is not for the Church. Jesus had to go to the cross or the Scripture would have been broken. When pretribulationists say that Jesus came to set up an earthly kingdom of Israel, they are taking Satan's side just as Peter did. Peter tried to prevent Jesus from fulfilling His purpose of going to the cross and ruling in His kingdom from heaven. Jesus did not have to wait two thousand years to set up the kingdom of Heaven. He is ruling the Church from heaven now. We must savor the things of God just as the Lord asked Peter to do: *And he began to teach them, that the Son of man must suffer many things, and be rejected of the elders, and of the chief priests, and scribes, and be killed, and after three days rise again. 32 And he spake that saying openly. And Peter took him, and began to rebuke him. 33 But when he had turned about and looked on his disciples, he rebuked Peter, saying, Get thee behind me, Satan: for thou savourest not the things that be of God, but the things that be of men* (Mark 8:31-33).

Peter was thinking of an earthly kingdom just like who teach that Jesus came to set up an earthly kingdom. They teach that because the Jews rejected Jesus, the kingdom was delayed until the millennium. If Jesus had come to set up an earthly kingdom, He would have called twelve legions of angels and conquered His enemies at that time. Jesus said the Scriptures of the prophets must be fulfilled: *Then said Jesus unto him, Put up again thy sword into his place: for all they that take the sword shall perish with the sword. 53 Thinkest thou that I cannot now pray to my Father, and he shall presently give me more than twelve legions of angels? 54 But how then shall the scriptures be fulfilled, that thus it must be? 55 In that same hour said Jesus to the multitudes, Are ye come out as against a thief with swords and staves for to take me? I sat daily with you teaching in the temple, and ye laid no hold on me. 56 But all this was done, that the scriptures of the prophets might be fulfilled. Then all the disciples forsook him, and fled* (Matthew 26:52-56).

Jesus taught his disciples about the greatness of the kingdom of heaven and our resurrected bodies in Heaven. He let His disciples know how great John the Baptist was, but He said that the least in the kingdom of Heaven would be greater because John the Baptist, in his natural body, still had infirmities and imperfections, and he came short of glorified saints. The glorified bodies of the Church will be equal with the angels. The dispensation of the Gospel and Grace far exceeds those who lived under the Law, but they which are of either do not compare to those in their resurrected state.

Jesus let His disciples know that, from the day of John the Baptist until the day He was talking to his disciples, the kingdom of heaven had suffered violence. The unbelieving Pharisees and Jews wanted to stop Jesus' ministry by force. They did put Jesus on the cross, but they did not stop the kingdom of heaven from coming into power by the King of Kings. I believe the prophets and the Law prophesied until John. From the day John the Baptist began to preach, *"Repent for the kingdom of heaven is at hand,"* the kingdom of heaven suffered violence. The Devil came to kill, steal, and destroy, but Jesus came to give eternal life. John's preaching of the kingdom of heaven was the beginning of a new dispensation fulfilling the prophecy of Isaiah saying, *"The voice of one crying in the wilderness, Prepare ye the way of the Lord, make his paths straight."* The Devil had done everything he could to stop the preaching of John about the kingdom of heaven. Those who have resurrected bodies in the kingdom of heaven will be stronger, and more powerful, and greater than John. Jesus said in Matthew 11:11-13: *Verily I say unto you, Among them that are born of women there hath not risen a greater than John the Baptist: notwithstanding he that is least in the kingdom of heaven is greater than he. 12 And from the days of John the Baptist until now the kingdom of heaven suffereth violence, and the violent take it by force. 13 For all the prophets and the law prophesied until John.*

John bore witness of the Light that all man might be saved by faith in Jesus. The new dispensation did not start after the Gospels; it started at the beginning of John's preaching about the promised One. The opportunity for salvation was immediate in receiving Jesus as savior: *There was a man sent from God, whose name was John. 7 The same came for a witness, to bear witness of the Light, that all men through him might believe. 8 He was not that Light, but was sent to bear witness of that Light. 9 That was the true Light, which lighteth every man that cometh into the world. 10 He was in the world, and the world was made by him, and the world knew him not. 11 He came unto his own, and his own received him not. 12 But as many as received him, to them gave he power to become the sons of God, even to them that believe on his name. The dispensation of grace had already started in the*

Gospel of John (John 1:6-12). *John bare witness of him, and cried, saying, This was he of whom I spake, He that cometh after me is preferred before me: for he was before me. 16 And of his fulness have all we received, and grace for grace. 17 For the law was given by Moses, but grace and truth came by Jesus Christ* (John 1:15-17).

Salvation did not come to the disciples on the day of Pentecost, but when they accepted Jesus and confessed he was the Christ, the Son of God (John 1:41). The disciples did not have to wait until the resurrection to receive salvation or start the Church. They were saved by faith the same way all Old and New Testament saints are saved. Jesus said the Father had already given the disciples to Jesus, and He kept them. This Scripture is further proof that the Church started before Pentecost: *These words spake Jesus, and lifted up his eyes to heaven, and said, Father, the hour is come; glorify thy Son, that thy Son also may glorify thee: 2 As thou hast given him power over all flesh, that he should give eternal life to as many as thou hast given him. 3 And this is life eternal, that they might know thee the only true God, and Jesus Christ, whom thou hast sent. 4 I have glorified thee on the earth: I have finished the work which thou gavest me to do. 5 And now, O Father, glorify thou me with thine own self with the glory which I had with thee before the world was. 6 I have manifested thy name unto the men which thou gavest me out of the world: thine they were, and thou gavest them me; and they have kept thy word. 7 Now they have known that all things whatsoever thou hast given me are of thee. 8 For I have given unto them the words which thou gavest me; and they have received them, and have known surely that I came out from thee, and they have believed that thou didst send me. 9 I pray for them: I pray not for the world, but for them which thou hast given me; for they are thine. 10 And all mine are thine, and thine are mine; and I am glorified in them. 11 And now I am no more in the world, but these are in the world, and I come to thee. Holy Father, keep through thine own name those whom thou hast given me, that they may be one, as we are. 12 While I was with them in the world, I kept them in thy name: those that thou gavest me I have kept, and none of them is lost, but the son of perdition; that the scripture might be fulfilled* (John 17:1-12).

Jesus never intended for a barrier to be put up between the Gospels and the Church. The book of Acts does not serve as a dividing line between the Law and the Church. The Acts of the Apostles was authored by the apostle Luke. The very first verse of Acts shows there is a continuation of all that Jesus began: *The former treatise have I made, O Theophilus, of all that Jesus began both to do and teach* (Acts 1:1). Luke is letting Theophilus know that Acts is a continuation of the account he had given in his first letter describing what Jesus began to do and teach. Since the book of Acts is a continuation of all that Jesus began both to do and teach, how is a doctrine possible that claims what Jesus taught in the Gospels about His coming is not for the Church, but for the Jew only, and under the dispensation of Law?

Luke had been with Jesus and was taught by Him about the promise of the Father concerning the enduement of power by the Holy Ghost (Luke 24:49). Luke repeated to the disciples what Jesus had already taught them concerning the power that would be needed in carrying out the great commission (Acts 1:4-5). The disciples were saved in the Gospels when they believed Jesus was the Messiah, but they did not have the power of the Holy Spirit that they were going to need in preaching the gospel. Luke quoted the words of Jesus in Acts 1:8: *But ye shall receive power, after that the Holy Ghost is come upon you: and ye shall be witnesses unto me both in Jerusalem, and in all Judaea, and in Samaria, and unto the uttermost part of the earth.*

The promise was fulfilled in Acts 2, not for salvation nor the establishing of the New Testament Church because they were already saved and were the first members of the Church, but they needed the promised power: *And when the day of Pentecost was fully come, they were all with one accord in one place. 2 And suddenly there came a sound from heaven as of a rushing mighty wind, and it filled all the house where they were sitting. 3 And there appeared unto them cloven tongues like as of fire, and it sat upon each of them. 4 And they were all filled with the Holy Ghost, and began to speak with other tongues, as the Spirit gave them utterance* (Acts 2:1-4).

Jesus charged the disciples to carry out the great commission. They were to teach all nations what Jesus had taught them. Therefore, the Gospels are as much for the Gentile as for the Jew: *Go ye therefore, and teach all nations, baptizing them in the name of the Father, and of the Son, and of the Holy Ghost: 20 Teaching them to observe all things whatsoever I have commanded you: and, lo, I am with you alway, even unto the end of the world. Amen* (Matthew 28:19-20).

The Gospels
and Salvation

If the Gospels were for the Jew only under the dispensation of the Law, then Jesus would have taught a salvation of works and not of faith. The Gospels give us a far different picture. Jesus offered salvation by faith to the Jew and the Gentile. Dispensationalists teach as if Paul's writings to the Romans are the primary mention of salvation by faith, but we can see the Gospels teach salvation by faith, the second birth, and the baptism of believers. It is a great error to place the Gospels for the Jew only under the dispensation of the Law when we can see a picture in the Gospel of John where Jesus baptized all who believed in Him. Jesus, the disciples, and all believers were baptized before Pentecost, making the Gospels the beginning of the Church, and not Acts 2: *When therefore the Lord knew how the Pharisees had heard that Jesus made and baptized more disciples than John, 2 (Though Jesus himself baptized not, but his disciples)* (John 4:1-2).

The foundation of soul-winning was laid in the Gospel of Matthew. Jesus prepared his disciples for soul-winning in the New Testament Church; this was not a salvation by the works of the law but by faith. This new kingdom of heaven was at hand, and was not a delayed kingdom: *From that time Jesus began to preach, and to say, Repent: for the kingdom of heaven is at hand. 18 And Jesus, walking by the sea of Galilee, saw two brethren, Simon called Peter, and Andrew his brother, casting a net into the sea: for they were fishers. 19 And he saith unto them, Follow me, and I will make you fishers of men. 20 And they straightway left their nets, and followed him* (Matthew 4:17-20).

It was in the beginning of Jesus' ministry when he told Nicodemus, a Jew, that he must be saved by the second birth. This does not sound like a salvation for the Jew only by the Law. We must not put the Gospels in with the dispensation of the law because it destroys the whole purpose of Jesus coming into the world: *There was a man of the Pharisees, named Nicodemus, a ruler of the Jews: 2 The same came to Jesus by night, and said unto him, Rabbi, we know that thou art a teacher come from God: for no man can do these miracles that thou doest, except God be with him. 3 Jesus answered and said unto him, Verily, verily, I say unto thee, Except a man be born again, he cannot see the kingdom of God. 4 Nicodemus saith unto him, How can a man be born when he is old? can he enter the second time into his mother's womb, and be born? 5 Jesus answered, Verily, verily, I say unto thee, Except a man be born of water and of the Spirit, he cannot enter into the kingdom of God. 6 That which is born of the flesh is flesh; and that which is born of the Spirit is spirit. 7 Marvel not that I said unto thee, Ye must be born again* (John 3:1-7).

Many soul-winners use the Gospel of John for soul-winning. It is heartbreaking to hear those who use some of these verses for the salvation of souls, and with the next breath tell their students that Matthew 24 does not apply to the Church. Matthew 24 applies to the Church the same as John 5:24: *Verily, verily, I say unto you, He that heareth my word, and believeth on him that sent me, hath everlasting life, and shall not come into condemnation; but is passed from death unto life.*

If the age of grace and salvation did not exist in the Gospels, then the Lord did not know what He was saying when Zacchaeus got saved. Salvation came to him before Acts. Salvation by grace through faith was taught in the Gospels: *And Zacchaeus stood, and said unto the Lord; Behold, Lord, the half of my goods I give to the poor; and if I have taken any thing from any man by false accusation, I restore him fourfold. 9 And Jesus said unto him, This day is salvation come to this house, forsomuch as he also is a son of Abraham. 10 For the Son of man is come to seek and to save that which was lost* (Luke 19:8-10). Salvation also came to the woman at the well immediately (John 4:23-30).

The Gospels make correction to dispensationalists' error. The Law of Moses stops with John the Baptist. The dispensation of the Law does not extend to Acts the second chapter, as dispensationalists teach. The following Scriptures set straight this terrible error of dispensationalists. The law and the prophets were until John. Since that time the kingdom of God has been preached for the salvation of all. The new dispensation of the Church started when John prepared the way of the Lord by preaching, *"The kingdom of heaven is at hand,"* and pointing to Jesus, saying, *Behold the Lamb of God, which taketh away the sin of the world.* This is what Jesus said: *The law and the prophets were until John: since that time the kingdom of God is preached, and every man presseth into it* (Luke 16:16). *For all the prophets and the law prophesied until John* (Matthew 11:13).

In the Gospel of Luke, the Holy Spirit revealed to Simeon how Jesus would be a light unto the Gentiles. I don't see where he was prophesying of an earthly kingdom to the Jews only. He knew Grace and Truth had arrived into the world for the Jew and Gentile. He knew Jesus was headed for the cross, and that the Church age would come before Jesus would set up the kingdom of Israel: *And, behold, there was a man in Jerusalem, whose name was Simeon; and the same man was just and devout, waiting for the consolation of Israel: and the Holy Ghost was upon him. 26 And it was revealed unto him by the Holy Ghost, that he should not see death, before he had seen the Lord's Christ. 27 And he came by the Spirit into the temple: and when the parents brought in the child Jesus, to do for him after the custom of the law, 28 Then took he him up in his arms, and blessed God, and said, 29 Lord, now lettest thou thy servant depart in peace, according to thy word: 30 For mine eyes have seen thy salvation, 31 Which thou hast prepared before the face of all people; 32 A light to lighten the Gentiles, and the glory of thy people Israel. 33 And Joseph and his mother marvelled at those things which were spoken of him. 34 And Simeon blessed them, and said unto Mary his mother, Behold, this child is set for the fall and rising again of many in Israel; and for a sign which shall be spoken against; 35 (Yea, a sword shall pierce through thy own soul also,) that the thoughts of many hearts may be revealed* (Luke 2:25-35).

The Gospels teach a salvation by faith in Jesus Christ and are for the Church. If we believe this we must also believe the Gospels are for the Church concerning Jesus' coming. Therefore, there will be no pretribulation rapture as the Church has been taught for over 150 years.

Every major doctrine has its roots in the Old Testament and the prophets. Jesus often quoted Old Testament Scriptures in the Gospels. The doctrine concerning the coming of the Lord was established in the

Old Testament, but the Jews rejected the message as recorded in the Gospels. Paul and the New Testament writers were building on the foundation of pure and true doctrine for the Church that had already been laid. Posttribulationists have a foundation built upon the Old Testament and the words of Jesus, but the doctrine of pretribulation rapture has no foundation in the prophets, the Gospels, nor the Epistles. Darby, Scofield, and pretribulation rapture teachers tell the Church that I Thessalonians 4:13-17 is the Church rapture and takes place before the tribulation begins. There is no foundation for such a doctrine. Look at I Thessalonians 5:1-9, and you will find a root of these verses in the prophets and the Gospels. The times and seasons are explained in the prophets. The times and seasons give us a time element in the Gospels of Matthew 24:29-31; Mark 13:24-27; Luke 21:25-28.

The Old Testament was the foundation for Jesus and the Gospels. The Gospels are the foundation for the Church and the Epistles. Let the Church begin to apply the Gospels, and know that Jesus gave the Gospels for the Church, both Jew and Gentile. To say the coming of the Lord and the Gospels does not apply to the Church is like saying the Ten Commandments that were given to Moses have no place in the Christian's life, because they were given under the Law and not under grace. We can see how foolish this would be.

Those who founded the pretribulation rapture have brought the Church to a form of Antinomianism, which taught that, when a person was saved by grace, that person was no longer bound to any obedience to the Law. They believe that under the gospel of grace, the moral law is of no use or obligation. Paul had to deal with the falsehood of this teaching (Romans 6:14-18). The people who teach a pretribulation rapture are making a terrible mistake, also, by saying that Jesus' words in the Gospels concerning His coming do not apply to the Church, because the Gospels were under the dispensation of the Law, and not under the dispensation of grace. They say the Gospels, therefore, cannot apply to the Church. We know this belief is wrong, because Jesus did not come to destroy the law or the prophets, but to fulfill. The Word always makes plain in the Gospels or the Epistles when the New Testament writers are talking only to Israel.

The Church is not the author of grace or faith, because the doctrine of grace reaches back to Adam, and the doctrine of faith reaches back to Abel. Paul wrote to the Corinthian Church that those things that happened to Israel were examples to the Church. Dispensational teachers often explain away many truths that should be applied to the Church. Faith and grace operated before the law—the Church was not the originator of either. Therefore, the Gospels and the prophets are not void to the Church. Jesus came to establish the Church. If a person would stop and think of what Jesus said to Peter, we would see the Gospels have their place for the Church. Jesus was not talking to just Peter or the Jew, but was talking to all who are part of the called-out assembly. Jesus was the Head of the Church; the disciples and the Jews were some of its first members. The Church has its beginning and foundation in the Gospels: *And I say also unto thee, That thou art Peter, and upon this rock I will build my church; and the gates of hell shall not prevail against it* (Matthew 16:18).

Jesus is the foundation on which we build our lives. His words are recorded in the Gospels in order to build our lives on a sure foundation. The Epistles are not the foundation of the Church. Jesus and the Gospels are the Church's foundation. Jesus confirms this in Luke 6:47-49: *Whosoever cometh to me, and heareth my sayings, and doeth them, I will show you to whom he is like: 48 He is like a man which built an house, and digged deep, and laid the foundation on a rock: and when the flood arose, the stream beat vehemently upon that house, and could not shake it: for it was founded upon a rock. 49 But he that heareth, and doeth not, is like a man that without a foundation built an house upon the earth; against which the stream did beat vehemently, and immediately it fell; and the ruin of that house was great.* Paul confirms this in I Corinthians 3:10-11: *According to the grace of God which is given unto me, as a wise masterbuilder, I have laid the foundation, and another buildeth thereon. But let every man take heed how he buildeth thereupon. 11 For other foundation can no man lay than that is laid, which is Jesus Christ.*

Jesus laid the foundation in the Gospels to bring both Jew and Gentile near to God through the blood of Christ. We cannot continue to discredit the Gospels to the Church to satisfy the pretribulation rapture theory. We must remember that it was the Gentiles who were without hope in the world, and were made nigh to God by the blood of Christ. It was Jesus who made both Jew and Gentile one in Him (Ephesians 2:11-16). The arrogance of pretribulationists must cease in thinking they have all truth concerning the second coming of the Lord. The rapture will not take place until Matthew 24:14 and I Thessalonians 2:1-5 is fulfilled. The Church must wait patiently until the Lord receives the early and latter rain (James 5:7-8). There must be a remnant of Jews saved in the latter rain as it was in the early rain.

THE KINGDOM
OF HEAVEN

When I realized how dispensationalists said the Gospels were not for the Church, I realized they also made a mistake in their interpetation of the kingdom of heaven, and the kingdom of God. This chapter and the next two are very important to the Church in knowing the true meaning of the kingdom of heaven and the kingdom of God. You will see God never delayed any kingdom, but all things are going forward as He planned from the beginning.

There has been much confusion about the teaching of what are the kingdom of heaven, the kingdom of God, and the kingdom of Israel, and their true meaning. I will try to untangle what dispensationalists and pretribulationists have wrongly interpreted about their meaning. Most dispensationalists say that the kingdom of heaven is the kingdom that Jesus came to set up for the Jews, but when the Jews rejected him as their king, God postponed the kingdom until after the Church age, at which time the Lord will restore the kingdom to the Jews. There are some who say the same about the kingdom of God, and interchange the two as meaning the same thing. I will give Bible proof of the true meaning of the kingdom of God in the next chapter. The great problem started when dispensationalism separated the Gospels from applying to the Church; consequently the kingdom of heaven could not have a meaning that would apply to the Church.

When Jesus speaks about the kingdom of heaven in the gospel of Matthew, and the kingdom of God in all four Gospels, He is not talking about setting up an earthly Messianic kingdom for the Jews and ruling them from an earthly temple in Jerusalem. This notion originated by pretribulationists who said that Jesus came to set up an earthly kingdom, but when the Jews rejected Jesus as the Messiah, God set into motion Plan B, which delayed the kingdom until after the rapture of the Church. There was never a Plan B, and I will give the historical and scriptural meaning of these two kingdoms. The two chapters on the subject will prove this part of their doctrine is in error.

Quotes from the Scofield Reference Bible concerning the kingdom of heaven in Matthew 3:2, and 11:12 reveal some of the mistakes that caused the error in doctrine:

1. The phrase, kingdom of heaven (lit. of Heavens), is peculiar to Matthew and signifies the Messianic earth rule of Jesus Christ, the Son of David. It is called the kingdom of the heavens because it is the rule of the heavens over earth (*Matthew 6:10.*) The phrase is derived from Daniel, where it is defined (*Daniel 2:34-36,44 and Daniel 7:23-27*) as the kingdom which *"the God of heaven"* will set up after the destruction by *"the stone cut out without hands"* of the Gentile world system. It is the kingdom covenanted to David's seed (*2 Samuel 7:7-10, refs.*) described in the prophets (*Zechariah 12:8., Note*): and confirms to Jesus Christ, the Son of Mary, through the angel Gabriel (*Luke 1:32&33*).

2. The kingdom of heaven has three aspects in Matthew: (a) *"at hand"* from the beginning of the ministry of John the Baptist (*Matthew 3:2*) to the virtual rejection of the King, and the announcement of the new brotherhood (*Matthew 12:46-50.*); (b) in seven *"mysteries of the kingdom of heaven,"* to be fulfilled during the present age (*Matthew 13:1-52.*), to which are to be added the parables of the kingdom of heaven which were spoken after those of (*Matthew 13.,* and which have to do with the sphere of Christian profession during this age; (c) the prophets aspect – the kingdom to be set up after the return of the King in glory (*Matthew 24:29-35 & Luke 19:12-19 & Acts 15:14-17*). See Kingdom (N.T.)" *Luke 1:33 & I Corinthians 15:28.*). Cf. "kingdom of God," *Matthew:6:33,* note.

3. John Baptist was as great, morally, as any man "born of woman," but as to the kingdom he but announced it at hand. The kingdom did not then come, but was rejected, and John martyred, and the King presently crucified.

Scofield said the Gospels were not for the Church in his introduction of the Bible, and that up to the second chapter of Acts was for the Jew only. He also said in his introduction to the Gospels that the doctrines of grace are to be sought in the Epistles, not in the Gospels, and further said that the Gospels do not unfold doctrines to the Church, but only the Epistles. He also states, (There is) "much in the Gospels which belongs in strictness of interpretation to the Jew or the kingdom." He is not changing his belief in the above concerning the kingdom of heaven. He is saying that the kingdom of heaven will be set up after "*the stone cut out without hands*" destroys the Gentile world system. I will show that the kingdom of heaven which Jesus preached had its beginning with Jesus, and will continue forever. We must not confuse the kingdom of heaven, which is now in effect, with the kingdom of Israel. The kingdom of Israel, will be set up after "*the stone cut out of the mountain without hands*" destroys the Gentile world system, and only one-third of the Jews will come through the fire and be refined as silver (Zech. 13:9). When we put the kingdom of heaven in its proper place, it makes a big difference of how we view the Gospels and apply them to our lives in the Church age. Scofield is saying that the new brotherhood is only announced, that whosoever does the will of the Father is his brother and sister and mother, and that part is true. He also states that the mysteries of the kingdom of heaven concerning the sowing of seed are fulfilled during the present age, and that part is also true, but his interpretation concerning the prophets' aspect of the kingdom of heaven to be set up after the return of Christ is incorrect. He claims concerning Matthew the second chapter that the phrase, "kingdom of heaven," signifies the Messianic earthly rule of Jesus Christ, the son of David, in the millennium. He takes out of context what Jesus and John the Baptist had to say about the kingdom of heaven. They said it was at hand, and drawing near: *And saying, Repent ye: for the kingdom of heaven is at hand* (Matthew 3:2 & 4:17).

Isaiah did not prophesy of a delayed kingdom, and Daniel makes it plain what would take place after the sixty-nine weeks were fulfilled

(Daniel 9:26). Neither Jesus nor any other writer of the Old or New Testament tells us that the kingdom of heaven will be delayed until after the tribulation period. God knew all things concerning the Jews and the Gentiles from the beginning of the world (Acts 15:13-18). If the kingdom of heaven was going to be set aside for two thousand years, surely there would have been some indication of it in the Old Testament, and surely Jesus would have given reference to it in the Gospels, but He didn't. Paul's defense before Agrippa was that he had spoken only of what was prophesied by Moses and the prophets concerning Jesus, the cross, and the resurrection, and that Jesus would be a light unto the Gentiles: *Having therefore obtained help of God, I continue unto this day, witnessing both to small and great, saying none other things than those which the prophets and Moses did say should come:23 That Christ should suffer, and that he should be the first that should rise from the dead, and should show light unto the people, and to the Gentiles* (Acts 26:22-23). I will also clarify what Jesus and the prophets taught concerning the coming of the Lord and the true meaning of the kingdom of heaven. The Church should know the mysteries of the kingdom of heaven.

Jesus commanded His disciples to go to the lost sheep of the house of Israel first because they were God's chosen people, and God wanted to fulfill His promise. When they preached to the Jews, Jesus told them to preach that the kingdom of heaven was at hand (Matthew 10:6-7). The Jews were Gods' chosen people, and chose to preach unto the Jews first, and then unto the Gentiles: *For I am not ashamed of the gospel of Christ: for it is the power of God unto salvation to every one that believeth; to the Jew first, and also to the Greek* (Romans 1:16). God said He is no respecter of persons, and as many as sin with, or without, the Law shall perish (Rom. 2:9-16). God's plan was to reach Jews and then the Gentiles in order to fulfill what Isaiah had prophesied: *Now I say that Jesus Christ was a minister of the circumcision for the truth of God, to confirm the promises made unto the fathers: 9 And that the Gentiles might glorify God for his mercy; as it is written, For this cause I will confess to thee among the Gentiles, and sing unto thy name. 10 And again he saith, Rejoice, ye Gentiles, with his people. 11 And again, Praise the Lord, all ye Gentiles; and laud him, all ye people. 12 And again, Esaias saith, There shall be a root of Jesse, and he that shall rise to reign over the Gentiles; in him shall the Gentiles trust* (Romans 15:8-12).

God gave the Jews many opportunities for salvation, but God had let the prophets know beforehand the condition of the hearts of the Jews. They prophesied the Jews would reject Jesus as the Messiah, and kill Him. After the Messiah's death, the Lord would bring judgment upon their nation, and let out His vineyard unto other husbandmen—the Gentiles which would bring Him fruit in their seasons (Matthew 21:33-41). Temple worship under the Jewish rulers and priests had ceased being true worship. They rejected the message of both John the Baptist and Jesus concerning repentance. The Messiah would soon be crucified, and the Stone, (Jesus) which the builders rejected would become the Head of the Corner and the very foundation of the Church, as recorded in the Old and New Testaments: Psalms 118:22-23; Isaiah 28:16-18; Mark 12:8-11; Luke 20:13-18; Acts 4:10-12; Romans 9:30-33; Ephesians 2:14-20; and I Peter 2:5-10. The Lord would rule His Church from heaven, and this heavenly kingdom would be called the kingdom of heaven. The Lord would take from the Jewish nation the kingdom of God, (Luke 17:20-21; John 3:3), and give it to a nation that would bring forth fruit, and whosoever shall fall on the Stone would be broken: *They say unto him, He will miserably destroy those wicked men, and will let out his vineyard unto other husbandmen, which shall render him the fruits in their seasons. 42 Jesus saith unto them, Did ye never read in the scriptures, The stone which the builders rejected, the same is become the head of the corner: this is the Lord's doing, and it is marvellous in our eyes? 43 Therefore say I unto you, The kingdom of God shall be taken from you, and given to a nation bringing forth the fruits thereof. 44 And whosoever shall fall on this stone shall be broken: but on whomsoever it shall fall, it will grind him to powder* (Matthew 21:41-44). Jesus broke down the wall between Jew and Gentile, making both one that He might reconcile both unto God in one body by the cross. The Church was built upon the foundation of the apostles and prophets, Jesus Christ Himself being the chief corner-stone (Ephesians 2:14-20).

John the Baptist began his ministry by preaching, "Repent for the kingdom of heaven is at hand." He prophesied how the ax is laid to the root, and how Israel would be hewn down because she had brought forth no fruit (Matt. 3:1-3). John the Baptist prepared the way of the Lord as was prophesied, and baptized Him in the river of Jordan where the Spirit of God descended like a dove, lighting upon Him. The Father's voice came from heaven identifying His only begotten Son in

Matthew 3:17. The Law and the prophets were until John, but at that point a new dispensation began. The eternal kingdom of the Father shows how He gave His only begotten Son all power in heaven and in earth. After John was the beginning of a new dispensation, and immediately after the baptism of Jesus, the Spirit drove Jesus into the wilderness to be tempted of Satan for forty days. John was put into prison, and Jesus began His ministry with the same message that John had preached, *Repent: for the kingdom of heaven is at hand,* and *went about all Galilee, teaching in their synagogues, and preaching the gospel of the kingdom* (Matt. 4:17, 23). The fig tree is a symbol of Israel, and Jesus ministered unto the Jewish nation for over three years. There was a remnant saved who believed that Jesus was the Messiah, but the majority of Jews rejected Jesus, saying, "Crucify Him." This rejection sealed their judgment because the Lord gave them three extra years to bring forth fruit before the final judgment was announced: *He spake also this parable; A certain man had a fig tree planted in his vineyard; and he came and sought fruit thereon, and found none. 7 Then said he unto the dresser of his vineyard, Behold, these three years I come seeking fruit on this fig tree, and find none: cut it down; why cumbereth it the ground? 8 And he answering said unto him, Lord, let it alone this year also, till I shall dig about it, and dung it: 9 And if it bear fruit, well: and if not, then after that thou shalt cut it down* (Luke 13:6-9).

John's message let us know that the kingdom of heaven was at hand, and it was the same kingdom that the prophet Isaiah spoke about concerning John preparing the way of the Lord (Matthew 3:1-3). John told the Jewish nation to repent, the same as the prophet Isaiah had spoke to them. Isaiah 40 is the source of the Old Testament prophecies concerning the kingdom of heaven. Isaiah tells how John the Baptist would prepare the way of the Lord, and verse 22 lets us know that it is the Lord who sits on His throne in heaven and will rule over the whole earth during the Church age, and forever. Isaiah tells about the Lord's first coming, and how the Lord would feed His flock, like a good shepherd, and His arm would rule (Isaiah 40:1-31). Chapter 40 is not about the Lord setting up an earthly kingdom, but, instead, a spiritual kingdom where the Lord will rule from heaven. This was accomplished when the Lord ascended to the right hand of the Father and was given all power in heaven and in earth (Matt. 28:18). Isaiah 40 and 42 tell about the Lord's first coming, which was a mystery to the Jews, but Jesus unfolded the mystery of the kingdom of heaven unto His disciples in parables (Matt.13:10-15). Isaiah 59 tells how the Messiah would come to save them from their sins, but their iniquities separated them from their God. Isaiah's prophecy came true concerning the Lord's first coming. Many of His people rejected Him as the Messiah, but as many as received them, to them gave He power to become sons of God (John 1:11-12). The mystery Isaiah and the Lord spoke about was not an earthly kingdom of Israel before the cross and the Church age, but that the Lord would rule from heaven. Jesus unfolded the mystery of the kingdom of heaven to His disciples in Matthew; 12:15-21; 13:1-52; 25:1-46. I show that the mystery of the kingdom of heaven is the Lord's rule from heaven over His Church in the Church age, and His kingdom is an eternal kingdom. Jesus let His disciples know that some of them would see the Son of Man coming into His kingdom before death (Matt. 16:28).

John's purpose was to prepare the way of the Lord, and the purpose of Jesus was the redemption of man (John 3:3, 16-17). When we understand the purpose of Jesus' coming into the world, we began to understand the kingdom of heaven. The Devil attempted to kill Jesus as a child, and did kill John after he had prepared the way of the Lord. The Father was in charge of heaven and earth, while His Son Jesus came to earth for the redemption of sinners. The kingdom of heaven suffered violence from the days of John because the Devil attempted by force to stop God's plan of salvation: *And from the days of John the Baptist until now the kingdom of heaven suffereth violence, and the violent take it by force* (Matthew 11:12). Jesus said, *And upon this rock I will build my church; and the gates of hell shall not prevail against it* (Matthew 16:18b). Jesus' death gained Him victory over death and the Devil. The Lord now rules over His Church from heaven, because the Father made Him head (Eph. 5:23). The Father gave His Son a kingdom, and He would reign with all power over heaven and earth as king (Matt. 28:18). Jesus let His disciples know that the prophets and the law prophesied until John, and from that point a new dispensation began: *For all the prophets and the law prophesied until John* (Matthew 11:13).

Jesus rebuked the cities where His mighty works were done because they repented not, and told them of the judgment that was to come. He thanked the Father, Lord of heaven and earth, because He had hidden these things which were done from the wise and the prudent, and revealed them unto babes (Matt. 11:25). Jesus let them know that the Father had delivered all things unto His hands in heaven and in earth (Matthew 11:27, 28:18). This overview shows that Jesus is in charge of all things in heaven and earth, and that John the Baptist and Jesus began their ministry by preaching the kingdom of heaven was at hand, not delayed. I will show in this chapter that it was Darby and Scofield who were in error about the true meaning of the kingdom of heaven.

The Gospel of Mathew teaches us about the kingdom of heaven and presents Jesus as King. All four Gospels and the Epistles teach us that the kingdom of God is God's reign in the hearts of His people. Jesus told the disciples that it was not for them to know the time when the earthly kingdom of Israel would be restored, to last one thousand years (Acts 1:6-7). I will give details about all three in this book. God in all His wisdom did not delay any kingdom, but is sovereign, and the universe is His dominion. I show that the problem started concerning the interpretation of the kingdom of heaven when dispensationalists said the Gospels were not for the Church, and that God delayed the kingdom of heaven when the Jews rejected Jesus as their king.

The Lord wants His Church (the Body of Christ) to understand what He is saying to the Church about the kingdom of heaven. The Lord does not want to talk to His Church in the Gospels, and have the Church say that the Gospels do not apply to them. When the Church does not recognize that the Lord was talking to them about the kingdom of heaven and the kingdom of God in the Gospels, this is a serious flaw in doctrine.

Most pretribulationists do not believe that the kingdom of heaven is the reign of Jesus over the Church, and began when Jesus ascended to the right hand of the Father and took charge of the heavenly kingdom. There is a big difference in what Jesus taught about the kingdom of heaven and what pretribulationists teach regarding how Jesus will set up the kingdom of heaven in the millennium after the rapture. Pretribulationists have made exactly the same mistake about what constitutes the kingdom of heaven as when Jesus and John were preaching their message to the Jews: *Repent; for the kingdom of heaven is at hand* (Matt. 3:2, & 4:17).

The Jews thought that when Jesus made His triumphal entry into Jerusalem, He was going to set up the kingdom of their father David (Mark 10:9-10). Jesus compared the barren fig tree to Israel, and then purified the temple by casting out those buying and selling. He over-threw the tables of the money changers and the seats of them that sold doves (Mark 11:12-21). Jesus spoke to them in parables concerning Israel and how He would be crucified, how their nation would be destroyed, and the Stone which the builders rejected becoming the head of the corner. Jesus clearly said this would be the LORD'S doing (Mark 12:1-12). Jesus wept over Jerusalem and said, "Your house is left unto you desolate," and departed from the temple. His disciples asked Him about the temple, and He told them that it would be destroyed, and the great tribulation would take place before He would come again (Mark 13:1-27 and Matt. 23:37-39, 24:1-30). Jesus was well aware of the prophecy God had given to Daniel, which was to take place after the fulfillment of the sixty-nine weeks. Jerusalem and the temple would be destroyed, and the end of the war would bring desolations. Daniel left a gap between week sixty-nine and seventy for the Church age (Daniel 9:26-27). Daniel or Jesus never offered the Jewish nation and earthly kingdom between the sixty-ninth and seventieth week. Dispensationalists were the ones who said that Jesus promised the Jews the kingdom and then withdrew it after they rejected Jesus.

Today's pretribulationists have been swayed by dispensational doc-trines concerning the meaning of the kingdom of heaven. Early dispen-sationalists taught that a great distinction must be made between Israel and the Church, and that the Gospels were primarily for the Jew. This caused God's people to believe that the kingdom of heaven was not for the Church but only for the Jew. Dispensationalists teach that the king-dom was offered to Israel, they rejected it, consequently the kingdom was held in abeyance until the Church age is completed and the Church is raptured. The pretribulation rapture theory has been taught in our churches and colleges, and now has become the dominant teaching. This teaching is the reason why pretribulationists believe the Church rapture takes place in Revelation 4:1, then the tribulation begins, and finally after the seven years of tribulation the Lord will come back to earth with His saints bringing judgment on the world. Only when the judgment is complete will the Lord set up the kingdom of heaven that was delayed at the Lord's first coming. This interpretation is against what Jesus taught, and against the historical teachings of the Church down through the Church age.

In Matthew 16:18-19 Jesus replies to Peter that He would build His Church upon this Rock, which is Christ. Jesus is the Foundation Stone upon whom the Church is built (I Peter 2:6). Christ is "that Rock" of which Israel drank in the wilderness (I Corinthians 10:4). Jesus let Peter know that the gates of hell, which are the powers of the Devil's Kingdom, would not prevail against the Church in the Church age. Jesus said to Peter that He would give him the keys of the kingdom of heaven, and whatsoever he bound on earth would be bound in heaven, and whatsoever he loosed on earth would be loosed in heaven: *And I say also unto thee, That thou art Peter, and upon this rock I will build my church; and the gates of hell shall not prevail against it. 19 And I will give unto thee the keys of the kingdom of heaven: and whatsoever thou shalt bind on earth shall be bound in heaven: and whatsoever thou shalt loose on earth shall be loosed in heaven* (Matthew 16:18-19). The kingdom of heaven in verse 19 is not referring to the kingdom of Israel in the millennium, but to saints in the Church age who have power to prohibit or permit on earth all things to which heaven had already agreed. These verses have nothing to do with the kingdom of Israel in the millennium but describes the power given to the Church by the Lord Himself in the Church age.

Immediately after Jesus taught His disciples about building His Church, He began to teach them how He must go to Jerusalem, be killed, and be raised again the third day. Then He talked to them about discipleship and His coming again (Matt. 16:20-27). Jesus promised that some of them would not taste death until they saw the Son of Man coming into His kingdom: *Verily I say unto you, There be some standing here, which shall not taste of death, till they see the Son of man coming in his kingdom* (Matt. 16:28). The disciples saw Jesus after His resurrection, and coming into His kingdom (Luke 19:12-15, Col. 1:13, II Peter 1:11). These verses prove the kingdom of heaven is the Lord's rule from heaven over the Church.

The disciples came to Jesus and asked Him, "Who is the greatest in the kingdom of heaven?" Jesus called a little child unto him, and set him in the midst of them and said: *Verily I say unto you, Except ye be converted, and become as little children, ye shall not enter into the kingdom of heaven. Whosoever therefore shall humble himself as this little child, the same is greatest in the kingdom of heaven* (Matt. 18:3-4). The conversion of saints that Jesus was talking about covers the whole Church age, not for the Jew only during a short seven-year period, and this is another proof that error was made by dispensationalists. Sinners who came to Jesus, humbled themselves as a little child, and accepted His way of salvation became the children of God, and the same are the greatest in the kingdom of heaven (present, not future). These Scriptures teach that the only way to enter into the kingdom of heaven in the Church age is to be converted to Christ. Jesus let it be known that this gospel of the kingdom must be preached in all the world before He will come again (Matt. 24:14). Preaching the gospel of the kingdom to the whole world is not accomplished in a short seven-year period, but throughout the entire Church age, and is commanded in the great commission (Matt. 28:19-20).

God did not change His plan when He sent His only begotten Son to earth as a Lamb slain before the foundation of the world, but gave Him sovereign power to rule over heaven and earth. When Jesus fulfilled His ministry, the majority of Israel had not changed. They still wanted an earthly kingdom. The LORD told Samuel, they have not rejected thee, but they have rejected me that I should reign over them (I Sam. 8:7). Most of Israel rejected the Lord as their king because they did not understand God's plan. Throngs in Israel praised Jesus as He entered into Jerusalem for the last time. They acknowledged Him as King, but a majority of the Jews rejected Him when they saw He did not come to set up an earthly kingdom, saying, "We will not have this man to reign over us." When Jesus was taken before Pilate, the Jews accused Jesus of not giving tribute to Caesar, saying that He claimed that He was a King (Luke 23:2). Jesus let Pilate know that He was King, but that His kingdom was not of this world. Jesus informed Pilate that if His kingdom were of this world, His servants would fight so He would not be delivered to the Jews. Jesus did not come to set up a temporal kingdom in opposition to Rome. The kingdom that Jesus was talking about had its origin in heaven for the salvation of all who believe in Him. He made this fact plain to Pilate: *Then Pilate entered into the judgment hall again, and called Jesus, and said unto him, Art thou the King of the Jews? 36 Jesus answered, My kingdom is not of this world: if my kingdom were of this world, then would my servants fight, that I should not be delivered to the Jews: but now is my kingdom not from hence. 37 Pilate therefore said unto him, Art thou a king then? Jesus answered, Thou sayest that I am a king. To this end was I born, and for this cause came I into the world, that I should bear witness unto the truth. Every one that is of the truth heareth my voice* (John 18:33, 36-37).

Dispensationalists changed the doctrine concerning the kingdom of heaven after 1830. The doctrine of many writers was still accurate in the late 1800s and early 1900s. Pretribulationists need to reclaim the truth concerning the kingdom of heaven. The next three references demonstrate that the Gospels are for the Church and the kingdom of heaven is the reign of Christ over the Church and all of God's creation in heaven and earth. This is what the 1890 *Cyclopedia of Religious Knowledge.* entry said about the kingdom of heaven:

> Kingdom of Heaven (*Gr. The heavens*); Of GOD. "The former is Matthew's phrase, the latter Mark's and Luke's; derived from *Dan. ii. 44; iv. 26; vii. 13,14,27*. Messiah's kingdom, as a whole, both in its present spiritual phase, the gospel dispensation of grace, and also in its present spiritual invisible phase, the gospel dispensation of grace, and also in its future manifestation on earth in glory, when finally heaven and earth shall be joined. (*John i. 51; Rev. xxi.; xxii.*) Our Lord's parables designate several aspects and phases of it by the one common phrase, 'the kingdom of the heavens,' or, "of God, is like, 'etc."

Another reference comes out of *The Popular and Critical Bible Encyclopaedia and Scriptural Dictionary.*

> Kingdom of Heaven. (a) The visible church, especially under the New Testament, is called a "kingdom;" Christ and the Father rule in it, and maintain order, safety, and happiness therein. It is called the "kingdom of heaven;" it is of heavenly origin, has a heavenly governor and laws; and is erected to render multitudes fit for heaven (*Matt. iii:2; iv:17; xiii:47; xvi:19; Col. I:13*).

Here is what Matthew Henry said about the kingdom of heaven which John the Baptist preached in Matthew 3:1-2: "Now repent, for the kingdom of heaven; the gospel dispensation of the covenant of grace, the opening of the kingdom of heaven to all believers, by the death and resurrection of Jesus Christ. It is a kingdom of which Christ is the Sovereign, and we must be willing, loyal subjects of it. It is a kingdom of heaven, not of this world, a spiritual kingdom; its original from heaven, its tendency to heaven. John preached this as at hand; then it was at the door; to us it is come, by the pouring out of the Spirit, and the full exhibition of the riches of gospel—grace. Now, this is a great inducement to us to repent."

Henry went on to comment about Jesus' preaching: "Repent for the kingdom of heaven is at hand" *Matthew 4:17*. "The kingdom of heaven is at hand; for it is not reckoned to be fully come, till the pouring out of the Spirit after Christ's ascension. John had preached the kingdom of heaven was at hand about a year before this; but now it was so much nearer, the argument was so much stronger; now is the salvation nearer, *Rom xiii. 11*. We should be so much the more quickened to our duty, as we see the day approaching, *Heb. x. 25*."

These three references are the historical and correct meaning of the kingdom of heaven. The correct meaning was replaced by dispensationalists and given a meaning contrary to the historical view that agreed with what Jesus taught in the Gospel of Matthew. From the beginning of Jesus' ministry, His will was to fulfill the Father's will, and fulfill what was prophesied of Him. Isaiah had prophesied how Jesus would be a light unto the Gentiles (Isa. 49:6, 60:3). When Jews or Gentiles get saved in the Church age, they have the Lord who reigns in the kingdom of heaven to protect, keep, and guide them. Dispensationalists erroneously teach that the kingdom of heaven has been delayed until after the rapture, and then Jesus will set up His earthly kingdom that the Jews rejected. Dispensational teachers changed fundamental doctrines after the year 1830 and deceived the Church. We need to compare what Henry and the other two references say about the kingdom of heaven with the teaching of dispensationalists. There is a wide gulf between them.

When Jesus heard that John was cast into prison, He immediately left Nazareth, and went to dwell in Capernaum to fulfill what was prophesied by Isaiah. His ministry started with this message: *From that time Jesus began to preach, and to say, Repent: for the kingdom of heaven is at hand* (Matthew 4:17). First Jesus chose His disciples and began to prepare them for the work they would have to do after the cross and in the

Church age. Jesus never promised or spoke to them one word about the Jews setting up an earthly kingdom. When we accept that the Gospels are for the Church, then the messages of John the Baptist and Jesus, "*Repent: for the kingdom of heaven is at hand*," makes sense. The kingdom of heaven was to come within a short time. Jesus did not come to set up an earthly kingdom of Israel, but go to the cross, die for man's sins, then ascend to heaven and rule all creation from the throne the Father had given Him, the kingdom of Heaven. He would give all believers the Holy Spirit, setting up the kingdom of God in their hearts.

The Father promised Jesus a kingdom. His kingdom began when He ascended to the right hand of the Father and was given all power in heaven and earth. The Lord's kingdom will never pass away. Daniel spoke of this kingdom in Daniel 2:44: *And in the days of these kings shall the God of heaven set up a kingdom, which shall never be destroyed: and the kingdom shall not be left to other people, but it shall break in pieces and consume all these kingdoms, and it shall stand for ever.* The stone that was cut out of the mountain without hands will break in pieces all kingdoms of men, and the Lord's kingdom will reign supreme (Daniel 2:34-35, 45; 7:9-14; Rev. 19:11-21). The Lord will then set up the kingdom of Israel, and the saints will rule with the Lord over the kingdom of Israel with a rod of iron (Matt. 19:28; I Cor. 6:2;Rev. 2:26-27).

It is not religion, nor works done in the flesh, that qualifies believers for the kingdom of heaven, but a change of mind and heart toward God by repentance. If there was no change, when they stand before Him in judgment, He will say to them, "*I never knew you: depart from me ye that work iniquity.*" This Scripture is not the fulfillment of a short seven-year period of time, but is speaking of all those down through the Church age who profess Christ, but never were converted by the second birth. They will give an account to the Lord in the day of judgment of why they never entered into the kingdom of heaven: *Not every one that saith unto me, Lord, Lord, shall enter into the kingdom of heaven; but he that doeth the will of my Father which is in heaven. 22 Many will say to me in that day, Lord, Lord, have we not prophesied in thy name? and in thy name have cast out devils? and in thy name done many wonderful works? 23 And then will I profess unto them, I never knew you: depart from me, ye that work iniquity* (Matthew 7:21-23).

Jesus spoke in parables about the kingdom of heaven. These parables describe the Lord's rule over the earth during the Church age. Jesus told his disciples in Matthew 13:11 the mystery of the kingdom of heaven, but unto the world it was not given. Jesus explained in Matthew 16:21, how He must go to Jerusalem and be killed, and would rise again on the third day. Jesus then told them in verse 28 that some of them would not see death until they saw the Son of Man coming in His kingdom. The kingdom of heaven was not to be His rule in the millennium alone, but would be His heavenly rule throughout all the ages. The parable concerning the wheat and the tares covers the Church age. There will be no end to His kingdom. His rule extends to all of creation, heaven and earth. Jesus makes the mystery of the kingdom of heaven plain to His disciples in Matthew 13:37-43. In verse 37 Jesus said that he that soweth the good seed is the Son of Man. In verse 38 He said that the field is the world, and the good seed is the children of the kingdom. The tares are the children of the wicked one. In verse 39 He said that the harvest is the end of the world, and the reapers are the angels. The tares will be gathered out of the world, and burned in the judgment, and then those who are left on earth will live in the thousand-year millennium, verses 40-43. The Lord's rule will extend throughout eternity. The Lord will destroy every unbeliever from the face of the earth who does not turn to Him when they see Him coming in the clouds for the rapture. Zechariah said the house of David would mourn, every family separately at that time. Those who are left in the earth will shine forth as the sun in the kingdom of the Father. The kingdom of heaven will never pass away because it is eternal.

Jesus gives us another parable about the kingdom heaven in Matthew 25:1-13. Jesus gives this parable about the ten virgins. The five wise virgins had oil in their lamps, but the five foolish virgins had no oil when the cry arose that the bridegroom was coming. This parable is not concerning the kingdom of Israel after the rapture of the Church but is warning the Church they must be ready for the rapture when the Lord comes or else they will be shut out of heaven, the same as the evil servants in Matthew 24:48-51.

The next parable concerning the kingdom of heaven is found in Matthew 25:14-46. It says the kingdom of heaven is like a man traveling into a far country, and he calls his servants, and delivers unto them his goods and talents. This parable is definitely talking about Jesus when He ascended to his throne in heaven, and left His servants (the

Church) in charge during the Church age. At the judgment seat of Christ, He will reward them for their labors according to their works. Before Jesus left, He gave the Church gifts to use until He returns. Every saint will give an account of what they have done, whether it be good or bad. These parables have nothing to do with the kingdom of Israel in the millenium but are for the Church.

In order to understand the kingdom of heaven, the kingdom of God, and the kingdom of Israel, we must understand that every kingdom has a place and origin. Before the cross, the Devil, the god of this world, held saints captive. Jesus went to the cross, died for sins, descended into the lower parts of the earth, took the keys of death and hell away from the Devil, and took the captive saints to heaven (Eph. 4:8-10). Jesus is now in control of the keys of death and hell (Rev. 1:18). The Devil was not going to stop Jesus from building His Church, and the gates of hell would not prevail against Him (Matt. 16:18). Jesus told Peter in verse 19 that He would give him the keys to the kingdom of heaven, and that he would be able to bind or loosen. Jesus had the key, and Jesus was the key. Jesus ascended to the right hand of the Father to rule in the kingdom the Father had given Him. Victory had been won at the cross, and all power was given Him in heaven and in earth. Jesus, the King of Kings and Lord of Lords, is now building His Church as He promised.

The creator of the heavens and the earth is ruler of the same. The whole universe and the earth are His domain. The Messiah, the Son of David, introduced a new era, and would not rule apart from Jehovah the Father or exercise a different authority. The kingdom of the Messiah would also be the kingdom of God. This kingdom would not be a worldly establishment and would never pass away. Daniel spoke of this kingdom that the Lord set up, which would never be destroyed, and said the stone cut out of the mountain would destroy all the other kingdoms, and would stand forever (Daniel 2:44-45). Nebuchadnezzar understood that God's heavenly kingdom is the only eternal kingdom (Daniel 4:2-3). Darius also understood that all earthly kingdoms will pass away, and only God's kingdom is eternal (Daniel 6:25-26).

The everlasting kingdom is the kingdom of heaven, not the kingdom of Israel that lasts only one thousand years. There is an earthly Jerusalem, and there is a heavenly Jerusalem. Abraham was looking for a city whose builder and maker was God, in the heavenly Jerusalem (Heb.11:10).

Israel brought forth a man child, who was to rule all nations with a rod of iron, and that man child was Jesus. He was caught up unto God, and to his throne (Rev. 12:5). Daniel spoke of the Lord's kingdom that would never pass away and would never be destroyed. The Lord's dominion reaches heaven and earth. He has ruled in His kingdom for two thousand years, His dominion is an everlasting dominion: *And there was given him dominion, and glory, and a kingdom, that all people, nations, and languages, should serve him: his dominion is an everlasting dominion, which shall not pass away, and his kingdom that which shall not be destroyed* (Daniel 7:14). The saints will have eternal life, and will rule and reign with Christ from the heavenly kingdom over the earthly Jerusalem for one thousand years (Rev. 20:6). The Lord will then offer up the kingdom to the Father when the last enemy, which is death has been destroyed (I Cor. 15:24-26). Daniel spoke of the saints, and the greatness of the Lord's kingdom *And the kingdom and dominion, and the greatness of the kingdom under the whole heaven, shall be given to the people of the saints of the most High, whose kingdom is an everlasting kingdom, and all dominions shall serve and obey him* (Daniel 7:27). Jesus let Pilate know that His kingdom was not of this world, and that He was born to be king of His kingdom (John 18:36-37).

The Jews thought that the Messiah at His first coming would reign as king over their nation, and would reside at Jerusalem. Many of the Jews wanted to make Jesus their king on earth to reign from Jerusalem. This notion was taken up by many of the Judaizing Christians. The apostles often entertained this notion because of their lack of understanding until after the ascension of Christ and the outpouring of the Holy Spirit. The apostles, being filled with the Holy Spirit, began to understand the mysteries of the Gospels. They abandoned the thought that Jesus had come to set up an earthly kingdom. They turned to what Jesus had said in the Gospels about His coming again. I believe Peter understood completely the second coming of Christ. I believe he understood Hosea 6:1-3 and knew it would be another two thousand years before Jesus would come back for the Church, and the judgment to follow. Peter did not say one word about Jesus coming at any moment, or a pretribulation rapture. He knew and understood clearly God's plan for the Church and Israel. Read what Peter said in II Peter 3:3-14.

God is calling man to repentance in this Church age because He has appointed a day in which He will judge the world in righteousness

(Acts 17:30-31). The everlasting kingdom starts in our lives at the time of our salvation, and we will receive our completeness at the coming of our Lord Jesus Christ. He will give us our new bodies, and we will be caught up to meet him in the air. The saints will be with the Lord in his kingdom forever (I Thessalonians 4:16-17).

Paul knew the truth concerning the kingdom of heaven, and that Jesus would reign over His Church from heaven until He comes again for the rapture, and then the judgment. He knew the kingdom of heaven is the reign of heaven over the heavens and earth. The Father gave Jesus all power in heaven and earth (Matthew 28:19). You cannot have a kingdom without a king, and you cannot have a king without a kingdom. Jesus is the King of kings and Lord of lords; and His kingdom will never pass away. If the kingdom that the Father gave Jesus is not called the kingdom of heaven, what is it called?

Darby and Scofield gave a wrong interpretation of the kingdom of heaven when they said the Gospel of Matthew was for the Jew only. This made other Church doctrines beside the pretribulation rapture be in error, also. When we go back to the point where Darby and Scofield went wrong and correct it, all those other doctrines will not be hard to correct. We must understand the meaning of the kingdom of heaven before we can understand that this kingdom was for the Church, both Jew and Gentile. Jesus reigns now from heaven. The Father has given His Son all power in heaven and in earth. What Jesus had taught them in the Gospels was to be taught in all the world: *And Jesus came and spake unto them, saying, All power is given unto me in heaven and in earth. 19 Go ye therefore, and teach all nations, baptizing them in the name of the Father, and of the Son, and of the Holy Ghost: 20 Teaching them to observe all things whatsoever I have commanded you: and, lo, I am with you alway, even unto the end of the world. Amen* (Matthew 28:18-20).

The kingdom of heaven is the reign of heaven over earth and all God's creation. Jesus, the King of Kings, would go to the cross, die, and ascend to heaven before He would set up His heavenly rule over His subjects on earth. There is only one body, composed of both Jew and Gentile. Jesus is now on the right hand of the Father, and He is the King of the kingdom of heaven. His dominion is heaven and earth, and He now reigns as head of the Church: *Which he wrought in Christ, when he raised him from the dead, and set him at his own right hand in the heavenly*

places, 21 Far above all principality, and power, and might, and dominion, and
every name that is named, not only in this world, but also in that which is to
come: 22 And hath put all things under his feet, and gave him to be the head
over all things to the church, 23 Which is his body, the fulness of him that filleth
all in all (Ephesians 1:20-23).

When Jesus began His ministry in Jerusalem, He already knew the
mystery of how the Gentiles would be grafted into the Body of Christ,
along with the Jews. Jesus knew the purpose for which He came into
the world, and that He was to go to the cross for the salvation of both
Jew and Gentile. The Gospels would be just as important to the Gentile
as to the Jew. Paul reveals this mystery that had been hidden: *For this*
cause I Paul, the prisoner of Jesus Christ for you Gentiles, 2 If ye have heard of
the dispensation of the grace of God which is given me to you-ward: 3 How that
by revelation he made known unto me the mystery; (as I wrote afore in few
words, 4 Whereby, when ye read, ye may understand my knowledge in the mys-
tery of Christ) 5 Which in other ages was not made known unto the sons of men,
as it is now revealed unto his holy apostles and prophets by the Spirit; 6 That
the Gentiles should be fellowheirs, and of the same body, and partakers of his
promise in Christ by the gospel (Ephesians 3:1-6).

The mystery concerning the Church and the salvation of the
Gentiles, who would be grafted in, was hidden from the eyes of the
unbelieving Jews. God gave them the spirit of slumber because their
hearts were far removed from the LORD. Isaiah looked forward to the
marvelous salvation of the Lord, which would be given to both Jews and
Gentiles, regardless of the unbelief of many of the Jews (Isaiah 29:9-14).
The Jews, whose eyes were blinded, could not see that the birth of Jesus
was the fulfillment of Isaiah 9:6-7; 11:1-2. They did not understand the
prophecies concerning the Gentiles and the Church age (Isaiah 62:1-2;
Jer. 16:19). They did not understand Isaiah 53:1-12 concerning the cross
and the death of Jesus. They did not understand that the Messiah would
be crucified, their city and temple destroyed, and their people scattered
to the ends of the earth after the end of Daniel's sixty-ninth week, and
before the seventieth week (Daniel 9:26). John the Baptist let them
know that because they had brought forth no fruit, the ax was laid unto
the root and their nation would be destroyed (Matt. 3:1-3, 10). Jesus
taught much about bearing fruit and gave the consequence (John 15:1-
6). Jesus spoke in parables concerning the prophecies of Isaiah, and how

only the disciples, and those Jews who had faith, would understand. The rest were blinded. The unbelieving Jews could not understand the mysteries of the kingdom of heaven because of unbelief just as Isaiah had prophesied: *And the disciples came, and said unto him, Why speakest thou unto them in parables? 11 He answered and said unto them, Because it is given unto you to know the mysteries of the kingdom of heaven, but to them it is not given. 12 For whosoever hath, to him shall be given, and he shall have more abundance: but whosoever hath not, from him shall be taken away even that he hath. 13 Therefore speak I to them in parables: because they seeing see not; and hearing they hear not, neither do they understand. 14 And in them is fulfilled the prophecy of Esaias, which saith, By hearing ye shall hear, and shall not understand; and seeing ye shall see, and shall not perceive: 15 For this people's heart is waxed gross, and their ears are dull of hearing, and their eyes they have closed; lest at any time they should see with their eyes and hear with their ears, and should understand with their heart, and should be converted, and I should heal them. 16 But blessed are your eyes, for they see: and your ears, for they hear. 17 For verily I say unto you, That many prophets and righteous men have desired to see those things which ye see, and have not seen them; and to hear those things which ye hear, and have not heard them* (Matthew 13:10-17). The Church must come back to sound doctrine and understand what Jesus was talking about concerning the kingdom of heaven or else their eyes will be blind to most important doctrines concerning the coming of the Lord.

Paul was well aware of Old Testament prophecies and what Jesus had taught, and knew these prophecies must be fulfilled. He knew that the disciples and many believing Jews would understand the mysteries of the kingdom of heaven, and those who did not believe that Jesus was the Messiah would be broken off, and the Gentiles grafted in. The Elect of God did get saved, and the rest were blinded, and through their fall, salvation came to the Gentiles (Romans 11:7-12). To take the Old Testament prophecies, and what Jesus taught and referred to in the Gospels, and then separate them from the Epistles is foolishness, and unscriptural. God intended for the gospel about the kingdom of heaven to be preached to the Gentiles. How could the Gentiles preach Christ in the Gospels if it was not for them? God had given all prophecies in the Old Testament about Jesus, His ministry, His death, and resurrection to the Jews for their knowledge, but because of unbelief the Jews were blinded from seeing the mysteries. The mystery that was hidden from the Jews was revealed unto the Gentiles: *Unto me, who am less than the least of all saints, is this grace given, that I should preach among the Gentiles the unsearchable riches of Christ; 9 And to make all men see what is the fellowship of the mystery, which from the beginning of the world hath been hid in God, who created all things by Jesus Christ: 10 To the intent that now unto the principalities and powers in heavenly places might be known by the church the manifold wisdom of God, 11 According to the eternal purpose which he purposed in Christ Jesus our Lord: 12 In whom we have boldness and access with confidence by the faith of him* (Ephesians 3:8-12).

God's eternal purpose was to have children through faith in His Son Jesus. All who receive Christ are Abraham's seed, whether they are Jew or Gentile. The very moment the disciples turned to Jesus and followed Him by faith and confessed they believed Him to be the Messiah, God made them children of Abraham by faith. They did not have to wait until Pentecost to be saved. They were justified by faith, the same as Abraham. The dispensation of Law ended to them the moment they believed in Jesus (John 1:12). This was the beginning of the Church, and I want to make plain to dispensationalists that the kingdom of heaven is for the saved (the Church, Abraham's seed): *But before faith came, we were kept under the law, shut up unto the faith which should afterwards be revealed. 25 But after that faith is come, we are no longer under a schoolmaster. 26 For ye are all the children of God by faith in Christ Jesus. 27 For as many of you as have been baptized into Christ have put on Christ. 28 There is neither Jew nor Greek, there is neither bond nor free, there is neither male nor female: for ye are all one in Christ Jesus. 29 And if ye be Christ's, then are ye Abraham's seed, and heirs according to the promise* (Galatians 3:23-29).

When Jesus preached the Sermon on the Mount, He taught His disciples how to pray: *After this manner therefore pray ye: Our Father which art in heaven, Hallowed be thy name. 10 Thy kingdom come. Thy will be done in earth, as it is in heaven* (Matthew 6:9-10). Jesus first taught them to recognize the Father in prayer, and to hallow His name. Jesus then asked them to pray that God's Kingdom come, and His will be done on earth as it is in heaven. The tenth verse has nothing to do with God delaying the earthly kingdom of Israel until the millennium as dispensationalists teach. The kingdom of heaven and the kingdom of God were at hand. Jesus was teaching the disciples to pray for God's kingdom, and the salvation of Man, because the kingdom of God does not come with observation, but is within the hearts of the believer (Luke 17:20-21). God made His only begotten Son head of the Church so God's will could be done in the life of every believer in the Church age, not the millennium.

When the Lord ascended to the throne of God, He was ruling in the kingdom of heaven as King of kings and Lord of lords, and He gave gifts unto man for the fivefold work of the ministry and the edifying of the Body of Christ so His kingdom on earth would be supplied with every good work as it is in heaven: *He that descended is the same also that ascended up far above all heavens, that he might fill all things. 11 And he gave some, apostles; and some, prophets; and some, evangelists; and some, pastors and teachers; 12 For the perfecting of the saints, for the work of the ministry, for the edifying of the body of Christ: 13 Till we all come in the unity of the faith, and of the knowledge of the Son of God, unto a perfect man, unto the measure of the stature of the fulness of Christ: 14 That we henceforth be no more children, tossed to and fro, and carried about with every wind of doctrine, by the sleight of men, and cunning craftiness, whereby they lie in wait to deceive;15 But speaking the truth in love, may grow up into him in all things, which is the head, even Christ: 16 From whom the whole body fitly joined together and compacted by that which every joint supplieth, according to the effectual working in the measure of every part, maketh increase of the body unto the edifying of itself in love* (Ephesians 4:10-16).

Jesus instructed them to pray for their daily needs: *Give us this day our daily bread. 12 And forgive us our debts, as we forgive our debtors* (Matthew 6:11-12). Jesus closes His teaching on prayer by teaching them to ask the Father in verse 13: *And lead us not into temptation, but deliver us from evil: For thine is the kingdom, and the power, and the glory, for ever. Amen.* Jesus is not asking them to pray about an earthly kingdom to come in the millennium, but to acknowledge that the kingdom of God, and the kingdom of heaven are the Father's eternal kingdom, which will never pass away: *The LORD hath prepared his throne in the heavens; and his kingdom ruleth over all* (Ps. 103:19). God's throne is in heaven from eternity to eternity, and His kingdom rules over all. Jesus went to the cross when under the reign of Caesar. He arose from the dead and rules from the heavenly kingdom over heaven and earth (Matt. 28:18). When Jesus ascended into heaven, the Father put His only begotten Son in charge of the heavenly kingdom. God's heavenly kingdom will never pass away, and when the Lord returns, the rapture will indeed take place, and then the Lord will break in pieces and consume all other kingdoms, fulfilling Daniel 2:44-45: *And in the days of these kings shall the God of heaven set up a kingdom, which shall never be destroyed: and the kingdom shall not be left to other people, but it shall break in pieces and consume all these kingdoms, and it shall stand for ever. 45 Forasmuch as thou sawest that the stone was cut out of the mountain without hands, and that it brake in pieces the iron, the brass, the clay, the silver, and the gold; the great God hath made known to the king what shall come to pass hereafter: and the dream is certain, and the interpretation thereof sure.*

Jesus did not postpone His reign in the kingdom of heaven. He must reign until He has put all enemies under His feet, and the last enemy is death. When death is destroyed the Lord will deliver up the kingdom unto the Father: *Then cometh the end, when he shall have delivered up the kingdom to God, even the Father; when he shall have put down all rule and all authority and power. 25 For he must reign, till he hath put all enemies under his feet. 26 The last enemy that shall be destroyed is death. 27 For he hath put all things under his feet. But when he saith all things are put under him, it is manifest that he is excepted, which did put all things under him. 28 And when all things shall be subdued unto him, then shall the Son also himself be subject unto him that put all things under him, that God may be all in all* (I Corinthians 15:24-28).

The Jewish rulers and priests rejected Jesus as ruler over them, and crucified Him. However, God took the Stone which the builders rejected, and made the same head of the corner. God took the kingdom of God (salvation as a nation) away from the Jew and gave it to the Gentile. The Jews' eyes were blinded because of unbelief. We can see in the Scripture below that the kingdom of God is the Spirit of God living inside the believer. It is the kingdom which the Lord rules as head in the Church age. Jesus became the cornerstone of the Church (Jew and Gentile), which is His body: *They say unto him, He will miserably destroy those wicked men, and will let out his vineyard unto other husbandmen, which shall render him the fruits in their seasons. 42 Jesus saith unto them, Did ye never read in the scriptures, The stone which the builders rejected, the same is become the head of the corner: this is the Lord's doing, and it is marvellous in our eyes? 43 Therefore say I unto you, The kingdom of God shall be taken from you, and given to a nation bringing forth the fruits thereof* (Matthew 21:41-43).

The Sermon on the Mount, which Jesus preached to the multitude, applies to the Gentile Church, the same as it applies to the disciples; there is no difference. Jesus was giving laws to the Church with his sermon. These were not laws for the Jews in the millennium only, but are for His children in the Church age. The Sermon on the Mount conveyed the Laws given to govern our conduct while we wait for His coming again. Those who teach these commandments are called great in the kingdom of heaven, but those who teach men to break them are called the least (Matthew 5:1-20).

Old Testament prophets let us know that God's heavenly kingdom rules over all from eternity to eternity. The Father does not rule apart from the Son, nor does the Son rule apart from the Father. The LORD is all powerful and is exalted above all: *Thine, O LORD, is the greatness, and the power, and the glory, and the victory, and the majesty: for all that is in the heaven and in the earth is thine; thine is the kingdom, O LORD, and thou art exalted as head above all* (I Chronicles 29:11). The Psalmist spoke of it: *The LORD hath prepared his throne in the heavens; and his kingdom ruleth over all* (Psalms 103:19). Zacharias prophesied in Luke 1:21-33 that the Lord's kingdom would be an everlasting kingdom, the same as in Psalms 145:13: *Thy kingdom is an everlasting kingdom, and thy dominion endureth throughout all generations.* The eternal kingdom of God has its origin in heaven, and rules over all. Jesus let Pilate know in John 18:36-37 that He was king, but His kingdom was not of this world.

The Gospel of Matthew presents Jesus as King of the kingdom of heaven, but in the Epistles the apostles no longer use the phrase "the kingdom of heaven," instead using phrases such as "the kingdom of our Lord." The kingdom of the Lord is the kingdom that the Father had given Him, where the Lord rules His Church from His heavenly throne. Many Scriptures infer that the apostles were already in the kingdom of God's dear Son. Paul shows us that the saints of Colossae were delivered from the powers of darkness, and translated into the kingdom of Jesus: *Who hath delivered us from the power of darkness, and hath translated us into the kingdom of his dear Son* (Colossians 1:13). The heavenly kingdom is called the kingdom of heaven in Matthew. Paul tells us God preserved him unto His heavenly kingdom: *And the Lord shall deliver me from every evil work, and will preserve me unto his heavenly kingdom: to whom be glory for ever and ever. Amen* (II Timothy 4:18). Paul said the saints should walk worthy of God, because He has called them unto His kingdom and glory (I Thessalonians 2:12). According to Peter, the Lord's kingdom is the everlasting kingdom: *For so an entrance shall be ministered unto you abundantly into the everlasting kingdom of our Lord and Saviour Jesus Christ* (II Peter 1:11). Hebrews lets the saints know that heaven and earth will be shaken once more, but the Church of the First Born will be safe in the Lord's kingdom, which can never be moved. This kingdom is the kingdom of heaven, where the saints are safe from God's wrath (Heb. 12:22-28).

When John wrote Revelation, he let us know that he is our brother and companion in tribulation, and in the kingdom of Jesus Christ: *I John, who also am your brother, and companion in tribulation, and in the kingdom and patience of Jesus Christ, was in the isle that is called Patmos, for the word of God, and for the testimony of Jesus Christ* (Revelation 1:9).

When the rapture and resurrection takes place at the last trump, judgment will follow because it is the last day the saints are on earth. The announcement is made that the kingdoms of this world are become the kingdoms of our LORD, and His Christ, and His kingdom will last forever and ever. When the announcement is made, the Devil, the Beast, the false prophet, and the rebellion against Jesus and His kingdom has run its course. The whole world will face Judgment, and the Lord's enemies will be made His footstool: *And the seventh angel sounded; and there were great voices in heaven, saying, The kingdoms of this world are become the kingdoms of our Lord, and of his Christ; and he shall reign for ever and ever. 18 And the nations were angry, and thy wrath is come, and the time of the dead, that they should be judged, and that thou shouldest give reward unto thy servants the prophets, and to the saints, and them that fear thy name, small and great; and shouldest destroy them which destroy the earth* (Revelation 11:15, 18).

The Lord's kingdom is an everlasting kingdom, and will never have an end, but the millennial kingdom of Israel will last only one thousand years. Only the Lord's kingdom that rules from heaven is the everlasting kingdom, which the Lord called the kingdom of heaven in the Gospel of Matthew.

The Kingdom of God

S ome pretribulationists are still teaching that the kingdom of heaven and the kingdom of God are the same.
I will show the true meaning of the kingdom of God, and will show it
was never a delayed kingdom. I can understand why unbelievers do not
understand the meaning of the kingdom of God, but it is unexcusable
for the saved to not know the meaning (Mark 4:11-12).

There are many dispensational teachings that have been handed
down from generation to generation since Darby. Most Christians
acknowledge that many Jewish people in Christ's day were looking for
the Messiah to establish the Messianic or Davidic kingdom. It was the
Jew's lack of understanding, and the wrong interpretations of Moses,
Isaiah, Daniel, and the Old Testament prophets that were their problem. The doctrines of men had blinded their eyes from knowing that
the Messiah must first go to the cross, fulfill all Scriptures concerning
the Gentiles, and the fulfillment of the Church age before the kingdom
of Israel can be set up. The division that Scofield made concerning the
Gospels up to Acts the second chapter, insisting that it was for the Jew
only, and that from that point to the fourth chapter of Revelation was
for the Church, still affects the way the kingdom of heaven, the kingdom of God, and the kingdom of Israel are interpreted.

Charles Caldwell Ryrie, Th.D., Ph.D. , Chairman of the
Department of Systematic Theology of Dallas Theological Seminary,

authored *The Ryrie Study Bible*. This is what he says about the kingdom of God in his notes concerning Mark 1:15, *The kingdom of God is at hand*. "The rule of Messiah on earth, promised in the Old Testament and earnestly longed for by the Jewish people, was near, for the Messiah had now come. However, the people rejected rather than accepted Him, and the fulfillment of the kingdom promises had to be delayed until God's purpose in saving Jews and Gentiles and forming His church was completed. Then Christ will return and set up God's kingdom on this earth (*Acts 15:14-16; Rev. 19:15*)."

Ryrie's reasoning about the kingdom of God does not hold true to the Word of God. Jesus never delayed the kingdom of God when the Jews rejected Him as the Messiah. The kingdom of God is established in the hearts of all believers when they get saved. When the Jews rejected Jesus as the Messiah, it did not stop the kingdom of God from coming into existence. Jesus states the kingdom of God is about the second birth, not an earthly kingdom: *Jesus answered and said unto him, Verily, verily, I say unto thee, Except a man be born again, he cannot see the kingdom of God* (John 3:3). Why would Jesus speak about the kingdom of God forty days after His resurrection, if God delayed the kingdom, and set it aside after the Jews rejected Him? (Acts 1:3). If Jesus set aside the kingdom of God after the Jews rejected Him as the Messiah, Paul would not used the term in most every Epistle he authored. Paul explains the meaning of the kingdom of God to the Roman Christians in Romans 14:17-19. Paul's letter to the Corinthian Church negates any indication that the Lord delayed the kingdom of God. He let them know that the unrighteous of the Church age will not inherit the kingdom of God because they were never washed from sins, sanctified, or justified by the Spirit of God (I Cor. 6:9-11). The kingdom of God is a spiritual kingdom, while the kingdom of Israel is an earthly kingdom. Jesus never promised the Jews that He would set up the kingdom of Israel before the prophecies concerning Himself, the cross, and the Church age were fulfilled. Isaiah 53 and Daniel 9:26 had to be fulfilled first. The kingdom of Israel will be established in the millennium.

Many Old Testament Scriptures concerning the kingdom of God are root Scriptures for the salvation of both Jew and Gentile in the Church age: I Chronicles 16:23-36; Psalm 37:39-40; 40:10-11; 62:6-8; 85:8-13; 96:1-13; 118:21-24. Isaiah prophesied how the Lord would become our salvation and a light to the Gentile in the Church age: Isaiah 12:1-6; 49:5-6; 60:1-3, and 62:1-2. At John's birth, his father Zechariah let us know that the God of Israel would send John to prepare the way of the Lord. He prophesied how God had raised up a horn of salvation for them in the house of His servant David to redeem them from their sins, as God had promised by His holy prophets since the world began (Luke 1:67-79). Simeon prophesied at the birth of Jesus how he had seen the salvation of the Lord, and how He would be a light to the Gentiles, and the glory of the people of Israel (Luke 2 25-32). John the Baptist prepared the way of the Lord, and preached; (Luke 3:2-9). The ministry of Jesus was about the salvation of Jew and Gentile and the kingdom of God, not about the kingdom of Israel, which will be set up in the millennium.

I want to make clear the meaning of the kingdom of God. The Gospels of Matthew, Mark, Luke, John and the Epistles deal with the kingdom of God. After the death of John the Baptist, Jesus began to preach, asking the Jews to repent for the kingdom of God was at hand; (Mark 1:14-15). If the kingdom of God was at hand, it could not be delayed, because God is sovereign and knows all things. He did not delay anything that was prophesied. Jesus plainly gave the time element of the kingdom of God at the beginning of His ministry: *The law and the prophets were until John: since that time the kingdom of God is preached, and every man presseth into it* (Luke 16:16). Jesus let the Pharisees know that the dispensation of Law extended only until John, and since that time the new dispensation of the kingdom of God is preached. Jesus said in Mark that the time of the kingdom of God had arrived, repent and believe the gospel: *Now after that John was put in prison, Jesus came into Galilee, preaching the gospel of the kingdom of God, 15 And saying, The time is fulfilled, and the kingdom of God is at hand: repent ye, and believe the gospel* (Mark 1:14-15).

Jesus established the meaning of the kingdom of God in the four Gospels. Jesus was the beginning of a new dispensation, where salvation would come to all who believed that Jesus was the Messiah and the savior of the world. The kingdom of God would not come about in an earthly kingdom that you could see, but would be a spiritual kingdom, where God would live inside the believer: *Jesus answered and said unto him, If a man love me, he will keep my words: and my Father will love him, and we will come unto him, and make our abode with him* (John 14:23). Jesus explains to them about the kingdom of God: *And when he was demanded of the Pharisees, when the kingdom of God should come, he answered them and said, The kingdom of God cometh not with observation: 21. Neither shall they say, Lo here! or, lo there! for, behold, the kingdom of God is within you. 22 And he said unto the disciples, The days will come, when ye shall desire to see one of the days of the Son of man, and ye shall not see it* (Luke 17:20-22). The Jews who did not believe in Jesus died in their sins and never saw salvation or the kingdom of God.

Jesus sent the twelve disciples to preach the kingdom of God (Luke 9:2). He then told them how He must suffer many things, and that He would be rejected of the elders, chief priest and scribes, and be slain, and would be raised the third day. He then taught them discipleship and told them that some would not taste death until they saw the kingdom of God. These verses show that the kingdom of God has been in effect for about two thousand years (Luke 9:22-27).

The apostle Paul continued with the same message as Jesus had preached, that sinners who have not been cleansed from their sins by the blood of Christ could not enter into the kingdom of Christ and of God (Eph. 5:5). Paul was not talking about a different kingdom, but was saying the kingdom of Christ is the *kingdom of God.* John the Baptist used the term kingdom of God, and then Jesus used it, and it is used from Matthew to Revelation. The kingdom of Christ and of God is a spiritual kingdom, where Christ lives within the heart of believers and rules from heaven. When a person accepts salvation, God seals them with the Holy Spirit, and sets up the kingdom of God or Christ in the heart of the believer. Paul said the saved are delivered from the powers of darkness and are made partakers of the Lord's kingdom the moment they believe: *Giving thanks unto the Father, which hath made us meet to be partakers of the inheritance of the saints in light: 13 Who hath delivered us from the power of darkness, and hath translated us into the kingdom of his dear Son: 14 In whom we have redemption through his blood, even the forgiveness of sins* (Colossians 1:12-14). Paul told the Thessalonian Church that God had already called them into His kingdom: *That ye would walk worthy of God, who hath called you unto his kingdom and glory* (I Thessalonians 2;12).

Paul made it plain to Timothy that heaven is for the saints. Paul knew the Lord had preserved him unto His heavenly kingdom. Paul knew that after his death he would be absent from the body but present with the Lord, and that he would be in the Lord's heavenly kingdom. Paul was not looking to return to earth to reign one thousand years: *And the Lord shall deliver me from every evil work, and will preserve me unto his heavenly kingdom: to whom be glory for ever and ever. Amen* (II Timothy 4:18). Paul makes it clear to Timothy that heaven will be home for the saints for ever and ever. There will be no end to the Lord's kingdom: *He shall be great, and shall be called the Son of the Highest: and the Lord God shall give unto him the throne of his father David: 33 And he shall reign over the house of Jacob for ever; and of his kingdom there shall be no end* (Luke 1:32-33).

Dispensationalists infer that there is a difference between a Jewish Christian and a Gentile Christian. However, they are both one in Christ. There is no difference, for both Jew and Gentiles who are saved are in the kingdom of Christ: *For the scripture saith, Whosoever believeth on him shall not be ashamed. 12 For there is no difference between the Jew and the Greek: for the same Lord over all is rich unto all that call upon him* (Romans 10:11-12). *And have put on the new man, which is renewed in knowledge after the image of him that created him: 11 Where there is neither Greek nor Jew, circumcision nor uncircumcision, Barbarian, Scythian, bond nor free: but Christ is all, and in all* (Colossians 3:10-11).

The Jew have a special place with God. God works through the Jew because they are His chosen people. Jesus was a Jew, the disciples were Jews, and the early Church members were Jews. Paul confirms this to the Roman Church: *Who are Israelites; to whom pertaineth the adoption, and the glory, and the covenants, and the giving of the law, and the service of God, and the promises* (Romans 9:4). God called both Jew and Gentile into His kingdom: *And that he might make known the riches of his glory on the vessels of mercy, which he had afore prepared unto glory, 24 Even us, whom he hath called, not of the Jews only, but also of the Gentiles?* (Romans 9:23-24).

Not all Jews were spiritual Jews. Those who were of the flesh were not made partakers of the kingdom of God, nor were they of the kingdom of Christ. Those who did not enter into the kingdom of God were broken off: *Not as though the word of God hath taken none effect. For they are not all Israel, which are of Israel: 7 Neither, because they are the seed of Abraham, are they all children: but, In Isaac shall thy seed be called. 8 That is, They which are the children of the flesh, these are not the children of God: but the children of the promise are counted for the seed* (Romans 9:6-8). Well;

because of unbelief they were broken off, and thou standest by faith. Be not high-minded, but fear: 23 And they also, if they abide not still in unbelief, shall be grafted in: for God is able to graft them in again (Romans 11:20, 23).

There should be no doubt concerning the meaning of the kingdom of God which Jesus and the apostles taught. The Word of God speaks for itself when all the facts are given and the Scripture has been rightly divided. I will show in this next chapter that God will establish the kingdom of Israel in its proper place and time.

The Kingdom
of Israel

When we understand the true meaning of the kingdom of heaven, and the kingdom of God, we then can understand that God will set up the kingdom of Israel in His timing. The first two have been in effect for about two thousand years. This chapter explains the meaning and the time element of the kingdom of Israel.

Now I want to make clear the meaning of the kingdom of Israel, which God promised David. The duration of the kingdom of Israel is only one thousand years because it is an earthly kingdom, but the duration of Jesus and His kingdom is forever. God will keep His promise to David, and the Lord will set up the promised kingdom of Israel in its appointed time.

The kingdom of heaven, the kingdom of God and the kingdom of Israel are not the same kingdom. I have given the scriptural and historical meaning of the first two, and will do the same concerning the kingdom of Israel. After the resurrection of Jesus, and just before He ascended unto His heavenly kingdom that the Father had given him (Luke 22:29-30), the disciples asked Him if he would restore the kingdom of Israel at that time. Jesus replied that the times and seasons the Father hath put in His own power: *When they therefore were come together, they asked of him, saying, Lord, wilt thou at this time restore again the kingdom to Israel? 7 And he said unto them, It is not for you to know the times or the seasons, which the Father hath put in his own power* (Acts 1:6-7). The

Scriptures could not be broken, and God knew from eternity that the religious leaders of Israel would not be fit to administer a spiritual kingdom in the Lord's first coming. The chief priest and elders were the ones who cried, "Crucify him," and claimed Caesar their king. The Jews' expectation was that Jesus would make the nation of the Jews as it was in the days of David and Solomon and roll back the Roman army, but Jesus was not sent to set up the earthly kingdom of Israel at that time. He was sent for the salvation of all, both Jew and Gentile.

After the resurrection, two had visited the sepulcher and were on the road to Emmaus. One of them, Cleopas, thought Jesus was a stranger who had chosen to walk with them. Jesus and Cleopas were talking together concerning the things that had come to pass. Jesus then revealed Himself, and let them know that it was necessary for Him to go to the cross and die for man's sins and then enter into glory. Jesus expounded to them from Moses and all the prophets concerning Himself. Jesus never came to set up an earthly kingdom of Israel before the cross. Jesus came to set up the kingdom of heaven and rule the Church from heaven until He comes to rapture the Church. At that time Jesus will set up the kingdom of Israel, fulfilling what Moses and the prophets have prophesied: *Then he said unto them; O fools, and slow of heart to believe all that the prophets have spoken: 26 Ought not Christ to have suffered these things, and to enter into his glory? 27 And beginning at Moses and all the prophets, he expounded unto them in all the scriptures the things concerning himself* (Luke 24:25-27).

After the Lord's resurrection, He ascended to sit on the heavenly throne, as King, and rule His Church from heaven. Jesus told Pilate that His kingdom was not of this world (John 18:36). Jesus knew that the kingdom of Israel would be set up in the Father's timing when all Scripture is fulfilled concerning the Church and Himself. Jesus showed the Pharisees that the Psalms pointed to Him as the son of David and the Messiah, and that He would sit on the right hand of the Father until he made His enemies His footstool: *While the Pharisees were gathered together, Jesus asked them, 42 Saying, What think ye of Christ? whose son is he? They say unto him, The son of David. 43 He saith unto them, How then doth David in spirit call him Lord, saying, 44 The Lord said unto my Lord, Sit thou on my right hand, till I make thine enemies thy footstool?* (Matthew 22:41-44).

The kingdom of Israel cannot be set up until after the rapture and the battle of Armageddon are fulfilled. It cannot be set up until the beginning of the millennium, and the fulfillment of Psalm 110:1-6: *The LORD said unto my Lord, Sit thou at my right hand, until I make thine enemies thy footstool. 2 The LORD shall send the rod of thy strength out of Zion: rule thou in the midst of thine enemies. 3 Thy people shall be willing in the day of thy power, in the beauties of holiness from the womb of the morning: thou hast the dew of thy youth. 4 The LORD hath sworn, and will not repent, Thou art a priest for ever after the order of Melchizedek. 5 The Lord at thy right hand shall strike through kings in the day of his wrath. 6 He shall judge among the heathen, he shall fill the places with the dead bodies; he shall wound the heads over many countries.*

Christians of today need to acknowledge that the kingdom of heaven and the kingdom of God have been in force for about two thousand years. God is fulfilling all that was prophesied concerning the Church and the nation of Israel, but the Church has not prepared herself for what lies ahead because of the false doctrines of dispensationalism. The Church has been conditioned to believe they will escape the tribulation period. When the tribulation period does come, and the saints are still on earth, it will be hard for pretribulationists to understand the persecution of saints. It will overthrow the faith of many, because they have not been prepared to suffer for Christ at the hands of the ungodly. Saints must be taught truth and be willing to suffer persecution as Jesus, the apostles, and the early Church suffered. Pretribulationists will not understand when they are called upon to suffer the fiery trials and be partakers of Christ's suffering. Truth must be taught about the tribulation period, about how the saints will be called upon to suffer the wrath of man, though not the wrath of God, for a short season: *Beloved, think it not strange concerning the fiery trial which is to try you, as though some strange thing happened unto you: 13 But rejoice, inasmuch as ye are partakers of Christ's sufferings; that, when his glory shall be revealed, ye may be glad also with exceeding joy. 14 If ye be reproached for the name of Christ, happy are ye; for the spirit of glory and of God resteth upon you: on their part he is evil spoken of, but on your part he is glorified* (I Peter 4:12-14).

By God's grace, Israel was established as a nation in 1948. God began bringing the Jews back to their land after 1900 years of being scattered unto all nations as Jesus prophesied. We can see how God is keeping the promise He made to David about the kingdom of Israel. In 1948 Israel declared themselves a Jewish nation. That was the first time the Jews were not under the rule of Gentiles since their captivity in Babylon. The Holy Spirit is calling them back to their land to fulfill

Ezekiel 37:1-28. The dry bones, which were dead, are taking on life. There are many Jews realizing Jesus is the Messiah, and being saved every day. In Revelation 7:4 there will be 144,000 of all the tribes of Israel saved and raptured (Rev. 14:1-4). The eyes of the Jewish nation have not been opened yet concerning their transgression of rejecting Jesus as the Messiah, but God will bring it to pass. Daniel's seventieth week must be fulfilled in the tribulation period in order to bring the Jews and their salvation to its completion. The end of the tribulation period will bring judgment on the Devil, the antichrist, the false prophet, and all Gentile nations.

Zechariah said only one-third of Israel will come through the fire and be refined as silver (Zech. 13:9). Those who are left on earth after the rapture and the first resurrection will not have resurrected bodies, but will have an earthly body and kingdom. The Jews who repent and believe Jesus is the Messiah after they see the nail prints in His hands will be in the kingdom of Israel (Zechariah 12:7-14, 13:6-9). They will be on earth when God pours out his wrath on a wicked world in the fifteenth, and sixteenth chapters of Revelation. After the battle of Armageddon, the Lord will establish the kingdom of Israel as He promised, and will rule them with a rod of iron (Rev. 2:27; 19:11-15). The Lord shows us the time when the kingdom of Israel is established; (Revelation 20:1-6). The kingdom of Israel will be established after the battle of Armageddon, and will last for a thousand years. When the thousand years are expired, Satan will be loosed for a short season to deceive the nations for the last time. He will be cast into the lake of fire and brimstone with the beast and false prophet. The great white throne judgment will then take place (Rev. 20:7-15).

Pretribulationists have a mindset that Jesus must sit in an earthly temple in Jerusalem to rule the children of Israel in the millennium. I want to remind pretribulationists that God did not sit in the temple so the people could see Him when He ruled Israel under the Judges. God's presence was in the Holy Place, but they wanted a king they could see, as had the heathen nations. God let Samuel know that it was not him they rejected, but God (I Sam. 8:1-8). Jesus has reigned over His church for two thousand years, and does not sit in an earthly temple in Jerusalem (Eph. 5:24-32). The Scriptures do not teach that Jesus will sit in an earthly temple for a thousand years, ruling the world from

Jerusalem. The following Scriptures written to the churches prove that Jesus will not rule from an earthly Jerusalem during the millennium, but from the New Jerusalem: *Him that overcometh will I make a pillar in the temple of my God, and he shall go no more out: and I will write upon him the name of my God, and the name of the city of my God, which is new Jerusalem, which cometh down out of heaven from my God: and I will write upon him my new name. 13 He that hath an ear, let him hear what the Spirit saith unto the churches* (Revelation 3:12-13). This promise was made to the church of Philadelphia before Revelation 4:1, therefore the promise was made to the Church. Scofield's belief does not conform to the promise made to the church of Philadelphia in Revelation 3:12-13.

Scofield's booklet, "Rightly Dividing The Word of Truth," said that after the rapture and tribulation period, the Lord will return to earth with His saints, and reign from Jerusalem over restored Israel and the earth for one thousand years. Most pretribulationists are still teaching the same thing, but it does not conform to what the Bible teaches. The saints who are in the first resurrection neither marry nor are given in marriage, because they are of two different worlds. It would be impossible for those who are in the resurrection to live on earth in the millennium with those who are of flesh and blood. Those in the resurrection are of a different world, and will be in heaven, which the Lord prepared for them (John 14:3). The saved will enter the New Jerusalem, and the nations which are saved will walk in the light of it (Rev. 21:1-2,9-10, 23-24). Nations cannot walk in the light of the New Jerusalem after the great white throne judgment when the Lord delivers up the kingdom of God to the Father that God may be all in all, because the kingdom of Israel will only last one thousand years. Paul gives us the order of events (I Cor. 15:23- 28).

Jesus makes a great distinction between the two resurrections: *Therefore in the resurrection whose wife of them is she? for seven had her to wife. 34 And Jesus answering said unto them, The children of this world marry, and are given in marriage: 35 But they which shall be accounted worthy to obtain that world, and the resurrection from the dead, neither marry, nor are given in marriage: 36 Neither can they die any more: for they are equal unto the angels; and are the children of God, being the children of the resurrection* (Luke 20:33-36).

I want to emphasize that after the seven last vials have been poured out and the millennium begins, one of the seven angels that had the seven last vials shows the bride, the Lamb's wife, in the New Jerusalem. This pictures the Church in the New Jerusalem at the beginning of the millennium and not the end: *And there came unto me one of the seven angels which had the seven vials full of the seven last plagues, and talked with me, saying, Come hither, I will show thee the bride, the Lamb's wife. 10 And he carried me away in the spirit to a great and high mountain, and showed me that great city, the holy Jerusalem, descending out of heaven from God* (Revelation 21:9-10). The Scripture below must be fulfilled during the millennium because the nations who are saved after the battle of Armageddon will walk in the light of the New Jerusalem: *And the nations of them which are saved shall walk in the light of it: and the kings of the earth do bring their glory and honour into it* (Revelation 21:24).

Jesus never promised the Jews an earthly kingdom until Daniel 9:26 and 27 are fulfilled. The kingdom of Israel can only be set up in God's timing after all prophecies are fulfilled. The earthly-minded Jews, who did not believe Jesus was the Messiah, were in the judgment of Jerusalem and perished because they rejected Jesus as the Messiah and rejected His salvation (John 1:11-12). They rejected the kingdom of heaven, the kingdom of God, and wanted the kingdom of Israel, but they did not want Jesus and His spiritual kingdom. The unbelieving Jews were blinded to the fact of why the Messiah came into the world. He did not come into the world to set up the kingdom of Israel, but to give salvation to all who believed. Jesus preached the kingdom of heaven and the kingdom of God for over three years, yet many priests and Pharisees still did not understand the message He preached. He preached about the Holy Spirit living within the believer and His heavenly kingdom that would rule from heaven. What Jesus was preaching, and what the Jews wanted to hear, did not sit well with the earthly minded Jews. We must bring our teachings in line with the Word of God, because there is not one single Scripture where Jesus said He came to set up an earthly kingdom of Israel before the cross.

John the Baptist preached to the Jews, and told them that the ax is laid to the root of Israel, and that they would be cut down because they had brought forth no fruit before Jesus began His ministry (Matthew 3:1-10). Jerusalem was destroyed, and the temple burned in A.D. 70. They were scattered throughout the earth, but the Lord told them he would bring them back to their own land in Ezekiel 36 and 37. After nineteen hundred years, God did bring them back to their land, but the promised righteous millennial kingdom of Israel has not been established. The timing is in the hands of the Father (Acts 1:6-7). The Jews who believe in Jesus up to the time of the rapture will be grafted into the Body of Christ, the same as the Gentiles. Those who do not believe Jesus is the Messiah until they see Him coming in the clouds will be left on earth to go through the seven last vials and the battle of Armageddon. Both the Jews and the Gentiles who survive the wrath of God when it is poured out on earth will remain on earth to be part of the kingdom of Israel. Everyone who is left of all the nations that came against Jerusalem will go up annually to worship the King, the Lord of hosts, and keep the feast of tabernacles (Zech. 14:16-17). The law will go forth from Jerusalem, and they will worship the Lord in the earthly Jerusalem.

The Jews wanted Jesus to set up the kingdom of Israel two thousand years ago. They could not see God's timing, nor understand His actions. When Jesus came into Jerusalem, the Jews hailed Him as their King, and believed He would set up the Kingdom of David at that time and turn back the Roman Empire and its rule. As the week went on, their hopes were dashed and they were ready to crucify Him. God knew from eternity that the cross and the Church age would be fulfilled before the kingdom of Israel could be set up. If the kingdom of Israel had been set up at the Lord's first coming, many Scriptures would have been broken, and the Word of God would have been counted void. This chapter proves Jesus never promised, or planned to set up the kingdom of Israel at the Lord's first coming.

Jesus never spoke or did anything contrary to the words of the prophets. He said that Jerusalem would be trodden down of the Gentiles until the time of the Gentiles was fulfilled. Therefore, Jesus never intended to set up an earthly kingdom of Israel until everything the prophets had prophesied was fulfilled: *And they shall fall by the edge of the sword, and shall be led away captive into all nations: and Jerusalem shall be trodden down of the Gentiles, until the times of the Gentiles be fulfilled* (Luke 21:24).

Daniel's seventieth week could not be fulfilled before the cross and the Church age. Jerusalem had to be destroyed, and the desolation of the land had to take place before the seventieth week could be fulfilled. The kingdom of Israel could not be set up contrary to the Word: *And after threescore and two weeks shall Messiah be cut off, but not for himself: and the people of the prince that shall come shall destroy the city and the sanctuary; and the end thereof shall be with a flood, and unto the end of the war desolations are determined. 27 And he shall confirm the covenant with many for one week: and in the midst of the week he shall cause the sacrifice and the oblation to cease, and for the overspreading of abominations he shall make it desolate, even until the consummation, and that determined shall be poured upon the desolate* (Daniel 9:26-27).

Paul's message preached to the Jews in the synagogue at Antioch should correct the false teaching about Jesus coming to set up the kingdom of Israel before the Church age. Paul started his message with Israel in Egypt and reviewed the events of the judges and kings. He preached how Jesus came through the lineage of David as the Messiah to save both Jew and Gentile, and was condemned and went to the cross. Paul let the Jews know that Jesus died for sins, was buried, and rose again, and was to be a light unto the Gentiles. Many Jews' believed Paul's message, but others contradicted and blasphemed his message. Paul and Barnabas told them that it was necessary that the Word of God should be spoken unto them first, but since they did not receive it, they would turn to the Gentiles. God had given the Jewish nation time to repent and bring forth fruit, and Paul's message was the last opportunity given to the Jewish nation before the judgment of Jerusalem. Paul's message: Acts 13:14-49.

Paul preached both to the Jew and Gentile the same message that the prophets and Moses had preached. Jesus would die first and arise from the dead, and would be light to Jew and Gentile (the Church Age). The Jews rejected Jesus and His salvation, and the kingdom of God (salvation) was taken from them and given to the Gentiles until the time of the Gentiles is fulfilled. All that Moses and the prophets prophesied must be fulfilled before God will set up the kingdom of Israel. Paul had to reason with King Agrippa, and tell him that he was only preaching what Moses and the prophets had taught. The Church would do well if they listen to these verses also, and see that the kingdom of Israel was not delayed. Jesus finished all that the Father had given Him to do (John 17:9). He went to the cross and paid for the sins of the whole world, and ascended back to heaven to set up the kingdom the Father had given Him (Acts 26:20-23).

The kingdom of Israel was not postponed, and God did not change his plan for Israel because God's prophets had already prophesied how the Messiah would be crucified in Isaiah 53. It was the priests of Israel who were blind in not distinguishing between the Lord's first coming in Isaiah 7:14-16; 9:6-7; Zechariah 9:9 and the cross that was to follow in Isaiah 53. Then Jesus would sit on the right hand of the Father and be a light unto the Gentiles in the Church age (Isaiah 60:3; Jeremiah 16:19). The Lord would sit on the right hand of the Father until His enemies were made His footstool (Psalms 110:1-6). The Jews who did not believe Jesus was the Messiah were blinded (Romans 11:5-8, 17-29). They were broken off and the Gentiles grafted in. Those who were broken off did not distinguish between the Lord's first coming, and His second coming at the end of the Church age. They did not see the Church age, the tribulation period and the rapture taking place in Isaiah 26:17-21, and that the day of the Lord would follow, and then the kingdom of Israel would be restored as set forth in many Old Testament prophecies. There were many in Israel who did not understand the order of events concerning the Lord's first coming and perished. There will also be many in the last days who will be in the apostasy, and will not understand the order of events concerning the Lord's second coming because of the pretribulation rapture theory.

When the saints are secure in the Lord's chambers, the Lord and the angels destroy all the kingdoms of this world. Only the kingdom of Israel under the rule of the Lord will remain on earth. This kingdom will last for one thousand years: *And in the days of these kings shall the God of heaven set up a kingdom, which shall never be destroyed: and the kingdom shall not be left to other people, but it shall break in pieces and consume all these kingdoms, and it shall stand for ever. 45 Forasmuch as thou sawest that the stone was cut out of the mountain without hands, and that it brake in pieces the iron, the brass, the clay, the silver, and the gold; the great God hath made known to the king what shall come to pass hereafter: and the dream is certain, and the interpretation thereof sure* (Daniel 2:44-45).

Jesus will come in the last days and rapture all who are ready for His coming, but will destroy all the powers of the kingdoms of this world, and set up the kingdom of Israel. His dominion is an everlasting dominion, and His heavenly kingdom will never pass away, nor be destroyed: *I saw in the night visions, and, behold, one like the Son of man came with the clouds of heaven, and came to the Ancient of days, and they brought him near before him. 14 And there was given him dominion, and glory, and a kingdom, that all people, nations, and languages, should serve him: his dominion is an everlasting dominion, which shall not pass away, and his kingdom that which shall not be destroyed* (Daniel 7:13-14).

The saints will rule with the Lord from heaven over the kingdom of Israel, and those on earth will have fleshly bodies. The kingdom of Israel will pass away after one thousand years, but the Lord's kingdom is an everlasting kingdom: *And the kingdom and dominion, and the greatness of the kingdom under the whole heaven, shall be given to the people of the saints of the most High, whose kingdom is an everlasting kingdom, and all dominions shall serve and obey him* (Daniel 7:27). The Lord will not dwell in an earthly temple (Psalms 11:4, I Kings 9:27, II Chro. 6:18, Acts 17:24).

Zechariah prophesied Jerusalem would be safely inhabited in the kingdom of Israel (Zech. 14:11). Daniel prophesied when the Lord would set up the kingdom of Israel, and said it would be set up after He comes in the clouds in the ancient of days (Daniel 7:13-14). Micah prophesied that the Lord would set up the kingdom of Israel in the last days after the battle of Armageddon (Micah 4:1-8). Isaiah prophesied how there will be few men left after the battle of Armageddon. Women will outnumber men seven to one, and all who are left will be called holy. Evil men will be destroyed, and holiness will run down as a mighty stream during the millennium (Isaiah 4:1-6).

Joel also prophesied about the restoration of Israel (Joel 3:17-21). Micah said peace would prevail in the millennium. The remnant of Jacob would be blessed. There will be no false gods or religions left in the earth (Micah 5:4-15). The Lord let the disciples know that the Father sets the time of the kingdom of Israel (Acts 1:6-7). If Jesus had set up the kingdom of Israel, then all the Old Testament prophets would have been in error concerning the last days and concerning Israel. I have heard dispensationalists say that the Church age was not mentioned in the Old Testament and that Paul revealed it to the Church. Yet in the next verses we see how God planned the Church age to come first, and then the kingdom of Israel would be established: *Simeon hath declared how God at the first did visit the Gentiles, to take out of them a people for his name. 15 And to this agree the words of the prophets; as it is written, 16 After this I will return, and will build again the tabernacle of David, which is fallen down; and I will build again the ruins thereof, and I will set it up: 17 That the residue of men might seek after the Lord, and all the Gentiles, upon whom my name is called, saith the Lord, who doeth all these things. 18 Known unto God are all his works from the beginning of the world* (Acts 15:14-18).

The main reason why there has been so much error and confusion concerning the coming of the Lord, the kingdom of heaven, the kingdom of God, and the kingdom of Israel is because those who teach dispensationalism teach that the Gospels are not for the Church, but only for the Jew. This is the reason why the kingdom of heaven has a wrong interpretation, and this is the reason why there is a pretribulation rapture theory. The following Scriptures will show the Church that the kingdom of Israel was not postponed, but will come after the rapture of the Church and the seven last vials have been poured out upon a wicked and unbelieving world. Jesus will secure Jerusalem first, and will destroy all nations that come against Jerusalem. Those Jews who did not believe Jesus was the Messiah will realize the terrible mistake they made when they see Jesus for the first time and look upon Him they pierced: *The LORD also shall save the tents of Judah first, that the glory of the house of David and the glory of the inhabitants of Jerusalem do not magnify themselves against Judah. 8 In that day shall the LORD defend the inhabitants of Jerusalem; and he that is feeble among them at that day shall be as David; and the house of David shall be as God, as the angel of the LORD before them. 9 And it shall come to pass in that day, that I will seek to destroy all the nations that come against Jerusalem. 10 And I will pour upon the house of David, and upon the inhabitants of Jerusalem, the spirit of grace and of supplications: and they shall look upon me whom they have pierced, and they shall mourn for him, as one mourneth for his only son, and shall be in bitterness for him, as one that is in bitterness for his firstborn. 11 In that day shall there be a great mourning in Jerusalem, as the mourning of Hadadrimmon in the valley of Megiddon. 12 And the land shall mourn, every family apart; the family of the house of David apart, and their wives apart; the family of the house of Nathan apart, and their wives apart; 13 The family of the house of Levi apart, and their wives apart; the family of Shimei apart, and their wives apart; 14 All the families that remain, every family apart, and their wives apart* (Zechariah 12:7-14).

Those Jews who missed the rapture will turn to Christ with all their hearts and be saved. Jesus went to the cross one time for all sin, whether it be in the Church age or the millennium. God will open a fountain of grace for them: *In that day there shall be a fountain opened to the house of David and to the inhabitants of Jerusalem for sin and for uncleanness* (Zechariah 13:1).

The Jews who are left will humble themselves and please God. Idol worship will be banished. The prophets will be ashamed of how wrong they were concerning the interpretation of the Word of God, and how they misled the people: *And it shall come to pass in that day, saith the LORD of hosts, that I will cut off the names of the idols out of the land, and they shall no more be remembered: and also I will cause the prophets and the unclean spirit to pass out of the land. 3 And it shall come to pass, that when any shall yet prophesy, then his father and his mother that begat him shall say unto him, Thou shalt not live; for thou speakest lies in the name of the LORD: and his father and his mother that begat him shall thrust him through when he prophesieth. 4 And it shall come to pass in that day, that the prophets shall be ashamed every one of his vision, when he hath prophesied; neither shall they wear a rough garment to deceive: 5 But he shall say, I am no prophet, I am an husbandman; for man taught me to keep cattle from my youth* (Zechariah 13:2-5).

The Jews will see the wounds in the hands of Jesus. They will realize why God scattered them to the four corners of the earth for nineteen hundred years. When they smote the Shepherd (Jesus on the cross), the sheep were scattered until He regathered them in 1948. When Jesus comes for the rapture and resurrection, all will see the nail prints in the Lord's hands: *And one shall say unto him, What are these wounds in thine hands? Then he shall answer, Those with which I was wounded in the house of my friends. 7 Awake, O sword, against my shepherd, and against the man that is my fellow, saith the LORD of hosts: smite the shepherd, and the sheep shall be scattered: and I will turn mine hand upon the little ones* (Zechariah 13:6-7).

Jesus will set up the kingdom of Israel for those that are left on earth after the battle of Armageddon. Zechariah 13:8-9 shows us there will only be one-third who will survive to go into the kingdom of Israel. Those who are left on earth who worship not, nor bow to the beast, will be in the kingdom of Israel. They will believe in the Lord, and will know Jesus is the only savior. There will be no other religions or gods that will be worshipped throughout the whole world. God will refine them as silver and will try them as gold is tried: *And it shall come to pass, that in all the land, saith the LORD, two parts therein shall be cut off and die; but the third shall be left therein. 9 And I will bring the third part through the fire, and will refine them as silver is refined, and will try them as gold is tried: they shall call on my name, and I will hear them: I will say, It is my people: and they shall say, The LORD is my God* (Zechariah 13:8-9). After the battle of Armageddon, the Lord will be king of the whole earth, because all rebellion against God has been conquered. All nations will confess Jesus as King of kings and Lord of lords: *And the LORD shall be king over all the earth: in that day shall there be one LORD, and his name one* (Zechariah 14:9).

There will be plagues that will be upon those nations that fought against Jerusalem: *And this shall be the plague wherewith the LORD will smite all the people that have fought against Jerusalem; Their flesh shall consume away while they stand upon their feet, and their eyes shall consume away in their holes, and their tongue shall consume away in their mouth. 13 And it shall come to pass in that day, that a great tumult from the LORD shall be among them; and they shall lay hold every one on the hand of his neighbour, and his hand shall rise up against the hand of his neighbour. 14 And Judah also shall fight at Jerusalem; and the wealth of all the heathen round about shall be gathered together, gold, and silver, and apparel, in great abundance. 15 And so shall be the plague of the horse, of the mule, of the camel, and of the ass, and of all the beasts that shall be in these tents, as this plague* (Zechariah 14:12-15).

Jew and Gentile that believe in Jesus when they see Him coming in the clouds for the rapture, and survive the seven last vials and the battle of Armageddon will be in the millennium, will come to Jerusalem to worship the Lord: *And it shall come to pass, that every one that is left of all the nations which came against Jerusalem shall even go up from year to year to worship the King, the LORD of hosts, and to keep the feast of tabernacles* (Zechariah 14:16).

The Law will go forth from Jerusalem in the millennium, and will be enforced. There will be holiness for once in the world. This is the judgment of those who will not come and worship the Lord in the millennium: *And it shall be, that whoso will not come up of all the families of the earth unto Jerusalem to worship the King, the LORD of hosts, even upon them shall be no rain. 18 And if the family of Egypt go not up, and come not, that have no rain; there shall be the plague, wherewith the LORD will smite the heathen that come not up to keep the feast of tabernacles. 19 This shall be the punishment of Egypt, and the punishment of all nations that come not up to keep the feast of tabernacles. 20 In that day shall there be upon the bells of the horses, HOLINESS UNTO THE LORD; and the pots in the LORD'S house shall be like the bowls before the altar. 21 Yea, every pot in Jerusalem and in Judah shall be holiness unto the LORD of hosts: and all they that sacrifice shall come and take of them, and seethe therein: and in that day there shall be no more the Canaanite in the house of the LORD of hosts* (Zechariah 14:17-21).

If the Church were on earth during the millennium, what need would there be for the Law to apply to saints who are sinless and have resurrected bodies? Obedience to the law will not be a choice, but a command. Those who missed the rapture and wanted the Law, not the grace of God, will receive what they wanted. The Law will go forth from Zion: *But in the last days it shall come to pass, that the mountain of the house of the LORD shall be established in the top of the mountains, and it shall be exalted above the hills; and people shall flow unto it. 2 And many nations shall come, and say, Come, and let us go up to the mountain of the LORD, and to the house of the God of Jacob; and he will teach us of his ways, and we will walk in his paths: for the law shall go forth of Zion, and the word of the LORD from Jerusalem* (Micah 4:1-2).

Even the animal world will be at peace with mankind during the millennium: *The wolf also shall dwell with the lamb, and the leopard shall lie down with the kid; and the calf and the young lion and the fatling together; and a little child shall lead them. 7 And the cow and the bear shall feed; their young ones shall lie down together: and the lion shall eat straw like the ox. 8 And the sucking child shall play on the hole of the asp, and the weaned child shall put his hand on the cockatrice' den. 9 They shall not hurt nor destroy in all my holy mountain: for the earth shall be full of the knowledge of the LORD, as the waters cover the sea* (Isaiah 11:6-9).

At the end of the millennium, Satan is loosed for a short season and makes war against the saints in Jerusalem. He is conquered and cast into the lake of fire to join the beast and the false prophet. The people of all ages whose names were not in the Book of Life will be judged and cast into hell, the lake of fire, which is the second death (Revelation 20:7-15). When the last enemy is destroyed, which is death, the Lord will offer up the kingdom to the Father, and all things will be put under Him. The Lord will be subject to the Father that God may be all in all: *For he must reign, till he hath put all enemies under his feet. 26 The last enemy that shall be destroyed is death. 27 For he hath put all things under his feet. But when he saith all things are put under him, it is manifest that he is excepted, which did put all things under him. 28 And when all things shall be subdued unto him, then shall the Son also himself be subject unto him that put all things under him, that God may be all in all* (I Corinthians 15:25-28). Eternity starts, and time will cease. Heaven and earth are made one in the heavenly Jerusalem. The unsaved will be judged at the great white throne judgment and cast into the lake of fire (Revelation 20:11-15). Those who accept salvation during the millennium and have their names written in the book of life will be changed and enter the New Jerusalem with the saints who were in the first resurrection (Revelation 22:1-7).

THE IMMINENT
RETURN OF CHRIST

Pretribulationists hear the phrase about the imminent return of Christ so much, and have it so instilled in them, that they never question whether it is true or not. I will show how pretribulationists erred in claiming that the Lord could come at any moment. This chapter will show there is no scriptural foundation for it, and that neither Jesus nor Paul taught such a doctrine. Pretribulationists coined the saying.

The word *imminent* has been used incorrectly by pretribulationists in describing the time of the coming of the Lord. Pretribulationists use this word to insinuate that Jesus could come at any moment, without warning, to the Church. Paul never used an expression like that. Paul did not want the people to assume that the coming of the Lord would be within their lifetime, but his plea was to look forward to the blessed hope: *Looking for that blessed hope, and the glorious appearing of the great God and our Saviour Jesus Christ; and always be ready* (Titus 2:13). *So that ye come behind in no gift; waiting for the coming of our Lord Jesus Christ: 8 Who shall also confirm you unto the end, that ye may be blameless in the day of our Lord Jesus Christ* (I Corinthians 1:7-8). *For our conversation is in heaven; from whence also we look for the Saviour, the Lord Jesus Christ: 21 Who shall change our vile body, that it may be fashioned like unto his glorious body* (Philippians 3:20-21).

Pretribulationists teach that the Lord could come at any moment without warning, and say the word *wait* is in its present tense in

Scriptures such as I Thessalonians 1:9-10; II Thessalonians 3:5; Titus 2:13, and I Corinthians 1:7-8. Certainly the Lord wanted every generation to be watching and waiting for His coming, but about two thousand years have passed since the Lord returned to heaven; therefore these Scriptures are not teaching the Lord could come at any moment. He will come, when all is fulfilled that was prophesied about His coming—and the fulfillment of Matthew 24:14, 29-31; I Corinthians 15:51-53, and II Thessalonians 2:1-3.

Paul wrote I and II Thessalonians to correct the errors that had arisen concerning the Lord's coming. He was not writing to establish a new doctrine. Paul said in I Thessalonians 5:1-8 that the Church should know the times and the seasons because they are the children of the light, and not of darkness. He instructed the Church that the Lord's coming should not overtake them as a thief. Paul let them know in verse 9 that God had not appointed them to wrath (hell) because they had obtained salvation by the Lord Jesus Christ. Pretribulationists have taken the word *imminent* and twisted Scripture to fit their doctrine instead of letting their doctrine fit the Word. There should be a distinction made between suddenness and immediacy. *Suddenness* is a scriptural word, but *imminent* is used by pretribulationists out of context. Pretribulationists have taken the two signs that were to take place before the Lord comes in II Thessalonians 2:3, and used human reasoning to say the Lord's coming is imminent. They say there can be no signs before the Lord comes for the rapture. This reasoning is only theological double-talk that has deceived the Church. Paul's epistles to the Thessalonian church were to remove misunderstandings and perplexities because of false teachers. Paul's two letters were letters of correction, not letters to teach a doctrine different than the Lord had taught him. The first letter's emphasis was on the suddenness of the Lord's coming, and some understood it to mean its immediacy. Paul left no doubts about when the Lord's coming would take place, and warned them not to let anyone deceive them. He let the Church know that the Lord's coming was not imminent because two things must take place before the Lord comes (II Thessalonians 2:1-3). In verse 2 he warns them not to be deceived, whether by an evil spirit, false prophet, or by a letter that was said to be from him. He let them know that the apostasy must take place, and the man of sin be revealed before the saints are gathered together unto the

Lord. We must believe what Paul wrote, not what pretribulationists tell us he said. This is what Paul wrote: *Now we beseech you, brethren, by the coming of our Lord Jesus Christ, and by our gathering together unto him, 2 That ye be not soon shaken in mind, or be troubled, neither by spirit, nor by word, nor by letter as from us, as that the day of Christ is at hand. 3 Let no man deceive you by any means: for that day shall not come, except there come a falling away first, and that man of sin be revealed, the son of perdition* (II Thessalonians 2:1-3). God's Word cannot be broken; these two things must take place before the saints are gathered unto the Lord (the rapture).

The Church has been misled about the imminent return of Christ. Preachers tell their congregations Jesus could come at any moment, and there is nothing that has to be fulfilled before He comes again. Then pretribulationists will say the signs in the Gospels are only for the Jew, and not for the Church. Jesus did not teach such a doctrine in the Gospels, nor Paul in the Epistles, nor John in Revelation. Pretribulationists are teaching false doctrine because Scofield discounted the Gospels for the Church, and taught the imminent return of Christ. Neither Jesus, Paul, nor John ever taught an any-minute coming of the Lord, but taught us to watch, because He would come quickly.

The word *imminent* is not found in the Bible. It means "ready to take place," "near at hand," "threatening to fall or occur." John said to show the things which are written to the Lord's servants, and to keep those things which are written, for the time is at hand. He is not saying that the Lord could come at any time: *The Revelation of Jesus Christ, which God gave unto him, to show unto his servants things which must shortly come to pass; and he sent and signified it by his angel unto his servant John: 3 Blessed is he that readeth, and they that hear the words of this prophecy, and keep those things which are written therein: for the time is at hand* (Revelation 1:1,3). God's timetable is not like man's. These Scriptures obviously are not talking about the imminent return of Christ, but are talking about His coming in these last days, because the time is at hand when these things will begin to be fulfilled. John is saying to keep these things in memory, for the time is at hand for these things to be accomplished. The time clock has been running for about two thousand years. Prophecies are being fulfilled every day, and the time is still at hand.

James tells the Church to be patient, and to establish their hearts, and not give up under the trials of life, because Jesus has already made plans for His return for the Church and judgment upon the wicked: *Be ye also patient; stablish your hearts: for the coming of the Lord draweth nigh* (James 5:8). God's Word is written in such a way that it causes every generation to look and watch for His coming. Certainly this generation should be excited about these things being fulfilled in our day. Although it has been close to two thousand years since these promises were made, God did not lie to us about the soon coming of Christ. We must listen to what the Word is saying to the Church, and the promises Jesus has made to us in the Gospels. When we do this, there is no room for discouragement or disillusionment.

In reality, pretribulationists are not teaching the imminent return of Christ. They teach that the Lord could come at any moment for the rapture of the Church, and that nothing has to be fulfilled before the Lord comes back for the rapture. With their next breath, they say the Lord is coming for the rapture first, then seven years later He is coming in the Revelation. If the Lord is going to come just before the tribulation, then certain things must be fulfilled leading up to the tribulation period before the Lord will come. If the pretribulationists truly believe what they teach concerning the imminent coming of Christ, there would be no set years between the rapture and the Revelation. Anyone can see that there could be no set time before the tribulation period if Jesus could come at any moment. In reality pretribulationists are not teaching an any-moment coming of the Lord, any more than the post-tribulationists, because their teachings are only seven years apart. In theology, pretribulationists teach the imminent return of Christ, but in practice they teach and give a time element for the Lord's coming, which they say will happen just before the tribulation period starts. This is not teaching the Lord could come at any moment.

There are certain things that must be fulfilled before the Lord will come. The man of sin must have his armies in place for him to have one of the greatest powers that the world has ever known. The false prophet will have already united the churches into the one world church, which all liberals will join. He that letteth will let the man of sin come to power in His timing. We can see there can be no any-minute coming of the Lord with out any signs being given. The coming of the Lord will be according to the Word.

Jesus said we cannot know the day nor the hour of His coming, but the Church can know that the coming of the Lord is drawing near when we see the signs He gave us in the Gospels being fulfilled (Matt. 24:33). Christians should take heed to I Thessalonians 5:4-6: *But ye, brethren, are not in darkness, that that day should overtake you as a thief. 5 Ye are all the children of light, and the children of the day: we are not of the night, nor of darkness. 6 Therefore let us not sleep, as do others; but let us watch and be sober.* Historians say that not one Christian perished when Jerusalem fell in A.D. 70, because Jesus had already said the city would be destroyed.

It has been close to two thousand years since Jesus ascended to the right hand of the Father. Jesus told us in Mark the time element of His coming so we won't be in darkness. Jesus taught that His coming is like a man taking a far journey, leaving his home and giving his servants authority (the Church). He told them to watch, for they knew not when their master would come. Jesus said to watch "lest I come and find you sleeping." God's people who are watching what is taking place in the world will not be taken by surprise. Jesus could not be speaking only to Israel as His servants, because Israel was to be broken off because of unbelief. Therefore, Jesus was talking to the Church, both Jew and Gentile. When we saw Israel become a nation in 1948, this was the beginning of this scripture being fulfilled. The fulfilling would not be in 40 or 57 years (a generation), that we could count off and calculate the date of Jesus coming. Jesus said, "When ye see these things come to pass know that summer is near," and, "This generation will not pass until all these things be done." I believe many of those living in this generation will see the coming of the Lord because we can see the signs being fulfilled (Mark 13:24-37).

Jesus Will Come Quickly

When Jesus said He would come "quickly," He did not mean immediately or soon. He means He will come suddenly and unexpectedly, without warning. These verses should not be used in the sense that Jesus could come at any minute, because Jesus will come in the appointed time that the Father has given him: *Behold, I come quickly: hold that fast which thou hast, that no man take thy crown* (Revelation 3: 11). When Jesus comes, the sinner will not have time to get saved. Jesus gave a parable concerning the kingdom of heaven, and compared it to five wise virgins and five foolish virgins. The five wise virgins had their lamps trimmed and full of oil, but the five foolish virgins had no oil in their lamps, and the call came at midnight to go out and meet the bridegroom: *And the foolish said unto the wise, Give us of your oil; for our lamps are gone out. 9 But the wise answered, saying, Not so; lest there be not enough for us and you: but go ye rather to them that sell, and buy for yourselves. 10 And while they went to buy, the bridegroom came; and they that were ready went in with him to the marriage: and the door was shut. 11 Afterward came also the other virgins, saying, Lord, Lord, open to us. 12 But he answered and said, Verily I say unto you, I know you not.13 Watch therefore, for ye know neither the day nor the hour wherein the Son of man cometh* (Matthew 25:8-13). This parable is for the Church, warning all people that they must be ready when the Lord comes for His Church. He will come quickly, and those not ready will be shut out of heaven and the marriage.

The Lord tells us what will happen when He comes for the rapture: *Then shall two be in the field; the one shall be taken, and the other left. 41 Two women shall be grinding at the mill; the one shall be taken, and the other left. 42 Watch therefore: for ye know not what hour your Lord doth come. 43 But know this, that if the goodman of the house had known in what watch the thief would come, he would have watched, and would not have suffered his house to be broken up. 44 Therefore be ye also ready: for in such an hour as ye think not the Son of man cometh* (Matthew 24:40-44). The separation between the saints and the wicked will be made. Two will be in the field. One will be taken in the rapture and the other left. Two women will be grinding at the mill. One will be taken and one left behind to suffer the wrath of God.

There is not going to be opportunity for the lost person who is not ready for the Lord's coming to get saved. The Lord said it would be as it was in the days of Noah. God told Noah and his family to get in the Ark, and God shut the door. The earth was cleansed by the flood. That evil generation was caught by surprise and perished. Jesus warned in Matthew 24:37: *But as the days of Noah were, so shall also the coming of the Son of man be.* Jesus told us what those days would be like in verse 38. *For as in the days that were before the flood they were eating and drinking, marrying and giving in marriage, until the day that Noe entered into the ark.* The unrighteous in the days of Noah did not believe that the judgment was coming, therefore they perished; verse 39: *And knew not until the flood came, and took them all away; so shall also the coming of the Son of man be.* Jesus said the unrighteous will have the same unbelief when He returns. Noah and his family were in the Ark above the water and the flood took the wicked away. When the Lord comes at the last trump, the saints will be caught up unto the Lord's chambers and will be safe, the same as Noah, while those who are left will perish. After the rapture, only those who do not worship the beast and believe Jesus is the Messiah will be spared to go into the millennium. The rest will be destroyed from the earth.

Those who are not ready for the Lord's coming at their death will not be ready for His coming at the resurrection. Only those who are saved and whose names are written in the book of life will hear the trumpet of the Lord and His voice in the resurrection. Those who are not ready for the Lord's coming in their death will be in the resurrection of the unjust at the great white throne judgment, which takes place at the end of the millennium. All the unsaved will be resurrected and judged and cast into the lake of fire where the Devil, the beast, and the false prophet are. This is the second death (Revelation 20:10-15, 21:8).

Many who died throughout the Church age were religious, but not saved. They will not be ready for the coming of the Lord because they followed a religion that was antichrist. These churches teach doctrines of men, not according to the Word of God. There are many over these two thousand years who started out right but did not continue in the faith. Some followed John and the disciples for a while, but turned back. God's people are commanded to continue in the faith: *Little children, it is the last time: and as ye have heard that antichrist shall come, even now are there many antichrists; whereby we know that it is the last time. 19 They went out from us, but they were not of us; for if they had been of us, they would no doubt have continued with us: but they went out, that they might be made manifest that they were not all of us* (I John 2:18-19).

Professing Christians who will not believe the true gospel are not ready for the Lord's coming. Those who turn to another gospel will be accursed. It is very important that each professing Christian search for truth concerning true doctrine and the way of salvation. There is only one true gospel of salvation by faith alone in Christ, and not by good works. The Christian is justified by faith. Paul marveled at the Galatian Church, because they were so quickly moved from truth (Galatians 1:6-9).

Seven times Jesus said to the seven churches of Asia, *He that hath an ear let him hear, what the Spirit saith unto the churches.* Jesus told every church the blessings of the obedient, and the judgment for those churches who did not repent and overcome their sinful ways. Jesus warned the church of Ephesus about their first love. Jesus asked them to repent and do the first work, or else He would come unto them quickly. Jesus is not teaching an any-minute coming of the Lord. He is talking about the suddenness of His coming in judgment if they don't repent: *Nevertheless I have somewhat against thee, because thou hast left thy first love. 5 Remember therefore from whence thou art fallen, and repent, and do the first works; or else I will come unto thee quickly, and will remove thy candlestick out of his place, except thou repent. 6 But this thou hast, that thou hatest the deeds of the Nicolaitanes, which I also hate. 7 He that hath an ear, let him hear what the Spirit saith unto the churches; To him that overcometh will I give to eat of the tree of life, which is in the midst of the paradise of God* (Revelation 2:4-7).

The message that Jesus gave to the seven churches of Asia can be applied to the Church today because He knew those local churches would not exist in our day, therefore, the quickness of His coming applies to all generations. Consider what Jesus told the church of Thyatira. He rebuked them for letting Jezebel, who called herself a prophetess, teach them to commit fornication and to eat things sacrificed to idols. The Lord gave Jezebel and her children time to repent, but they did not. Then Jesus told them in verse 25: *But that which ye have already hold fast till I come.* Jesus is telling God's people of all generations there is not going to be time to get things right with God after death or at His coming, both come quickly (Revelation 2:18-26).

Jesus told the church of Philadelphia that He would come quickly. We know that the church of Philadelphia does not exist today; therefore Jesus is telling God's people of all ages to be ready because His judgments will come without warning on the world or to a backslidden Church. The Church is to hold this message fast. Jesus is not teaching a pretribulation rapture, but the quickness of His coming: *Behold, I come quickly: hold that fast which thou hast, that no man take thy crown* (Revelation 3:11).

It would be senseless for Jesus to tell only Israel that He was going to come quickly in Revelation 22:7 if the Church had already been raptured. Jesus is talking to the Church because the rapture does not take place in the chapter 4, but at the seventh trumpet: *Behold, I come quickly: blessed is he that keepeth the sayings of the prophecy of this book* (Revelation 22:7). *And, behold, I come quickly; and my reward is with me, to give every man according as his work shall be (Revelation 22:12).*

All of Revelation is to be taught to the Church because it concerns the Church. Those who teach that the rapture takes place in Revelation chapter 4 and say the Church is not mentioned again need to take note of this next verse. God's people should obey the Word and not man's doctrine: *I Jesus have sent mine angel to testify unto you these things in the churches. I am the root and the offspring of David, and the bright and morning star (Revelation 22:16).*

The final words the Lord gave John were that He was going to come "quickly." I pray God's people now better understand what the word means: *He which testifieth these things saith, Surely I come quickly. Amen. Even so, come, Lord Jesus (Revelation 22:20).*

The saints are warned to be ready for the Lord's coming in Matthew 24:44. Why would they be warned to be ready if the Lord had raptured the Church seven years earlier? *Therefore be ye also ready: for in such an hour as ye think not the Son of man cometh* (Matthew 24:44).

When Jesus ascended into heaven, the two men in white apparel standing by the disciples explained to them concerning how Jesus is going to come: *Which also said, Ye men of Galilee, why stand ye gazing up into heaven? this same Jesus, which is taken up from you into heaven, shall so come in like manner as ye have seen him go into heaven* (Acts 1:11). Every generation is to watch and be ready for the Lord's coming. Jesus warned His people to watch and not let that day come as a thief in the night, for we are of the day. Waiting for the coming of the Lord is like a relay race where the Word of God is the baton. Each member of the relay team is to pass the Gospel to the next member until the last member is added to the race. Then Jesus will come. I believe in this generation we are getting close to the last runners of the team. Every generation that is on the team has been instructed how to run the race, and to look for that blessed hope and glorious appearing of our savior Jesus Christ at the end of the journey. Every runner who has died while running the race will be resurrected to be with the last runners and they will finish the race together. Every team member will be greeted by Jesus Himself at the finish line. Paul instructs each runner how they must conduct themselves in the race. We are to be looking and ready for the Lord's coming: *Teaching us that, denying ungodliness and worldly lusts, we should live soberly, righteously, and godly, in this present world; 13 Looking for that blessed hope, and the glorious appearing of the great God and our Saviour Jesus Christ; 14 Who gave himself for us, that he might redeem us from all iniquity, and purify unto himself a peculiar people, zealous of good works. 15 These things speak, and exhort, and rebuke with all authority. Let no man despise thee* (Titus 2:12-15).

THE TRIBULATION PERIOD

The Church should understand the tribulation period and how it will affect the Church. Pretribulationists say that the tribulation period is the wrath of God on those who are left on earth after the rapture of the Church. There is not one word in the Bible that tells the Church that the entire tribulation period is the wrath of God. The wrath of God comes at the end of the tribulation period upon the beast and unbelieving world. Whether or not the Church goes through the tribulation is not the issue. It is a question of what the Word of God teaches about when the rapture takes place. We need to earnestly seek out the Word and will of God; truth always sets free. Those who perish in God's wrath will perish because they loved not the truth that they might be saved: *Even him, whose coming is after the working of Satan with all power and signs and lying wonders, 10 And with all deceivableness of unrighteousness in them that perish; because they received not the love of the truth, that they might be saved. 11 And for this cause God shall send them strong delusion, that they should believe a lie: 12 That they all might be damned who believed not the truth, but had pleasure in unrighteousness* (II Thessalonians 2:9-12).

The tribulation period is the time fulfilling Daniel's seventieth week (Daniel 9:27). Jesus told His disciples about the events that were to come upon the earth in Matthew 24:21: *For then shall be great tribulation, such as was not since the beginning of the world to this time, no, nor ever shall be.* The tribulation period will be a time of making a choice of whether a person will believe and serve the Lord, or will bow to the beast and worship him as God. It will be a time for Jewish eyes to be opened, and salvation given to all who will believe that Jesus is the Messiah. Israel, which was broken off as a nation because of unbelief, will be grafted back into the Body of Christ at that time. I will give details on this subject later.

When Paul said in Romans 11:23 that God was able to graft Israel back into the Body of Christ, he was referring to the fulfillment of Isaiah 66:7-9. It was the suffering of World War II that made the Jews determined to return to their land after being dispersed in A.D. 70. Israel became a nation again in 1948. The opening of the sixth seal will play an important part in the judgment of those nations that attack Israel, the apple of God's eye. It will be the travail of Ezekiel 38 and 39 that will bring Israel to the light. Their eyes will be opened, and they will see that Jesus was the savior and Messiah. The 144,000 of all the tribes of Israel, the first fruits, will be grafted back into the Body of Christ before the trumpet judgments start in the eighth chapter of Revelation. Jesus was brought forth before her pain, but the pain of the tribulation period will cause her to bring forth children unto God: *Before she travailed, she brought forth; before her pain came, she was delivered of a man child.8 Who hath heard such a thing? who hath seen such things? Shall the earth be made to bring forth in one day? or shall a nation be born at once? for as soon as Zion travailed, she brought forth her children. 9 Shall I bring to the birth, and not cause to bring forth? saith the LORD: shall I cause to bring forth, and shut the womb? saith thy God* (Isaiah 66:7-9).

The tribulation period will be a time when both Jewish and Gentile Christians will understand what has been prophesied about Daniel's 70th week and the Lord's coming. The Jewish Christians in Israel will understand the part of Matthew 24 that applies to them, but the Gentile Christians will also understand the time element of the Lord's coming as recorded in Matthew 24:15-44.

The tribulation period will be the time when the Jews and the Gentile Church will be suffering by the hands of the Devil, the beast, and the false prophet. The beast will make war with the two witnesses and kill them: *And when they shall have finished their testimony, the beast that ascendeth out of the bottomless pit shall make war against them, and shall overcome them, and kill them* (Revelation 11:7). It will be a time when the Devil will make war with the remnant of Israel who have been grafted back into the Body of Christ, and have a testimony of Jesus Christ. The woman is Israel: *And the dragon was wroth with the woman, and went to make war with the remnant of her seed, which keep the commandments of God, and have the testimony of Jesus Christ* (Revelation 12:17).

It also will be a time when the beast makes war against the Church and demands God's people worship him as God. It will be a time of decision, and most who do not have their names written in the book of life will worship the beast. The saints are to be patient and have faith when the beast makes war on the saints: *And it was given unto him to make war with the saints, and to overcome them: and power was given him over all kindreds, and tongues, and nations. 8 And all that dwell upon the earth shall worship him, whose names are not written in the book of life of the Lamb slain from the foundation of the world. 9 If any man have an ear, let him hear. 10 He that leadeth into captivity shall go into captivity: he that killeth with the sword must be killed with the sword. Here is the patience and the faith of the saints* (Revelation 13:7-10).

The false prophet will give power to the beast, and will cause all those who do not understand to worship the beast. The false prophet will deceive many by those miracles which he has power to do. God's word tells us that His people should understand these things and not be in darkness (Revelation 13:11-18).

Saints will overcome the Devil just as Jesus overcame him in the wilderness. Saints will overcome just as the early Church and all other saints down through the Church age, who have suffered and given their lives for Christ. When the Devil is cast out of heaven and comes down to earth, God will give His saints the grace that is needed in that hour just as in the early Church. A young man who was sentenced to be burned at the stake cried to Polycarp in agony when he burnt his hand. "How can I stand it, this little burn hurts so bad?" Polycarp looked at the young man and replied, "God will give grace when that hour comes." God will not forsake his children in the hour of the tribulation, but will give them the grace to endure, and overcome (Revelation 12:7-11).

The beast will enter the temple and demand he be worshipped as God. He will stop the offering of sacrifices in the temple. From that point to his end will be three and one-half years: *And arms shall stand on his part, and they shall pollute the sanctuary of strength, and shall take away the daily sacrifice, and they shall place the abomination that maketh desolate* (Daniel 11:31). *And from the time that the daily sacrifice shall be taken away, and the abomination that maketh desolate set up, there shall be a thousand two hundred and ninety days* (Daniel 12:11).

The beast will come to his end at Jerusalem, the city of David, where Jesus paid the price for our sins: *And he shall plant the tabernacles of his palace between the seas in the glorious holy mountain; yet he shall come to his end, and none shall help him* (Daniel 11:45).

I believe the following Scriptures identify the false prophet as coming out of Rome, because Rome is built on seven hills. The woman in Revelation is the apostate church that will be headed up by the Pope. The Pope will give the beast his power, uniting all religions into a one-world apostate Church. Even Catholic doctrine teaches that an evil Pope will arise in the last days and deceive the people. This apostate church is called the Mother of Harlots, and will sell out to the Devil. Many Protestant Churches will be joined to her again in a united church that will sit on the city that has seven hills. The beast will make war with Jesus, but Jesus will destroy the false prophet and the beast at His coming. Revelation 17 tells of their judgment. The following Scriptures identify the false prophet that sits on the seven hills of Rome: Revelation 17:9 and 14-18.

When I was in my twenties, my Bible was a Scofield and my pastor was a pretribulation rapture preacher. I was teaching a class of young people from Scofield on the coming of Christ. I went to the pastor concerning some of the material of Scofield and his teachings. I began to see some of the things that Scofield was saying concerning the pretribulation rapture theory were not proven by the Scriptures. I began to search the Scriptures on the subject, and in the late 1950s I read II Thessalonians 2:1-12. I read in verse 3 where Paul said, *Let no man deceive you by any means: for that day shall not come, except there come a falling away first, and that man of sin be revealed, the son of perdition;* A strange feeling came over me when I read what the Word said. I saw the difference between what I had been taught about pretribulation rapture and what the Bible was saying. At that time, I did not know about the different teachings concerning the coming of the Lord, but I began to search the Word diligently to find the truth. There were very few books I could find outside the pretribulation rapture theory, therefore it had to be just me and the Bible to find the answer. The more I studied the subject, the more I was convinced pretribulation rapture was not according to the Word of God, but was a doctrine established by Darby and then spread by Scofield.

When I realized that Paul was teaching that the rapture of the Church would be after the apostasy and the man of sin was revealed, I began to realize the great errors that had been made concerning the coming of the Lord, and all the other doctrines that it affected. There is not one Scripture that says there will be a seven-year period between the rapture of the Church and Jesus coming back to earth with His saints. This doctrine and others were formulated by dispensationalists and have no foundation.

The tribulation period is not the wrath of God. The tribulation period comes first, then immediately after the tribulation, the sun will be darkened, the moon will not give her light, the stars shall fall, and the powers of heaven shall be shaken. Only then will appear the sign of the coming of the Son of Man in the clouds. When the trumpet sounds, the rapture will take place. The wrath of God follows the rapture. Jesus will come on a white horse for the judgment. Revelation 19:11-21 and Revelation 14:14-20 explain how the Lord and His angels will reap the earth after the rapture. Revelation chapters 15 and 16 tell God's people about the seven last plagues or vials that will be world-wide on all the wicked. The sixth vial prepares the way for the kings of the east and the battle of Armageddon. All those who opposed the Lord will be destroyed in the battle of Armageddon. Every false god and religion will be destroyed from the earth. Jesus will reign supreme as King of kings and Lord of lords. The kingdom of Israel will be set up at that time and last for a thousand years. Those who were not in the rapture but did not worship the beast, and survived the wrath of God, will come to Jerusalem and worship the Lord yearly.

One of the great mistakes of those who teach that the tribulation period is the wrath of God is they never go into detail of what the words *tribulation* or *wrath* really mean.

Tribulation comes from the Latin word *Tribulum*. It was a word used in the ancient times that describes a threshing instrument that separates wheat from the chaff.

The Great Tribulation will be a time when man will choose to serve Christ, or follow the man of sin. When Jesus comes, He will separate the chaff from the wheat, gather the wheat into His garner, and burn the chaff. God has not promised His saints that He would deliver them from tribulation or the Great Tribulation, but He did promise to deliver them from His wrath: *Whose fan is in his hand, and he will thoroughly purge his floor, and gather his wheat into the garner; but he will burn up the chaff with unquenchable fire. Zephaniah 2:1-3: Gather yourselves together, yea, gather together, O nation not desired; 2 Before the decree bring forth, before the day pass as the chaff, before the fierce anger of the LORD come upon you, before the day of the LORD'S anger come upon you. 3 Seek ye the LORD, all ye meek of the earth, which have wrought his judgment; seek righteousness, seek meekness: it may be ye shall be hid in the day of the LORD'S anger* (Matthew 3:1).

I give detail later in the book concerning the wrath of God on a sinful world, but His wrath will never be on His people. I want to clearly show the difference in meaning between the word *tribulation* and the word *wrath*. These two words do not have the same meaning, yet nearly all who teach a pretribulation rapture call the entire tribulation period the wrath of God. Here is the meaning of the word, *wrath*.

Wrath—Strong vengeful anger or indignation. Retributory punishment for an offense or crime. Divine chastisement.

- To say that the tribulation period is the wrath of God is misleading to believers.
- Tribulation and wrath of God must be looked at individually, so we will not be misled in God's Word.

God's people should be able to distinguish between the word tribulation and the wrath of God. The following Scripture has been used by pretribulationists trying to prove a pretribulation rapture, but this verse is not calling the whole tribulation period the wrath of God. The day of the Lord is the beginning of the wrath of God (Rev. 11:18). The rapture comes first at the seventh trump, and then the wrath of God is poured out. The fifth chapter of I Thessalonians is telling the saints they should not be in darkness about the Day of the Lord, but should be ready for the rapture before God pours out His wrath: *For God hath not appointed us to wrath, but to obtain salvation by our Lord Jesus Christ* (I Thessalonians 5:9). The tribulation period will be a time of the beast and the false prophet pouring out their satanic wrath on man. At the end of the tribulation period the Lord will come to be glorified in the saints, and then pour out His wrath on those who are not ready for His coming. Paul makes this plain in II Thessalonians 1:7-10: *And to you who are troubled rest with us, when the Lord Jesus shall be revealed from heaven with his mighty angels, 8 In flaming fire taking vengeance on them that know not God, and that obey not the gospel of our Lord Jesus Christ: 9 Who shall be punished with everlasting destruction from the presence of the Lord, and from the glory of his power; 10 When he shall come to be glorified in his saints, and to be admired in all them that believe (because our testimony among you was believed) in that day.*

I Thessalonians 5 is about the Day of the Lord that comes at the end of the tribulation period, and it does not call the whole tribulation period the wrath of God. It is telling God's people that God did not appoint them to His wrath or hell, because He gave them salvation by the Lord Jesus Christ. When Noah got into the Ark and God shut the door, the wrath of God followed. When Lot and his family were safely out of Sodom, the wrath of God followed. In the tribulation period, God will give grace to those who give their lives for Christ. God seals the 144,000 thousand before the seven trumpet judgments begin. God's grace and salvation will be available for all who will believe and be saved. The wrath of God comes after the rapture in the seventh trumpet, and then God will pour out His wrath with the seven last vials and the battle of Armageddon (Revelation 16:1-21). In the middle of the chapter 16, Jesus spoke these words, verse 15: *Behold, I come as a thief. Blessed is he that watcheth, and keepeth his garments, lest he walk naked, and they see his shame.* Jesus put this verse in the middle of this chapter as a warning to God's people to watch, and keep themselves from evil. The Lord is warning His Church in this Scripture so they will be ready for the coming of the Lord, because God has not appointed them to wrath.

Isaiah gives us a Scripture concerning the resurrection and the wrath of God: *Hell from beneath is moved for thee to meet thee at thy coming: it stirreth up the dead for thee, even all the chief ones of the earth; it hath raised up from their thrones all the kings of the nations* (Isaiah 14:9).

THE CHURCH
WILL SUFFER
TRIBULATION

It is very important that God's people understand the difference between the wrath of the beast and the wrath of God. Pretribulationists have planted fear in the hearts and minds of God's people about how the wrath of God covers all the tribulation period and will be so terrible on those left behind after the rapture of the Church. It's time God's people understand the truth of when the Lord will come, and how God will never forsake His people in tribulation, or the tribulation period. This chapter clears up the misunderstandings.

Tribulation Scriptures tell us that we will have tribulation. How can the Church prepare to suffer the Great Tribulation if the Church does not teach the saints the truth? The following Scriptures need to be taught in this generation. The Gospels, Epistles, and Revelation teach that the Church will have tribulation. Preachers need to prepare the Church for the tribulation period and the trials that lie ahead for them: *These things I have spoken unto you, that in me ye might have peace. In the world ye shall have tribulation: but be of good cheer; I have overcome the world* (John 16:33). *And not only so, but we glory in tribulations also: knowing that tribulation worketh patience* (Romans 5:3). *Who shall separate us from the love of Christ? shall tribulation, or distress, or persecution, or famine, or nakedness, or peril, or sword?* (Romans 8:35). *Who comforteth us in all our tribulation, that we may be able to comfort them which are in any trouble, by the comfort wherewith we ourselves are comforted of God* (II Corinthians 1:4).

Great is my boldness of speech toward you, great is my glorying of you: I am filled with comfort, I am exceeding joyful in all our tribulation (II Corinthians 7:4).

The early Church in the book of Acts is filled with the accounts of the disciples suffering tribulation at the hands of wicked religious leaders and evil men. Do those who today teach a pretribulation rapture count themselves better than those who suffered for Christ during the early days of the Church when the disciples suffered great persecution? All but John gave their lives for Christ, and he was thrown into a pot of hot oil. Why do pretribulationists think it impossible for the Church to suffer in the tribulation period by the hands of the beast and false prophet? The early Church grew under persecution, and the Church will also become bold and strong during the tribulation period. Under persecution the Church has always been purified and made stronger. When you read the following Scripture in Acts, can you then say that this is the wrath of God on His people? If you cannot call this the wrath of God, neither can you call the tribulation period the wrath of God when the beast and the ungodly are persecuting the saints. Please read every Scripture concerning the early church, because it will change your thinking about God's people suffering tribulation.

Acts 4:1-4:

And as they spake unto the people, the priests, and the captain of the temple, and the Sadducees, came upon them,2 Being grieved that they taught the people, and preached through Jesus the resurrection from the dead. 3 And they laid hands on them, and put them in hold unto the next day: for it was now eventide. 4 Howbeit many of them which heard the word believed; and the number of the men was about five thousand.

Acts 5:17-20:

Then the high priest rose up, and all they that were with him, (which is the sect of the Sadducees,) and were filled with indignation, 18 And laid their hands on the apostles, and put them in the common prison. 19 But the angel of the Lord by night opened the prison doors, and brought them forth, and said, 20 Go, stand and speak in the temple to the people all the words of this life.

Acts 7:54-60:

When they heard these things, they were cut to the heart, and they gnashed on him with their teeth. 55 But he, being full of the Holy Ghost, looked up stedfastly into heaven, and saw the glory of God, and Jesus standing on the right hand of God, 56 And said, Behold, I see the heavens opened, and the Son of man standing on the right hand of God. 57 Then they cried out with a loud voice, and stopped their ears, and ran upon him with one accord, 58 And cast him out of the city, and stoned him: and the witnesses laid down their clothes at a young man's feet, whose name was Saul. 59 And they stoned Stephen, calling upon God, and saying, Lord Jesus, receive my spirit. 60 And he kneeled down, and cried with a loud voice, Lord, lay not this sin to their charge. And when he had said this, he fell asleep.

Acts 8:1-4:

And Saul was consenting unto his death. And at that time there was a great persecution against the church which was at Jerusalem; and they were all scattered abroad throughout the regions of Judaea and Samaria, except the apostles. 2 And devout men carried Stephen to his burial, and made great lamentation over him. 3 As for Saul, he made havock of the church, entering into every house, and haling men and women committed them to prison. 4 Therefore they that were scattered abroad went every where preaching the word.

Acts 11:19-21:

Now they which were scattered abroad upon the persecution that arose about Stephen travelled as far as Phenice, and Cyprus, and Antioch, preaching the word to none but unto the Jews only. 20 And some of them were men of Cyprus and Cyrene, which, when they were come to Antioch, spake unto the Grecians, preaching the Lord Jesus. 21 And the hand of the Lord was with them: and a great number believed, and turned unto the Lord.

Acts 12:1-4:

Now about that time Herod the king stretched forth his hands to vex certain of the church. 2 And he killed James the brother of

John with the sword. 3 And because he saw it pleased the Jews, he proceeded further to take Peter also. (Then were the days of unleavened bread.) 4 And when he had apprehended him, he put him in prison, and delivered him to four quaternions of soldiers to keep him; intending after Easter to bring him forth to the people.

Acts 13:50-53:

But the Jews stirred up the devout and honourable women, and the chief men of the city, and raised persecution against Paul and Barnabas, and expelled them out of their coasts. 51 But they shook off the dust of their feet against them, and came unto Iconium. 52 And the disciples were filled with joy, and with the Holy Ghost.

Those who believe in a pretribulation rapture should look at what happened to Paul. This is no different than what the Church will suffer during the tribulation period. Paul said we enter into the kingdom of God through much tribulation: *And there came thither certain Jews from Antioch and Iconium, who persuaded the people, and, having stoned Paul, drew him out of the city, supposing he had been dead. 20 Howbeit, as the disciples stood round about him, he rose up, and came into the city: and the next day he departed with Barnabas to Derbe. 21 And when they had preached the gospel to that city, and had taught many, they returned again to Lystra, and to Iconium, and Antioch, 22 Confirming the souls of the disciples, and exhorting them to continue in the faith, and that we must through much tribulation enter into the kingdom of God. Acts 21:30-33: And all the city was moved, and the people ran together: and they took Paul, and drew him out of the temple: and forthwith the doors were shut. 31 And as they went about to kill him, tidings came unto the chief captain of the band, that all Jerusalem was in an uproar. 32 Who immediately took soldiers and centurions, and ran down unto them: and when they saw the chief captain and the soldiers, they left beating of Paul. 33 Then the chief captain came near, and took him, and commanded him to be bound with two chains; and demanded who he was, and what he had done* (Acts 14:19-22).

I cannot see how anyone could have read the history in the book of Acts concerning the persecution of the early Church, or read *Fox's Book of Martyrs* without it changing their thinking about the Church and the tribulation period. None of these saints suffered the wrath of God, neither will the saints in the tribulation period suffer the wrath of God. Paul is letting the Church of the Thessalonians know that the Church will suffer tribulation, but not the wrath of God. Paul assures the saints why they will suffer tribulation even up to the time of the coming of Lord. The following Scripture immediately precedes the rapture of the Church in the fourth chapter of I Thessalonians. Paul was not trying to frighten the Church, but they needed to know that saints are appointed to affliction and tribulation, and Paul gives them this information before he revealed the rapture of the Church in I Thessalonians 4:13-18. Pretribulationists disregard, or explain away, the verses Paul gave to the Church about suffering tribulation. Paul instructed them not to be moved by these afflictions, but is telling them that saints have been appointed to suffer tribulation. We should not teach a doctrine designed to hide these truths from the Church: *Wherefore when we could no longer forbear, we thought it good to be left at Athens alone; 2 And sent Timothy, our brother, and minister of God, and our fellow laborer in the gospel of Christ, to establish you, and to comfort you concerning your faith: 3 That no man should be moved by these afflictions: for yourselves know that we are appointed thereunto. 4 For verily, when we were with you, we told you before that we should suffer tribulation; even as it came to pass, and ye know. 13 To the end he may stablish your hearts unblameable in holiness before God, even our Father, at the coming of our Lord Jesus Christ with all his saints* (I Thessalonians 3:1-4, 13).

The tribulation saints will come through the terrible time of persecution the same as Old Testament saints came through times of severe persecution and testing of their faith. It is faith that brings every generation to victory, as the book of Hebrews records. God is showing all dispensations that God's people will suffer great persecution and tribulation, but it is faith that keeps them, and brings them through to victory. It will be faith that brings the tribulation saints to victory, and they will see the glorious appearing of our Lord Jesus Christ. Read the account of those saints in Hebrews 11:30-40.

Saints are told they will suffer tribulation from Genesis to Revelation. Over and over the Lord gives comfort to those who suffer in tribulation. It is wicked to tell the Church they will escape the tribulation period when God wants to prepare them. The Church needs truth, not a myth. The Church needs to be comforted through the following verses by seeing how God will be with them, and has promised to come in flaming fire, taking vengeance on them that know not God: Revelation 1:9, II Thessalonians. 1:3-9.

There is already an increase in earthquakes, floods, fires, epidemics, and disease. These disasters will increase until Jesus comes. God's people need to know how to deal with those things that are coming upon the earth. The Gospel of Matthew tells what to look for in these last days: *And ye shall hear of wars and rumours of wars: see that ye be not troubled: for all these things must come to pass, but the end is not yet. 7 For nation shall rise against nation, and kingdom against kingdom: and there shall be famines, and pestilences, and earthquakes, in divers places. 8 All these are the beginning of sorrows* (Matthew 24:6-8).

There will be many disasters that will come on the earth that Christians will face. When pretribulationists tell the Church that they will be raptured before the tribulation and it does not happen, when all these things begin to come upon the world, the faith of many will be shaken. Jesus told us with His own mouth that we would not see Him coming in the clouds until after the tribulation. I have chosen to believe what Jesus said in His word: *And there shall be signs in the sun, and in the moon, and in the stars; and upon the earth distress of nations, with perplexity; the sea and the waves roaring; 26 Men's hearts failing them for fear, and for looking after those things which are coming on the earth: for the powers of heaven shall be shaken. 27 And then shall they see the Son of man coming in a cloud with power and great glory. 28 And when these things begin to come to pass, then look up, and lift up your heads; for your redemption draweth nigh* (Luke 21:25-28).

Ezekiel 14 is an edifying chapter that shows the Church how God protects His people when these four judgments come upon the land because of sin. These judgments have come upon parts of the world before, and they will come again. The prophet uses Noah, Daniel, and Job concerning the righteous, because God wants His people to know that by using these three men, God's grace is spread across all dispensations. These Scriptures can be applied to the tribulation saints, also. God always protects and delivers His saints. God has promised to be with His people in famine. The righteous will not perish by the hand of God: *Son of man, when the land sinneth against me by trespassing grievously, then will I stretch out mine hand upon it, and will break the staff of the bread thereof, and will send famine upon it, and will cut off man and beast from it: 14 Though these three men, Noah, Daniel, and Job, were in it, they should deliver but their own souls by their righteousness, saith the Lord GOD* (Ezekiel 14:13-14:).

When noisome beasts plague the land, God has given us His word, assuring us that He will keep us in those terrible times: *If I cause noisome beasts to pass through the land, and they spoil it, so that it be desolate, that no man may pass through because of the beasts: 16 Though these three men were in it, as I live, saith the Lord GOD, they shall deliver neither sons nor daughters; they only shall be delivered, but the land shall be desolate* (Ezekiel 14:15-16).

When war comes, as the Lord said it would in Matthew 24, God has promised He will not forsake us: *Or if I bring a sword upon that land, and say, Sword, go through the land; so that I cut off man and beast from it: 18 Though these three men were in it, as I live, saith the Lord GOD, they shall deliver neither sons nor daughters, but they only shall be delivered themselves* (Ezekiel 14:17-18).

When pestilence increases, as Jesus said it will, we should understand that it is coming upon the earth because of great sin. It will be as it was when God destroyed Sodom and Gomorrah. Pestilence is a contagious or infectious epidemic disease that is virulent and devastating. It is a disease such as bubonic plague, or AIDS, which medicine will not cure. When these things come upon the earth, we will have prayer and faith for our protection and security. God's people will be protected because of their faith in the great physician (Jesus): *Or if I send a pestilence into that land, and pour out my fury upon it in blood, to cut off from it man and beast: 20 Though Noah, Daniel, and Job, were in it, as I live, saith the Lord GOD, they shall deliver neither son nor daughter; they shall but deliver their own souls by their righteousness* (Ezekiel 14:19-20).

Our trust must be in the Lord when these four judgments come upon the earth because of a sinful world. God's people need to be aware of what is to come upon the earth. God is the same yesterday, today, and forever. He does not change concerning His promises. His promises to His people will still be the same in the tribulation period: *For thus saith the Lord GOD; How much more when I send my four sore judgments upon Jerusalem, the sword, and the famine, and the noisome beast, and the pestilence, to cut off from it man and beast? 22 Yet, behold, therein shall be left a remnant that shall be brought forth, both sons and daughters: behold, they shall come forth unto you, and ye shall see their way and their doings: and ye shall be comforted concerning the evil that I have brought upon Jerusalem, even concerning all that I have brought upon it* (Ezekiel 14:21-22).

God has promised not to forsake those who are in tribulation in the latter days:

But if from thence thou shalt seek the LORD thy God, thou shalt find him, if thou seek him with all thy heart and with all thy soul. 30 When thou art in tribulation, and all these things are come upon thee, even in the latter days, if thou turn to the LORD thy God, and shalt be obedient unto his voice; 31 (For the LORD thy God is a merciful God;) he will not forsake thee, neither destroy thee, nor forget the covenant of thy fathers which he sware unto them (Deuteronomy 4:29-31).

THE WRATH
OF GOD

God will never let the saints suffer His wrath. Pretribulationists use this one verse in I Thessalonians 5:9 to teach their students they will miss the tribulation period, because God has not appointed us to wrath. Paul is not telling the Thessalonians they will miss the great tribulation period, but Paul is saying God has given them salvation so they will not suffer the wrath of God in Revelation 16:1-21 and in Revelation 19:11-16. God does not appoint His people to wrath or hell, because He gives them salvation. This verse has nothing to do with the saints missing the tribulation period: *For God hath not appointed us to wrath, but to obtain salvation by our Lord Jesus Christ* (I Thessalonians 5:9).

Paul let the Thessalonian church know how God had turned them from idols to serve the living God. The following verses will again show God's people that they can suffer tribulation, but because of the resurrection of Jesus, they will be delivered from His wrath or punishment. God will let the saints go through the tribulation, but he will not let them suffer His wrath or hell because He gave them salvation. Verse 10 shows plainly that I Thessalonians 5:9 is not about the saints avoiding the tribulation period, but is telling the saints they will not suffer God's wrath in the judgment because Jesus had already saved them: *And ye became followers of us, and of the Lord, having received the word in much affliction, with joy of the Holy Ghost: 7 So that ye were ensamples to all that believe in Macedonia and Achaia. 8 For from you sounded out the word of the Lord not only in Macedonia and Achaia, but also in every place your faith to God-ward is spread abroad; so that we need not to speak any thing. 9 For they themselves show of us what manner of entering in we had unto you, and how ye turned to God from idols to serve the living and true God; 10 And to wait for his Son from heaven, whom he raised from the dead, even Jesus, which delivered us from the wrath to come* (I Thessalonians 1:6-10).

The Scripture above does not show a deliverance from the tribulation period, but a deliverance from the judgment to come at the appearing of our Lord Jesus Christ. Saints will come with Jesus to receive our resurrected bodies. This is our hope, joy and rejoicing: *For what is our hope, or joy, or crown of rejoicing? Are not even ye in the presence of our Lord Jesus Christ at his coming? 20 For ye are our glory and joy* (I Thessalonians 2:19-20).

God's people are to abound and increase in love until Jesus comes so we will be unblameable and holy before God at the coming of our Lord Jesus Christ with all His saints. Paul gave the Thessalonian Church this charge just before he gave them the true doctrine concerning the rapture: *And the Lord make you to increase and abound in love one toward another, and toward all men, even as we do toward you: 13 To the end he may stablish your hearts unblameable in holiness before God, even our Father, at the coming of our Lord Jesus Christ with all his saints* (I Thessalonians 3:12-13).

Paul gives the saints a revelation concerning those who have died in the Lord and those who are living when Jesus appears. There is not one word below in these verses concerning a pretribulation rapture of the Church. Paul gives the time element in I Corinthians 15:51-53; I Thessalonians 5:1-10, and II Thessalonians 1:3-10; 2:1-5. If Jesus came a different time than what His Word reveals, it would break His Word, and we all know that cannot be. The Bible does not teach Jesus can come at any moment before the tribulation period. This theory was developed by Darby and Scofield, and the errors they made can be eliminated when pretribulationists accept the time element Paul gives for the Lord's coming in II Thessalonians 2:1-3, and Jesus in Matthew 24:29-31. These scriptures give the time element for I Thessalonians 4:13-18: *But I would not have you to be ignorant, brethren, concerning them which are asleep, that ye sorrow not, even as others which have no hope.14 For if we believe that Jesus died and rose again, even so them also which sleep in Jesus will God bring with him. 15 For this we say unto you by the word of the Lord, that we which are alive and remain unto the coming of the Lord shall not prevent them which are asleep. 16 For the Lord himself shall descend from heaven with a shout, with the voice of the archangel, and with the trump of God: and the dead in Christ shall rise first: 17 Then we which are alive and remain shall be caught up together with them in the clouds, to meet the Lord in the air: and so shall we ever be with the Lord. 18 Wherefore comfort one another with these words.*

God chose Israel, and spoke unto them by the mouth of the prophets. Old and New Testament Scriptures let us know that the saints will be safe in heaven when God pours out His wrath on earth. Daniel 12:1 tells about the tribulation period and how everyone written in the book of life will be delivered, and in verse 2 tells about the resurrection. Zephaniah 2:1-3 says to seek the Lord before the day of the Lord so the saints will be hid in the day of the Lord's anger. Isaiah 26:17-21 tells about the tribulation period, the resurrection, and in verse 20 tells God's people to enter into their chambers and shut the door for a little moment until the indignation be overpast. These Old Testament scriptures are just shadows of the rapture and resurrection of the New Testament.

Jesus spoke to us in these last days and gave light to the shadows concerning His coming, the rapture and resurrection. He told the disciples that at the end of the tribulation period all things which were written would be fulfilled, and immediately after the tribulation period they would see the Son of Man coming in the clouds, and He would gather the elect from the four winds. Paul's second letter to the Thessalonians let them know that the coming of the Lord and our gathering together unto Him would not take place until the apostasy came and the man of sin be revealed. The Revelation let us know all the shadows of the Old Testament concerning the mystery of God are finished at the last trump as he hath declared to His servants the prophets (Rev. 10:7). After seeing the whole picture in the New Testament, Isaiah's prophecy is no longer a great mystery concerning the tribulation period, the rapture and resurrection, and the day of the Lord which follows: *Like as a woman with child, that draweth near the time of her delivery, is in pain, and crieth out in her pangs; so have we been in thy sight, O LORD.18 We have been with child, we have been in pain, we have as it were brought forth wind; we have not wrought any deliverance in the earth; neither have the inhabitants of the world fallen.19 Thy dead men shall live, together with my dead body shall they arise. Awake and sing, ye that dwell in dust: for thy dew is as the dew of herbs, and the earth shall cast out the dead.20 Come, my people, enter thou into thy chambers, and shut thy doors about thee: hide thyself as it were for a little moment, until the indignation* be overpast.21 For, behold, the LORD cometh out of his place to punish the inhabitants of the earth for their iniquity: the earth also shall disclose her blood, and shall no more cover her slain (Isaiah 26:17-21). In verses 20 and 21 the Lord takes His saints into a place of safety before the wrath of God, just as Noah entered the Ark the same day the rain began. Lot was taken out of Sodom before the judgment fell. Christians were safe in Pella when Jerusalem was destroyed in A.D. 70. The mystery of God will be finished, as He hath declared unto His servants the prophets when the seventh trumpet begins to sound (Rev. 10:7).

God has never sent His wrath and indignation upon His own people. He will keep His word. When the Lord comes to rapture the saints and send His judgments on the wicked, it should not take His people by surprise. Paul tells the church of Thessalonica about the times and seasons of the Lord's coming, because the Lord's coming was not to come on them as a thief. They were to understand the times and the seasons concerning Jesus coming for the saints. The times and seasons were taught in the Old Testament, and taught also by Jesus in the Gospels. Paul is telling them they should know these things already: *But of the times and the seasons, brethren, ye have no need that I write unto you. 2 For yourselves know perfectly that the day of the Lord so cometh as a thief in the night. 3 For when they shall say, Peace and safety; then sudden destruction cometh upon them, as travail upon a woman with child; and they shall not escape. 4 But ye, brethren, are not in darkness, that that day should overtake you as a thief. 5 Ye are all the children of light, and the children of the day: we are not of the night, nor of darkness. 6 Therefore let us not sleep, as do others; but let us watch and be sober. 7 For they that sleep sleep in the night; and they that be drunken are drunken in the night. 8 But let us, who are of the day, be sober, putting on the breastplate of faith and love; and for an helmet, the hope of salvation. 9 For God hath not appointed us to wrath, but to obtain salvation by our Lord Jesus Christ* (I Thessalonians 5:1-9).

In I Thessalonians 5:9, Paul was not talking about God's people being spared from the tribulation period, but that God would spare them from His wrath or judgment because they were already saved. Those saints have been dead for many years—they cannot be in the tribulation period. Therefore, Paul was not talking about the tribulation period as the wrath of God. Paul confirms this again in the book of Romans. He was not talking about God sparing the Church from the tribulation period, but was talking about giving salvation, not the judgment of God. The following verses make this plain. God said He commended His love toward us while we were yet sinners, and that we shall be saved from wrath. We should not twist the Word to fit our doctrine, but let our doctrine conform to the Word: *But God commendeth his love toward us, in that, while we were yet sinners, Christ died for us. 9 Much more then, being now justified by his blood, we shall be saved from wrath through him.10 For if, when we were enemies, we were reconciled to God by the death of his Son, much more, being reconciled, we shall be saved by his life* (Romans 5:8-10).

The saints of all ages, who died for Christ, are crying out to the Lord to avenge their blood (Revelation 6:9-11). These Scriptures below show both groups are of the Church, and of the Body of Christ. Why would they be crying out, if they had already came back to earth to receive their new bodies in the rapture? These saints are told to rest a little season until their fellow servants and brethren be killed as they were. We cannot say those who were killed in the early Church, and the Dark Ages, suffered the wrath of God any more than we can say those killed for Christ in the tribulation period suffer the wrath of God: *And when he had opened the fifth seal, I saw under the altar the souls of them that were slain for the word of God, and for the testimony which they held: 10 And they cried with a loud voice, saying, How long, O Lord, holy and true, dost thou not judge and avenge our blood on them that dwell on the earth? 11 And white robes were given unto every one of them; and it was said unto them, that they should rest yet for a little season, until their fellowservants also and their brethren, that should be killed as they were, should be fulfilled* (Revelation 6:9-11).

Zephaniah also mentions how the saints will be hidden from danger when the Lord pours out His wrath in the day of the Lord: *Gather yourselves together, yea, gather together, O nation not desired; 2 Before the decree bring forth, before the day pass as the chaff, before the fierce anger of the LORD come upon you, before the day of the LORD'S anger come upon you. 3 Seek ye the LORD, all ye meek of the earth, which have wrought his judgment; seek righteousness, seek meekness: it may be ye shall be hid in the day of the LORD'S anger* (Zephaniah 2:1-3). The Lord is our hope; we do not have to fear God in the tribulation period, because He is our refuge (Psalms 46:1-11).

The Lord will gather His saints unto Himself when He comes. The rapture and His devouring fire that goes before Him are not seven years apart. Look at what the Word says. There is not a rapture for the Church before the tribulation period, and then another for the Jews after the tribulation period. There is only one rapture. We are told to look for the signs of His coming mmediately after the tribulation as recorded in Matthew 24. The Psalmist gives us another root in the Old Testament for the rapture, and says the saints will be gathered unto the Lord before His wrath: *A Psalm of Asaph. The mighty God, even the LORD, hath spoken, and called the earth from the rising of the sun unto the going down thereof. 2 Out of Zion, the perfection of beauty, God hath shined. 3 Our God shall come, and shall not keep silence: a fire shall devour before him, and it shall be very tempestuous round about him. 4 He shall call to the heavens from above, and to the earth, that he may judge his people. 5 Gather my saints together unto me; those that have made a covenant with me by sacrifice. 6 And the heavens shall declare his righteousness: for God is judge himself. Selah* (Psalms 50:1-6).

Saints will suffer persecution, and even death by the Devil and evil people in the Church age, but God has never appointed the saved, Jew or Gentile, to wrath. Christians get the victory even in death: *O death, where is thy sting? O grave, where is thy victory? 56 The sting of death is sin; and the strength of sin is the law. 57 But thanks be to God, which giveth us the victory through our Lord Jesus Christ. 58 Therefore, my beloved brethren, be ye stedfast, unmoveable, always abounding in the work of the Lord, forasmuch as ye know that your labour is not in vain in the Lord* (I Cor. 15:55-58). The faithfulness of the saints in the tribulation period will be rewarded at the judgment seat of Christ: *And the great dragon was cast out, that old serpent, called the Devil, and Satan, which deceiveth the whole world: he was cast out into the earth, and his angels were cast out with him. 10 And I heard a loud voice saying in heaven, Now is come salvation, and strength, and the kingdom of our God, and the power of his Christ: for the accuser of our brethren is cast down, which accused them before our God day and night.11 And they overcame him by the blood of the Lamb, and by the word of their testimony; and they loved not their lives unto the death.* (Rev. 12:9-11). We can see the saints are winners even in death in the tribulation period. How could they be delivered if they are suffering the wrath of God? All will be delivered whose names are written in the Book of Life: *And at that time shall Michael stand up, the great prince which standeth for the children of thy people: and there shall be a time of trouble, such as never was since there was a nation even to that same time: and at that time thy people shall be delivered, every one that shall be found written in the book* (Daniel 12:1).

God Will Not Forsake His People

We need to understand that the entire tribulation period is not the wrath of God. It is a time when the seventieth week of Daniel will be fulfilled. It is a time when the last Gentile ruling world power and the false prophet join forces against the true God and His people. It will be a time when the beast persecutes Israel and the saints of God. The Lord will come in the clouds at the end of the seventieth week to rapture the saints, and then will pour out His wrath (Daniel 7:13-14).

God revealed what was going to happen in the last days to Daniel the prophet. Then Daniel revealed to God's people how the beast would make a peace treaty with Israel during the seventieth week of Daniel. Since each day stands for a year, after three and one-half years, the beast will break this treaty and set himself up as God. The beast will try to enforce his worship around the world. He will wage war against the saints, Israel, the two witnesses. The Lord will intervene in the war of the sixth trumpet before all flesh is destroyed and every eye will see the Lord coming in the clouds. The rapture and the resurrection take place at the end of the seventieth week, and not before, as pretribulationists teach. Then occurs the judgment of the beast and the false prophet. The last seven vials and the battle of Armageddon are the wrath of God at the end of the tribulation period. God's wrath at the end of the tribulation period must be separated from the wrath of the beast during the tribulation period. The two are not the same.

The first response for saints when they are told that the Church must go through the tribulation period is unbelief, because they have been taught that the Church will be raptured before the tribulation period. The very thought of the Church going through the tribulation period fills their hearts with fear. When they are told the truth about what Paul said would happen before the Lord comes, they become worried about what the future holds, but preaching a lie does not change what the Word says. The apostasy and the man of sin must be revealed before the rapture of the Church, as Paul stated in II Thessalonians 2:1-5. The Church has not been taught how the Lord will be there to comfort and strengthen the saints. The tribulation period is not going to be a time when every Christian is going to be killed, or starved to death. It will be a time when great victories are won by God's people. It's time to put away the fear that pretribulationists have planted in the minds of God's people about the tribulation period. John said it best: *There is no fear in love; but perfect love casteth out fear: because fear hath torment. He that feareth is not made perfect in love* (I John 4: 18). We need to remember He that is in us is greater than he that is in the world.

The tribulation period will be a golden opportunity for the saints of God, who know the truth, to be witnesses and soul-winners. Our God will supply all our needs according to His riches in glory by Christ Jesus. Daniel said many will be saved and made white during that time. God's people will be able to remind the unsaved that God will bring persecution and wrath upon all those who persecute God's people. Prayer, the Word, and the promises of God will become very important to the saints: *Who shall separate us from the love of Christ? shall tribulation, or distress, or persecution, or famine, or nakedness, or peril, or sword? 36 As it is written, For thy sake we are killed all the day long; we are accounted as sheep for the slaughter. 37 Nay, in all these things we are more than conquerors through him that loved us* (Romans 8:35).

The tribulation period will be a time when the saints' prayers ascend up before God. We are told to pray for our enemies and those who persecute us (Matthew 5:10-11, 44-46; Romans 12:14). Paul said the Church will suffer persecution for the cross of Christ (Galatians 6:12).

God is not going to send His wrath upon His children, because the rapture takes place before the wrath of God. God protects the 144,000 Jews who are sealed in the tribulation period. He keeps the two witnesses until they have completed their ministry. The saints who are in the light will be a light in those troubled times, reminding others how God is bringing judgment on the wicked, and how the saints should be patient until the Lord comes. It will be a glorious time of victory for many saints, because the Lord will overwhelm saints with His love. Their witness will be as strong as Stephen's, when he was martyred: *There will be a great move of the Holy Spirit for the salvation of many* (Acts 7:54-56, 59-60). *And I heard a loud voice saying in heaven, Now is come salvation, and strength, and the kingdom of our God, and the power of his Christ: for the accuser of our brethren is cast down, which accused them before our God day and night. 11 And they overcame him by the blood of the Lamb, and by the word of their testimony; and they loved not their lives unto the death* (Revelation 12:10-11).

Jews who understand and become believers in the Lord will be protected during the tribulation period. The Lord prepared a place for them: *And the woman fled into the wilderness, where she hath a place prepared of God, that they should feed her there a thousand two hundred and threescore days* (Revelation 12:6). Believers should not think they will be helpless, nor that God is going to forsake them in that time of need. The Lord has promised never to leave nor forsake us. Believe His promise and let the Holy Spirit reveal truth (John 14:26). God's people have listened to pretribulationists so long that fear builds up in them at the very thought of going through the tribulation period.

God has never let His people suffer His wrath. He did not let Noah and his family suffer His wrath when He destroyed every living thing that was not on the Ark. He did not let Lot suffer His wrath when He destroyed Sodom, and Gomorrah, and He will not let His people suffer His wrath in the tribulation period, either. God's people will suffer the wrath of the beast and the false prophet, but they will not suffer the wrath of God. Jesus instructed His disciples not to fear what man would do to them, but to respect and fear God because of His awesome power to destroy both the soul and body, and cast them into hell: *And fear not them which kill the body, but are not able to kill the soul: but rather fear him which is able to destroy both soul and body in hell* (Matthew 10:28).

The righteous will not have to fear God in the tribulation period, because the righteous walk with God. Moses instructed the children of Israel not to fear God when He came to prove them, and gave them His

Commandments. God has instructed us in Revelation that we are not to worship the beast or bow down to him. God has already warned us, just as God warned the children of Israel, not to have any other god before Him. God did not come to destroy the children of Israel. He came to prove them: *And Moses said unto the people, Fear not: for God is come to prove you, and that his fear may be before your faces, that ye sin not. 21 And the people stood afar off, and Moses drew near unto the thick darkness where God was. 22 And the LORD said unto Moses, Thus thou shalt say unto the children of Israel, Ye have seen that I have talked with you from heaven. 23 Ye shall not make with me gods of silver, neither shall ye make unto you gods of gold. 24 An altar of earth thou shalt make unto me, and shalt sacrifice thereon thy burnt offerings, and thy peace offerings, thy sheep, and thine oxen: in all places where I record my name I will come unto thee, and I will bless thee* (Exodus 20:20-24).

The tribulation period will be a time of purification for both Jew and Gentile. The righteous will understand because God's people are in the light. It is the wicked who will be in darkness, and not understand: *Many shall be purified, and made white, and tried; but the wicked shall do wickedly: and none of the wicked shall understand; but the wise shall understand* (Daniel 12:10).

Jesus told us we would have tribulation. That is the very reason God gave His people the Word of God so His people would know the truth, and the truth would set them free from fear. God will intervene in the darkest hour, to rapture the Church, and then bring judgment upon a wicked world. God's elect will not be deceived, because they will understand what the Lord said about His coming: *For then shall be great tribulation, such as was not since the beginning of the world to this time, no, nor ever shall be. 22 And except those days should be shortened, there should no flesh be saved: but for the elect's sake those days shall be shortened. 23 Then if any man shall say unto you, Lo, here is Christ, or there; believe it not. 24 For there shall arise false Christs, and false prophets, and shall show great signs and wonders; insomuch that, if it were possible, they shall deceive the very elect. 25 Behold, I have told you before* (Matthew 24:21-25).

The tribulation must come before the rapture of the Church, but God will not forsake His people. Jesus knew what was to take place before the cross, and depended on the Father completely. We must depend on the same God that kept His son in the hour of temptation.

God will never forsake His Children until Jesus comes. The Lord did not deceive the saints but told them the rapture would take place after the tribulation. The two Scriptures below are talking about the same rapture. Paul taught the same coming as Jesus taught: *Then shall two be in the field; the one shall be taken, and the other left. 41 Two women shall be grinding at the mill; the one shall be taken, and the other left. 42 Watch therefore: for ye know not what hour your Lord doth come. 43 But know this, that if the goodman of the house had known in what watch the thief would come, he would have watched, and would not have suffered his house to be broken up. 44 Therefore be ye also ready: for in such an hour as ye think not the Son of man cometh.* Paul taught the same coming as Jesus taught (Matthew 24:40-44). *For this we say unto you by the word of the Lord, that we which are alive and remain unto the coming of the Lord shall not prevent them which are asleep. 16 For the Lord himself shall descend from heaven with a shout, with the voice of the archangel, and with the trump of God: and the dead in Christ shall rise first: 17 Then we which are alive and remain shall be caught up together with them in the clouds, to meet the Lord in the air: and so shall we ever be with the Lord. 18 Wherefore comfort one another with these words* (I Thessalonians 4:15-18).

The Great Apostasy

Paul said Jesus will return after the great apostasy and the man of sin is revealed (II Thessalonians 2:1-3). Pretribulationists are very vague about this portion of Scripture, and try to explain away its true meaning about the time element of the Lord's coming. Paul tells the saints what takes place before the saints are raptured. There will be no secret rapture. The greatest harm in teaching pretribulation rapture is that when those things which pretribulationists have been taught do not come to pass before the tribulation period, many will turn to unbelief. When the man of sin is revealed, and the Lord still has not come, many will become disillusioned about the Bible and the return of the Lord. This may actually cause part of the apostasy. This falling away is not a falling away from earth but a falling away from truth. The Devil knows how to deceive the people who become disillusioned. The man of sin will sit in the temple and say that he is God (II Thessalonians 2:4). He will say to the people that Jesus is not going to come, and if they will worship him as god, they can continue to buy and sell, and be free. Many will choose to follow the antichrist rather than to suffer for the Lord. The false prophet will add to the deception by making fire come down from heaven and deceiving those on earth by means of various miracles (Revelation 13:11-18). Many will be deceived and worship the image of the beast, because they did not believe the truth about the coming of the Lord. If the rapture were before the tribulation period, how could the man of sin stand in the temple and tell the people that he is God? There would be few that would believe him if the rapture had already occurred.

George Muller, a great saint of God, lived in the time when the pretribulation rapture theory was being developed. He was grieved over the error that was being taught concerning the coming of the Lord. Being a student of the Word, he was grieved over Darby and the Brethren developing the pretribulation rapture theory, which later occasioned a split between Darby and Muller. It was said of Muller that the older he got, the more he preached about the Second Advent. In the book, *George Muller*, the account is given by William Harding of Muller and his wife while in Toronto attending a conference. Muller spoke several times upon the subject of the second coming of Christ. Written questions were given to him about the subject. Mrs. Muller preserved one, with her husband's answer:

Question: "Are we to expect our Lord's Return at any moment, or that certain events must be fulfilled before He comes again?"

Answer: "I know that on this subject there is great diversity of judgment, and I do not wish to force on other persons the light that I have myself. The subject, however, is not new to me; for, having been a careful, diligent student of the Bible for nearly fifty years, my mind has long been settled on this point, and I have not the shadow of a doubt about it. The Scriptures declare plainly that the Lord Jesus will not come until the Apostasy shall have taken place, and the man of sin, the 'son of perdition' (or personal Antichrist) shall have been revealed, as seen in II Thessalonians 2:1-5. There are many other portions of the Word of God that distinctly teach that certain events must be fulfilled before the return of the Lord."

God has used great men like Muller to preserve the truth concerning the Lord's coming, just as He has preserved His Word. It's time the Church of today corrects the damage done concerning the pretribulation rapture theory. False teachers brought great confussion to the Thessalonian Church concerning the Lord's coming. Paul told them they must first endure the persecution and tribulation that they were experiencing with faith and patience (II Thess. 1:3-5).

In order to understand I Thessalonians 5:9 we look at II Thessalonians 1:1-4. Paul, Silas, and Timothy are praising the Thessalonian Church for the patience and faith they have shown in enduring persecutions and tribulations: *Paul, and Silvanus, and Timotheus, unto the church of the Thessalonians in God our Father and the Lord Jesus Christ: 2 Grace unto you, and peace, from God our Father and the Lord Jesus Christ. 3 We are bound to thank God always for you, brethren, as it is meet, because that your faith groweth exceedingly, and the charity of every one of you all toward each other aboundeth; 4 So that we ourselves glory in you in the churches of God for your patience and faith in all your persecutions and tribulations that ye endure* (II Thessalonians 1:1-4). The suffering of the saints in the Thessalonian church is no different than the saints suffering under the reign of the beast in the tribulation period.

In II Thessalonians 1:4-5 below, Paul is telling the Thessalonian Church that God has made them grow in faith and love through their persecutions and tribulations. In verse 3 Paul was assuring the Church that this is the method God uses in order to show His righteous judgments to His Church. Paul told them that the endurance of their suffering shows they are worthy of the kingdom of God (Salvation). Let me put verses 4 and 5 together: *So that we ourselves glory in you in the churches of God for your patience and faith in all your persecutions and tribulations that ye endure: 5 Which is a manifest token of the righteous judgment of God, that ye may be counted worthy of the kingdom of God, for which ye also suffer.* In verses 6-9 below, Paul tells the Church that God will repay those who are persecuting them with His righteous judgments. He is assuring them that when Jesus comes with His mighty angels, He will come in flaming fire to take vengeance on those who do not know God, and do not obey the Gospel of our Lord Jesus Christ. He lets the Church know that the Lord will punish the persecutors with an everlasting destruction from the presence of the Lord at His coming. This is what Paul is explaining in *For God has not appointed us to wrath, but to obtain salvation, by our Lord Jesus Christ* (I Thessalonians 5:9). This is God's wrath: *Seeing it is a righteous thing with God to recompense tribulation to them that trouble you; 7 And to you who are troubled rest with us, when the Lord Jesus shall be revealed from heaven with his mighty angels; 8 In flaming fire taking vengeance on them that know not God, and that obey not the gospel of our Lord Jesus Christ: 9 Who shall be punished with everlasting destruction from the presence of the Lord, and from the glory of his power* (II Thessalonians 1:6-9).

We are to wait for God's Son from heaven because God has already delivered us from His wrath, which was accomplished when He raised

Jesus from the dead. The blood of Jesus justifies us, and we will be saved from the wrath of God in II Thessalonians 1:6-9. I Thessalonians 5:9 has nothing to do with delivering God's people from the tribulation period, but from God's wrath. These following verses should further clarify what Paul meant in I Thessalonians 5:9, and shows it in the past tense, not future. If this Scripture were talking about wrath in the tribulation period it would be in the future tense: *And to wait for his Son from heaven, whom he raised from the dead, even Jesus, which delivered us from the wrath to come* (I Thessalonians 1:10). *Much more then, being now justified by his blood, we shall be saved from wrath through him. 10 For if, when we were enemies, we were reconciled to God by the death of his Son, much more, being reconciled, we shall be saved by his life* (Romans 5:9-10).

It has been over forty years since I first taught a church youth class about the coming of the Lord. The pastor was a pretribulationist. I had purchased a Scofield Bible, and the pastor gave me some of Scofield's teaching books concerning the coming of the Lord. I began to teach the subject and found that Scofield gave I Thessalonians 4:13-17 as the rapture of the Church, which is correct, but he gave no scriptural evidence of the event taking place before the tribulation period. I knew very little about pretribulation or posttribulation back then; therefore I asked the pastor questions as to why Scofield gave no scriptural evidence about the time element of when the rapture was to take place in I Thessalonians 4:13-17. Neither he nor anyone else has ever given me any scriptural evidence to prove I Thessalonians 4:13-17 is a pretribulation rapture of the Church. Many can give a lot of words, and author a lot of books, but none give scriptural proof, but only theory. I knew something was wrong and began to question my pastor as to why Matthew 24 could not be used concerning the time element of the Lord's coming. I was told that Jesus was addressing only the Jews in the Gospels, and not to take what Jesus said in the Gospels and apply it to the Church. I know now where the pastor's teaching came from, but I wondered at the time how Jesus could be head of the Church, come to save us, and not say one word to the Church about His coming again, or about a pretribulation rapture.

I continued to study the Word on the subject, and then in the early '60s I broke my leg and was in a cast for six months. This gave me plenty of time to study the Word! I stayed up one night after everyone had gone to bed and found in I Thessalonians 2:1: *Now we beseech you, brethren, by the coming of our Lord Jesus Christ, and by our gathering together unto him.* I realized this verse was concerning the rapture and our gathering together unto Him. Then I read verse 2: *That ye be not soon shaken in mind, or be troubled, neither by spirit, nor by word, nor by letter as from us, as that the day of Christ is at hand.* This Scripture fortified me that I should not let anyone deceive me in any fashion concerning the coming of the Lord. Then I read verse 3: *Let no man deceive you by any means: for that day shall not come, except there come a falling away first, and that man of sin be revealed, the son of perdition;* When I read this verse the strangest feeling came over me. It was telling me something completely different from what I had been taught. I saw that two things must happen before the Lord would come for the rapture of the Church—first the apostasy, and then the man of sin would be revealed. That night the deception that I had been taught concerning the coming of the Lord became clear. I saw in this verse that Paul was saying the same thing about the coming of the Lord as Jesus taught in the Gospels. There are many scriptures that say the apostasy must take place before the Lord comes; (I Tim. 4:1-3; II Tim. 3:1-5; II Pet. 2:10-21; 3:3-4; Matt. 24:48-51; Luke 17:26-30). Pretribulationists misinterpret what Paul said about the man of sin being revealed after the rapture because of dispensationalism. The man of sin is revealed before the Lord comes; (I Thes. 2:3; Matt. 24:15-31; Mark 13:14-27; Dan. 7:7-27; 9:26-27; 11:36-45; 12:11; Rev. 13:1-10; 17:8-14). I found the key in II Thessalonians 2:3 that unlocked the door to truth concerning the second advent. This was the beginning of the end in solving the pretribulation rapture theory.

Paul makes it plain in II Thessalonians 2:1-6 that this is the rapture of the Church and our gathering together unto Him. The Church is to heed what Paul said concerning the Lord's coming. They are not to let anyone deceive them. Paul told the Church there would come a falling away first and the man of sin would be revealed before Jesus would come, yet pretribulationists explain away what Paul said to the Church. It is difficult to see how so many of God's people can read these Scriptures day after day, and not realize the truth of what they are saying. God's people should be in the light and not be fooled by the doctrines of man concerning the Lord's coming. The Thessalonians were disturbed by false teaching of their day concerning the coming of the

Lord and the rapture. Paul tells them plainly not to believe when some-one claims to prophesy by the spirit, as did Margaret MacDonald, or by teachings which they claim was the Word, or by letter. Darby and Scofield brought the false teaching of the pretribulation rapture theory into the Church. Now it is up to God's people to rectify it.

The Church of today has committed the great sin of teaching a false pretribulation rapture which has invaded a large percentage of our churches, and religious radio, and TV programing. The Church of today has accepted deception when they will not interpret the following Scripture with its true meaning: *Now we beseech you, brethren, by the coming of our Lord Jesus Christ, and by our gathering together unto him, 2 That ye be not soon shaken in mind, or be troubled, neither by spirit, nor by word, nor by letter as from us, as that the day of Christ is at hand. 3 Let no man deceive you by any means: for that day shall not come, except there come a falling away first, and that man of sin be revealed, the son of perdition; 4 Who opposeth and exalteth himself above all that is called God, or that is worshipped; so that he as God sitteth in the temple of God, showing himself that he is God. 5 Remember ye not, that, when I was yet with you, I told you these things?* (II Thessalonians 2:1-5).

Today's Church has been coddled and put to sleep concerning the troublesome end times that the Church will soon face. Paul taught believers they would suffer trials and tribulations. Pretribulationists do not have a message for the Church concerning any preparation for those dark days just before the Lord comes. Peter instructed the saints in his day that the devil would try to deceive and destroy them, and they would suffer for Christ. Is the Church of today more worthy than the early Church to suffer for Christ? *Casting all your care upon him; for he careth for you. 8 Be sober, be vigilant; because your adversary the devil, as a roaring lion, walketh about, seeking whom he may devour: 9 Whom resist sted-fast in the faith, knowing that the same afflictions are accomplished in your brethren that are in the world. 10 But the God of all grace, who hath called us unto his eternal glory by Christ Jesus, after that ye have suffered a while, make you perfect, stablish, strengthen, settle you. 11 To him be glory and dominion for ever and ever. Amen* (I Peter 5:7-11). He warned the Church of his day that they would have severe testing to try them, and that they would be partakers of Christ's suffering. If judgment starts at the house of God, and the Church is purified during the tribulation period, why should the Church think they are above suffering tribulation? God has never exempted the Church from suffering trials and tribulations. God's people will need to commit the keeping of their souls to Him: *Beloved, think it not strange concerning the fiery trial which is to try you, as though some strange thing happened unto you: 13 But rejoice, inasmuch as ye are partakers of Christ's sufferings; that, when his glory shall be revealed, ye may be glad also with exceeding joy. 14 If ye be reproached for the name of Christ, happy are ye; for the spirit of glory and of God resteth upon you: on their part he is evil spoken of, but on your part he is glorified. 15 But let none of you suffer as a murderer, or as a thief, or as an evildoer, or as a busybody in other men's matters. 16 Yet if any man suffer as a Christian, let him not be ashamed; but let him glorify God on this behalf. 17 For the time is come that judgment must begin at the house of God: and if it first begin at us, what shall the end be of them that obey not the gospel of God? 18 And if the righteous scarcely be saved, where shall the ungodly and the sinner appear? 19 Wherefore let them that suffer according to the will of God commit the keeping of their souls to him in well doing, as unto a faithful Creator* (I Peter 4:12-19).

The Jews had built false doctrines in their theology before Jesus was born. Their doctrines would allow for a conquering king to deliver them from Roman rule, but would not allow for a cross-bearing Messiah. Their theology concerning the major and minor prophets about Jesus' coming as savior of the world was misguided. They did not take heed to Daniel's sixty-nine weeks, that the Messiah would be crucified, and the Romans would destroy Jerusalem and their temple, and then they would be scattered throughout the earth before God would bring them back to their own land to fulfill the seventieth week (Daniel 9:24-27).

I believe the same thing is happening to the Gentile churches. False doctrine about the Lord's second coming is setting up the Gentiles for part of the great apostasy in the end time. Paul said God broke off the Jews because of unbelief, and the Gentiles stood by faith. We will see the reverse take place in these last days. A remnant of Jews will be grafted back into the Body of Christ, while many Gentiles will depart from the faith (I Tim. 4:1-2, II Thess. 2:3). Part of the problem will be the false doctrines that have been taught concerning the pretribulation rapture theory and the time element of the Lord's coming. Just as Jewish doctrines did not allow the Gentiles to be grafted into the Body of Christ with the Jews, now the Gentiles do not have doctrines that allow for the 144,000 of the twelve tribes of Israel to be grafted into the

Body of Christ before the rapture. Neither does pretribulationist doctrine allow for the Gentiles to be broken off because of unbelief as the Jews were. The Holy Spirit showed Paul these things when he wrote Romans 11:1-36. Many in Gentile churches are not ready to face the tribulation period because they call Daniel's entire seventieth week the wrath of God. The Jews wanted an earthly kingdom, and did not want their Messiah setting up a spiritual kingdom to rule from heaven. Now the Gentile Church is separating themselves from Israel in saying the rapture will take place before the tribulation period, and all of Israel will go through the tribulation period and the wrath of God.

Preachers must start preparing God's people to find comfort when tribulation begins to come upon the Church. If they reject this book, and all the documented evidence given of error, pretribulationists will be as blind as the Pharisees concerning truth. Some pretribulationist say they will change their minds if there is no pretribulation rapture, but I remind them that the leaders of the one-world church, "the false prophet," and one-world government, "the beast," will take away religious freedom. Now is the time to preach truth concerning the Lord's coming. The Church needs to be taught that the Lord is not going to forsake His people when those troubles begin to come upon the world. Paul taught the Corinthian church how to handle tribulation in II Corinthians 1:2-11.

The Church of today has been so busy telling the world that the Jews will suffer the wrath of God during the tribulation period that they have neglected to warn the saints how the devil is going to persecute saints, both Jew and Gentile. Our message must change and begin to tell the Church what a mighty God we serve, and the Lord will be our refuge in the time of trouble. The following Scriptures will be of great value in preparing God's people for the tribulation period. Our God will be with His people: Psalms 9:9-10, 32:7, 46:1-11.

The Man of Sin

Pretribulationists tell us that the Holy Spirit will be taken from the earth, and the rapture will take place at that time in II Thessalonians 2:7: *For the mystery of iniquity doth already work: only he who now letteth will let, until he be taken out of the way.* However, this Scripture is not saying the Holy Spirit will be taken from the earth. If the Holy Spirit were taken from the earth, no one could be saved during the tribulation period. This Scripture is saying that the man of sin will not come to power until the Lord lets him. The man of sin will be revealed in the Lord's time, and not one minute before. It is the Lord who sets the time for him to be revealed. The Lord will take Himself out of the way and let the man of sin come to power in His timing: *Remember ye not, that, when I was yet with you, I told you these things? 6 And now ye know what withholdeth that he might be revealed in his time. 7 For the mystery of iniquity doth already work: only he who now letteth will let, until he be taken out of the way. 8 And then shall that Wicked be revealed, whom the Lord shall consume with the spirit of his mouth, and shall destroy with the brightness of his coming: 9 Even him, whose coming is after the working of Satan with all power and signs and lying wonders, 10 And with all deceivableness of unrighteousness in them that perish; because they received not the love of the truth, that they might be saved* (II Thessalonians 2:5-10).

The following verses will show how all things happen in God's timing. The timing of the crucifixion was set by God (Acts 4:26-28, Daniel

11:35-36). Jesus the creator has the preeminence in all things. He will set the time for the man of sin to be revealed (Colossians 1:16-18), and all things will happen in God's timing. Michael the prince withheld the prince of Persia until God's timing was fulfilled, and then he came forth. The Lord touched Daniel, and strengthened him, and told him He would return and fight with the prince of Persia. Michael was used as the Lord's helper in withholding (Daniel 10:18-21). God set the time for his only begotten Son to be born and die (Luke 1:26-27, 30-32, 38, John 7:8). No one could lay hands on Jesus until God's timing (John 8:20). The man of sin will come forth in God's timing and not one minute before. The Holy Spirit does not have to be removed from the earth for the man of sin to be revealed. The Father sets the time for all things even to the timing of the Lord's return: *But of that day and hour knoweth no man, no, not the angels of heaven, but my Father only* (Matthew 24:36). Jesus is not coming back in a split coming or secret rapture of the Church. He is coming back as they saw Him go into Heaven, and every eye is going to see Him (Acts 1:10-11, Rev. 1:7). There will be no secret coming or rapture as pretribulationists teach. All will take place in God's timing.

THE COMING
OF THE LORD
IN THE CLOUDS

God is consistent concerning the Lord's coming in the clouds, whether it be in the Old or New Testament. Jesus comes in the clouds in Daniel, Matthew, Mark, Luke, Acts, Thessalonians, and Revelation. There is only one return for the rapture and resurrection of the saints. All of mankind will see Jesus coming in the clouds, and all the world will see Him and the rapture taking place at His coming. Those who are not ready when the Lord comes will suffer God's judgment and wrath. Jesus said the time of His coming is going to be immediately after the tribulation and that we should be looking for the signs of His coming. I think we should put more confidence in what Jesus said in the Gospels than what man says. The following Scriptures are for the Church and give the Church the time element of when the Lord is going to come, beginning in the Old Testament and ending in Revelation.

Daniel 7:13:
I saw in the night visions, and, behold, one like the Son of man came with the clouds of heaven, and came to the Ancient of days, and they brought him near before him.

Matthew 24:29-31:
Immediately after the tribulation of those days shall the sun be darkened, and the moon shall not give her light, and the stars shall

fall from heaven, and the powers of the heavens shall be shaken: 30 And then shall appear the sign of the Son of man in heaven: and then shall all the tribes of the earth mourn, and they shall see the Son of man coming in the clouds of heaven with power and great glory. 31 And he shall send his angels with a great sound of a trumpet, and they shall gather together his elect from the four winds, from one end of heaven to the other.

Mark 13:24-27:

But in those days, after that tribulation, the sun shall be darkened, and the moon shall not give her light, 25 And the stars of heaven shall fall, and the powers that are in heaven shall be shaken. 26 And then shall they see the Son of man coming in the clouds with great power and glory. 27 And then shall he send his angels, and shall gather together his elect from the four winds, from the uttermost part of the earth to the uttermost part of heaven.

Luke 21:25-28:

And there shall be signs in the sun, and in the moon, and in the stars; and upon the earth distress of nations, with perplexity; the sea and the waves roaring; 26 Men's hearts failing them for fear, and for looking after those things which are coming on the earth: for the powers of heaven shall be shaken. 27 And then shall they see the Son of man coming in a cloud with power and great glory. 28 And when these things begin to come to pass, then look up, and lift up your heads; for your redemption draweth nigh.

Paul said Jesus was coming in the clouds just as Jesus said in the Gospels. Daniel, the Gospels, and the Epistles do not teach two different comings. There is only one return of Jesus in the clouds for His saints: *Then we which are alive and remain shall be caught up together with them in the clouds, to meet the Lord in the air: and so shall we ever be with the Lord* (I Thessalonians 4:17). John said the Lord comes in the clouds: *Behold, he cometh with clouds; and every eye shall see him, and they also which pierced him: and all kindreds of the earth shall wail because of him. Even so, Amen* (Revelation 1:7:).

When the trumpet of the Lord sounds in I Thessalonians 4:16, the whole world is going to hear it. The dead and the living will hear the trumpet of the Lord. That blast will arouse and shake the whole earth as it did in Exodus 19:16: *And it came to pass on the third day in the morning, that there were thunders and lightnings, and a thick cloud upon the mount, and the voice of the trumpet exceeding loud; so that all the people that was in the camp trembled.*

We see in the verses below that when the seventh trumpet sounds, the nations will be angry because the wrath of God has come. The seventh trumpet is the day for the resurrection of the saints who have died in the Lord and will be rewarded at the judgment seat of Christ. When the seventh trumpet sounds, it will be the last day the saints are on earth (John 6:40). The same day of the rapture and resurrection, the wrath of God begins: *But in the days of the voice of the seventh angel, when he shall begin to sound, the mystery of God should be finished, as he hath declared to his servants the prophets.11:15: And the seventh angel sounded; and there were great voices in heaven, saying, The kingdoms of this world are become the kingdoms of our Lord, and of his Christ; and he shall reign for ever and ever. 18 And the nations were angry, and thy wrath is come, and the time of the dead, that they should be judged, and that thou shouldest give reward unto thy servants the prophets, and to the saints, and them that fear thy name, small and great; and shouldest destroy them which destroy the earth* (Revelation 10:7, 11:15, 18).

The rapture and resurrection do not take place before the tribulation period begins, as pretribulationists teach. The mystery of the coming of the Lord, the rapture, and resurrection are complete only when the last trump sounds (I Cor. 15:52, Rev. 10:7). When the seventh trumpet sounds, it brings us to the end of Daniel's seventieth week. The same day of the rapture and resurrection, the saints will be ushered into the Lord's chambers until the wrath is over (Isaiah 26:19-21). The wrath of God starts the same day that the Church is raptured (Revelation 11:18). The man of sin must be revealed in I Thessalonians 2:3, before the saints are gathered unto the Lord. The saints will meet the Lord in the air and be secured in His chambers, and then the seven last vials of God's wrath begins (Rev. 15:1-8, 16:1-21). The Lord and His angels are the reapers (Rev. 14:14-20). The Lord will come to earth on a white horse to judge and make war on the beast, and all who took the mark of the beast (Rev. 19:11-16). The eastern gate will be closed until the Lord enters it (Ezek. 44:1-2), and the Lord's feet will stand upon the Mount of Olives (Zech. 14:4), and Jerusalem shall be delivered, and all who are left in the earth after the wrath of God will serve the Lord.

Luke 17:26-27 tells us that the same day Noah entered the Ark, the door was shut and judgment started, and the same day Lot went out of Sodom, judgment fell. We can see the rapture in Luke 17:34-36. The wrath of God starts after the tribulation and the rapture. The Bible is always consistent concerning Jesus' coming. The problems start when dispensationalists say the Gospels are not for the Church, and go on to devise a pretribulation rapture by discounting the Gospels for the Church. This error is corrected by listening to what Jesus said in the Gospels. We can see in the verses below that judgment starts the same day after the rapture. Fire and brimstone rained down upon Sodom the same day Lot went out. The same day that the Son of Man is revealed, and the rapture and resurrection take place in verse 30, is the same day judgment starts: *And as it was in the days of Noe, so shall it be also in the days of the Son of man. 27 They did eat, they drank, they married wives, they were given in marriage, until the day that Noe entered into the ark, and the flood came, and destroyed them all. 28 Likewise also as it was in the days of Lot; they did eat, they drank, they bought, they sold, they planted, they builded; 29 But the same day that Lot went out of Sodom it rained fire and brimstone from heaven, and destroyed them all. 30 Even thus shall it be in the day when the Son of man is revealed. 31 In that day, he which shall be upon the housetop, and his stuff in the house, let him not come down to take it away: and he that is in the field, let him likewise not return back. 32 Remember Lot's wife. 33 Whosoever shall seek to save his life shall lose it; and whosoever shall lose his life shall preserve it. 34 I tell you, in that night there shall be two men in one bed; the one shall be taken, and the other shall be left. 35 Two women shall be grinding together; the one shall be taken, and the other left. 36 Two men shall be in the field; the one shall be taken, and the other left* (Luke 17:26-36).

Pretribulationists erroneously teach that there are two phases in the second coming of Christ. First, Christ descends from heaven in the air above the earth and calls out the saints in a secret rapture. Then, seven years later, Jesus comes to the earth with His saints when every eye will see Him, referred to as the revelation. The judgment of nations will follow and then Jesus will set up His kingdom on earth where the saints will be with Christ on earth for one thousand years ("Rightly Dividing The Word of Truth" by Dr. C. I Scofield). In truth there is no secret rapture, nor seven years between the rapture and revelation. The Church is headed for heaven, not an earthly kingdom (John 14:3).

Schaff's 1889 commentary on Corinthians, found in Lange's, states the trump in I Thessalonians 4:16 is the same as the last trumpet in Revelation 10:7 and 11:15. Therefore, this could not be a secret blast of the trumpet that no one hears but the dead and the saints. Indeed the whole world will hear the trumpet of the Lord and tremble. Every eye shall see the Lord coming in the air.

The trumpet in the Old Testament was used to call an assembly, announce judgment, or proclaim the king's victory. In Revelation 11:15-18, the trumpet of the Lord will sound for all three reasons. It will signal the whole earth that the kingdom of this world has become the kingdom of our Lord. It will signal that God's wrath is ready to be poured out upon the earth. It will signal the resurrection of the just and the rapture of the saints to be awarded by the Lord. It signals to the whole world to get ready for the Battle of Armageddon and the wrath of God.

God's Dealings
with the Jews
in the Last Days

God fulfills all Scripture, and will fulfill what was prophesied concerning the Jews in the last days. While Paul was in the desert for three years, the Lord taught him concerning the things that were to take place and his ministry: *But the Lord said unto him, Go thy way: for he is a chosen vessel unto me, to bear my name before the Gentiles, and kings, and the children of Israel: 16 For I will show him how great things he must suffer for my name's sake* (Acts 9:15). Paul had preached to the Jews but they rejected His message, and he said unto them, *Your blood be upon your own heads; I am clean: from henceforth I will go unto the Gentiles* (Acts 18:6). Paul wrote the book of Romans, which tells about the Jews and how the Lord will deal with them. Paul quotes Isaiah regarding Israel and how the Lord will do a short work with them. There will be a remnant saved and grafted back into the body of Christ in the last days. Pretribulationists have overlooked the short work the Lord will do concerning a remnant being saved before the rapture of the Church: *Isaiah also crieth concerning Israel, Though the number of the children of Israel be as the sand of the sea, a remnant shall be saved: 28 For he will finish the work, and cut it short in righteousness: because a short work will the Lord make upon the earth. 29 And as Isaiah said before, Except the Lord of Sabaoth had left us a seed, we had been as Sodom, and been made like unto Gomorrha* (Romans 9:27-29).

The Gentiles were shown mercy because they sought righteousness by faith. Jews who sought righteousness by the Law were rejected when they did not believe Jesus was the Messiah, and He became their stumbling stone and rock of offense: *What shall we say then? That the Gentiles, which followed not after righteousness, have attained to righteousness, even the righteousness which is of faith. 31 But Israel, which followed after the law of righteousness, hath not attained to the law of righteousness. 32 Wherefore? Because they sought it not by faith, but as it were by the works of the law. For they stumbled at that stumblingstone; 33 As it is written, Behold, I lay in Zion a stumblingstone and rock of offense: and whosoever believeth on him shall not be ashamed* (Romans 9:30-33).

God broke off Israel because of their unbelief, and will graft a remnant back into His Body before the rapture. God said He would also break off the Gentiles if they did not continue in the faith. The Bible talks of one Body, and one coming of the Lord for the Church, Jew and Gentile. The Jews did not understand the prophecies of the Old Testament concerning the Messiah and His relationship to the Jew, and the Jew and Gentile being molded into one Body, "the Church." Isaiah prophesied how the light would come to the Gentiles. Jesus fulfilled Isaiah's prophecy, and laid the foundation in the Gospels. The Church was in the mind of God from eternity. Jesus said to Peter, "upon this rock I will build my Church."

Jesus was the covenant of salvation and the light to the Gentiles: *Behold my servant, whom I uphold; mine elect, in whom my soul delighteth; I have put my spirit upon him: he shall bring forth judgment to the Gentiles. 2 He shall not cry, nor lift up, nor cause his voice to be heard in the street. 3 A bruised reed shall he not break, and the smoking flax shall he not quench: he shall bring forth judgment unto truth. 4 He shall not fail nor be discouraged, till he have set judgment in the earth: and the isles shall wait for his law. 5 Thus saith God the LORD, he that created the heavens, and stretched them out; he that spread forth the earth, and that which cometh out of it; he that giveth breath unto the people upon it, and spirit to them that walk therein: 6 I the LORD have called thee in righteousness, and will hold thine hand, and will keep thee, and give thee for a covenant of the people, for a light of the Gentiles; 7 To open the blind eyes, to bring out the prisoners from the prison, and them that sit in darkness out of the prison house* (Isaiah 42:1-7). The covenant of salvation was for both Jews and Gentiles. We start in the Old Testament, and continue through the Gospels, Epistles, and Revelation in order to understand the mysteries revealed. The first indications of the Gentiles being grafted in are found in Isaiah, and follow through the New Testament. The Gentiles were grafted in and becoming part of Church, just like the Jews who were broken off, a remnant will be grafted into the Body of Christ again before the rapture.

There is one doctrine in particular that is very misleading concerning Israel. Replacement theology states that when the Jews rejected Jesus as the Messiah, God set the nation aside forever and the Church took Israel's place. They believe Israel's becoming a nation in 1948 means nothing in prophecy. This doctrine cannot be true because Daniel shows us there is a gap between the sixty-ninth and seventieth week. The seventieth week can only be fulfilled in the last days. The seventieth week is the tribulation period when the antichrist will be made known, and will make war on Israel, the saints, and the two witnesses. God brought Israel back to their land as promised. The Jews must now fulfill Ezekiel 36 through 39 in the last days in order to complete the prophecy concerning the dry bones.

There was a remnant of Jews saved in the early rain, and there must be a remnant also saved in the latter rain. The book of James speaks of being" *patient therefore, brethren, unto the coming of the Lord. Behold, the husbandman waiteth for the precious fruit of the earth, and hath long patience for it, until he receive the early and latter rain. 8 Be ye also patient; stablish your hearts: for the coming of the Lord draweth nigh*" (James 5:7-8).

The disciples and the three thousand saved on the day of Pentecost were in the beginning of the early rain. God promised Israel an early and latter rain in a prophecy in the book of Hosea which has not yet been fulfilled. He said after two days (or two thousand years), Israel would be revived in the third day, and *he shall come unto us as the rain, as the latter and former rain unto the earth* (Hosea 6:1-3). Zechariah spoke of the early and latter rain. Israel has been without a shepherd for two thousand years. Jesus will be made known to a remnant in the latter rain (Zech. 10:1-6). Joel spoke of the early and latter rain (Joel 2:23). Joel spoke of the Holy Spirit being poured out on all flesh in the early rain, and how signs would be given in the heavens and earth before the day of the Lord. Salvation was promised to all who call upon the name of the Lord (Joel 2:28-32).

Peter knew what was taking place on the day of Pentecost, and quoted Joel's prophecy concerning the early rain and the Holy Spirit being poured out upon all flesh. There were about three thousand who gladly received the Word, and were baptized and added to the Church (Acts 2:14-41). The latter rain, and the signs which are to be given before the Day of the Lord, are yet to be fulfilled. Daniel's sixty-nine weeks have been fulfilled: the Messiah was crucified, the Jews were scattered, and are being gathered together again. About two thousand years have passed in the gap between the sixty-ninth and seventieth week of Daniel. The latter rain concerning Israel must be fulfilled, and because Israel is back in her own land, this proves God will fulfill His promise. The Lord will not forget Jerusalem and the Jews (Ps. 137:5-6; Isa. 49:15).

The Lord said Jerusalem would be trodden down of the Gentiles until the time of the Gentiles is fulfilled, and the Jews are back in their land. We Gentiles must not make the same mistake as was made by the Jews in thinking that Gentiles could not be in the same Body with the Jews. The Gentile Church must remember Paul revealed the mystery concerning the Gentiles being grafted into the Body of Christ. I show in this book how the Church was started in the Gospels and not in the book of Acts, and how the Gentiles were grafted into the Body of Christ. Will the Gentiles now say they are better than the Jew, and deny the Jew being grafted back into the Body of Christ in doctrine? We must remember the Gentiles were made fellow heirs and partakers of His promise in Christ by the gospel. The Scriptures could not be fulfilled for the Jews if there were a pretribulation rapture. How could the Jews be grafted back into the Body of Christ if the rapture takes place before the seventieth week of Daniel begins? Only by the grace of God were the Gentiles grafted into the Body of Christ, to be fellow heirs: *How that by revelation he made known unto me the mystery; (as I wrote afore in few words, 4 Whereby, when ye read, ye may understand my knowledge in the mystery of Christ) 5 Which in other ages was not made known unto the sons of men, as it is now revealed unto his holy apostles and prophets by the Spirit; 6 That the Gentiles should be fellowheirs, and of the same body, and partakers of his promise in Christ by the gospel* (Ephesians 3:3-6).

God desires all Israel to be saved: *Brethren, my heart's desire and prayer to God for Israel is, that they might be saved* (Romans 10:1).

Paul showed Jew and Gentile how to be saved: *That if thou shalt confess with thy mouth the Lord Jesus, and shalt believe in thine heart that God hath raised him from the dead, thou shalt be saved. 10 For with the heart man believeth unto righteousness; and with the mouth confession is made unto salvation. 13 For whosoever shall call upon the name of the Lord shall be saved* (Romans 10:9-10,13).

God stretched out His hand to Israel to be saved but they would not, but He found the Gentiles were ready for salvation: *But Isaiah is very bold, and saith, I was found of them that sought me not; I was made manifest unto them that asked not after me. 21 But to Israel he saith, All day long I have stretched forth my hands unto a disobedient and gainsaying people* (Romans 10:20-21).

God has not utterly cast away His people Israel, but a remnant will be saved according to the election of grace. A remnant was saved in the early church, and there will be 144,000 and many others who will accept salvation and be in the rapture of the Church. Two-thirds of the Jews who miss the rapture will loose their lives, but one-third will not worship the beast, and will survive the battle of Armageddon (Zech. 13:8-9). These will be the Jews who make up the kingdom of Israel on earth in the millennium while a remnant of Jews will be grafted back into the Body of Christ (the Church) and will be in the rapture: *I say then, Hath God cast away his people? God forbid. For I also am an Israelite, of the seed of Abraham, of the tribe of Benjamin. 2 God hath not cast away his people which he foreknew. Wot ye not what the scripture saith of Elijah? how he maketh intercession to God against Israel, saying, 3 Lord, they have killed thy prophets, and digged down thine altars; and I am left alone, and they seek my life. 4 But what saith the answer of God unto him? I have reserved to myself seven thousand men, who have not bowed the knee to the image of Baal. 5 Even so then at this present time also there is a remnant according to the election of grace. 6 And if by grace, then is it no more of works: otherwise grace is no more grace. But if it be of works, then is it no more grace: otherwise work is no more work* (Romans 11:1-6).

The elect received salvation because they believed; the rest of Israel was blinded: *What then? Israel hath not obtained that which he seeketh for; but the election hath obtained it, and the rest were blinded* (Romans 11:7).

Through Israel's fall, salvation came to the Gentiles in order to provoke Israel to jealousy. Through their fall the Gentiles were made rich. God said it will be a greater blessing to the world during the tribulation period when the remnant's eyes are opened: *I say then, Have they stumbled that they should fall? God forbid: but rather through their fall salvation is come unto the Gentiles, for to provoke them to jealousy. 12 Now if the fall of them be the riches of the world, and the diminishing of them the riches of the Gentiles; how much more their fulness? 15 For if the casting away of them be the reconciling of the world, what shall the receiving of them be, but life from the dead?* (Romans 11:11-12,15).

The remnant of Jews saved before the rapture will be a blessing to both Jew and Gentile. There will be many purified and made white in the tribulation preiod; Dan. 12:10. They will understand the events that are unfolding concerning the tribulation period, and what Jesus said in Matt. 24:15-28, and Paul in I Thes. 5:1-10. The apostasy of the Gentiles will take place because of failed teachings concerning the pretribulation rapture theory but the saved Jewish remnant will be a blessing to the Church in those dark hours of the tribulation period. The Jewish first-fruits in Rev. 7:3 and the two witnesses in Rev. 11:3 will be an encouragement to the Church with their message and mighty power. Those who walk in the light will not be in darkness as the world, concerning the time element of the Lord's coming as recorded in Matt. 24:28-31, and II Thes. 2:1-8.

God broke off Israel because of unbelief. God is able to graft them in again (Rom. 11:23). This must be done in order to fulfill all prophecy. There must be a latter rain for Israel just as there was an early rain. There will be a remnant who believe in the Lord and will be in the rapture. These will be redeemed from among men, being the firstfruits unto God and to the Lamb, and are before the throne of God in heaven (Rev. 14:1-5).

GRAFTING
GENTILES AND JEWS
INTO THE
BODY OF CHRIST

God hid the mystery of how the Gentiles should be fellow heirs and of the same body by salvation by faith in Christ. Jesus began to reveal the mystery by quoting Isaiah in Matthew 4:12-17. Other verses are found in Isaiah 9:1-2; 42:6-7; 49:22-23; 53:1-12; 60:1-16; 62:2; 66:12-19. Paul revealed this secret in its completeness (Eph. 3:2-11).

The Holy Spirit revealed to Simeon when he prophesied concerning baby Jesus how Jesus would be a light to the Gentiles and the glory of Israel (Luke 2:32). Jesus prophesied how Jerusalem would be trodden down of the Gentiles until the time of the Gentiles be fulfilled (Luke 21:24). The eyes of the Pharisees were blind concerning the mysteries of how Israel would be broken off because of unbelief and the Gentiles grafted in. They could not see that the Messiah must come as a servant and savior, and go to the cross, and die for the sins of the whole world before He would come back as the conquering King. The Pharisees completely misunderstood Isaiah 53. Pretribulationists also have made a great mistake in not believing what Jesus said about His coming again in the Gospels, and what Paul said in II Thessalonians 2:1-5. Paul made it plain to the Church that the apostasy and the man of sin would be revealed before the saints would be gathered unto the Lord. Pretribulationists are blinded to Israel being grafted in again (Romans 11:23). This darkness of pretribulationists will cause many problems for them in these last days, just as it caused problems for the Pharisees.

Writers before the pretribulation theory was developed saw that there was not going to be a rapture of the Church prior to Israel being grafted back into the Church. They saw how God took the Gentiles, a wild olive branch, and grafted them into a good olive tree, and understood how easy it would be to graft the natural olive branch back in. Henry wrote in his commentary concerning Romans the eleventh chapter that there would be a conversion of the Jews and that they would be grafted back into the Church. "The conversion of the Jews will bring great joy to the church. See *Luke xv. 32; He was dead, and is alive; and therefore it was meet we should make merry and be glad*, (3) It is called the *grafting of them in again* (*v. 23*, into the church, from which they had been broken off. They shall be *grafted into their own olive-tree* (*v. 24*); that is, into the church of which they had formerly been the most eminent and conspicuous members."

John did not tell us in Revelation when Israel would be grafted back into the Body of Christ. He only tells us that the 144,000 will be sealed before the four angels that hold the four winds hurt the earth in Revelation chapter 7. These Jews have already been saved and grafted into the body of Christ in the chapter 7. The conversion of the Jews will bring great joy to the Church just as when the prodigal son came home. In God's timing, it will be easier to graft the natural branches back into the Body of Christ than the Gentiles, who were a wild olive tree. When the gospel has had its intended success in the Gentile world, God will turn to the Jews as He promised in Romans 11:25-26. After the early rain in the early Church, Paul turned to the Gentiles. The Gentiles accepted the gospel readily, and the Church was replenished. When the Gentiles have had their opportunity to carry the Gospel to all the world and begin to grow disillusioned and cold, some will depart from the faith as Paul said would happen in the last days in I Timothy 4:1. The Church will be replenished by the Jews when they are grafted back into the Body of Christ. Revival will come as it did in the early Church.

There will be a great persecution of the Church during the tribulation period under the hands of the beast, the revived Roman Empire, and the apostate world church that will sit on the seven hills of Rome as stated in Revelation 17:9. Jews in the early Church showed themselves strong under the persecution of Rome, and the Jews will show themselves strong once again to the floundering Gentile Church. I believe the pretribulation rapture theory is going to play a big part in the disillusionment of the Gentiles in the later days because they have been lulled to sleep by a promise that will not come to pass.

Gentiles should understand that the remnant of the early Church and those Jews saved during the Tribulation period are the same Body, the Church. It is very prideful and wrong to tell the Jew they will not be grafted into the Body of Christ, but will suffer the wrath of God. The Jew will be grafted in again. God help us if we Gentiles do not open our eyes to the truth concerning Israel, while putting the Gentiles in a more blessed place in God's eyes than the Jews. There is no pretribulation rapture. The Church will be one Body comprised of both Jew and Gentile. God has promised to open the eyes of the Jews again as a nation, and will graft them back into the body of Christ again during the tribulation period. The 144,000 of the twelve tribes of Israel in Revelation chapter 14 will no longer be on earth to be exposed to trials, but is shown around the throne triumphant with the Lord. They will be the firstfruits unto God and to the Lamb, and will be in the rapture. The 144,000 of the children of Israel and the tribulation saints are both in heaven around the throne of God (Rev. 7:9, 14-15, 14:1-4). Both will be safe in the Lord's chambers until the Lord and His angels judge the earth (Rev. 15:14-16:21). There will be only one Body of Christ.

The Old Testament prophets gave us only a glimpse of how Jesus would be a light to the Gentiles. The Gentiles being grafted into the Body of Christ was a great mystery that will be finished when the seventh trumpet sounds, as God has declared to His servants the prophets in Revelation 10:7. Jesus came with a message of salvation and truth to fulfill the Old Covenant and establish the New. The Old Covenant is a covenant of works. The New Covenant is a covenant of the grace of God. All who would receive God's Son by faith would become sons of God, because He was the Lamb slain before the foundation of the world. Many Jews rejected his message because they wanted the Messiah to defeat the Roman army and give them their freedom. This would allow them to continue in the Old Covenant of the Law. There were a remnant that received Jesus as the Messiah, and were saved. Most rejected Jesus and the New Covenant of salvation—their eyes were blinded and they were broken off from being saved (Romans 11:7). The Lord opened the door to other sheep who would hear His voice and be saved. The Lord has only one fold for Jew and Gentile

(John 10:16). God included all in unbelief so He could have mercy on all (Romans 11:32). If the Gentiles were a wild olive tree and were grafted into the Body of Christ, how can Gentiles think God is not going to graft the natural branches back into the Body before the rapture? Paul tells us in Romans that God is going to do exactly that: *And if some of the branches be broken off, and thou, being a wild olive tree, wert grafted in among them, and with them partakest of the root and fatness of the olive tree; 18 Boast not against the branches. But if thou boast, thou bearest not the root, but the root thee. 19 Thou wilt say then, The branches were broken off, that I might be grafted in. 20 Well; because of unbelief they were broken off, and thou standest by faith. Be not highminded, but fear: 21 For if God spared not the natural branches, take heed lest he also spare not thee. 22 Behold therefore the goodness and severity of God: on them which fell, severity; but toward thee, goodness, if thou continue in his goodness: otherwise thou also shalt be cut off. 23 And they also, if they abide not still in unbelief, shall be grafted in: for God is able to graft them in again. 24 For if thou wert cut out of the olive tree which is wild by nature, and wert grafted contrary to nature into a good olive tree: how much more shall these, which be the natural branches, be grafted into their own olive tree? 25 For I would not, brethren, that ye should be ignorant of this mystery, lest ye should be wise in your own conceits; that blindness in part is happened to Israel, until the fulness of the Gentiles be come in. 26 And so all Israel shall be saved: as it is written, There shall come out of Zion the Deliverer, and shall turn away ungodliness from Jacob: 27 For this is my covenant unto them, when I shall take away their sins. 28 As concerning the gospel, they are enemies for your sakes: but as touching the election, they are beloved for the fathers' sakes. 29 For the gifts and calling of God are without repentance* (Romans 11:17-29).

God included both Jew and Gentile in unbelief that He might show mercy on all. God wants one Body, the Church: *For God hath concluded them all in unbelief, that he might have mercy upon all. 33 O the depth of the riches both of the wisdom and knowledge of God! how unsearchable are his judgments, and his ways past finding out! 34 For who hath known the mind of the Lord? or who hath been his counsellor?* (Romans 11:32-34).

A majority of the Jews did not believe in Jesus when He came to His own, but all who received Him were saved. This truth has been our confidence down through the Church age for both Jew and Gentile: *He came unto his own, and his own received him not. 12 But as many as received him, to them gave he power to become the sons of God, even to them that believe on his name* (John 1:11-12).

THE EARLY AND LATTER RAIN

The Old and New Testament teaches about the early and latter rain. I began to see how pretribulationists made void to the Church the latter rain because they said it takes place after the rapture of the Church. The early rain at Pentecost was very important to the early Church, and so will the latter rain be.

Individual Jews have been saved throughout the Church age and admitted to the Church through faith in Christ. God brought the Jews back to their own land in 1948, and will deal with the nation of Israel again concerning their salvation in the latter rain. We should not be ignorant of this mystery, and God promised in His Word that blindness in part has happened to Israel, until the fullness of the Gentiles comes in. We must remember we as Gentiles did not bear the root, but the root bore us. Israel will come forth by God's grace out of the root, Jesus, and be grafted back into the Body of Christ, and they will receive the latter rain as God promised. James let us know that the Father is waiting for the precious fruit of the earth, and "hath long patience until He receive the early and latter rain." This must take place before the Lord comes (James 5:7-8).

The pouring out of the Holy Spirit that is spoken of in Joel was fulfilled in Acts. The Holy Spirit was poured out upon Jew and Gentile, the Church in the early rain. I believe we will have the latter rain also for the Jew and Gentile in the tribulation period, but it will be for the whole Church, not for the Jew only. This prophecy has not yet come to pass. Under pretribulation rapture doctrine it cannot be fulfilled because the Church is raptured and the Holy Spirit removed from the earth. Pretribulationists teach that the Jews must go through the wrath of God, which is the tribulation period. If their doctrine were true, Joel and James's prophecy could not be fulfilled. However the remnant of Jews will have the latter rain just as they had the early rain before the Lord comes again. We must remember that (1) Israel must be grafted back into the Body of Christ. (2) The Jews must have the latter rain just like they had the early rain. These two things must happen to Israel before the Lord is going to come. All prophecy must be fulfilled: *Be glad then, ye children of Zion, and rejoice in the LORD your God: for he hath given you the former rain moderately, and he will cause to come down for you the rain, the former rain, and the latter rain in the first month* (Joel 2:23).

Peter combined the early rain, the latter rain, and the signs of the Lord's coming in his message to the Jews on the day of Pentecost. The Church should be looking for the latter rain before the Lord's return. Peter says the same thing as the Gospels: *But Peter, standing up with the eleven, lifted up his voice, and said unto them, Ye men of Judaea, and all ye that dwell at Jerusalem, be this known unto you, and hearken to my words: 15 For these are not drunken, as ye suppose, seeing it is but the third hour of the day. 16 But this is that which was spoken by the prophet Joel; 17 And it shall come to pass in the last days, saith God, I will pour out of my Spirit upon all flesh: and your sons and your daughters shall prophesy, and your young men shall see visions, and your old men shall dream dreams: 18 And on my servants and on my handmaidens I will pour out in those days of my Spirit; and they shall prophesy* (Acts 2:14-18).

Peter is talking about the coming of the Lord, and how there will be signs and wonders before the Lord is going to come. We will see the latter rain and the grafting in of the Jews to the Body of Christ. It shows there will be salvation for all, both Jew and Gentile. These things must happen before the Lord comes: *And I will show wonders in heaven above, and signs in the earth beneath; blood, and fire, and vapour of smoke: 20 The sun shall be turned into darkness, and the moon into blood, before that great and notable day of the Lord come: 21 And it shall come to pass, that whosoever shall call on the name of the Lord shall be saved* (Acts 2:19-21).

Hosea said the return of the Jews to the Lord would be on the third day. A day in God's calendar is one thousand years. After two days the

Lord promised to raise them up. God gave them the early rain. He also will give them the latter rain: *Come, and let us return unto the LORD: for he hath torn, and he will heal us; he hath smitten, and he will bind us up. 2 After two days will he revive us: in the third day he will raise us up, and we shall live in his sight. 3 Then shall we know, if we follow on to know the LORD: his going forth is prepared as the morning; and he shall come unto us as the rain, as the latter and former rain unto the earth* (Hosea 6:1-3).

Jesus promised the Centurion (Gentiles) a place in His Body in the kingdom of heaven. How can Gentiles not believe God? Will He not honor His promise to the Gentiles? Will He not also honor His promise to His chosen people, the Jews? The Jews will be grafted back into the Body of Christ. The following Scripture shows that both Jew and Gentile will be in the kingdom of heaven along with Abraham, Isaac, and Jacob. We know that these three men are dead. After the resurrection, they, along with saints of all generations, will be in heaven (the kingdom of heaven), the heavenly Jerusalem. This is the same place the Lord promised us in John 14:3 as well as Matthew 8:5-11, 13: *And when Jesus was entered into Capernaum, there came unto him a centurion, beseeching him, 6 And saying, Lord, my servant lieth at home sick of the palsy, grievously tormented. 7 And Jesus saith unto him, I will come and heal him. 8 The centurion answered and said, Lord, I am not worthy that thou shouldest come under my roof: but speak the word only, and my servant shall be healed. 9 For I am a man under authority, having soldiers under me: and I say to this man, Go, and he goeth; and to another, Come, and he cometh; and to my servant, Do this, and he doeth it. 10 When Jesus heard it, he marvelled, and said to them that followed, Verily I say unto you, I have not found so great faith, no, not in Israel. 11 And I say unto you, That many shall come from the east and west, and shall sit down with Abraham, and Isaac, and Jacob, in the kingdom of heaven. 13 And Jesus said unto the centurion, Go thy way; and as thou hast believed, so be it done unto thee. And his servant was healed in the selfsame hour.* Verse 11 is fulfilled in the millennial kingdom in heaven. Abraham and the saints, Jew and Gentile, will receive the city Abraham was looking for: *For he looked for a city which hath foundations, whose builder and maker is God. 12:22: But ye are come unto mount Sion, and unto the city of the living God, the heavenly Jerusalem, and to an innumerable company of angels* (Hebrews 11:10).

THE EXAMPLES OF
EGYPT AND ISRAEL

Paul instructed the Corinthian church, warning them how God dealt with Israel in their deliverance from bondage in Egypt. He warned them not to follow after the example of those who sinned in the wilderness. Paul went on to tell how God had made Jew and Gentile one bread in Christ (I Corinthians 10:1-17). The example of Egypt will be of great importance in helping the Church during the tribulation period to understand how God is dealing with His Church.

When pretribulationists call the entire tribulation period the wrath of God, they should understand that it is a time when the beast and the false prophet will bring great persecution on the Church. The wrath of God is not poured out until the end of the tribulation period. We must understand that God has promised to protect His own from His judgments. God promised in Matthew 24:21-22 that He would cut the time short or else no lives would be saved. Great persecution will be upon the two prophets, Israel, and the Church during this time. The following verses are about the wrath of the Devil and the beast, not the wrath of God: *And I will give power unto my two witnesses, and they shall prophesy a thousand two hundred and threescore days, clothed in sackcloth. 7 And when they shall have finished their testimony, the beast that ascendeth out of the bottomless pit shall make War against them, and shall overcome them, and kill them* (Revelation 11:3,7). The Devil will make war against Israel: *And the dragon was wroth with the woman, and went to make war with the remnant of her seed, which keep the commandments of God, and have the testimony of Jesus Christ* (Revelation 12:17). The beast will make war with the saints: *And it was given unto him to make war with the saints, and to overcome them: and power was given him over all kindreds, and tongues, and nations. 8 And all that dwell upon the earth shall worship him, whose names are not written in the book of life of the Lamb slain from the foundation of the world. 9 If any man have an ear, let him hear* (Revelation 13:7-9).

Many saints will give their lives for Christ, just as they did in the early Church and also in times of persecution down through Church history. It is false to assume that today's saints are more privileged than the Lord, the disciples, or saints who have given their lives for Christ throughout Church history: *After this I beheld, and, lo, a great multitude, which no man could number, of all nations, and kindreds, and people, and tongues, stood before the throne, and before the Lamb, clothed with white robes, and palms in their hands; 10 And cried with a loud voice, saying, Salvation to our God which sitteth upon the throne, and unto the Lamb. 14 And I said unto him, Sir, thou knowest. And he said to me, These are they which came out of great tribulation, and have washed their robes, and made them white in the blood of the Lamb. 15 Therefore are they before the throne of God, and serve him day and night in his temple: and he that sitteth on the throne shall dwell among them* (Revelation 7:9-10, 14-15).

God does not forsake His people. He hears the prayers of His people, and prepares the trumpet judgment for all who do not have their names in the Book of Life: *And I saw the seven angels which stood before God; and to them were given seven trumpets. 3 And another angel came and stood at the altar, having a golden censer; and there was given unto him much incense, that he should offer it with the prayers of all saints upon the golden altar which was before the throne. 4 And the smoke of the incense, which came with the prayers of the saints, ascended up before God out of the angel's hand* (Revelation 8:2-4).

Those who do not have the seal of God will suffer during the trumpet judgments just as those in Egypt who were not covered by the blood: *And it was commanded them that they should not hurt the grass of the earth, neither any green thing, neither any tree; but only those men which have not the seal of God in their foreheads. 5 And to them it was given that they should not kill them, but that they should be tormented five months: and their torment was as the torment of a scorpion, when he striketh a man. 6 And in those days shall men seek death, and shall not find it; and shall desire to die, and death shall flee from them* (Revelation 9:4-6).

The tribulation period will be a time when God will use the trumpet judgments as He used the plagues in Egypt. The plagues of Egypt caused Pharaoh to change his mind and let God's people go. Pharaoh did not know he was headed for judgment. The Lord will cut the time short before all flesh is destroyed in the great war of the sixth trumpet. The Lord will come for His people in the rapture, and the Day of the Lord begins: *For then shall be great tribulation, such as was not since the beginning of the world to this time, no, nor ever shall be. 22 And except those days should be shortened, there should no flesh be saved: but for the elect's sake those days shall be shortened* (Matthew 24:21-22).

When the sixth trumpet sounds, the four angels which are bound by the great river Euphrates will be loosed. This battle is between the kings of the East and the antichrist, who would destroy all life if the Lord did not intervene with His coming. There will be over two hundred million men at war. Even after the sixth trumpet sounds, and a third part of the population is killed, they will show no remorse or repentance for their evil. God will judge them as He did Pharaoh. Jesus said it would be as it was before the flood, when their every thought was evil (Revelation 9:13-21).

In Revelation 10:1, the Lord comes down for the rapture and resurrection, and the Day of the Lord follows. When the seventh trumpet sounds, the mystery of God should be finished: *But in the days of the voice of the seventh angel when he shall begin to sound, the mystery of God should be finished, as he hath declared to his servants the prophets* (Revelation 10:7). The nations will be angry, because it is time for the wrath of God to be poured out on the wicked, and the fulfillment of Revelation 11:18: *And the nations were angry, and thy wrath is come, and the time of the dead, that they should be judged, and that thou shouldest give reward unto thy servants the prophets, and to the saints, and them that fear thy name, small and great; and shouldest destroy them which destroy the earth.* There will be weeping and gnashing of teeth for those who were religious but not saved (Matt. 24:51; 25:30). They will see the Lord coming in the clouds, and realize they are not ready (Rev. 22:7,12).

God will keep the promise He made to His children. They will be able to rest in those promises when the tribulation begins to come upon the world because of the evil generation: *For he hath said, I will never leave thee, nor forsake thee* (Hebrews 13:5b). *Who shall separate us from the love of Christ? shall tribulation, or distress, or persecution, or famine, or nakedness, or peril, or sword? 36 As it is written, For thy sake we are killed all the day long; we are accounted as sheep for the slaughter. 37 Nay, in all these things we are more than conquerors through him that loved us. 38 For I am persuaded, that neither death, nor life, nor angels, nor principalities, nor powers, nor things present, nor things to come, 39 Nor height, nor depth, nor any other creature, shall be able to separate us from the love of God, which is in Christ Jesus our Lord* (Romans 8:35-39).

THE BOOK
OF REVELATION

Millions of books have been printed, and messages preached, of how the rapture takes place in Revelation 4:1. This teaching has caused a big portion of the Church to disregard the rest of Revelation as being for the Church. Just because the word *Church* is not mentioned after the fourth chapter is not a valid reason to say the rest of Revelation is not for the Church. Jesus Himself tells us in Revelation 22:16 to testify these things unto the churches. The angel said to John in Revelation 1:3: *Blessed is he that readeth, and they that hear the words of this prophecy, and keep those things which are written therein: for the time is at hand.* Jesus said in Revelation 22:16: *I Jesus have sent mine angel to testify unto you these things in the churches. I am the root and the offspring of David, and the bright and morning star.*

Pretribulationists say the rapture takes place in Revelation 4:1, and because of this error, they cram all prophecy into the seven-year tribulation period from that point. Pretribulationists should examine what John said, and not what pretribulationists say he said. When the door was opened in heaven, the first voice said to John, *Come up hither, and I will show thee things which must be hereafter.* This verse does not say one word about the Church rapture. It is only telling John to come up hither so he can be shown the things to write which happen hereafter. This fulfills what was said in Revelation 1:19: *Write the things which thou hast seen, and the things which are, and the things which shall be hereafter.* John was immediately in the spirit and beheld the throne of the Lord. This is the throne the Father promised Jesus: *And immediately I was in the spirit; and, behold, a throne was set in heaven, and one sat on the throne. 3 And he that sat was to look upon like a jasper and a sardine stone: and there was a rainbow round about the throne, in sight like unto an emerald* (Revelation 4:2-3). These Scriptures have nothing to do with the tribulation period, but picture the Lord on His throne. The fourth and fifth chapters picture the saints who had died in the Lord around the throne with Him, waiting to receive their resurrected bodies: *To the end he may stablish your hearts unblameable in holiness before God, even our Father, at the coming of our Lord Jesus Christ with all his saints* (I Thessalonians 3:13). In Revelation 5:5, the Lord alone is worthy to open the seals for the Church. These seals are open for the Church down through Church history: *And one of the elders saith unto me, Weep not: behold, the Lion of the tribe of Juda, the Root of David, hath prevailed to open the book, and to loose the seven seals thereof* (Revelation 5:5).

The book of Revelation is very important to the Church in unveiling the end times. God does not leave His people in darkness. When pretribulationists begin to see the errors that have been made concerning the pretribulation rapture theory, Revelation will become a very important book to the Church, and they will know it is for them, and not for the Jew only. It details events that happened in John's day, and the things which were to happen thereafter. The Church must have knowledge concerning the Jews and Gentiles in these last days. They should know about the beast and the one-world government, and be warned about the false prophet that is to arise and deceive many. The Church should be able to identify Mystery Babylon the Great, the Mother of Harlots, and the Abominations of the Earth. Revelation lets the Church know when the rapture will take place, and the time of the first resurrection. Revelation reveals to the Church much truth about our eternal destiny and the New Jerusalem, the eternal home for the Church. We are commanded to teach these things to the Church. It should make us weep over the many false doctrines that are taught in churches today (Revelation. 22:16).

In my study of the many different doctrines concerning the interpretation of Revelation, I found that the key determining point is where writers place the rapture. Pretribulationists say the rapture takes place in Revelation 4:1, and the rest of Revelation is for the Jew only. Pre-Wrath and others say the rapture takes place at the sixth seal, and the wrath of God begins. Posttribulationists say that the rapture takes place at the seventh trumpet. Only one of these three are right, and the other two are wrong. The Church is confused over the many doctrines concerning the Lord's coming, and surely God's people should be able to separate truth from error. The next chapter will show that the rapture at the seventh trumpet is the only one of three that conforms to the Word.

POSTTRIBULATION COMING IS THE ONLY SCRIPTURAL COMING OF THE LORD

This chapter will give scriptural proof that the Lord will come at the end of the tribulation period, and not the beginning, or the middle. I pray this chapter brings some uniformity of the time element of the Lord's coming.

The posttribulation coming of the Lord is well established in the Old Testament; the Lord taught it in the Gospels; Luke taught it in the book of Acts; Paul taught it in the Epistles; and John taught it in Revelation. Luke made it plain by the inspiration of the Holy Spirit that there would be signs in heaven and earth before the Lord comes: *The sun shall be turned into darkness, and the moon into blood, before that great and notable day of the Lord come: 21 And it shall come to pass, that whosoever shall call on the name of the Lord shall be saved* (Acts 2:20-21). The Lord said in Luke that signs would take place before He comes in the clouds with power and great glory: *And they shall fall by the edge of the sword, and shall be led away captive into all nations: and Jerusalem shall be trodden down of the Gentiles, until the times of the Gentiles be fulfilled. 25 And there shall be signs in the sun, and in the moon, and in the stars; and upon the earth distress of nations, with perplexity; the sea and the waves roaring; 26 Men's hearts failing them for fear, and for looking after those things which are coming on the earth: for the powers of heaven shall be shaken. 27 And then shall they see the Son of man coming in a cloud with power and great glory. 28 And when these things begin to come to pass, then look up, and lift up your heads; for your redemption draweth nigh* (Luke 21:24-28).

The posttribulation coming was the message that the apostles preached in the early Church, and then the Catholic Church established a postmillennial coming. But reformers rejected this view and taught the premillennial coming of the Lord, the same message that Jesus and the early Church had taught. The Bible teaches us that the second advent of Jesus takes place after the tribulation, not before: *Immediately after the tribulation of those days shall the sun be darkened, and the moon shall not give her light, and the stars shall fall from heaven, and the powers of the heavens shall be shaken: 30 And then shall appear the sign of the Son of man in heaven: and then shall all the tribes of the earth mourn, and they shall see the Son of man coming in the clouds of heaven with power and great glory. 31 And he shall send his angels with a great sound of a trumpet, and they shall gather together his elect from the four winds, from one end of heaven to the other* (Matt. 24:29-31). Paul taught the same message, and said the apostasy and the man of sin would be revealed before the saints would be gathered unto the Lord (II Thessalonians. 2:1-3).

Paul let us know that both Jew and Gentile were reconciled unto God by Jesus, and that the Church was built upon the foundation of the apostles and prophets (Eph. 2:11-20). The prophets of the Old Testament began laying a foundation concerning the Lord's coming. Joel gives us the signs that will take place before the Lord comes, and the day of the Lord: *The sun shall be turned into darkness, and the moon into blood, before the great and the terrible day of the LORD come* (Joel 2:31). Luke spoke of these signs in Acts 2:20. The sign concerning the moon being turned into blood is fulfilled in the sixth seal (Revelation 6:12). The rapture and resurrection cannot take place at the sixth seal because the moon turns into blood before the great and terrible day of the LORD comes. The signs given in the sixth seal are different than the signs given by Jesus in the Gospels. Jesus said in Matthew 24:29-30: *Immediately after the tribulation of those days shall the sun be darkened, and the moon shall not give her light, and the stars shall fall from heaven, and the powers of the heavens shall be shaken: 30 And then shall appear the sign of the Son of man in heaven: and then shall all the tribes of the earth mourn, and they shall see the Son of man coming in the clouds of heaven with power and great glory.*

The signs in Matthew 24 must be fulfilled after the sixth seal, the 144,000 sealed, and the great multitude of saints who come out of great tribulation in Revelation 7:9, 13-15. The signs in Matthew 24:29 are fulfilled when the third and fourth angels sound in Revelation 8:10-13. When the seven angels began to sound in Revelation 8:7, it will be the beginning of the signs Jesus said would take place before He comes: *And there shall be signs in the sun, and in the moon, and in the stars; and upon the earth distress of nations, with perplexity; the sea and the waves roaring; 26 Men's hearts failing them for fear, and for looking after those things which are coming on the earth: for the powers of heaven shall be shaken. 27 And then shall they see the Son of man coming in a cloud with power and great glory* (Luke 21:25-28). Jesus will not come until the mystery is finished at the sounding of the last trumpet (Revelation 10:7).

The prophets gave a shadow of the rapture and resurrection taking place at the end of the tribulation period, but before the day of the Lord (Isa.26:17-21, Zeph. 2:1-3). The day of the Lord and His wrath starts immediately after the rapture. Peter speaks of the judgment concerning the day of the Lord, and how the saints will look for a new heaven before the day of the Lord: *But the day of the Lord will come as a thief in the night; in the which the heavens shall pass away with a great noise, and the elements shall melt with fervent heat, the earth also and the works that are therein shall be burned up. 11 Seeing then that all these things shall be dissolved, what manner of persons ought ye to be in all holy conversation and godliness, 12 Looking for and hasting unto the coming of the day of God, wherein the heavens being on fire shall be dissolved, and the elements shall melt with fervent heat? 13 Nevertheless we, according to his promise, look for new heavens and a new earth, wherein dwelleth righteousness* (II Peter 3:10-13).

The Lord is preparing a place for the saints before the day of the Lord (John 14:2). Jesus said the same day that Lot went out of Sodom it rained fire and brimstone from heaven and destroyed them all, and thus shall it be in the day when the Son of man is revealed (Luke 17:29-30). II Peter 3:10-13 is fulfilled after the rapture and resurrection at the last trump in Rev.10:7, 11:15. The day of the Lord, which is the wrath of God, begins the same day. The time element of the judgment seat of Christ and the day of the Lord's wrath is revealed in Revelation. 11:18: *And the nations were angry, and thy wrath is come, and the time of the dead, that they should be judged, and that thou shouldest give reward unto thy servants the prophets, and to the saints, and them that fear thy name, small and great; and shouldest destroy them which destroy the earth.*

The heathen nations will be angry when they see the rapture take place, and heaven opened, and the Lord coming on a white horse for judgment (Rev. 19:11-21, 14:17-20, 15:1–19:10). Old Testament prophets gave much about the day of the Lord, and how the righteous would be hid in the day of judgment (Zeph. 1:14-18, 2:1-3, Isa. 26:20-21, 2:12-22, 13:6-13, 34:1-8, Joel 1:15-2:11, 3:9-16, Obed.15-21, Zech. 14:1-7, 12-16, Mal. 4:1-2). Paul said the saints should not be ignorant concerning the time element of the day of the Lord, because they are the children of light and not darkness (I Thess. 5:1-9). James asked the brethren to be patient unto the coming of the Lord, because the latter rain must take place first. The latter rain will take place in Daniel's seventieth week before the Lord comes for the rapture: *Be patient therefore, brethren, unto the coming of the Lord. Behold, the husbandman waiteth for the precious fruit of the earth, and hath long patience for it, until he receive the early and latter rain. 8 Be ye also patient; stablish your hearts: for the coming of the Lord draweth nigh* (James 5:7-8). The Lord must receive the latter rain before He comes, the same as He received the early rain which began on the day of Pentecost.

The Old Testament is the source of all New Testament doctrines, and tells us about the tribulation period, the rapture and resurrection, and how the saints will be safe in the Lord's chambers before God pours out His wrath in the day of the Lord (Isa. 26:17-21). Daniel tells how God's people will be delivered in the time of trouble, and about the resurrection (Daniel 12:1-3). Joel described the signs that will take place before the Day of the Lord. After the rapture and resurrection, the day of the Lord begins, which is the wrath of God (Isa. 13:6, 9-16). Daniel said the Lord would come in the clouds in the ancient of days, and the kingdoms of this world will become the kingdoms of our Lord, and His Christ (Daniel 7:13-14, Rev. 11:15). The day of the Lord and the battle of Armageddon take place after the rapture and resurrection. The kingdom of Israel and the millennium follow (Zech. 14:1-21). Many of God's people stopped using these root scriptures concerning the second advent when the pretribulation rapture theory was established in 1830. These Scriptures are the very foundation Peter used in his message after Pentecost concerning the time element of the Lord's first and second advent. Both advents have their root in the Old Testament and the prophets (Acts 3:19-26).

The restitution of all things cannot take place in Revelation 4:1, or the sixth seal in Revelation 6:12-17. Paul tells us the mystery of the rapture and resurrection takes place at the last trumpet (I Cor. 15:51-53). There is no other place in the Bible except the last trumpet in Revelation where this Scripture could be fulfilled. Revelation tells us the mystery of God is finished when the seventh angel begins to sound (Rev. 10:7). When the seventh trumpet sounds, the kingdoms of this world will become the kingdoms of our Lord, and of His Christ; and He shall reign forever and ever (Rev. 11:15). This is the same time sequence concerning the coming of the Lord and the restitution of all things that Peter preached (Acts 3:19-21). The nations will be angry when they see the rapture and resurrection. The time has come for Christ to reward His servants—the prophets, saints, and all who fear His name. The day of the Lord begins the same day that the rapture and resurrection takes place (Rev. 11:18; Luke 17:29-30).

Sound doctrine rests on a scriptural and historical foundation. The pretribulation rapture has neither. The theory of evolution is not taught because people have a foundation of truth, but because people are willing to accept a theory of man, which has no foundation of truth. Pretribulation theory can only survive if people are willing to accept a theory that is based on dispensational teachings discounting the Gospels for the Church. Pretribulationists use I Thessalonians 5:9, which tells us that God has not appointed us to wrath, in trying to prove a pretribulation rapture. They take this verse out of context. This verse has nothing to do with the Church being exempted from the tribulation period, but tells the Church they will not suffer the wrath of God, or hell, because they are saved. In verse 10 Paul says, whether we are alive or dead, we shall live together with the Lord; therefore Paul is not talking to the Church about escaping the tribulation period. He is telling the Church they will not suffer God's wrath because they are God's children.

Pretribulationists believe that the rapture takes place in Revelation 4:1, and from that point on is the beginning of the tribulation period, which they mistakenly call the wrath of God. Authors of the Pre-Wrath doctrine believe that the rapture takes place in the sixth seal, and the wrath of God follows. They believe the trumpet judgments are the wrath of God. I believe this view of the time sequence of the rapture is incorrect. I have already shown that the sixth seal is the fulfillment of Joel 2:31 and Acts 2:20-21. The sun is turned into darkness, and the moon into blood before the Lord comes; therefore the Lord must come after the sixth seal and the tribulation in Revelation 6:9 and 14 as Jesus said in Matthew 24:29. We must not mislead ourselves in the interpretation of the verse of the sixth seal: *For the great day of his wrath is come; and who shall be able to stand?* (Revelation 6:17). This Scripture does not mean that the time for the rapture has come, nor the day of the Lord. God's people should be careful not to take the word *wrath* and think it only applies to those who are left behind after the rapture in the tribulation period. The word has a much broader meaning, and implies punishment, anger, indignation, or vengeance. God has poured out His wrath on nations, and has never let His wrath come upon His people. The word *wrath* was used in Scripture to describe punishment against the ungodly long before it was used against the wicked in Revelation. The Lord did not take the righteous out of the world in any of the judgments below, but protected them from His judgments.

The children of Israel provoked the LORD to wrath in the wilderness (Deu. 9:7). Jehu told King Jehoshaphat that the wrath of God was upon him because he helped the ungodly and loved them that hate the LORD (II Chro. 19:2). The Word of the LORD came to Ezekiel, and let him know that when the land sins against the LORD, and God stretches out his hand against the wicked by famine, noisome beast, and the sword, that He will keep His children from harm (Ezek. 14:12-23). God judged Pharaoh while the children of Israel were still in Egypt, and God's judgments did not hurt one person of the children of Israel. These things happened for examples for the Church (I Cor. 10:1-11). Down through the ages God has never let His people suffer His wrath when He judged the wicked. God sealed the righteous in Israel upon their foreheads when He used the army of Nebuchadnezzar to destroy Jerusalem (Ezek. 9:1-11). When the four angels are sent to hurt the earth and the sea in the tribulation period, God seals and protects His servants from harm as the trumpet judgments begin to sound (Rev. 7:1-3). God has always kept His people from harm in His judgments, because He did not appoint them to wrath.

Paul counseled the Thessalonians that the tribulation and afflictions they were suffering were not to destroy their faith, but to prefect it, and that in the end hearts, would be stablished "unblameable in holiness before God." *That no man should be moved by these afflictions: for yourselves know that we are appointed thereunto. 4 For verily, when we were with you, we told you before that we should suffer tribulation; even as it came to pass, and ye know. 5 For this cause, when I could no longer forbear, I sent to know your faith, lest by some means the tempter have tempted you, and our labour be in vain. 10 Night and day praying exceedingly that we might see your face, and might perfect that which is lacking in your faith? 11 Now God himself and our Father, and our Lord Jesus Christ, direct our way unto you. 12 And the Lord make you to increase and abound in love one toward another, and toward all men, even as we do toward you: 13 To the end he may stablish your hearts unblameable in holiness before God, even our Father, at the coming of our Lord Jesus Christ with all his saints* (I Thessalonians 3:3-5, 10-13).

Paul's first letter to the Thessalonian church kindled great excitement. He forewarned them not to be moved by the affliction coming upon the Church because it was appointed for them to suffer tribulation. Paul then revealed the rapture and resurrection of the saints (I Thess. 4:16-17). He told them that the Lord would *descend from heaven with a shout, with the voice of the archangel, and with the trump of God: and the dead in Christ would rise first: 17 Then we which are alive and remain shall be caught up together with them in the clouds, to meet the Lord in the air: and so shall we ever be with the Lord,.* Paul explained the times and seasons, which the Lord had already taught in the Gospels. Paul later had to write them a second letter because new persecution had come upon the Church, and false prophets were teaching error. Paul assured them that the day of the Lord had not come, and let them know they would suffer persecution from the enemy, but the Lord in His righteous judgment would recompense tribulation to them that troubled them: *Which is a manifest token of the righteous judgment of God, that ye may be counted worthy of the kingdom of God, for which ye also suffer: 6 Seeing it is a righteous thing with God to recompense tribulation to them that trouble you; 7 And to you who are troubled rest with us, when the Lord Jesus shall be revealed from heaven with his mighty angels, 8 In flaming fire taking vengeance on them that know not God, and that obey not the gospel of our Lord Jesus Christ: 9 Who shall be punished with everlasting destruction from the presence of the Lord, and from the glory of his power; 10 When he shall come to be glorified in his saints, and to be admired in all them that believe (because our testimony among you was believed) in that day* (II Thessalonians 1: 5-10).

Dispensationalist and pretribulationists have been teaching since the days of Darby that the second coming of Christ could take place at any moment without any preliminary signs or prophesied event. This is the same mistake the false prophets were making in the church at Thessalonica. They were making prophecies that the Lord could come at any moment, and Paul interceded, encouraged, and exhorted the Thessalonians to stand fast in the faith, and not to be alarmed at rumors they heard concerning the imminent coming of Christ. Paul corrected the false prophets, and let the Thessalonian saints know that prior to the Lord's coming and our gathering together unto Him would come the great apostasy from the faith, and the antichrist would be revealed to deceive and pervert the world—particularly those who do not have a love for truth, but have pleasure in unrighteousness. Paul asked them not to let anyone by any means deceive them on these two issues: *Now we beseech you, brethren, by the coming of our Lord Jesus Christ, and by our gathering together unto him, 2 That ye be not soon shaken in mind, or be troubled, neither by spirit, nor by word, nor by letter as from us, as that the day of Christ is at hand. 3 Let no man deceive you by any means: for that day shall not come, except there come a falling away first, and that man of sin be revealed, the son of perdition; 4 Who opposeth and exalteth himself above all that is called God, or that is worshipped; so that he as God sitteth in the temple of God, showing himself that he is God. 5 Remember ye not, that, when I was yet with you, I told you these things? 9 Even him, whose coming is after the working of Satan with all power and signs and lying wonders,10 And with all deceivableness of unrighteousness in them that perish; because they received not the love of the truth, that they might be saved.11 And for this cause God shall send them strong delusion, that they should believe a lie: 12 That they all might be damned who believed not the truth, but had pleasure in unrighteousness* (II Thessalonians 2:1-5, 9-12). That which Paul warned against, dispensationalists and pretribulationists have broken, and teach the very same message that the false prophets were teaching.

I read *Zwingli and Bullinger*, edited by G. W. Bromiley, about reformers who wanted truth and purity of doctrine. They brought back to the Church the doctrine of the premillinnial coming of Christ. Zwingli wrote about the errors of the Catholic Church and the Lord's supper, and gave his belief concerning the Lord's coming. He did not discount the Gospels for the Church or accept a pretribulation rapture theory. He believed the Lord would come in the last day before judgment:

"For the whole context and meaning show us that Christ's aim was to teach them that he would ascend up bodily into heaven and sit at the right hand of the Father until the last day. The omnipotence of God accomplishes all things according to the Word of God: it never does that which is contrary to that word.

"Second, we point out that until the last day Christ cannot be anywhere but at the right hand of God the Father. In Psalm 110 it is written: *Sit thou at my right hand, until I make thine enemies thy footstool.* Paul refers to this text in I Corinthians 15, when he teaches that Christ will sit at the right hand of the Father until the last day. If Christ is seated there, he is not here. And if he were here, we could not speak of his return, for he would have returned already. The proof of this is in Matthew 26:64: *Jesus saith unto him, Thou hast said: nevertheless I say unto you, Hereafter shall ye see the Son of man sitting on the right hand of power, and coming in the clouds of heaven.* What could be clearer than that? The word ap arti, 'hereafter,' is of itself enough to show us that we must seek him at the right hand of the Father until that day when he returns in the clouds for judgment. That 'hereafter' extends to the last day. And that is the basis of the third article in the Creed: 'From thence he shall come to judge the quick and the dead.'"

There is no secret coming of the Lord. The Lord will come visibly, exactly as He departed. In Acts 1:9-11 it is written: *And when he had spoken these things, while they beheld, he was taken up; and a cloud received him out of their sight. 10 And while they looked stedfastly toward heaven as he went up, behold, two men stood by them in white apparel; 11 Which also said, Ye men of Galilee, why stand ye gazing up into heaven? this same Jesus, which is taken up from you into heaven, shall so come in like manner as ye have seen him go into heaven.*

Dispensationalists make a distinction between the coming of the Lord for the Church and His return to earth with His saints at the end of the tribulation period. Matthew 24 is looked upon as Christ coming back to earth with His saints for the judgment of nations. Pretribulationists say the Jewish remnant will preach the gospel of the kingdom unto all nations during the seven-year tribulation period, and when the Lord comes back to earth with his Church, He will separate the sheep from the goats. The sheep represent those saved during the tribulation period. They and the saints who were in the rapture will be in the kingdom of heaven on earth which lasts one thousand years. This doctrine puts those who went through the tribulation period and have fleshly bodies in the same kingdom with the Church which have resurrected bodies. This cannot be true; you cannot mix the heavenly Jerusalem with the earthly, or the fleshly bodies with the spiritual. Paul made this plain in I Corinthians 15:35-57. Verse 50: *Now this I say, brethren, that flesh and blood cannot inherit the kingdom of God; neither doth corruption inherit incorruption.*

Two comings of the Lord are given by dispensationalists: one for the Church before the tribulation starts, and the other after the tribulation, in which the Lord is coming back to earth with His saints for the judgment of nations. This is only theological reasoning concerning a pretribulation rapture, and it does not hold true to the Word. Jesus told His disciples, who were the first members of the New Testament Church, when He would come again. The signs of His coming would occur immediately after the tribulation, and He would send His angels to gather His elect before the judgment (Matthew 24:29-31). The elect are Jews and Gentiles who are saved (Mark 13:27; I Peter 1:2; Tit. 1:1; Rom. 8:33). The rapture of the Church is found in Matthew 24:31, 40-42, and is the same rapture that Paul gives us in I Thessalonians 4:13-17. The rapture and resurrection of saints will take place at the last trumpet (I Cor. 15:51-53; Thes. 4:16; Rev. 10:7; 11:15-18; Daniel 12:1-2). The angels are the reapers, not the saints (Matthew. 13:30,39).

The judgment of nations begins immediately after the rapture and resurrection, which takes place at the last trumpet, and then comes the judgment seat of Christ (Rev.10:7; 11:15,18). In order to understand the time element of the rapture and resurrection, we must understand what takes place before that great event. It will be like in Joshua when seven priest were given seven trumpets. They blew their trumpets each day for six days warning of the coming judgment, and on the seventh day after sounding their trumpets seven times the city fell. The fall of Jericho was a type of the coming judgment. The saints will find safety behind the blood in the rapture as did Rahab, and the rest in Jericho suffered judgment. When the seventh seal is opened in Revelation 8:1-6, seven angels are given seven trumpets. The angels will sound warning, and the saints will understand what is taking place (I Thess. 5:4-9). The seven trumpets will be seven distinct events, which will bring to a close Daniel's seventieth week. The seven angels that have the seven trumpets are not pouring out the wrath of God on the saints, but are allowed to hurt only those who do not have the seal of God in their foreheads (Rev. 9:4).

God's angels were behind the destroying armies of Nebuchadnezzar when Jerusalem was destroyed. God showed Ezekiel that Nebuchadnezzar's army was acting as the agent of God, under the supervision of angels. The angel placed a mark upon the forehead of the righteous, and no hurt was allowed to anyone who had the mark (Ezek. 9:6). It will be the same in the tribulation period, when the four angels are assigned to hurt the earth and the sea. God protects the 144,000 who are sealed (Rev. 7:1-4).

We must consider the two witnesses, and the power they are given in the 1,260 days of their ministry. This will help us understand that the seven angels are not pouring out God's wrath on the saints: *And if any man will hurt them, fire proceedeth out of their mouth, and devoureth their enemies: and if any man will hurt them, he must in this manner be killed. 6 These have power to shut heaven, that it rain not in the days of their prophecy: and have power over waters to turn them to blood, and to smite the earth with all plagues, as often as they will. 7 And when they shall have finished their testimony, the beast that ascendeth out of the bottomless pit shall make war against them, and shall overcome them, and kill them* (Revelation 11:5-7).

The trumpet judgments will be similar to the plagues of Egypt before the children of Israel were delivered. The two witnesses will be able to bring judgment on the wicked as Moses brought on Egypt. Paul, Silvanus, and Timothy rejoiced in the saints of the church of Thessalonica because of their patience and faith in all their persecution and tribulation. God brought tribulation on those that persecuted God's children, and said it was a manifest token of the righteous judgment of God, which they suffered to recompense tribulation on them that troubled them. The saints going through the six trumpet judgments will be no different, because the Lord will come in flaming fire on them that know not God, when He comes to be glorified in the saints (II Thessalonians 1:1-10).

When the sixth angel sounds and the four angels which are bound by the river Euphrates are loosed, the great army of two hundred million will slay the third part of men (Rev. 9:13-21). This great army is making war against the beast, and is the fulfillment of (Daniel 11:44-45). The Lord will intervene in this great war by His coming for the rapture and resurrection before man destroys all flesh; (Matt. 24:21-22). Daniel 12:1-2 shows the rapture and resurrection taking place after the war. This takes us back to the fulfillment of where we started, and the sounding of the last trumpet in Revelation 10:7, 11:15, after which comes the judgment of nations, and then the judgment seat of Christ (Rev. 11:18).

The war of the sixth trumpet is not the battle of Armageddon, nor is it the fulfillment of Ezekiel 38, and 39, but is the fulfillment of Daniel 11:44-45. The war in Ezekiel 38 and 39 refers to Russia and her allies making war on Israel when she is resting in peace, and I believe it takes place at the sixth seal. I believe God will use the beast to bring defeat to Russia and her allies in Daniel 11:40-43. After the war of Ezekiel 38 and 39 the beast will make his palace in Jerusalem as recorded in Daniel 11:41. This will make China, the kings of the East, and the nations which border the Euphrates feel threatened by the beast and his mighty power, and they will prepare for war: *But tidings out of the east and out of the north shall trouble him: therefore he shall go forth with great fury to destroy, and utterly to make away many. 45 And he shall plant the tabernacles of his palace between the seas in the glorious holy mountain; yet he shall come to his end, and none shall help him* (Daniel 11:44-45). The war of the sixth trumpet with China and her allies, as recorded in Revelation 9:13-21, will be interrupted by the Lord's coming before all flesh is destroyed. Every eye will see the Lord coming in the clouds, the rapture and resurrection will take place. The war will cease, and the beast and the kings of the earth with their armies will gather together to make war with the Lord in the battle of Armageddon (Rev. 19:11-21). This is where the beast will come to his end.

The following Scriptures will confirm I have put the time element of the Lord's coming in its proper place. The Lord leaves heaven, and is on His way to earth to fulfill the mystery which takes place at the seventh trump: *And I saw another mighty angel come down from heaven, clothed with a cloud: and a rainbow was upon his head, and his face was as it were the sun, and his feet as pillars of fire. 5 And the angel which I saw stand upon the sea and upon the earth lifted up his hand to heaven, 6 And sware by him that liveth for ever and ever, who created heaven, and the things that therein are, and the earth, and the things that therein are, and the sea, and the things which are therein, that there should be time no longer: 7 But in the days of the voice of the seventh angel, when he shall begin to sound, the mystery of God should be finished, as he hath declared to his servants the prophets* (Revelation 10:1, 5-7). The sixth and seventh verses let us know that there will be no longer any delay in fulfilling the mystery of God, which He declared unto His servants, the prophets of the Old and New Testament, concerning the two advents, the second coming of the Lord, the Church age, the rapture and resurrection. This mystery was not made plain to Old Testament saints concerning Deuteronomy 4:30-31, Isaiah 26:17-21, Daniel 9:24-27,12:1-3, Joel:2:30-32, and many other Scriptures concerning the Lord's coming. Jesus began to explain all that was prophesied of Him concerning the events leading up to His coming in Luke 21:21-28, Matt. 24:29-31, and Mark 13:14-27, 32-37. Paul corrected the doctrines of false prophets that had gotten into the church of the Thessalonians, and let them know that rapture and resurrection had not taken place (I Thess. 4:13-17). He let them know that the saints had already been taught the times and the seasons, and how the day of the Lord should not come on them as a thief in the night, because they were of the light and not darkness (I Thess. 5:1-9). Paul let them know that the rapture could not take place until the apostasy comes, and the man of sin be revealed, and then the day of the Lord would take place (II Thess. 2:1-12). Paul made it plain that the mystery of the rapture and resurrection takes place at the last trump (I Cor. 15:51-52), and is the same time element as the seventh trumpet in Revelation 10:7. Prophecies in the Old Testament, the Gospels, the Epistles, and Revelation are fulfilled to their completeness when the seventh trumpet sounds in Revelation 10:7 and 11:15.

All the prophecies of the mystery, which God declared unto His servants the prophets, must be fulfilled before the seventh trumpet sounds. Jesus revealed the mystery of the kingdom of God (Mark 4:11). The kingdom of God was a spiritual kingdom that would not come with observation (Luke 17:20-21), but would be given to the believer by the second birth (John 3:3-8). Paul wrote how the mystery of Christ was not made known in other ages, but was made known unto him. He said, *That the Gentiles should be fellowheirs, and of the same body, and partakers of his promise in Christ by the gospel* (Ephsians. 3:6). The next mystery is found in Romans 11:24-25, how blindness in part happened to Israel until the fullness of the Gentiles be come in. The Jews stumbled that the Gentiles be grafted in, and how great will be the fullness of the Jews (Rom. 11:11-12). A remnant of Jews must be grafted in before the Lord will come (Rom. 11:15-23). Jesus was the beginning of the mystery of the preaching of the gospel (Heb. 2:3). The preaching of the gospel for the redemption and salvation of both Jew and Gentile was a mystery, and kept secret in Old Testament times. Only types and shadows of it were given in the ceremonial Law. It was not made plain by the prophets, but only pointed to (Heb. 9:1-15; 10:1-14). The veil of the Old Testament was taken away in Christ (II Cor. 3:13-18). The Old Testament needed the light of Jesus, and the New Covenant, which revealed the things that had been hid. This gospel must be preached unto all the world before the mystery can be complete, and the end come (Rom. 16:24-27; Matt. 24:14). The man of sin, the mystery of iniquity in II Thessalonians 2:7, and the mystery of blindness in part which happened unto Israel, (Rom. 11:25) will be fully made known. When the seventh trumpet sounds all the mysteries of God will be finished as He declared unto His servants the prophets; (Rev. 10:7).

The message that Peter preached after Pentecost let the unbelieving Jews know that repentance, and conversion, is the only way to miss the coming judgment of the Lord. He let them know that the Lord would remain in heaven until the time for the complete restoration of all the things, which God had spoken by the mouth of His holy prophets since the world began (Acts 3:18-21). The first part of Acts 3:21 will be fulfilled when Jesus leaves heaven to come to earth for the rapture and resurrection in Revelation 10:1. The second part will be fulfilled when the seventh trumpet begins to sound, and the announcement is made that the kingdoms of this world are become the kingdoms of our Lord, and of His Christ (Rev. 11:15). The nations will be angry when they see all these events taking place before their eyes. The day of the Lord has arrived, and the Lord will destroy them that destroyed the earth (Rev. 11:18). The judgment of the day of the Lord begins immediately after the rapture and resurrection, the same as when Noah entered the ark, the flood began, and destroyed them all (Luke 17:17).

When dispensationalists separated the Old Testament prophets, and what Jesus taught about His coming for the Church, and put both under the Law, it caused blindness to the Church concerning the fulfillment of the mystery. All the mysteries must come to their fulfillment and completion when the seventh trumpet sounds. There is no other place in Revelation where the coming of the Lord fulfills all that was prophesied by the prophets except the seventh trump (Revelation 10:7; 11:15). When the seventh trumpet sounds, the seven seals have been opened, and completed, and six trumpets have blown, before the Lord intervenes. The mystery is now complete, and it's time for the coming of the Lord, the rapture and resurrection. The wrath of God follows in Revelation 11:18.

After the saints are raptured and safe in the Lord's chambers, He will come back to earth with His angels to reap the earth and pour out the wrath of God. Revelation 19:11-21 shows Jesus and His armies coming in judgment, but it does not mention any saints coming with them back to earth. The saints are safe in heaven until the seven last vials and the battle of Armageddon are completed. Every eye will see these things taking place on earth, and great fear will come upon everyone who is left, because the judgment starts immediately. The judgment will be the same as when Noah entered the Ark, God shut the door, and judgment started, or as when Lot was safe out of Sodom, the fire fell in judgment (Luke 17:28-36). The coming of the Lord for the rapture takes place at the last day, the same day that the wrath of God begins. The Jews who are not in the rapture will see the wounds in the Lord's hands, and will mourn for Him, realizing Jesus was the Messiah. Only one-third will come through the fire and will go into the millennium. The Lord will take Jerusalem first when the judgment starts, and will stand upon the Mount of Olives (Zech. 13:6-9; 14:1-5). The wrath of God will be poured out by the seven angels which have the seven last vials, and ends with the battle of Armageddon (Rev. 16:1-21). After the Church is raptured, the Lord will gather all nations to Jerusalem for the big battle and the reaping of the earth (Joel 3:2, 11-16).

There will not be two resurrections for the righteous. John said the first resurrection includes those who gave their lives for Christ in the tribulation period (Rev. 20:4-6). We can trace the early indications of the rapture to Enoch and Elijah, but for Old Testament Scripture for

Israel in the last days, the tribulation period, the rapture and resurrection of saints, we go to Isaiah 26:17-21. Daniel tells us of the same event in Daniel 12:1-2. Jesus said all that the Father had given Him, He would raise up in the last day. The last day is not the beginning of the tribulation period, but is the last day the saints will be on earth before the judgment (John 6:39-40, 44, 54). Jesus also affirmed His coming and that the rapture would take place immediately after the tribulation (Matt. 24:29-31, 37-42). Paul did not change the doctrine that the prophets and Jesus taught concerning the rapture and resurrection. He made clear and confirms what had already been taught: that the coming of the Lord would take place at the last trumpet after the tribulation (I Cor. 15:20-23, 51-53). Paul's letter to the Thessalonian church was to correct false teaching about the coming of the Lord, not to develop a new doctrine. Paul instructed the Thessalonian church that they were not to let anyone deceive them concerning the Lord's coming because that day would not take place until the apostasy comes first and the man of sin is revealed (II Thess. 2:1-5). Pretribulationists have added another resurrection before the tribulation period to satisfy dispensational teachings, but this is not scriptural. All New Testament doctrine must be built upon the foundation of the apostles and prophets (Ephesians 2:20).

Pretribulationists and midtribulationists say that believing in a posttribulation rapture of the Church does not give enough time for the judgment seat of Christ if the rapture of the Church comes at the end of Daniel's seventieth week. Their reasoning does not hold true when all the facts are presented concerning the judgment seat of Christ, and the marriage of the Lamb to His bride. Pretribulationists teach that the judgment seat of Christ and the marriage to the Lamb take place in a seven-year period of time, between the rapture and the revelation. If all stood before the Lord, and were judged one by one for seven years, twenty-four hours a day, judging one per minute until the revelation of Jesus Christ, this would give enough time to judge 3,679,235 people. Midtribulationists would have time enough to have 1,839,612 people judged. What would happen to all the other millions of saints still standing in line to be judged? Their reasoning cannot be right because the judgment seat of Christ cannot take place until after the seventh trumpet sounds. No one knows on earth the length of time the Lord will take in the Bema seat judgment, or what method He will use. Pretribulationists' concepts of the judgment seat of Christ and God's are oceans apart. If God can hear all the prayers of His people at one time, I am sure, time will be no object with the Lord. We do know that the Lord keeps records of our works, whether good or bad, and we will be judged and rewarded for our works. The time sequence of when this is to take place is after the seventh trumpet. These Scriptures must be fulfilled first: *But in the days of the voice of the seventh angel, when he shall begin to sound, the mystery of God should be finished, as he hath declared to his servants the prophets. 15. And the seventh angel sounded; and there were great voices in heaven, saying, The kingdoms of this world are become the kingdoms of our Lord, and of his Christ; and he shall reign for ever and ever* (Revelation. 10:7; 11:15). Verse 18 makes plain the time element of the judgment seat of Christ, which takes place after the rapture at the last trump. The nations will be angry when they see the coming of the Lord and the rapture take place before their eyes. The Lord said it is time for the judgment seat to take place, and for Him to give rewards to His servants: *18: And the nations were angry, and thy wrath is come, and the time of the dead, that they should be judged, and that thou shouldest give reward unto thy servants the prophets, and to the saints, and them that fear thy name, small and great; and shouldest destroy them which destroy the earth.* This makes the pretribulationists concept to be in error.

Revelation teaches the same message Jesus taught in the Gospels concerning the judgment seat of Christ and the reward of the saints. Both are connected with the Lord's coming: *For the Son of man shall come in the glory of his Father with his angels; and then he shall reward every man according to his works* (Matt. 16:27). Paul revealed the mystery of the resurrection to take place at the last trumpet: *Behold, I show you a mystery; We shall not all sleep, but we shall all be changed, 52 In a moment, in the twinkling of an eye, at the last trump: for the trumpet shall sound, and the dead shall be raised incorruptible, and we shall be changed. 53 For this corruptible must put on incorruption, and this mortal must put on immortality* (I Cor. 15:51-53).Paul made it plain that the Lord would not come until the apostasy come first, and the man of sin be revealed (II Thess. 2:1-3). All three set the same time for the coming of the Lord and the judgment seat of Christ.

Interpreting the 1,260 days in Revelation 11:3 and 12:6 to be years as in Daniel's seventy weeks, where a day is counted for a year, cannot apply concerning the seventieth week because there can only be a seven-year period of time. God gave forty-two months, a time, times, and half a time as being the same length of time as the 1,260 days. The 1,260 days in Revelation 11:3 and 12:6 are the same length as the time, times, and half a time in Revelation 12:14. Power is given to the beast to continue forty-two months in Revelation 13:5, which is the same length of time as the time, times, and the dividing of time in Daniel 7:25. The man clothed in fine linen will hold up His right hand and His left unto heaven and will declare all things are finished. This will take place at the end of the time, times, and one-half time (Dan. 12:7). The extra 30 days in Daniel 12:11 is the time needed for the beast to scatter the power of God's people before judgment (Dan. 12:7). There are another 45 days in Daniel 12:12, making a total of 75 days beyond the 1,260 days, which I believe is the time needed for the judgment. The Gentiles are allowed to control the Holy City for forty-two months before the Lord intervenes (Rev. 11:2). The beast is allowed to continue 42 months before the Lord comes for the rapture, and announces judgment on the beast (Rev 13:5). The two witnesses witness for 1,260 days before the beast makes war and kills them (Rev.11:3,7). The big war of the sixth trumpet is also raging (Rev. 13-21, Dan. 11:36-45). The Lord leaves heaven in Revelation 10:1-6, and will intervene by his coming at the last trump before all flesh is killed (I Cor. 15:51-52, Rev.10:7, 11:15). Immediately after the rapture and resurrection, the Day of the Lord begins.

Daniel's seventieth week and the Revelation tie together concerning the time element of the Lord's coming. Daniel 12:1-2 shows the resurrection, and in Daniel 12:6, the man clothed in linen, who is Jesus, is asked the question of how long shall it be to the end of these wonders? The man in linen lifts up His hands to heaven and says, *It shall be for a time, times, and an half; and when he shall have accomplished to scatter the power of the holy people, all these things shall be finished* (Dan. 12:7). Daniel 12:11 is the fulfillment of verses 6 and 7: *And from the time that the daily sacrifice shall be taken away, and the abomination that maketh desolate set up, there shall be a thousand two hundred and ninety days.* Daniel 12:11 starts in the middle of Daniel's seventieth week, when the beast breaks his covenant with Israel and stops the sacrifices being offered in the temple. This verse extends beyond the 1,260 days to 1,290 days where the abomination that makes desolate is set up, and shows the fulfillment of an extra 30 days where the beast makes war on Israel, as well as the ful-fillment of verses 6 and 7.

In Revelation 11:2, the Gentiles tread Jerusalem under foot for forty-two months, and in verse 3 the two witnesses prophesy for 1,260 days before the beast makes war against them, and kills them. This is the same time element as Daniel's chapter 12, and the Revelation chap-ter 12. In Revelation 12:6, Israel flees into the wilderness, and is pro-tected for 1,260 days, which is the same time as the time, times, and half a time in verse 14. After the 1,260 days is finished, the Devil is angry with Israel and goes to make war with her. This verse shows that there are many in Israel who are already saved, and have the testimony of Jesus Christ: *And the dragon was wroth with the woman, and went to make war with the remnant of her seed, which keep the commandments of God, and have the testimony of Jesus Christ* (Revelation 12:17). The seventh trumpet sounds in Revelation 11:15 when the rapture and resurrection take place, and must sound after the 1,260 days is finished, and the two wit-nesses are killed (Rev. 11:7). The mystery of the rapture and resurrec-tion will be finished when the seventh trumpet sounds as He hath declared unto His servants the prophets (Rev. 10:7). The time element concerning the rapture and resurrection are the same in Daniel as it is in Revelation.

The tribulation period, or the fulfillment of Daniel's seventieth week, is much more than God dealing with the nation of Israel. The antichrist will magnify himself above every god, and will prosper until the time of the judgment (Dan. 11:36). He will honor the god of power (Dan. 11:36). He will conquer many nations (Dan. 11:39-41). He will control money (Dan. 11:43). The Devil and his angels will be cast out of heaven unto the earth, and this will lead to the salvation of many. The saints will be endued with the mighty power of God, and will over-come the Devil by the blood. It will be a time of rejoicing in heaven and earth, because the Devil will only have a short time left before the Lord comes. The Lord will give much grace to His people (Rev. 12:9-16). The Devil will make war against Israel and the remnant of her seed who keep the commandments of God, and have the testimony of Jesus Christ (Rev. 12:17). The beast will blaspheme God, and against His tab-ernacle, and them that dwell in heaven, and will make war against the saints, and power will be given him over all nations (Rev. 13:6-7). The false prophet will deceive many by miracles, and cause people to worship the image of the beast (Rev. 13:11-14). Those who do not understand the times and the seasons will be deceived into taking the mark of the beast, and worshipping the beast as god (Rev. 13:15-18). God's people should not be in darkness, but be in the light, and know that God did not appoint His people to wrath, but they will suffer tribulation by the hands of the wicked (II Thess. 5:1-10).

If we want to know how long the judgment will last, we go to Daniel 12:12: *Blessed is he that waiteth, and cometh to the thousand three hundred and five and thirty days.* I believe the extra 45 days is the time needed from the beginning of the day of the Lord until the close of the seven last vials and the battle of Armageddon (Rev.15:1-8; 16:1-21, & 19:11-21). God's judgment will be swift. The judgment seat of Christ will take place afterwards: *And the nations were angry, and thy wrath is come, and the time of the dead, that they should be judged, and that thou shouldest give reward unto thy servants the prophets, and to the saints, and them that fear thy name, small and great; and shouldest destroy them which destroy the earth* (Revelation 11:18). There will be many who will be saved after the rapture when they see Jesus coming in the clouds, and see the nail prints in His hands and feet (Zech. 13:6-9). The people left on earth after the judgment in Daniel 12:12-13 are the people who were not in the rapture, but believed when they saw Jesus coming, and will live in the millennium on earth (Zech. 13:9; 14:16-21).

Prior to the rapture and resurrection, the saints before the throne are given white robes (Rev. 6:11, 7:9, 13-14), but after the rapture and resurrection, the bride of Christ dresses in fine linen for the marriage: *Let us be glad and rejoice, and give honour to him: for the marriage of the Lamb is come, and his wife hath made herself ready. 8 And to her was granted that she should be arrayed in fine linen, clean and white: for the fine linen is the righteousness of saints. 9 And he saith unto me, Write, Blessed are they which are called unto the marriage supper of the Lamb. And he saith unto me, These are the true sayings of God* (Revelation 19:7-9). These Scriptures show the preparation of the bride for her marriage, which cannot take place before the seven last vials and the battle of Armageddon is fulfilled (Rev. 15:5-8). The verses that follow this Scripture show Jesus coming on a white horse, to judge and make war, and end with the battle of Armageddon. The beast and the false prophet are cast into the lake of fire (Rev. 19:11-21). If the marriage and marriage supper take place before the battle of Armageddon, that would make the judgment seat of Christ, the marriage and the marriage supper, take place in heaven while the wrath of God is being poured out on earth during the 45 days of God's wrath (Rev. 19:11-21). The Lord will not be in both places at the same time. The Lord and His angels as the reapers will bring judgment on earth first. The following paragraph will explain the mystery.

If Jesus follows Jewish marriage customs, He is only getting His bride ready by the rapture, resurrection, and the judgment seat of Christ. In Revelation 7:14-15 the tribulation saints are serving the Lord in the temple before the throne of God, and this takes place before the saints leave heaven with the Lord to receive their resurrected bodies (Rev. 10:1,7). After the rapture and resurrection, the saints will be safe in the Lord's chambers (Isa. 26:19-21) while the Lord and His angels are bringing judgment upon the earth. According to marriage laws, a Jewish groom was not to leave his bride for war during the first year of marriage, therefore I believe the marriage supper of the Lamb will take place after the seven last vials and the battle of Armageddon: *When a man hath taken a new wife, he shall not go out to war, neither shall he be charged with any business: but he shall be free at home one year, and shall cheer up his wife which he hath taken* (Deuteronomy 24:5). In Revelation 14:1-4, we see the redeemed 144,000 standing before the throne, and the only way they could be in heaven is to be in the rapture before the marriage. If Jesus follows the pattern of a Jewish marriage, the Day of the Lord must be fulfilled before the marriage ceremony as these Scriptures demonstrate: Isaiah 26:20-21; 27:1; II Thessalonians 1:7-10, and Revelation 19:11-21. The last seven vials and the battle of Armageddon are recorded in Revelation 15 and 16. One of the seven angels which had the seven last vials shows the judgment of the great whore, *Mystery, Babylon the Great, the Mother of Harlots and Abominations of the Earth,* in chapters 17 and 18. Revelation 19:7 announces the time for the marriage has come, and the Lord's bride has made herself ready. If the marriage and marriage supper takes place after the judgments are complete, the Lord would be able to stay with His bride after the marriage (John 14:3).

Jesus makes two promises to the saints who overcome in Revelation 3:12. He promised to make them a pillar in the temple of God, and to write upon them the name of His God, and the city of God, which is New Jerusalem. The first part of the promise had its beginning when Jesus ascended to the throne in Revelation 4:2, and the saints were gathered before Him. The redeemed saints who died in the tribulation period are also pictured before the throne, where they serve the Lord day and night in the temple (Rev. 7:9, 14-15). The Lord leaves heaven with His saints and comes to the earth for the rapture and resurrection in Revelation 10:1 at the last trump (Rev. 10:7, 11:15). The time for the judgment of the earth and the judgment seat of Christ has arrived (Rev. 11:18). Immediately after the rapture and resurrection, the seven angels which have the seven last plagues will began to pour them out on the wicked, ending with the battle of Armageddon, Revelation 15 and 16. Paul tells about the same coming of the Lord as John taught in Revelation, and Jesus taught in the Gospels. Paul lets the saints know that the same day the Lord comes to be glorified in the saints is the same day judgment starts for the wicked: *And to you who are troubled rest with us, when the Lord Jesus shall be revealed from heaven with his mighty angels, 8 In flaming fire taking vengeance on them that know not God, and that obey not the gospel of our Lord Jesus Christ: 9 Who shall be punished with everlasting destruction from the presence of the Lord, and from the glory of his power; 10 When he shall come to be glorified in his saints, and to be admired in all them that believe (because our testimony among you was believed) in that day* (II Thessalonians 1:7-10).

The temple of God is opened in Revelation 11:19, but no one is able to enter the temple until the seven last plagues of the seven angels are fulfilled (Rev. 15:5-8). The saints who were victorious over the antichrist are standing on a glassy sea singing the song of Moses and the song of the Lamb (Rev. 15:1-4). These verses show both Jew and Gentile are singing praises to God for His deliverance, just as Israel sang when delivered from the bondage of Egypt in Exodus 15, and Deuteronomy 31:30, 32:1-47. The temple is filled with smoke from the glory of God, and no one is able to enter until the seven angels pour out the seven last plagues (Rev. 15:8). The second part of Revelation 3:12, concerning the promise of the New Jerusalem is fulfilled after the rapture, and resurrection. When the marriage of the Lamb takes place the Lord will take His bride to the New Jerusalem (Rev. 21:2, 9-11).

Paul gives the same time element in II Thessalonians 1:7-10 as Peter concerning the coming of the Lord, and the Day of the Lord, which follows. Peter tells the saints that the Day of the Lord will come as a thief on the wicked, but the saints will have the New Jerusalem, which the Lord has prepared for His bride-to-be: *But the day of the Lord will come as a thief in the night; in the which the heavens shall pass away with a great noise, and the elements shall melt with fervent heat, the earth also and the works that are therein shall be burned up. 11 Seeing then that all these things shall be dissolved, what manner of persons ought ye to be in all holy conversation and godliness, 12 Looking for and hasting unto the coming of the day of God, wherein the heavens being on fire shall be dissolved, and the elements shall melt with fervent heat? 13 Nevertheless we, according to his promise, look for new heavens and a new earth, wherein dwelleth righteousness. 14 Wherefore, beloved, seeing that ye look for such things, be diligent that ye may be found of him in peace, without spot, and blameless* (II Peter 3:10-14).

The source of this Scripture, which Peter gave to the Church concerning the Day of the Lord and the saints being gathered unto the Lord in order to escape the wrath of God, are found in the Gospels and also in Psalms 50:3-6: *Our God shall come, and shall not keep silence: a fire shall devour before him, and it shall be very tempestuous round about him. 4 He shall call to the heavens from above, and to the earth, that he may judge his people. 5 Gather my saints together unto me; those that have made a covenant with me by sacrifice. 6 And the heavens shall declare his righteousness: for God is judge himself. Selah.* These verses let God's people know that the posttribulation coming of the Lord is the only scriptural second advent, and Luke confirms this in Acts 3:21. The posttribulation advent is spoken by the mouth of God's holy prophets from Genesis through Revelation. Man changed the teaching by unfounded dispensational theology, which has brought many untrue doctrines into the Church, but I have shown how the Old Testament, the Gospels, Acts, the Epistles, and Revelation are all connected leading to the correct conclusion of a posttribulation second advent of the Lord.

Revelation chapter 16, 17, and 18 deal with the judgments, and in Revelation 19:1-6 the saints are praising the Lord for His righteous judgments, rejoicing because the time of the marriage and marriage supper has arrived (Rev. 19:7-9). Revelation 19:11–20:6 is fulfilled before the marriage and marriage supper. The bride, the Lamb's wife, is dressed in fine linen for the marriage, but the saints who went to be with the Lord before the rapture and resurrection are dressed in white robes. There is a difference in the dress of the saints before and after the resurrection. After the marriage, the Lord will take His bride to the place He promised in John 14:3 (the New Jerusalem). This fulfills the second part of the promise He made in Revelation 3:12. The saints will not be on earth during the millennium, but will reign with Christ from heaven in the New Jerusalem (Rev. 21:1-7). The bride, the Lamb's wife, is pictured in the New Jerusalem (Rev. 21:9-10). There is no temple there because the Lord is the temple, and the nations which were saved on earth, will walk in the light of it. These Scriptures could not be fulfilled after the millennium in Revelation 21:22-27.

Paul gives an illustration about the two covenants in Galatians 4:19-31. One concerns the earthly Jerusalem, and the other the heavenly Jerusalem. The bondwoman was born after the flesh (Hagar), which stands for Mount Sinai, and answers to an earthly Jerusalem. The other covenant was by promise (Isaac), in which Paul viewed Christians as the children of promise who are free, and answereth to Jerusalem above. Those who receive Jesus and the New Covenant will receive the New Jerusalem, and those who rejected Him as Messiah, until they see Him coming in the clouds, will weep for Him, and will be in the earthly Jerusalem during the millennium. The Law will go forth from the earthly Jerusalem, and many nations will come to worship (Micah 4:1-8). If the saints come back to earth during the millennium, they would be answering to an earthly Jerusalem, the same as those who missed the rapture. The Church is the freewoman, and will receive the promise Jesus made in Revelation 3:12. I believe the New Jerusalem in chapter 21 of Revelation is for the saints, and comes into effect after the rapture, not after the millennium, because the saints will rule over the nations with the Lord from the New Jerusalem (Rev. 21:22-24).

I want to bring attention to Revelation 5:10: *And hast made us unto our God kings and priests: and we shall reign on the earth.* The *Interlinear Greek-English New Testament* by Zondervan, tells us that the last part of that verse should read, "*and we shall reign over the earth.*" This makes a big difference, because the saints will rule from heaven with the Lord over the earth (II Tim. 2:12). The saints will be able to ascend or descend, just as the angels, because they will have resurrected bodies (John 1:51, I John 3:2, Matt. 22:30). Jacob dreamed of a ladder set up on earth that reached heaven, and the Lord stood above it. The angels were ascending and descending on it, and this shows we have no other way into heaven, but by Jesus (Gen. 28:10-17).

The posttribulation coming of the Lord is the only one which is scriptural. There is no secret pretribulation coming of the Lord, and rapture. The Lord will come in like manner as He was seen going into heaven (Acts 1:11). Nor is there a Pre-Wrath rapture between the opening of the sixth and seventh seal. There is nothing in Revelation 4:1, or in the sixth seal that fulfills the resurrection in the last day (John 6:44), or the coming of the Lord at the last trumpet (I Cor. 15:51-52). The seventh trumpet fulfills both (Rev.10:7; 11:15). John said He will come in the clouds, and every eye will see Him (Rev. 1:7). Every eye will see the Lord coming in the clouds when the rapture and resurrection takes place. Jesus made it plain that the resurrection takes place at the last day. The last day is the same day the rapture and resurrection take place, and the Day of the Lord begins (John 6:39, 40, 44, 54). The seventh angel sounds the last day and the mystery of the coming of the Lord; the rapture and resurrection will be completed (Rev. 10:7, 11:15).

Immediately after the seventh trumpet sounds, all the world will see Jesus coming with power and great glory; the nations will be angry because they have seen all these things take place, and will know that the time of God's wrath has come: *And the nations were angry, and thy wrath is come, and the time of the dead, that they should be judged, and that thou shouldest give reward unto thy servants the prophets, and to the saints, and them that fear thy name, small and great; and shouldest destroy them which destroy the earth* (Revelation.11:18). Verse 18 tells us it's time for the judgment seat of Christ, and shows both Old and New Testament saints standing before the Lord to be judged and rewarded for their works. The coming of the Lord, the rewarding of the saints, and the judgment is spoken of in Isaiah 40:10: *Behold, the Lord GOD will come with strong hand, and his arm shall rule for him: behold, his reward is with him, and his work before him.* It will be a joyful day for the saints, but not for the wicked. The saints will behold His glory, but the wicked will see His power. This illustrates how the saints will be safe, but the wicked will be judged in the same day when the Son of man is revealed: *But the same day that Lot went out of Sodom it rained fire and brimstone from heaven, and destroyed them all. 30 Even thus shall it be in the day when the Son of man is revealed* (Luke 17:29). The wicked all over the world will be angry and will gather themselves to battle against the Lord in the battle of Armageddon.

A misinterpretation by dispensationalism corrupted the time element concerning the coming of the Lord, setting the rapture and resurrection in Revelation 4:1. According to their doctrine, the saints go to be with the Lord in heaven for seven years, while the judgment seat of Christ takes place. In those seven years God pours out His wrath on earth. Pretribulationists teach that at the end of the seven years, the Lord comes back to earth with the saints for the revelation of Jesus, and the battle of Armageddon following. The Lord then sets up the thousand-year kingdom of heaven on earth. This places the saints who have resurrected bodies on earth with those who were not in the rapture, and have fleshly bodies. This is completely against everything the Bible teaches about the separation of corruption from incorruption in I Corinthians 15:20-57. Pretribulationists sing about going to heaven, but in doctrine they teach that the saints will be reigning on earth in the millennium with Christ. If pretribulationists believe the Church is coming back to earth in the millennium and will not be in heaven, it would be useless and without meaning to sing the following songs: "Beulah Land," "Everybody Will Be Happy Over There," "He the Pearly Gates Will Open," "How Beautiful Heaven Must Be," "I'll Meet You in the Morning," "Just Over in Glory Land," "Looking for a City," "Mansion over the Hilltop," "No Tears in Heaven," "We're Marching to Zion," "When the Roll Is Called Up Yonder," "When We All Get to Heaven," and "Won't It Be Wonderful There." I don't believe these songs err in doctrine. It's pretribulationists who sing one thing, and believe another.

Pretribulationist doctrine completely destroys what the prophets and Jesus said about heaven for the saints, and the New Jerusalem. The saints do not come back to earth after the rapture and resurrection. Jesus said He would go to prepare a place for the saints, and if He went, He would come again and receive them unto Himself. Jesus is preparing a place for the Church, therefore why would He bring the saints back to earth for the battle of Armageddon if angels are the reapers (Matt. 13:39)? Heaven is the place the Lord is preparing for the Church, not an earthly Jerusalem. The Church saints who have incorruptible resurrected bodies cannot be mixed with those who have corruptible bodies in the millennium. Paul's letter to the Corinthians makes it plain that the two cannot be mixed (I Cor. 15:40-57).

Abraham looked for a city whose builder and maker was God, not an earthly kingdom for the saints (Heb. 11:8-10). If Abraham looked for a city whose builder and maker was God, it would be foolish for the Church to look for a lesser kingdom on earth during the millennium, and be ruled by a rod of iron. The Church will rule with the Lord over the earth from heaven. Moses saw the heavenly Jerusalem and the Church of the first-born in heaven (Heb. 12:18-24). Jesus died outside the camp because on earth we have no continuing city, but we seek one to come (Heb. 13:10-14). One of the seven angels which had the seven last vials full of the seven last plagues shows the bride, the Lamb's wife, immediately after the seven last vials and the battle of Armageddon in the New Jerusalem (Rev. 21:9-10). These Scriptures could not have their fulfillment after the great white throne judgment because the kingdom is delivered up to God (I Cor. 15:24), and when the last enemy is destroyed which is death, the Lord will offer up the kingdom unto the Father, and the Son Himself will be subject unto Him that put all things under Him, that God may be all in all (I Cor. 15:24-28). Eternity will start because God is eternal, and He gave eternal life to His children, and all things will be made new. There will be no sin, nor corruption entering the New Jerusalem that would defile. Eternity begins, and time ceases.

I have given scriptural proof that the posttribulation coming of the Lord takes place at the last trump. When dispensationalists took the Gospels and put them under the dispensation of Law, and not under the dispensation of grace and truth of Jesus, Church doctrines became confused. That is the reason why pretribulationists say that Matthew 24 is not for the Church but for the Jew only. Jesus said what He meant, and meant what He said about His second advent.

The Lord's Coming in the Gospels

Pretribulationists have discredited what Jesus said in the Gospels as not being for the Church, until most believe it. I pray your mind and heart has already been changed before you got to this chapter. If there is still a little doubt, I pray you will see how important the Gospels are, and that what Jesus taught about His coming again is very vital and must not be cut off from the Church by dispensational teaching.

Some say that Matthew appealed more to the Jew, Mark to the Romans, and Luke appealed more to the Greek, but when Scripture concerning the Lord's coming appears in all three, it applies both to the Jew and the Gentiles. Therefore it is not rightly dividing the Word of truth when someone that believes in the pretribulation rapture says that the coming of the Lord that appears in the Gospels can only apply to the Jews. I trust your eyes will be opened to see what Darby and Scofield have done to the minds of God's people concerning the coming of the Lord.

Jesus gave the Great Commission to His disciples and the Church. He commanded them, *Go ye therefore, and teach all nations, baptizing them in the name of the Father, and of the Son, and of the Holy Ghost: Teaching them to observe all things whatsoever I have commanded you.* This command includes teaching the posttribulation coming of the Lord as Jesus gave us in the Gospels. Since the disciples were the first members of the Church, the words that Jesus spoke in the Gospels were for both Jew and Gentile. Jesus gave the Church the same command as He gave to His disciples: *And Jesus came and spake unto them, saying, All power is given unto me in heaven and in earth. 19 Go ye therefore, and teach all nations, baptizing them in the name of the Father, and of the Son, and of the Holy Ghost: 20 Teaching them to observe all things whatsoever I have commanded you: and, lo, I am with you alway, even unto the end of the world. Amen (Matthew 28:18-20).*

The Gospels give to the Church, both Jew and Gentile, a perfect description of when the Lord is going to come in Matthew 24:29-31; Mark 13:24-27 and Luke 21:25-28. There is no pretribulation rapture. The Lord does not come in two advents as pretribulationists teach, one for the rapture of the Church before the tribulation period, and then another when the Lord comes back to earth with the saints when every eye shall see Him in the Revelation. When the Lord comes for the rapture of the Church at the end of the tribulation period, He will secure His people in His chambers (Isa. 26:20). Jesus will then come back to earth with His angels for the reaping and the battle of Armageddon (Isa. 26:21; Zech. 14:1-5; Rev.16:1-21; 19:11-19). Pretribulationists believe in a spilt-coming because it was planted in their minds by pretribulation teachers, and not because of facts found in the Bible. Paul told the Thessalonian church they should not be in darkness concerning the coming of the Lord in I Thessalonians 5:1-8. The Gospels and Epistles were given to God's people so they would not be in darkness concerning the coming of the Lord. The Scriptures are not of a private interpretation.

If we believe Matthew 24, Mark 13 and Luke 21 are for the Jew only, then we must believe also that Jesus did not teach one word to the Church concerning any doctrine. Can you imagine the rebellion that policy would cause if it were enforced on preachers. Jesus came to establish and die for the Church. Jesus was not silent on the matter concerning His coming, but revealed to His Church about His coming again in Matthew 24:27-46; Mark 13:24-37 and Luke 21:25-28. Jesus was teaching Jew and Gentile about His coming again to take place after the tribulation (Matt. 24:31,40-42; Mark 13:27).

All pretribulationists do not teach exactly the same thing. One may say that the Gospel of Matthew is for the Jew only, while another will say that Matthew 24:36 is for the Church, along with verses 40-42, which are for the rapture of the Church. Either Matthew 24 is for the Jew only, or is for Jew and Gentile. Man should not take a few verses in Matthew 24 and apply them to the rapture, and then say the rest is for the Jew. If a person sees that the Gospels are for the Church, then that person must also believe what Jesus said about His coming again is for the Church, and see dispensationalists are wrong concerning the pretribulation rapture theory.

We must put Matthew 24 into its proper setting in order to understand it. Jesus did not spend the three and one-half years of His ministry in Jerusalem, but was entering it for the last time in order to fulfill all prophecy. His triumphal entry is found in chapter 21, where He cleanses the temple for a second time, and speaks in parables about the dishonest husbandman and the King's marriage feast. He then pronounced judgment on Jerusalem in Matthew 23:37-39. Jesus went out of the temple and said to the disciples that not one stone would not be left upon another. Later as He sat upon the mount of Olives, the disciples asked Him, *Tell us, when shall these things be? and what shall be the sign of thy coming, and of the end of the world?* Jesus answered them in verses 4-12 of the events and persecutions that would follow. Verse 15 concerning the Abomination of Desolation, spoken of by Daniel the prophet, standing in the Holy Place could not be talking about the destruction of the temple by Titus in A.D. 70, but the Lord was giving the disciples the answer to their question about His posttribulation coming. Matthew 24:15-44 deals with the fulfillment of Daniel's seventieth week.

A great multitude of saints are pictured in heaven before the throne who come out of great tribulation at the end of the sixth seal (Rev. 7:9,14). The seventh seal is opened in chapter 8, and the trumpet judgments begin. When the trumpet judgments begin to sound, it will be the beginning of the fulfillment of what Jesus said would take place before He comes: *And there shall be signs in the sun, and in the moon, and in the stars; and upon the earth distress of nations, with perplexity; the sea and the waves roaring; 26 Men's hearts failing them for fear, and for looking after those things which are coming on the earth: for the powers of heaven shall be shaken. 27 And then shall they see the Son of man coming in a cloud with power and great glory. 28 And when these things begin to come to pass, then look up, and lift up your heads; for your redemption draweth nigh* (Luke 21:25-28).

The Gospels help us to understand the seven seals, the seven trumpet judgments, the last seven vials, and the battle of Armageddon. What Jesus said in the Gospels about His coming is for the Church the same as the Revelation. The outline Jesus gave us in Mathew 24 will not contradict the Old or New Testament if our doctrine is correct. The two verses in Matthew 24:29-30 are very important in determining the time element of when Jesus is going to come. *Immediately after the tribulation of those days shall the sun be darkened, and the moon shall not give her light, and the stars shall fall from heaven, and the powers of the heavens shall be shaken:* This must happen before the Lord will come for the rapture. Jesus continued in verse 30: *And then shall appear the sign of the Son of man in heaven: and then shall all the tribes of the earth mourn, and they shall see the Son of man coming in the clouds of heaven with power and great glory.* Jesus said after the signs appear, He will send His angels with a great sound of a trumpet, and would gather his elect (the rapture): *And he shall send his angels with a great sound of a trumpet, and they shall gather together his elect from the four winds, from one end of heaven to the other* (Matthew 24:31). In verse 31, the angels gather the saints from the four winds, from one end of heaven to the other for the rapture. I believe this verse is talking about the Lord gathering the saints that are in heaven in order to bring them back to earth to receive their resurrected bodies, and gathering the saints on earth for the rapture, fulfilling I Thessalonians 4:13-17.

NINETEEN HUNDRED
YEARS OF CHURCH
HISTORY RESTORED

Most everyone agrees that the first three chapters of
Revelation concerning the seven churches of Asia
were the things John had seen, and the things which are (Revelation
1:19). If you start with A.D. 95, when Revelation was written, and say
the rapture takes place in Revelation 4:1, this leaves a nineteen hundred
year gap between the chapter 3 and 4 of Revelation. Its time these nineteen hundred years be put back in their place in the Revelation.
Revelation covers a much wider revelation for the Church than taught
by pretribulationists.

John wrote Revelation in A.D. 95 by the inspiration of the Holy
Spirit. Jesus ends His address to the seven churches of Asia with: *He
that hath an ear, let him hear what the Spirit saith unto the churches*
(Revelation 3:22). John begins chapter 4 with this verse: *After this I
looked, and, behold, a door was opened in heaven: and the first voice which I
heard was as it were of a trumpet talking with me; which said, Come up hither,
and I will show thee things which must be hereafter* (Rev. 4:1). John begins
this verse with the words, *After this I looked, and behold a door was opened
in heaven.* This verse does not contain one word about the rapture of the
Church before the tribulation period. The voice was telling John to
come up hither so he could see the things that were to take place from
A.D. 95 and forward. Jesus did the talking in the first three chapters and
told John in Revelation 1:19: *Write the things which thou hast seen, and the*

things which are, and the things which shall be hereafter; John wrote the things which he had seen, and the things which are in the first three chapters of Revelation, and now the voice is saying to John in Revelation 4:1: *Come up hither, and I will show thee things which must be hereafter.* Jesus is not talking to the Church, but to John; therefore it cannot be the time of the rapture. If Jesus were talking to the Church to "come up hither," it would be contrary to what He had taught in the Gospels, and to what Paul said would take place before the Church would be gathered unto the Lord (II Thess. 2:1-5). Paul warned the Church that the apostasy and the man of sin would be revealed before the Lord comes. It is not possible to skip early Church history in chapters 4 and 5 of Revelation, and say the rapture of the Church takes place in Revelation 4:1. Scripture does not stop for the Church after Revelation 4:1, nor is the rest of Revelation for the Jew only. John is showing the Church what will be after A.D. 95, and saying these great truths should be taught to the Church: *I Jesus have sent mine angel to testify unto you these things in the churches. I am the root and the offspring of David, and the bright and morning star* (Revelation 22:16).

Chapters 4 and 5 of Revelation are not teaching that the Church has been raptured, nor that these saints have resurrected bodies. It is teaching that John saw Jesus on His throne, with the Old and New Testament saints (which includes the early Church) around the throne of God with the Lord. It also gives the work of the Holy Spirit in the Church age (Rev. 5:6). The saints shown in the chapters 4 and 5 will remain with the Lord until they come back to earth to receive their resurrected bodies at the last trumpet. When a person understands that the Bible does not teach a pretribulation rapture it changes the meaning of the fourth chapter from being the rapture, and the tribulation period back to John's day when he saw Jesus on the throne. John saw the Old Testament and early New Testament saints gathered before the throne. This will close the nineteen-hundred-year gap in Revelation that dispensationalists make when they claim Revelation 4:1 is the rapture of the Church and the beginning of the tribulation period.

In Revelation 4:2 John was caught up into the third heaven in the spirit and saw Jesus sitting on the throne that the Father had promised Him; therefore Jesus was already on His throne when Revelation was written. As Stephen was stoned he said, *Behold, I see the heavens opened,* and the Son of man standing on the right hand of God (Acts 7:56). The fourth chapter of Revelation is not about Scripture being fulfilled in the tribulation period, but about saints in heaven around the throne with the Lord, which was seen by Stephen, and then by John in A.D. 95. A throne is used as a seat of honor. Jesus is sovereign, and all power is given Him over heaven and earth (Matt. 28:18). His throne is forever (Ps. 45:6; 93:1-2; Hebrews 1:8,13). *But unto the Son he saith, Thy throne, O God, is for ever and ever: a sceptre of righteousness is the sceptre of thy kingdom. 13 But to which of the angels said he at any time, Sit on my right hand, until I make thine enemies thy footstool?* When God raised Jesus from the dead, He set Him at His own right hand in heavenly places, and made Him ruler above all things: *Far above all principality, and power, and might, and dominion, and every name that is named, not only in this world, but also in that which is to come: 22 And hath put all things under his feet, and gave him to be the head over all things to the church* (Ephesians 1:21-22).

Jesus is head of the Church, and has ruled the Church from His throne since the day He was caught up to heaven (Acts 1:10-11). In Revelation 4:2 John saw Jesus on His throne immediately. Ezekiel had a vision of heaven and of God on His throne in Ezekiel 1:26-28. Revelation 4:1-9 is a continuation of the vision of heaven for the Church age. Ezekiel was both priest and prophet, and called the son of man. Jesus also is our High Priest and Prophet, and is called the Son of Man. This shows He is the Prophet and High Priest of all men (Luke 7:16; Heb. 2:17). Ezekiel saw four living creatures (Ezek. 1:4-21), and each of them had faces, which pictures Jesus as (1) a "man" incarnate; (2) an ox (suffering servant and sacrifice for sin) (3) a lion (ruler). Judah had the lion as its standard, and the Messiah is the Lion of the tribe of Judah, the root of David. This shows He is the King of kings and Lord of lords, and rules over heaven and earth: *And one of the elders saith unto me, Weep not: behold, the Lion of the tribe of Juda, the Root of David, hath prevailed to open the book, and to loose the seven seals thereof.* (4) an eagle, all-seeing and all-knowing, and those who wait upon Him fulfill Isaiah 40:31: *But they that wait upon the LORD shall renew their strength; they shall mount up with wings as eagles; they shall run, and not be weary; and they shall walk, and not faint* (Revelation 5:5).

John was given a view of heaven and of the throne of God, which Ezekiel had seen. He saw the Lord on His throne with the saints who had died in the Lord before A.D. 95. In order for pretribulationists to be correct in their doctrine concerning a pretribulation rapture, the word *immediately* would have to be removed from Revelation 4:2. The time element in this verse is not in the future tense to be fulfilled after the year A.D. 2000, but in its present tense, which had the beginning of its fulfillment in A.D. 95. *And immediately I was in the spirit; and, behold, a throne was set in heaven, and one sat on the throne* (Revelation 4:2). John saw Jesus on His throne, not the raptured Church. John was seeing heaven in the Church age, while Ezekiel saw God on His throne, and a picture of heaven in his day: *Now it came to pass in the thirtieth year, in the fourth month, in the fifth day of the month, as I was among the captives by the river of Chebar, that the heavens were opened, and I saw visions of God. 26 And above the firmament that was over their heads was the likeness of a throne, as the appearance of a sapphire stone: and upon the likeness of the throne was the likeness as the appearance of a man above upon it. 27 And I saw as the colour of amber, as the appearance of fire round about within it, from the appearance of his loins even upward, and from the appearance of his loins even downward, I saw as it were the appearance of fire, and it had brightness round about. 28 As the appearance of the bow that is in the cloud in the day of rain, so was the appearance of the brightness round about. This was the appearance of the likeness of the glory of the LORD. And when I saw it, I fell upon my face, and I heard a voice of one that spake* (Ezekiel 1:1,26-28).

John saw a picture of heaven as Ezekiel had seen, and the rainbow signifies the covenant God made with Noah, when God showed him mercy because of his faith: *And he that sat was to look upon like a jasper and a sardine stone: and there was a rainbow round about the throne, in sight like unto an emerald* (Revelation 4:3). John saw round about the throne twenty-four seats with twenty-four elders sitting upon those seats in Revelation 4:4. The elders in the New Testament were the same as the bishops. It was an office derived from the Jewish usage of elder, or ruler, of synagogues. Peter asked the elders, or bishops, to take oversight of the Church, and to feed the flock of God. Peter was an apostle, and he also was an elder: *The elders which are among you I exhort, who am also an elder, and a witness of the sufferings of Christ, and also a partaker of the glory that shall be revealed: 2 Feed the flock of God which is among you, taking the oversight thereof, not by constraint, but willingly; not for filthy lucre, but of a ready mind;3 Neither as being lords over God's heritage, but being ensamples to* the flock. 4 And when the chief Shepherd shall appear, ye shall receive a crown of glory that fadeth not away (I Peter 5:1-4).

I believe the twenty-four elders in Revelation 4:4 are the twelve patriarchs of the Old Testament and the twelve apostles of the New Testament. Stephen spoke of the twelve patriarchs of Jacob in Acts 7:8: And he gave him the covenant of circumcision: and so Abraham begat Isaac, and circumcised him the eighth day; and Isaac begat Jacob; and Jacob begat the twelve patriarchs. The Bible does not list all of them in order, or say who they will be, but the Lord did mention some in Matthew 8:11: And I say unto you, That many shall come from the east and west, and shall sit down with Abraham, and Isaac, and Jacob, in the kingdom of heaven.

Jesus told the twelve apostles that when He sits upon His throne, those who followed Him in regeneration would rule over Israel as judges (Matt. 19:28). I have already stated that the kingdom of heaven is not just the millennial kingdom of Israel on earth. Jesus now reigns in the heavenly kingdom over His Church. The saints who have died are with Him in heaven, and the saints who are living should also be under His leadership and rule. The twelve patriarchs and the twelve apostles of the New Testament make twenty-four, and God brought the Church of the Old and New Covenants together to make one body in Christ (Gal 3:28). The four beasts full of eyes before and behind in Revelation 4:6 are the representatives of God's redeemed Church. The twenty-four elders in Revelation 4:5 and the four beasts with eyes before and behind in Revelation 4:6 make up the saints found in Revelation 5:8-9. Paul said the spirits of the saints go to be with the Lord at the moment of death. All who have died in Christ are now present with the Lord: We are confident, I say, and willing rather to be absent from the body, and to be present with the Lord (II Corinthians 5:8).

The four beasts in the fourth chapter of Revelation are more literally translated "living creatures." They are heavenly creatures with the nature of angels, seraphim, or cherubim. Seraphim are mentioned one time in the Bible. Isaiah sees them, with six wings, singing praises unto the Lord grouped above Jehovah's throne: In the year that king Uzziah died I saw also the Lord sitting upon a throne, high and lifted up, and his train filled the temple. 2 Above it stood the seraphims: each one had six wings; with twain he covered his face, and with twain he covered his feet, and with twain he did fly. 3 And one cried unto another, and said, Holy, holy, holy, is the LORD of *hosts: the whole earth is full of his glory* (Isaiah 6:1-3). Cherubim are mentioned many times, and played a big part in the Old Testament temple. They are identified as the four living creatures in Ezekiel chapters 1 and 10. The Devil was the anointed cherub which fell (Ezek. 28:13-15). Cherubim are guardians of the tree of life (Gen. 3:24). *The Dictionary of the Bible*, edited by James Hastings, tells us that in Jewish theology the cherubim were one of the highest classes of angels, the other two being seraphim and ophanim, which guard the throne of the Most High. I find no place in the Bible where "ophanim" is ever mentioned.

There is nothing in Revelation that lets us know for sure if the four beasts are seraphim or cherubim. The Lord put the focus on the redeemed saints, which the four beasts represent. Revelation 5:8-10 gives us the answer of how the four beasts and the twenty-four elders represent the saints who have been redeemed by the blood of Christ. They are before the throne of God giving praise unto the Lord.

The four beasts in Revelation 4:6 and 8 are full of eyes before and behind. In Revelation 4:7 the first having a face as of a lion, the second like a calf, the third had a face as of a man, and the fourth was like a flying eagle, and the four beasts had each of them six wings. The four living creatures in Ezekiel 1:10, all four have the face of a man, and the face of a lion on the right side, the face of an ox on the left side, and also the face of an eagle and four wings. The cherubim (or living creatures) that Ezekiel sees each have four wings and four faces, whereas in Revelation the living creatures each have six wings and only one face. The living creatures in Ezekiel 1:18 have rings full of eyes round about them four, and in Revelation 4:6 the living creatures have eyes before and behind. I believe the eyes in the living creatures represent the saints. The eyes in the beasts are not the same as those found in the Lamb that had been slain, having seven horns and seven eyes, which are the seven Spirits of God sent forth unto all the earth (Rev. 5:6).

God chose to explain the likeness of the four beasts, or living creatures, in the fourth chapter of Revelation, but in the fifth chapter He choose to identify the four beasts, the twenty-four elders, and the saints as being one and the same. Revelation 5:8-9 shows the four beasts and twenty-four elders falling down before the Lamb and worshipping Him because the Lord has redeemed them by His blood. We know that neither cherubim nor seraphim get saved by the blood of Christ, only sinful people. How can the living creatures (or cherubim) in Ezekiel 10:15 be called saints in Revelation 5:8-9,14, if only the saints were redeemed by the blood of Christ? When saints die, they go to be with the Lord around the throne, and at that time are under the wings of the cherubim giving glory to the Lamb of God. When the Word speaks of the four beasts and the twenty-four elders in the fifth chapter of Revelation, it includes all saints who have been redeemed by the blood of Christ. I believe God is showing us the unity of heaven and how all are made one in Christ (John 10:16, 17:21).

Cherubim played a big part in the tabernacle in the wilderness, and also in Solomon's temple. They were placed at each end of the mercy seat (Exod. 25:18-22). They were represented upon the hanging veil, which separated the Holy of Holies from the Holy Place (Exod. 26:31-35). Solomon also used cherubim in his temple (I Kings 6:23-30; II Chronicles 3:7). The four living creatures with four wings which Ezekiel saw in his vision were cherubim (Ezek. 1:5-21; 10:18-21). Revelation 5:8-11 shows the four beasts and the four and twenty elders falling down before the Lamb of God and worshipping him: *And when he had taken the book, the four beasts and four and twenty elders fell down before the Lamb, having every one of them harps, and golden vials full of odours, which are the prayers of saints. 9 And they sung a new song, saying, Thou art worthy to take the book, and to open the seals thereof: for thou wast slain, and hast redeemed us to God by thy blood out of every kindred, and tongue, and people, and nation; 10 And hast made us unto our God kings and priests: and we shall reign on the earth. 11 And I beheld, and I heard the voice of many angels round about the throne and the beasts and the elders: and the number of them was ten thousand times ten thousand, and thousands of thousands.*

There must be an explanation of why the four beasts, or living creatures in Revelation 5:8-11, can be called saints that were redeemed by the blood of Christ, when the four living creatures in Ezekiel 10:12-16 are called cherubim. We can see in Revelation 5:11 that the four beasts represent millions of saints in heaven, not just four beasts. Revelation 4:6 lets us know that the four beasts are full of eyes before and behind. Therefore I believe the eyes in the four beasts represent the saints, so that when John uses the word *beasts* he is including the redeemed saints. The four living creatures, which have four faces each in Ezekiel 1:5-10, are four created cherubim as explained in Ezekiel 10:12,14. Cherubim cannot be redeemed by the blood, because they were created without sin. They are angelic beings, but the saints who were formerly sinners are redeemed by the blood of Christ, and after death go to be with the Lord before the throne. They are under the wings and protection of the cherubim, or seraphim, and are singing a new song before the throne with the twenty-four elders, and there is no distinction between the four living creatures and the saints in Revelation 4:6; 5:8-10,14, except for their wings.

The saints around the throne in the fourth and fifth chapters of Revelation are not tribulation saints because the first seal is not opened until the sixth chapter. They are saints who died down through history who repented of their sins and were saved by faith. These will include Old Testament saints, the disciples, and early Church saints. The four beasts, or living creatures, represent the Church saints that are saved from the four winds of the earth, because Revelation 5:9 tells us that these saints are redeemed by the blood out of every kindred, and tongue, and people, and nation. It appears God uses "four beasts" as He used four standards or ensigns of the four divisions of the tribes of Israel. The lion was the emblem on the ensign for Judah, Issachar, and Zebulon on the east. The calf or ox was the emblem on the ensign of Ephraim, Manasseh, and Benjamin on the west. The face of a man was the emblem on the ensign for Reuben, Simeon, and Gad on the south. The flying (spread) eagle was the emblem on the ensign of Dan, Asher, and Naphtali on the north. The lion has courage. The ox or calf is diligent. The beast that has the face of a man shows the saints that they need knowledge, wisdom, prudence, and discretion to carry the gospel to the ends of the earth. The fourth beast like a flying eagle shows that those who wait upon the Lord mount up with wings as eagles.

If Jesus had shown the Church cherubim which have four faces to represent the Lord and His work carrying the gospel to the four winds, we would start with Jerusalem and the early Church. The disciples and the early Church began to reach out to many other nations. Many saints gave their lives for the Lord down through Church history, and after the Reformation, the Protestant missionary movement began. Great Britain had the emblem of the lion, though I do not believe John is identifying all the nations involved by emblems, but we do know the English-speaking people in Great Britain, America, Canada, and

Australia have played a large part in sending missionaries around the world. In Great Britain alone there were between thirty-five and forty foreign missionary societies in 1888. Europe once had fervency in sending missionaries to evangelize the world. America was strong in missions in the 1800s, but it appears all have cooled in their missionary zeal in these last days.

Another reason why the redeemed saints are called beasts in Revelation 5:8-9 is found when we go back to Peter's vision of heaven in the book of Acts. The Old Testament ceremonial dietary laws were no longer in force. Peter saw in a vision all manner of clean and unclean wild beasts, creeping things, and fowls of the air, and the voice told him to kill and eat. His reply was, *I have never eaten any thing that is common or unclean:. And the voice spake unto him again the second time, What God hath cleansed, that call not thou common.* The heavenly picture that Peter was shown is about how God can cleanse the Gentiles as well as the Jews, and make both acceptable unto God. God had to show Peter a picture from heaven in order for him to see that what God cleanses is clean. The great sheet that Peter saw represents the four winds, or four corners of the earth, with all manner of beasts, symbolizing all of mankind in the sheet. Those whom the Lord saves and cleanses become part of the Church. The Lord had to show Peter that Cornelius and the Gentiles could be cleansed from their sins as well as the Jews, and all can be made one in the Lord: *On the morrow, as they went on their journey, and drew nigh unto the city, Peter went up upon the housetop to pray about the sixth hour: 10 And he became very hungry, and would have eaten: but while they made ready, he fell into a trance, 11 And saw heaven opened, and a certain vessel descending unto him, as it had been a great sheet knit at the four corners, and let down to the earth: 12 Wherein were all manner of fourfooted beasts of the earth, and wild beasts, and creeping things, and fowls of the air. 13 And there came a voice to him, Rise, Peter; kill, and eat. 14 But Peter said, Not so, Lord; for I have never eaten any thing that is common or unclean. 15 And the voice spake unto him again the second time, What God hath cleansed, that call not thou common. 16 This was done thrice: and the vessel was received up again into heaven. 17 Now while Peter doubted in himself what this vision which he had seen should mean, behold, the men which were sent from Cornelius had made inquiry for Simon's house, and stood before the gate, 21 Then Peter went down to the men which were sent unto him from Cornelius; and said, Behold, I*

am he whom ye seek: what is the cause wherefore ye are come? 22 And they said,
Cornelius the centurion, a just man, and one that feareth God, and of good
report among all the nation of the Jews, was warned from God by an holy angel
to send for thee into his house, and to hear words of thee. 34 Then Peter opened
his mouth, and said, Of a truth I perceive that God is no respecter of persons: 35
But in every nation he that feareth him, and worketh righteousness, is accepted
with him (Acts 10:9-17, 21-22, 34-35).

These verses help us to understand why the four beasts in Ezekiel
are called saints in Revelation. The four beasts represent the saints and
show how God has cleansed both Jews and Gentiles by the blood of
Christ, and they are made one in Him.

If the rapture took place in Revelation 4:1, as pretribulationists
teach, the Church would appear before the throne with resurrected
bodies, and there could be no tribulation saints who would appear
before the throne in heaven. The first thing John sees after seeing Jesus
sitting on His throne were the twenty-four elders and the four beasts.
These are the redeemed saints, who died in Christ before A.D. 95 (Rev.
5:8-9). The saints were given white robes, and told to rest a little season, until their fellow servants are killed as they were (Rev. 6:11). The
tribulation saints are given white robes before the rapture and resurrection in Revelation 7:9,13-14. These saints are clothed in white raiment, and are before the throne of God with the Lord. The saints
before the throne in Revelation 4:6 were not in the rapture and resurrection, but both the 144,000 standing before the throne of God and
the tribulation saints will be in the rapture (Rev. 14:1-4; 15:1-3). This is
the fulfillment of what Isaiah prophesied how God's people would
enter the Lord's chambers until the indignation be finished (Isa. 26:19-
21). No one will be able to enter into the temple in heaven until the
seven plagues of the seven angels are fulfilled (Rev. 15:7-8). The seven
angels pour out the seven last vials in Revelation 16:1-21.

There is a big difference between the saints who appear in heaven
before the throne of God dressed in white robes prior to the rapture,
and those arrayed in fine linen for the marriage of the Lamb and the
marriage supper (Rev. 19:7-9). The redeemed saints of the early Church
appearing before the throne are dressed in white and have a white covering, just as Jesus did when His raiment was changed to white and glis-
tened before the disciples. Jesus talked to Moses and Elijah in the

transfiguration (Luke 9:27-34). Enoch and Elijah did not die, but ascended into heaven with their physical bodies, yet did not have a resurrected body. God gave the two angels a body when they came to Sodom to deliver Lot and his family. The angels washed their feet, and stayed all night with Lot and ate unleavened bread with him (Gen. 19:1-3). This Scripture destroys pretribulationists' teaching that clothes cannot be hung on a spirit in heaven. Since God let the angels have the appearance of men, and had clothes on their bodies, and they washed their feet and ate bread, God is able to give saints a temporary body and a covering of white when they ascend to the throne of God after death. When our souls and spirits go to be with the Lord after death, we will not be disembodied spirits that cannot praise and glorify God. Revelation makes this plain in the next paragraph.

Jesus promised the Church of Sardis that those who overcome the world would walk with Him in white. The following Scripture shows that saints are given a temporary body after death until the resurrection. I believe the saints of Sardis at death ascended to be with the Lord, and were given white robes: *Thou hast a few names even in Sardis which have not defiled their garments; and they shall walk with me in white: for they are worthy. 5 He that overcometh, the same shall be clothed in white raiment; and I will not blot out his name out of the book of life, but I will confess his name before my Father, and before his angels* (Revelation 3:4-5). The saints dressed in white in Revelation 4:4: *And round about the throne were four and twenty seats: and upon the seats I saw four and twenty elders sitting, clothed in white raiment; and they had on their heads crowns of gold* is the fulfillment of Revelation 3:4-5. The saints dressed in white robes in Revelation 4:4 is different than the fine linen wedding garments in Revelation 19:7-8: *Let us be glad and rejoice, and give honor to him: for the marriage of the Lamb is come, and his wife hath made herself ready. 8 And to her was granted that she should be arrayed in fine linen, clean and white: for the fine linen is the righteousness of saints.*

The saints in the marriage ceremony received their resurrected bodies, but the twenty and four elders around the throne that ascended to heaven with the Lord, and are dressed in white, have not left heaven to receive their resurrected bodies. Paul clarifies the difference between the two, and says if our earthly house is dissolved, we have a building of God not made with hands. John R. Rice said in his notes on the

Scripture below that Paul was implying he would have a temporary body after death before he received his resurrected body. These verses confirm how saints can appear in white raiment in heaven before the coming of the Lord: *For we know that if our earthly house of this tabernacle were dissolved, we have a building of God, an house not made with hands, eternal in the heavens. 2 For in this we groan, earnestly desiring to be clothed upon with our house which is from heaven: 3 If so be that being clothed we shall not be found naked. 4 For we that are in this tabernacle do groan, being burdened: not for that we would be unclothed, but clothed upon, that mortality might be swallowed up of life. 5 Now he that hath wrought us for the selfsame thing is God, who also hath given unto us the earnest of the Spirit. 6 Therefore we are always confident, knowing that, whilst we are at home in the body, we are absent from the Lord: 7 (For we walk by faith, not by sight:) 8 We are confident, I say, and willing rather to be absent from the body, and to be present with the Lord. 9 Wherefore we labour, that, whether present or absent, we may be accepted of him* (II Corinthians 5:1-9).

The saints who die are not disembodied spirits floating around the throne until the resurrection, but are given a temporary body wearing a white robe. When the saints return to earth with the Lord in the rapture and resurrection, they will receive their new body, and will be given their wedding garments of fine linen (Rev. 19:7-9).

Jesus gives John a picture of heaven and what is taking place in the Church age. He shows John that there are seven lamps of fire burning before the throne, which are the seven Spirits of God. These seven Spirits of God are sent throughout the earth for the salvation of man. John saw before the throne a sea of glass like crystal, and four beasts full of eyes before and behind, which represent the saints. The Greek word, *beasts* in Revelation 4:6, means "living creatures," not wild animals of the forest. He proceeds to tell us the appearance of the four beasts: *And out of the throne proceeded lightnings and thunderings and voices: and there were seven lamps of fire burning before the throne, which are the seven Spirits of God. 6 And before the throne there was a sea of glass like unto crystal: and in the midst of the throne, and round about the throne, were four beasts full of eyes before and behind. 7 And the first beast was like a lion, and the second beast like a calf, and the third beast had a face as a man, and the fourth beast was like a flying eagle. 8 And the four beasts had each of them six wings about him; and they were full of eyes within: and they rest not day and night, saying, Holy, holy,*

holy, Lord God Almighty, which was, and is, and is to come (Revelation 4:5-8). This eighth verse gives definite proof that the rapture did not take place in Revelation 4:1, because the saints in heaven are giving praise unto the Lord which was, and is, and is to come.

When the seventh trumpet sounds, the saints who have died down through the Church age will leave the throne of God with the Lord, and come back to earth to receive resurrected bodies. The temple in heaven will be shut, and no one will be able to enter until the seven last plagues of the seven angels are fulfilled. The saints around the throne who had robes of white, leave the throne of God. They will leave the throne with the Lord, and come to earth in order to receive their resurrected bodies. They will be given their wedding attire of pure white linen for the marriage: *And one of the four beasts gave unto the seven angels seven golden vials full of the wrath of God, who liveth for ever and ever. 8 And the temple was filled with smoke from the glory of God, and from his power; and no man was able to enter into the temple, till the seven plagues of the seven angels were fulfilled. 19:7-9. Let us be glad and rejoice, and give honour to him: for the marriage of the Lamb is come, and his wife hath made herself ready. 8 And to her was granted that she should be arrayed in fine linen, clean and white: for the fine linen is the righteousness of saints. 9 And he saith unto me, Write, Blessed are they which are called unto the marriage supper of the Lamb. And he saith unto me, These are the true sayings of God* (Revelation 15:7-8).

The fifth chapter of Revelation shows the crucified, atoning Christ on His throne with the twenty-four elders and the millions of saints around the Lord, giving praise to Him. He died for the sins of Old and New Testament saints. Jesus gave the disciples the great commission in Matthew 28:19-20, and the gospel went forth from Jerusalem. The disciple's ministry was far-reaching, and Paul spread the gospel in his four missionary journeys. I believe those are the saints who had died and are before the throne singing to the Lord, saying He alone is worthy to open the seven seals to the Church (Rev. 5:1-14). Revelation 5:8-9 tells us that the four beasts and the four and twenty elders are redeemed by the blood of Christ out of every kindred, tongue, and nation. The Lord shows John a picture of the redeemed saints around the throne of God so all generations will know that to be absent from the body is to be present with the Lord. The fourth and fifth chapters of Revelation need to be restored to their proper beginning in A.D. 95 and not after the year

2,000, as according to the pretribulation rapture theory. This closes the gap of over 1,900 years where dispensationalists have made the error of placing the rapture in Revelation 4:1.

We may not know for sure what kind of body the saints will have after they are absent from the body and present with the Lord, but we do know this earthly house is a temporary tabernacle that will be dissolved. The earthly body will return to dust, and our souls and spirits return to God, Who made them. Death can separate the soul and spirit from the body, but death cannot separate the soul and spirit from God. Souls will not be found naked in heaven while waiting for their resurrected bodies, but God will clothe them with robes of righteousness made white by the blood of the Lamb. The verses below identify all Christians who suffered martyrdom in the early Church, the millions of Christians who died for the cause of Christ in the Dark Ages, and during the Reformation, and the millions who have died under Communism and other nations up to the time before the great tribulation period begins. These saints are given white robes, and are told to rest for a little season, until their fellow servants and brethren in the tribulation should be killed as they were: *And when he had opened the fifth seal, I saw under the altar the souls of them that were slain for the word of God, and for the testimony which they held: 10 And they cried with a loud voice, saying, How long, O Lord, holy and true, dost thou not judge and avenge our blood on them that dwell on the earth? 11 And white robes were given unto every one of them; and it was said unto them, that they should rest yet for a little season, until their fellow servants also and their brethren, that should be killed as they were, should be fulfilled* (Revelation 6:9-11).

The Lord will not come, nor will the rapture take place, before the seventh trumpet sounds, because Revelation 10:1 pictures Jesus coming down from heaven, clothed in a cloud, and a rainbow upon His head, which is a symbol of God's mercy and the covenant He made with Noah. This verse shows Jesus leaving heaven and His throne and coming to earth for the rapture and resurrection, before the wrath of God is poured out on the wicked, fulfilling I Thessalonians 3:13 and 4:13-17. After the seventh trumpet sounds in Revelation 10:7, the rapture and resurrection take place in Revelation 11:15, the nations are angry because the wrath of God has come, and it's time to give reward unto the saints (Rev. 11:18). The temple of God is opened in heaven (Rev.

11:19). Starting at Revelation 15:8 God's Word shows the events that take place after the temple is opened. The time has finally come for the seven angels that have the seven last vials to come out of the temple, and pour out the vials upon the earth. The temple will be filled with smoke from the glory of God and from His power, and no one will be able to enter until the seven last plagues of the seven angels are fulfilled (Rev. 15:6-8). Revelation 16 tells us about the seven last vials being poured out. When the sixth vial is poured out, all nations will gather together for the battle of Armageddon, which takes place when the seventh vial is poured out: *And the sixth angel poured out his vial upon the great river Euphrates; and the water thereof was dried up, that the way of the kings of the east might be prepared. 13 And I saw three unclean spirits like frogs come out of the mouth of the dragon, and out of the mouth of the beast, and out of the mouth of the false prophet. 14 For they are the spirits of devils, working miracles, which go forth unto the kings of the earth and of the whole world, to gather them to the battle of that great day of God Almighty. 15 Behold, I come as a thief. Blessed is he that watcheth, and keepeth his garments, lest he walk naked, and they see his shame. 16 And he gathered them together into a place called in the Hebrew tongue Armageddon* (Revelation 16:12-16).

The sixth angel pours out his vial upon the great river Euphrates, and all the water is dried up to make way for the kings of the East. They are gathered to a place called Armageddon (Rev. 16:12-16). When the seventh vial is poured out it will end the rule of the false prophet and the antichrist. All the nations of the world, called "Great Babylon," fall after the seventh vial is poured out: *And the seventh angel poured out his vial into the air; and there came a great voice out of the temple of heaven, from the throne, saying, It is done. 18 And there were voices, and thunders, and lightnings; and there was a great earthquake, such as was not since men were upon the earth, so mighty an earthquake, and so great. 19 And the great city was divided into three parts, and the cities of the nations fell: and great Babylon came in remembrance before God, to give unto her the cup of the wine of the fierceness of his wrath. 20 And every island fled away, and the mountains were not found. 21 And there fell upon men a great hail out of heaven, every stone about the weight of a talent: and men blasphemed God because of the plague of the hail; for the plague thereof was exceeding great* (Revelation 16:17-21). Revelation 17 unfolds to the Church why Mystery Babylon the Great, the Mother of Harlots and Abomination of the Earth, the beast, and all the nations who committed fornication with the Mother of Harlots are judged. When the seven last vials are finished, the raptured and resurrected saints will be able to enter the temple.

This chapter closes the 1900-year gap created by pretribulationists who believe the rapture takes place in Revelation.4:1. We can see how detrimental it has been to the Church when a division was made in Revelation and the fourth chapter was allocated only for the Jew. The fourth and fifth chapters of Revelation give a lot of comfort to the saints who have lost loved ones because they can see that their saved loved ones are around the throne with the Lord. It is a real comfort to know God gave all the Revelation of Jesus Christ to the Church in order to see how it affects the Church after Revelation. 4:1.I have given scriptural and historical proof that the pretribulation rapture is only a theory, and not fact. The next three pages give time-line charts which shows the Law vanishing away, and the beginning of the Church until the last enemy is destroyed, which is death, and eternity begins.

THE CHURCH AGE

(I) When John finished preparing the way of the Lord, Jesus began His ministry. The Old Covenant had served its purpose, and began the process of vanishing away; *Luke 16:16-17, Heb. 8:13.* The beginning of the New Testament Church was when Jesus called His disciples, and they followed the Messiah by faith; *Matt. 4:18-22.* The New Covenant would be a salvation by Grace through faith in Jesus; *Hab.2:1-4, Rom. 1:17, Gal. 3:11, Col. 2:6-7, Heb. 10:35-38.*

Jesus began to preach the gospel of the kingdom, said "repent for the kingdom of God is at hand," and began to call His disciples *Mark 1:14-15.* The kingdom of God is when God makes His abode in the heart of the believer; *Luke 17:20-21.*

Jesus preached those things pertaining to the kingdom of God 40 days after His resurrection; *Acts 1:3.* The disciples continued to preach salvation, and the kingdom of God; *Acts:8:12, 14:22, 19:8, 20:25, 28:23, 31, Rom. 14:17, I Cor. 4:20, 6:9-10, 15:24, 30.* The kingdom of God never passes away.

Pentecost was not the beginning of the Church. When Jesus called His disciples, and they believed and followed Him, that was the beginning, but they needed the power of the Holy

(II) Ghost. Jesus instructed them to tarry at Jerusalem until they were endued with power from on high. The power came on the day of Pentecost, and 3,000 were saved, and added to the Church; *Acts 1:8, 2:41.*

The Jews established Israel as a nation once again in 1948, and after 2000 years, God is reviving them. They received the early rain, and they must receive the latter rain also; *Hos.6:1-3.*

The antichrist will make a 7-year peace covenant with Israel, and will break it after three and one-half years; *Dan. 7:7-14, 9:27, Rev. 13:1-18, 17:8-18.*

The Day of the Lord begins the same day of the rapture and resurrection; *Luke 17:26-27.* The judgement, or the wrath of God will last 45 days; *Dan12:12.* The Day of the Lord which is the wrath of God will be swift and short; *Joel 3:9-16, Zech. 14:1-7, I. Thes. 5:2-5, II Peter 3:10-14, Rev. 15:1-8, 16:1-26, 19:11-21*

Israel hid 1,260 days; *Revelation 12:6,14.* Daily sacrifices taken away, desolate set up, 1,290 days *Dan. 12:11,*

The rapture and resurrection
I Thes.4:16-17, II Thes. 2:1-3, I Cor. 15:51-52. Rev. 10:7, 11:15.

Antichrist revealed
Dan. 9:27, Rev. 17:8-18.

Titus destroys Jerusalem 70 A.D.

Daniel's 70th wk. begins →

The Law vanishes away	The Church age, and the gap between Daniel's 69th and 70th week	3½ yrs.	1,260 days	30 days	45 days wrath
John	Jesus, Church age begins				ends

Apostasy, *I Tim. 4:1, II Tim. 3:1-7, II Peter 3:3-7, II Thes. 2:3.*

(III) The great persecution of saints in all nations *Rev. 7:9, 14-15,* lasts much longer than a few days. Daniel tells how the Antichrist will not regard the true God, and how he will conquer many nations, and will come to his end in Jerusalem; *Dan. 11:36-45.* These two prophecies are taking place while the two witnesses witness 1,260 days before being killed; *Rev. 11:3-12.*

THE DAY OF THE LORD

(I) Isaiah explains the Day of the LORD. He said it comes as a destruction from the Almighty, and pangs and sorrows shall take hold of them. It would be a day, cruel both with wrath and fierce anger, and to lay the land desolate; and He shall destroy the sinners thereof out of it, and He will punish the world for their evil (*Isa. 13:6-13*).

Jesus said the Day of the Lord begins the same day of the rapture (*Luke 17:26-29*). The extra 45 days found in *Daniel 12:12* is the time needed for God's wrath (*Rev. 11:18, 15:1-8, 16:1-21*). The day of the Lord will be quick and just. Only a third in Israel will be left after judgment which enter into the kingdom of Israel (*Zech. 13:8-9*). There is no 7-year gap between the rapture and resurrection in I *Thess. 4:13-17*, and the day of the Lord in I *Thess. 5:2*. Paul immediately gave saints instructions about the Day of the Lord, and let them know he had already taught them about the times and and seasons. He let them know that the day of the Lord would not come on the children of light as a thief in the night, because they were of the day, and that God did not appoint them to wrath because they had obtained salvation in the Lord (I *Thess. 5:1-10*). Paul did not tell them they would escape the tribulation period, when the wrath of man is poured out on God's people, but taught them they would escape the Day of the Lord, when God pours out His wrath.

THE MILLENNIUM

(II) In Paul's second letter to the Thessalonians, he asked those who were troubled to rest with him, because the Lord would come in flaming fire with His mighty angels, taking vengeance on them that know not God (II *Thes. 1:7-10*). The saints will be safe in the LORD'S chambers when the wrath of God is poured out (*Isa. 26:17-21*). The rapture takes place at the last trump (*Rev. 11:15*), and the temple of God was opened in heaven, and the ark of His Testament was seen (*Rev. 11:18, 15:1-8, Rev. 11:19*). No one was able to enter the temple in heaven until the seven last vials of the wrath of God were fulfilled (*Rev.15:8*). The marriage and marriage supper will take place after the wrath of God, and the harlot is judged (*Rev. 19:1-9*). Then the bride and groom will be together forever.

Those who missed the rapture and did not worship the beast, and survived the fires of judgment, will be the people on earth during the millennium. They will see the scars in the Lord's hands and feet, and will mourn for Him, and the Lord will show them grace (*Zech. 12:1-14; 13:1-9; 14:1-21*). The Lord will be king over the whole earth (*Zech 14:9*). The millennium begins and lasts for 1,000 years (*Rev. 20:5*). The saints who overcame the world will have power over the nations, and will rule from above with the Lord (*Rev. 2:26*). The earth will be ruled with a rod of iron (*Ps. 2:8-9; Rev. 2:26-27; 12:5; 19:15*).

NEW JERUSALEM above is for the bride of Christ. Rev. 21:9;21, Jn. 14:3, Heb. 11:8-10, 12:18-24, 13:10-14.

ETERNAL KINGDOM; John 18:36-37, II Peter 1:11, Col.1:13, Daniel 4:3, 7:25-27, Luke 1:32-32, Heb. 1:8, 10-13, Gal. 4:26.

The marriage & marriage supper; Rev. 19:7-9. ⟶

See chapter, (kingdom of heaven.) It is the eternal kingdom, Rev.3:12, 21:2, 9-10, 21:22-27, Heb. 12:22, Ps.23:6.

Judgment seat of Christ; Rev. 11:18. ⟶

Wrath of God, Rev. 11:18, 16:1-21, 19:11:18.

The rapture and resurrection ⟶

| CHURCH AGE AND DANIEL'S 70th WEEK | 3½ yrs. | 1,260 days | 30 days | wrath 45 days | Millennium and the earthly kingdom of israel, Rev. 20:1-15 Nations saved walk in light of New Jerusalam, Rev. 21:22,27 | 1,000 yrs. ends |

GREAT WHITE THRONE JUDGMENT

(I) After the thousand years have ended, the Devil will be loosed from the bottomless pit a little season. He will go out to deceive the nations again, and surround the camp of saints, and Jerusalem. Fire comes down from heaven and devours them all. The Devil and all those who rebelled against the Lord will be cast into the lake of fire and brimstone where the beast and the false prophet were cast, and they shall be tormented forever (*Rev. 20:7-10*).

The time for the great white throne judgment has come. The Lord will sit upon His throne, and all the unsaved dead will be brought before Him. The Lord will have two books before Him, one for the unsaved, who will be judged and cast into the lake of fire, and the other for the saved saints in the millennium, "and whosoever was not found in the book of life was cast into the lake of fire. This is the second death" (*Rev. 20 11-15*). I believe the saved of the millennium will be judged, and rewarded, and given a place in the New Jerusalem with the Church saints because *Rev. 20:11* tells us that the Lord sits upon the great white throne, and the earth and the heaven fled away, and there was found no place for them. *Revelation 20:11* is in unity with what Jesus said in (*Matt.24:35*): *Heaven and earth shall pass away, but my words shall not pass away.*

ETERNITY BEGINS

(II) The New Jerusalem is the place the Lord prepared for the saints (*John 14:3*). When the last enemy is destroyed, which is death,the Lord will offer up the kingdom unto the Father, and the Son Himself will be subject unto Him that put all things under Him, that God may be all in all (*I Cor. 15:24-28*). Eternity starts at this point because God is eternal, and He gave eternal life to His children, and all things are made new. There is nothing that can enter into the New Jerusalem that can defile. When the devil and all the unsaved are cast into the lake of fire, eternity will begin, and time will cease to be.

Revelation 22:12-16. And, behold, I come quickly; and my reward is with me, to give every man according as his work shall be. I am Alpha and Omega, the beginning and the end, the first and the last. Blessed are they that do his commandments, that they may have the right to the tree of life, and may enter in through the gates into the city. For without are dogs, and sorcerers, and whoremongers, and murderers, and idolaters, and whosoever loveth and maketh a lie. I have sent mine angel to testify unto you these things in the churches. I am the root and the offspring of David, and the bright and morning star.

NEW JERUSALEM ABOVE   ETERNITY BEGINS; I Cor. 15:23-28.
Christ delivers up the kingdom to God

Saints in Book of Life

GREAT WHITE THRONE JUDGMENT
THE DEAD STAND BEFORE GOD

Unsaved cast into lake of fire

DANGER OF PRETRIBULATION RAPTURE THEORY

The pretribulation rapture theory has become so entrenched in Church doctrine all over the world, it will take the work of the Holy Spirit to change hearts and minds. It's time God's people began to pray for God's grace and forgivness until unity of doctrine concerning the coming of the Lord is brought back into the Church concerning the second advent.

The doctrine concerning the coming of the Lord has become very important to me because the Church needs to prepare herself with truth concerning the end time so she will be able to stand strong in tribulation. I believe Jesus came near to Jerusalem and wept because He knew the suffering that lay ahead for them due to their unbelief. The Church is not prepared for what lies ahead: *And when he was come near, he beheld the city, and wept over it, 42 Saying, If thou hadst known, even thou, at least in this thy day, the things which belong unto thy peace! but now they are hid from thine eyes. 43 For the days shall come upon thee, that thine enemies shall cast a trench about thee, and compass thee round, and keep thee in on every side, 44 And shall lay thee even with the ground, and thy children within thee; and they shall not leave in thee one stone upon another; because thou knewest not the time of thy visitation* (Luke 19:41-44).

History tells us that the early Church disciples and saints who believed the apostles and what Jesus had prophesied left the city before its destruction of the city in A.D. 70. And there is no doubt the Apostles'

Doctrine included what Daniel had prophesied: *And after threescore and two weeks shall Messiah be cut off, but not for himself: and the people of the prince that shall come shall destroy the city and the sanctuary; and the end thereof shall be with a flood, and unto the end of the war desolations are determined* (Daniel 9:26). Daniel's prophecy covers the sixty-nine weeks from Babylon to John the Baptist and the end of the Law, to the cross, the fall of Jerusalem, through the Church age, the rapture and resurrection, and to the end of Daniel's seventieth week in the tribulation period: *And at that time shall Michael stand up, the great prince which standeth for the children of thy people: and there shall be a time of trouble, such as never was since there was a nation even to that same time: and at that time thy people shall be delivered, every one that shall be found written in the book. 2 And many of them that sleep in the dust of the earth shall awake, some to everlasting life, and some to shame and everlasting contempt. 3 And they that be wise shall shine as the brightness of the firmament; and they that turn many to righteousness as the stars for ever and ever. 10 Many shall be purified, and made white, and tried; but the wicked shall do wickedly: and none of the wicked shall understand; but the wise shall understand. 11 And from the time that the daily sacrifice shall be taken away, and the abomination that maketh desolate set up, there shall be a thousand two hundred and ninety days. 12 Blessed is he that waiteth, and cometh to the thousand three hundred and five and thirty days. 13 But go thou thy way till the end be: for thou shalt rest, and stand in thy lot at the end of the days* (Daniel 12:1-3, 10-13).

There was an uprising in China in 1900 called the Boxer Rebellion. It was directed against foreigners and Chinese Christians, many of whom were brutally killed. David Wilkerson relates in *America's Last Call* that certain missionaries told the Chinese converts Jesus would come and rapture them away before they had to face any coming violence. When the violence hit, no such rapture occurred, and many of the hundreds of thousands Chinese Christians lost their faith, because they weren't ready to face suffering. They were persecuted, lost their homes, land and possessions, and were beaten, bloodied and killed. Tragically, their leaders hadn't prepared them for what was coming, and the Christians who survived felt lied to, cheated, and deceived. Do you think people will listen to pretribulationists when the tribulation period comes? We need to stop and think what great harm the pretribulation rapture theory is going to cause all over the world when the man of sin comes to power and tells Christians that he is God, and begins to persecute them. The Boxer Rebellion will be mild in comparison.

If pretribulationists continue to tell people the rapture will take place at any time, but when things do not happen as people have been taught, many will be vulnerable to join forces with Rome for the one-world church. Their faith will be shaken, and they will become discouraged. Many will think the Lord has delayed His coming and go back to living wickedly, fulfilling: *But and if that evil servant shall say in his heart, My lord delayeth his coming; 49 And shall begin to smite his fellowservants, and to eat and drink with the drunken; 50 The lord of that servant shall come in a day when he looketh not for him, and in an hour that he is not aware of, 51 And shall cut him asunder, and appoint him his portion with the hypocrites: there shall be weeping and gnashing of teeth* (Matthew 24:48-51).

I come to the end of this book, and I have given enough evidence to prove the pretribulation rapture theory to be in error. You must look at all the evidence yourself as if you were on a jury and not make your decision on emotion, but on facts presented. If your mind is still confused because of past teaching on the pretribulation rapture theory, you must not let any bias sway you. The Conclusion of the Death Sentence to Pretribulation Rapture Theory shows how the Church has been deceived in one of the most important doctrines in the Bible outside of salvation. God's people should not put their faith in a doctrine that has no foundation, or evidence of truth.

In these last days true doctrine will be the Christians' greatest asset.

THE CONCLUSION OF
THE PRETRIBULATION
RAPTURE THEORY

I write this conclusion especially for those who still have some doubt concerning a pretribulation rapture. I hope you do not continue to search for some technicality in this book only to find fault. There are many things, such as the kingdom of heaven, the kingdom of God, the kingdom of Israel, or some other area you may disagree with, however untruths concerning the pretribulation rapture are the most important issue. It was necessary to put those other things in this book because they are related subjects. When a person's doctrine is wrong concerning the time element of the coming of the Lord, their doctrine will also be wrong about heaven, the kingdom of heaven, the kingdom of God, and the kingdom of Israel.

I have documented evidence of how dispensationalists put the Old Testament and the Gospels under the dispensation of Law, and said the Gospels were only for the Jews. Scofield said in his notes that from the second chapter of Acts to the fourth chapter of Revelation were for the Church. Out of this method of dispensationalism, the pretribulation rapture theory was born. All true doctrine is rooted in the Old Testament, and continues through the Gospels, the Epistles, and Revelation. There is no source in the Old Testament or the Gospels to prove a pretribulation rapture. Jesus used Moses and the prophets as a foundation for His ministry concerning Himself (Luke 24:25-27). Paul was accused of preaching heresy and teaching the Jews that were among the Gentiles to forsake Moses, saying that they ought not to circumcise their children, neither to walk after the customs (Acts 21: 21). He defended his ministry of what they called heresy, and showed how he used the Old Testament law and prophets as a foundation. He said he believed all things which were written in the law and in the prophets, and was not teaching contrary to them: *But this I confess unto thee, that after the way which they call heresy, so worship I the God of my fathers, believing all things which are written in the law and in the prophets* (Acts 24:14). Paul connects his ministry to the Gentiles and the Church with a verse going back to Moses and the prophets. *Having therefore obtained help of God, I continue unto this day, witnessing both to small and great, saying none other things than those which the prophets and Moses did say should come: 23 That Christ should suffer, and that he should be the first that should rise from the dead, and should show light unto the people, and to the Gentiles* (Acts 26:22-23).

The Church should also start in the Law and the prophets as a witness, just as Paul did in Romans. The book of Romans deals with our justification and lets us know that the saved are not justified by the Law, but by faith in Jesus Christ. The Law was given to bring the sinner to Christ so we could be justified by faith. This following verse lets us know that *the righteousness of God without the law is manifested, being witnessed by the law and the prophets* (Romans 3:21). There were types, prophecies, and promises in the Old Testament that pointed to this. The witnesses by the Law and the prophets are very numerous (Gen. 3:15, 15:1-6, 22:17-18; Isa. 53; Jer. 31:31-33; John 5:46; I Pet. 1:10): *Of which salvation the prophets have inquired and searched diligently, who prophesied of the grace that should come unto you.* Jesus is the theme of the Bible from Genesis to Revelation. He fulfilled all that was written of Him in the Old Testament (Acts 13:29), and you cannot separate the Jesus of the Old Testament and His teachings in the Gospels from the Epistles by dispensationalism, and say it is rightly dividing the Word of truth. Paul let us know that the Church was built upon the foundation of the apostles and the prophets, so both Jew and Gentile could be reconciled to God (Eph. 2:14-20). The foundation concerning the Lord's coming must also start in the Old Testament and the prophets, and come through what Jesus taught in the Gospels, continuing through the Epistles and Revelation.

I will begin in the Old Testament an continue through the Gospels, the Epistles, and Revelation concerning the rapture and the Lord's coming. It is an error to separate what Jesus said in the Gospels about His coming, saying it is only for the Jew, and then say that what Paul taught in the Epistles is for the Church. Neither Jesus nor Paul taught such a doctrine.

Abraham was the father of our faith in Jesus Christ (Gal. 3:7) and saw that Jesus was the Messiah. He also saw the Church age, heaven, and the New Jerusalem: *Your father Abraham rejoiced to see my day: and he saw it, and was glad* (John 8:56). *By faith Abraham, when he was called to go out into a place which he should after receive for an inheritance, obeyed; and he went out, not knowing whither he went. 9 By faith he sojourned in the land of promise, as in a strange country, dwelling in tabernacles with Isaac and Jacob, the heirs with him of the same promise: 10 For he looked for a city which hath foundations, whose builder and maker is God* (Hebrews 11:8-10). Abraham was looking for the heavenly Jerusalem, whose builder and maker is God. He was not looking for the earthly Jerusalem for the saints, which will last only one thousand years.

The Scriptures show how Jacob saw the ladder that reached to heaven (Jesus). He saw the angels of God ascending and descending. He saw a glimpse of the heavenly Jerusalem, far superior to the earthly kingdom of Israel in the Millennium. The saints will be as the angels, able to ascend and descend in the Heavenly Jerusalem after the rapture and resurrection (Luke 20:34-38). In Abraham's seed all the families of the earth will be blessed: *And he lighted upon a certain place, and tarried there all night, because the sun was set; and he took of the stones of that place, and put them for his pillows, and lay down in that place to sleep. 12 And he dreamed, and behold a ladder set up on the earth, and the top of it reached to heaven: and behold the angels of God ascending and descending on it. 13 And, behold, the LORD stood above it, and said, I am the LORD God of Abraham thy father, and the God of Isaac: the land whereon thou liest, to thee will I give it, and to thy seed; 14 And thy seed shall be as the dust of the earth, and thou shalt spread abroad to the west, and to the east, and to the north, and to the south: and in thee and in thy seed shall all the families of the earth be blessed* (Genesis 28:11-14).

Jesus knew what the future held for Him, and how His own people would reject Him. Jesus spoke of Isaiah's prophecy concerning Israel's spiritual blindness. They did not understand the purpose of His first advent to die for man's sins, and then His ascension back to the Father to set up the heavenly kingdom that the Father gave Him. The Jews rejected Jesus as the Messiah, but there was a remnant who believed and were saved according to the election of grace, while the rest were blinded (Rom. 11:1-8). Those who did believe were the good seed in the Church age, of which Jesus spoke quoting Isaiah the prophet. Only those Jews who believed that Jesus was the promised Messiah understood the meaning of the kingdom of heaven. Pretribulationism has given a wrong interpretation of the kingdom of heaven by changing its meaning, which has caused blindness in God's people. Jesus explains the kingdom of heaven in His parables, and gave great detail about its meaning. Jesus let the believing Jews know that the good seed heareth the word, understands it, and bears fruit (Matt. 13:11-23).

Many Jews did not understand the prophecies about the Lord's first coming, just as many in this Church age are in darkness about the time sequence of the Lord's second coming. When dispensationalists claim the Old Testament prophecies, the Gospels, and after the fourth chapter of Revelation are for the Jews only, and not for the Church, it changes what the Lord wanted the Church to understand about His second coming. The major prophets prophesied about both comings, and the Church needs to understand that Isaiah had much to say about the Church age, the Gentiles, and the coming of the Lord. I believe Isaiah, the Lord, Paul, and John prophesied about the same coming of the Lord, the rapture and resurrection. In the following Scripture, Isaiah tells about the great tribulation, and how God's children will be safe in His chambers (the rapture) when the Lord comes to judge the world: *Like as a woman with child, that draweth near the time of her delivery, is in pain, and crieth out in her pangs; so have we been in thy sight, O LORD. 18 We have been with child, we have been in pain, we have as it were brought forth wind; we have not wrought any deliverance in the earth; neither have the inhabitants of the world fallen. 19 Thy dead men shall live, together with my dead body shall they arise. Awake and sing, ye that dwell in dust: for thy dew is as the dew of herbs, and the earth shall cast out the dead. 20 Come, my people, enter thou into thy chambers, and shut thy doors about thee: hide thyself as it were for a little moment, until the indignation be overpast. 21 For, behold, the LORD cometh out of his place to punish the inhabitants of the earth for their iniquity: the earth also shall disclose her blood, and shall no more cover her slain* (Isaiah 26:17-21).

Zephaniah wrote how the saints of God will be hidden when God judges the earth because they are in the rapture as found in I Thessalonians 4:13-18. Saints do not suffer the wrath of God, Jew or Gentile; The meek of the whole earth are asked to seek the Lord before the Day of the LORD, so they will be safe from God's wrath: *Gather yourselves together, yea, gather together, O nation not desired; 2 Before the decree bring forth, before the day pass as the chaff, before the fierce anger of the LORD come upon you, before the day of the LORD'S anger come upon you. 3 Seek ye the LORD, all ye meek of the earth, which have wrought his judgment; seek righteousness, seek meekness: it may be ye shall be hid in the day of the LORD'S anger* (Zephaniah 2:1-3).

The Psalms describes the Lord's second coming and the rapture: *Our God shall come, and shall not keep silence: a fire shall devour before him, and it shall be very tempestuous round about him. 4 He shall call to the heavens from above, and to the earth, that he may judge his people. 5 Gather my saints together unto me; those that have made a covenant with me by sacrifice* (Psalm 50:3-5).

Daniel tells us about the time of trouble in the tribulation period, that those whose names are written in the Book shall be delivered, and about the resurrection (Daniel 12:1-2). The Bible does not teach one resurrection before the tribulation period and then another seven years later. Revelation 20:5 is the first resurrection, and is the same as recorded in Daniel 12:1-2: *And at that time shall Michael stand up, the great prince which standeth for the children of thy people: and there shall be a time of trouble, such as never was since there was a nation even to that same time: and at that time thy people shall be delivered, every one that shall be found written in the book. 2 And many of them that sleep in the dust of the earth shall awake, some to everlasting life, and some to shame and everlasting contempt.*

The Minor Prophets also refer to Jesus' second coming. Joel tells us how the sun is darkened and the moon turned to blood before the terrible day of the wrath of the Lord. This corresponds to the time element of Jesus' coming as found in Matthew, Mark, and Luke. If there were a pretribulation rapture of the Church, there would be some mention of it in the Old Testament and the Gospels. Jesus would not have left the Church in darkness concerning such an important subject: *The sun shall be turned into darkness, and the moon into blood, before the great and the terrible day of the LORD come. 32 And it shall come to pass, that whosoever shall call on the name of the LORD shall be delivered: for in mount Zion and in Jerusalem shall be deliverance, as the LORD hath said, and in the remnant whom the LORD shall call* (Joel 2:31-32).

Malachi speaks to the Jew about when God "make up His jewels." He will not forget those whose names are written in God's book of remembrance. God promised to spare those who serve Him, and these are some of the last verses God gives to the Jew before Jesus comes and gives the Gospels: *Then they that feared the LORD spake often one to another: and the LORD hearkened, and heard it, and a book of remembrance was written before him for them that feared the LORD, and that thought upon his name. 17 And they shall be mine, saith the LORD of hosts, in that day when I make up my jewels; and I will spare them, as a man spareth his own son that serveth him. 18 Then shall ye return, and discern between the righteous and the wicked, between him that serveth God and him that serveth him not* (Malachi 3:16-18).

References to the rapture and resurrection are found in the Major and Minor Prophets. Jesus often quoted them in His ministry. He makes His coming plain to the Church, both Jew and Gentile, in the Gospels. He said He would come after the tribulation period. I believe Jesus knows more about the subject than man: *Immediately after the tribulation of those days shall the sun be darkened, and the moon shall not give her light, and the stars shall fall from heaven, and the powers of the heavens shall be shaken: 30 And then shall appear the sign of the Son of man in heaven: and then shall all the tribes of the earth mourn, and they shall see the Son of man coming in the clouds of heaven with power and great glory. 31 And he shall send his angels with a great sound of a trumpet, and they shall gather together his elect from the four winds, from one end of heaven to the other* (Matthew 24:29-31).

Jesus gave information in the Gospels concerning the rapture, prior to Paul's two letters to the Thessalonians. It took 1800 years before dispensationalists separated the Gospels from the Epistles. This made the interpretation of what Jesus said in the Gospels different from what Paul said. The following Scripture concerning the rapture is for Jew and Gentile, not for the Jew only: *And he shall send his angels with a great sound of a trumpet, and they shall gather together his elect from the four winds, from one end of heaven to the other. 40 Then shall two be in the field; the one shall be taken, and the other left. 41 Two women shall be grinding at the mill; the one shall be taken, and the other left. 42 Watch therefore: for ye know not what hour your Lord doth come* (Matthew 24:31, 40-42).

Mark also gives the Lord's words to the Church concerning the Lord's coming (Mark 13:34-37). Jesus explains that He is going to take a far journey (heaven, after His resurrection), but He will come again. Jesus warns the Church to watch and be ready for His coming: *For the Son of man is as a man taking a far journey, who left his house, and gave authority to his servants, and to every man his work, and commanded the porter to watch. 35 Watch ye therefore: for ye know not when the master of the house cometh, at even, or at midnight, or at the cockcrowing, or in the morning: 36 Lest coming suddenly he find you sleeping. 37 And what I say unto you I say unto all, Watch* (Mark 13:34-37).

Luke gave the Lord's words to the Church concerning His second coming in Luke 21:5-36. Jesus gave us the signs of his coming in verses 25-33. These signs are what Paul instructed the Thessalonian Church about in I Thessalonians 5:1-8, and he said the Lord would not come as a thief, because they are of the light. The Lord Himself had given the Church all they needed to know about His coming, but Paul and the apostles were establishing the apostles' doctrine until the Church had the completed Bible in their hands.

Paul did not tell the confused Thessalonian church about a different coming from that which Jesus had established. He told them about the same coming which has its root in the Old Testament and the Gospels. Paul's letters to the Thessalonian church only corrected the errors that false prophets had made concerning the rapture, resurrection, and the Lord's coming. He was not forming a new doctrine concerning a pretribulation rapture. Paul confirms the same coming, rapture, and resurrection that the Lord taught while He was on earth. If this was a new doctrine, where is its foundation in the Old Testament and the Gospels? *But I would not have you to be ignorant, brethren, concerning them which are asleep, that ye sorrow not, even as others which have no hope. 14 For if we believe that Jesus died and rose again, even so them also which sleep in Jesus will God bring with him. 15 For this we say unto you by the word of the Lord, that we which are alive and remain unto the coming of the Lord shall not prevent them which are asleep. 16 For the Lord himself shall descend from heaven with a shout, with the voice of the archangel, and with the trump of God: and the dead in Christ shall rise first: 17 Then we which are alive and remain shall be caught up together with them in the clouds, to meet the Lord in the air: and so shall we ever be with the Lord. 18 Wherefore comfort one another with these words* (I Thessalonians 4:13-18).

After Paul gives the truth in the fourth chapter of Thessalonians concerning the rapture and resurrection, He then says in I Thessalonians 5:1: *But of the times and the seasons, brethren, ye have no need that I write unto you. 2 For yourselves know perfectly that the day of the Lord so cometh as a thief in the night.*

Jesus had already given the times and seasons of His coming in the Gospels, and Luke records the trouble Paul endured in the Thessalonian church (Acts 17:10-14). Paul gives the time element of when Jesus comes, the rapture, and resurrection, and is in agreement with what Jesus had already taught. The tribulation period is the wrath of man on man, not the wrath of God on man. The following Scriptures tell the saints about the Day of the Lord, and how it will come upon the unbelievers by surprise. Paul lets the saints know that it should not come on them as a thief in the night because they are the children of light. He said in verse 8: *But let us, who are of the day, be sober, putting on the breastplate of faith and love; and for an helmet, the hope of salvation.*

God did not appoint the saints to wrath because they are children of God, and are raptured before the Day of the Lord takes place. Paul did not give a different Day of the Lord to the Thessalonian church than Isaiah, Zephaniah, or Jesus taught. The Day of the Lord is at the end of the tribulation period: *For yourselves know perfectly that the day of the Lord so cometh as a thief in the night. 3 For when they shall say, Peace and safety; then sudden destruction cometh upon them, as travail upon a woman with child; and they shall not escape. 4 But ye, brethren, are not in darkness, that that day should overtake you as a thief. 5 Ye are all the children of light, and the children of the day: we are not of the night, nor of darkness. 6 Therefore let us not sleep, as do others; but let us watch and be sober. 7 For they that sleep sleep in the night; and they that be drunken are drunken in the night. 8 But let us, who are of the day, be sober, putting on the breastplate of faith and love; and for an helmet, the hope of salvation. 9 For God hath not appointed us to wrath, but to obtain salvation by our Lord Jesus Christ, 10 Who died for us, that, whether we wake or sleep, we should live together with him* (I Thessalonians 5:2-10).

He warns them not to let anyone deceive them about the apostasy and the man of sin being revealed before the Lord would come. Listen to Paul: *Now we beseech you, brethren, by the coming of our Lord Jesus Christ, and by our gathering together unto him, 2 That ye be not soon shaken in mind, or be troubled, neither by spirit, nor by word, nor by letter as from us, as that the day of Christ is at hand. 3 Let no man deceive you by any means: for that day shall not come, except there come a falling away first, and that man of sin be revealed, the son of perdition; 4 Who opposeth and exalteth himself above all that is called God, or that is worshipped; so that he as God sitteth in the temple of God, showing himself that he is God. 5 Remember ye not, that, when I was yet with you, I told you these things?* (II Thessalonians 2:1-5).

Paul tells us that the rapture will take place at the last trumpet: *Behold, I show you a mystery; We shall not all sleep, but we shall all be changed, 52 In a moment, in the twinkling of an eye, at the last trump: for the trumpet shall sound, and the dead shall be raised incorruptible, and we shall be changed. 53 For this corruptible must put on incorruption, and this mortal must put on immortality* (I Corinthians 15:51-53).

John tells us in Revelation that the Lord is going to come with clouds, and every eye will see Him. There is no secret rapture: *Behold, he cometh with clouds; and every eye shall see him, and they also which pierced him: and all kindreds of the earth shall wail because of him. Even so, Amen* (Revelation 1:7).

There is no rapture in Revelation 4:1 as pretribulationists teach. The voice is telling John to "come up hither," and be shown what would happen afterward. There is not ONE word in this Scripture that sets forth a time element of the rapture and resurrection. The door is in heaven, and the voice invites John up to the throne so he can see future events: *After this I looked, and, behold, a door was opened in heaven: and the first voice which I heard was as it were of a trumpet talking with me; which said, Come up hither, and I will show thee things which must be hereafter. 2 And immediately I was in the spirit; and, behold, a throne was set in heaven, and one sat on the throne* (Revelation 4:1-2).

John did not change the time element of the rapture and resurrection in Revelation, which Paul already established in I Corinthians 15:51-53. The rapture and resurrection take place when the seventh trumpet sounds, which is the last trumpet. The mystery of God concerning the coming of the Lord is completed, or finished, when the seventh trumpet sounds. The mysteries of all the prophets concerning the coming of the Lord and the judgment to follow will lay bare for all to see. God never promised His servants a pretribulation rapture: *But in the days of the voice of the seventh angel, when he shall begin to sound, the mystery of God should be finished, as he hath declared to his servants the prophets* (Revelation 10:7).

When the seventh trumpet sounds, it will signal to the whole world that resurrection day has arrived. At the rapture of the saints, the kingdoms of this world will become the kingdoms of the Lord: *And the seventh angel sounded; and there were great voices in heaven, saying, The kingdoms of this world are become the kingdoms of our Lord, and of his Christ; and he shall reign for ever and ever* (Revelation 11:15).

The wrath of God comes immediately after the rapture of the Church, and the judgment seat of Christ takes place after the wrath of God has been poured out on a sinful world. Both must take place after the seventh trumpet sounds: *And the nations were angry, and thy wrath is come, and the time of the dead, that they should be judged and that thou shouldest give reward unto thy servants the prophets, and to the saints, and them that fear thy name ,small and great; and shouldest destroy them which destroy the earth* (Revelation 11:18).

There is not one scriptural evidence that pretribulationists can give to show that the rapture and resurrection take place in Revelation 4:1. Every evidence given in the Old Testament, the Gospels, the Epistles, and Revelation always take place just before the day of the Lord at the end of the tribulation period, not before.

Jesus will come without warning on a sinful world, and we are to testify these things unto the churches. We are to let saints know that Jesus has prepared a beautiful city for us, the heavenly Jerusalem. We are not to add or take away from the Word of God. God wants those who are thirsty for salvation to come and drink of the water of life freely: *And, behold, I come quickly; and my reward is with me, to give every man according as his work shall be. 13 I am Alpha and Omega, the beginning and the end, the first and the last. 14 Blessed are they that do his commandments, that they may have right to the tree of life, and may enter in through the gates into the city. 15 For without are dogs, and sorcerers, and whoremongers, and murderers, and idolaters, and whosoever loveth and maketh a lie. 16 I Jesus have sent mine angel to testify unto you these things in the churches. I am the root and the offspring of David, and the bright and morning star. 17 And the Spirit and the bride say, Come. And let him that heareth say, Come. And let him that is athirst come. And whosoever will, let him take the water of life freely. 18 For I testify unto every man that heareth the words of the prophecy of this book, If any man shall add unto these things, God shall add unto him the plagues that are written in this book: 19 And if any man shall take away from the words of the book of this prophecy, God shall take away his part out of the book of life, and out of the holy city, and from the things which are written in this book. 20 He which testifieth these things saith, Surely I come quickly. Amen. Even so, come, Lord Jesus. 21 The grace of our Lord Jesus Christ be with you all. Amen* (Revelation 22:12-21).

Pure Doctrine

In a single generation we have seen Americans give away most of the God-given rights, values, and principles that made this nation great. Our courts and government removed the Bible from our schools, and many of our public schools have become jungles. The American home is being broken apart by sin and a growing disconnection between family members, and to God. The divorce rate is over 50 percent, and is the same in professing Christian homes as it is in the world. Our legal system no longer uses the Bible as a guide. The Ten Commandments are publicly ridiculed. Darkness is now setting in. Over seventy-two churches close their doors every week in America, and only one-third are replaced. We have lost close to 10 percent of the membership in Protestant churches in the last ten years. Most political leaders are calling evil good and good evil. The apostasy has already begun.

Because of this darkness, our government clamors for the New World Order (One World Government). In other words, they have the spirit of the antichrist but do not know it. This calamity has come about because those in athority no longer look to God for direction as did our forefathers. Drugs, alcohol, crime, adultery, fornication, gambling, lotteries, abortion, homosexuality, and every evil way have replaced the fear of God.

The other side of the coin is that our spiritual leaders, our pastors, evangelists, and prophets are giving back what our forefathers died for.

Church unity at any cost has become a priority for many denominations today. There are twenty-three groups which form a new organization called "Christian Churches Together in the USA." They tell us that unity is for the common good of all. These groups focus on areas of agreement, not disagreement. These groups are working to get the Roman Catholic, evangelical mainline Protestants, and the NCC into one group. The leaders of all involved will sacrifice God's plan for man, and substitute their plan. They totally disregard what the Bible says about the end-time One World Church. The rationale is, "Put away doctrines, because doctrines divide." God's people are blind concerning true oneness in Christ, thinking that putting away pure and sound doctrine will make the Body of Christ into one body. Yet this only increases division between the true and the false. The nation's largest Lutheran denomination is preparing to unite with the Episcopal Church. These two Protestant denominations united will further a One World Church, and the issues which caused the Reformation in the sixteenth century are being swept under the rug. In 1997, the Lutheran Church entered into full communion with the Presbyterian Church (USA), the United Church of Christ, and the Reformed Church in America. The Roman Catholic and the Eastern Orthodox are on the verge of closing the division between them. Complete denominational unity is only a matter of time, fulfilling what was prophesied.

Before the turn of this century many pretribulationists prophesied how the rapture would soon take place. The year 2000 has come and gone and no rapture has occurred. Books and films by pretribulationists, such as Left Behind, are very popular today, but many prophecies made by pretribulationists will fail because of the wrong interpretation of vital Scriptures. When prophecies begin to fail and tribulations begin to come, there will be much dissolution. Paul told the Thessalonian church the time element of the Lord's coming, the rapture, and our gathering together unto Him. Paul let them know that the apostasy will happen and the man of sin will be revealed before our gathering together unto the Lord. When the Lord is revealed, and the saints raptured and safe in the Lord's chambers, He will consume the antichrist with the spirit of His mouth, and the brightness of His coming.

The world is already laying the groundwork to receive the antichrist with globalization of trade, a one-world government, and a one-world religion. The time is coming when the unified churches will follow the false prophet, and will no longer offer salvation to the people. They will be religious but unsaved. The antichrist's *coming is after the working of Satan with all power and signs and lying wonders, And with all deceivableness of unrighteousness in them that perish; because they received not the love of the truth, that they might be saved* (II Thess. 2:9-10). Those who are deceived by the antichrist and the false prophet will perish because they loved not the truth: *And for this cause God shall send them strong delusion, that they should believe a lie: 12 That they all might be damned who believed not the truth, but had pleasure in unrighteousness* (II Thess. 2:11-12). All of these great truths are found in II Thessalonians 2:1-17.

When doctrine is found to be in error, it should be corrected to fit the Word. Denominations should reevaluate, and rightly divide the Word of truth to learn if there has been error. Fundamentalists of the faith must not compromise doctrine for church unity. If doctrine is found to be in error, correct only the error. When Fundamental churches throw away good doctrine for Church unity, they stand for nothing. We must not forget what the Reformation was all about in the sixteenth century. Let us hunger for truth once again, and never forsake the truth of the Word.

Those who understand what is taking place concerning the apostasy and the one-world church will do well to heed what George Muller had to say:" What will help us, who believe in Christ, to be more united together? One might say: 'Oh, we must give up our differences.' Allow me affectionately and humbly to say: 'I do not think so.' According to my judgment, a closer union would not be brought about by us giving up our views of what we consider to be taught by God and the scriptures. Not thus, but the great point is to let the foundation truths of our holy Faith have their proper place. We have not to say: 'Now I will put away for the time being all that I hold distinctively from my brethren.' No; nor do I expect this from my brethren. With great diligence and prayerfulness, and, if necessary, great sacrifice, ought we to 'buy the truth'; but, having obtained it, for no price whatever is it to be sold."

We must not disregard what the prophets have prophesied about the end time. We must sift out the truth, and discard the false. We have two groups of religious people in these last days. One will be for church unity in order to have a one-world church and government. They will compromise truth for unity's sake. The other group will seek for truth in order to be in unity with Christ and the Word of God. This is the group that the world will hate and persecute. This group will be ready for the rapture and the Lord's coming.

For those who realized they made a mistake in teaching and preaching the pretribulation rapture theory should not keep silent on the subject. Admit to your people that you were wrong, then preach with power what the New Testament teaches. Each one of us should preach the Word as God asked us to do (II Tim. 4:2-5). I pray this book will bring the Church of Jesus Christ back to truth concerning the second advent and the posttribulation rapture.

Judgment Starts at the House of God

The Church is not going to be taken out by a secret rapture. God's people must deal with false doctrine, false teaching, and the false hopes they have created. This book is not about denominational teachings, but about correcting a great error. Judgment starts at the House of God and we all shall give an account before God for every word which we have spoken in error. If we are to give an account to God, what will be the end of those that will not obey the gospel of God? *For the time is come that judgment must begin at the house of God: and if it first begin at us, what shall the end be of them that obey not the gospel of God?* (I Peter 4:17).

Many deceivers and cults are arising as we enter the twenty-first century. The Church must teach true doctrine about the coming of the Lord or else the Church will be among the great deceivers. All writings should be tested by the Word to make sure doctrine is right.

The Lord gave a parable that is very fitting to what it will be like when the call is given: *Behold, the bridegroom Cometh; go out to meet him.* There are five wise virgins who have oil in their lamps and are ready to go in to the marriage feast, but there are five foolish virgins who have no oil in their lamps and when the cry is made to go out and meet the bridegroom they are not ready, and are shut out. This is how it will be when the Lord comes; some will be shut out of heaven, and will perish in the wrath of God (Matt. 25:1-13).

HEAVEN OR HELL

Choices we make today will determine where we will spend eternity. There are many unsaved people who love prophecy, yet don't change in response to it. The following verses aptly illustrate this: *There was a certain rich man, which was clothed in purple and fine linen, and fared sumptuously every day: 20 And there was a certain beggar named Lazarus, which was laid at his gate, full of sores, 21 And desiring to be fed with the crumbs which fell from the rich man's table: moreover the dogs came and licked his sores. 22 And it came to pass, that the beggar died, and was carried by the angels into Abraham's bosom: the rich man also died, and was buried; 23 And in hell he lift up his eyes, being in torments, and seeth Abraham afar off, and Lazarus in his bosom. 24 And he cried and said, Father Abraham, have mercy on me, and send Lazarus, that he may dip the tip of his finger in water, and cool my tongue; for I am tormented in this flame. 25 But Abraham said, Son, remember that thou in thy lifetime receivedst thy good things, and likewise Lazarus evil things: but now he is comforted, and thou art tormented. 26 And beside all this, between us and you there is a great gulf fixed: so that they which would pass from hence to you cannot; neither can they pass to us, that would come from thence. 27 Then he said, I pray thee therefore, father, that thou wouldest send him to my father's house: 28 For I have five brethren; that he may testify unto them, lest they also come into this place of torment. 29 Abraham saith unto him, They have Moses and the prophets; let them hear them. 30 And he said, Nay, father Abraham: but if one went unto them from the dead, they will repent. 31 And he said unto him, If they hear not Moses and the prophets, neither will they be persuaded, though one rose from the dead* (Luke 16:19-31).

The doctrine of Heaven and Hell has been preached, shouted, and sung across the ages. By one of these destinies every soul is bound—we must make a choice in this life. We must choose between two masters, the Lord or the Devil, between living the Christian life, or living a sinful life. Everyone must make a choice of which road they will follow, the narrow or the broad road. We will each die as a sinner, or die as a saint. We have only two destinies—heaven or hell. The rich man chose the world and the things of this life. Destiny was not determined because the rich man was rich and went to hell, or because the poor man was poor,and went to heaven. Destiny is determined by what we do with Jesus (John 3:18).

Many who once preached there was a literal hell have softened their message to fit the liberals' view, preaching that a loving God would not let someone burn in hell forever. The Bible teaches hell is a literal place, the same as heaven. Hell is spoken of as from beneath, and heaven is spoken of as from above: *The way of life is above to the wise, that he may depart from hell beneath* (Proverbs 15: 24). The Hebrew word for hell in the Old Testament is "Sheol," to which "Hades" corresponds in the New Testament. It means "grave" or the "condition of the dead," or hell. The final place for the punishment of sinners is Gehenna, which is translated "hell" in Luke 12:5: *But I will forewarn you whom ye shall fear: Fear him, which after he hath killed hath power to cast into hell; yea, I say unto you, Fear him.*

Hell is an eternal place for the wicked, where the suffering of the souls of the damned by the judgment of God is without intermission. They are deprived of the sight of God forever. Those in hell will feel pain. Jesus said their "worm dieth not," and the "fire is not quenched." It's better to tell people the truth concerning hell than to deceive them with a lie and say that it won't last long. If God made this place for the Devil and his angels, the Lord should know what it is: *Where their worm dieth not, and the fire is not quenched* (Mark 9:44). The beast and the false prophet will be cast into the lake of fire, as will all those who worship him:*And the beast was taken, and with him the false prophet that wrought miracles before him, with which he deceived them that had received the mark of the beast, and them that worshipped his image. These both were cast alive into a lake of fire burning with brimstone* (Revelation 19: 20). The Devil which was released for a short season will be cast into the lake of fire: *And the devil that deceived them was cast into the lake of fire and brimstone, where the beast* and the false prophet are, and shall be tormented day and night for ever and ever (Revelation 20:10). After the resurrection of the unsaved at the great white throne judgment, they will be judged, and also cast into the lake of fire, which is the second death: *And I saw a great white throne, and him that sat on it, from whose face the earth and the heaven fled away; and there was found no place for them. 12 And I saw the dead, small and great, stand before God; and the books were opened: and another book was opened, which is the book of life: and the dead were judged out of those things which were written in the books, according to their works. 13 And the sea gave up the dead which were in it; and death and hell delivered up the dead which were in them: and they were judged every man according to their works. 14 And death and hell were cast into the lake of fire. This is the second death. 15 And whosoever was not found written in the book of life was cast into the lake of fire* (Revelation 20:11-15).

After the great white throne judgment, death, the last enemy, will be destroyed. Death and hell will be cast into the lake of fire. The Lord will offer up the kingdom to the Father. The Son will be subject to the Father so that God may be all in all: *But every man in his own order: Christ the firstfruits; afterward they that are Christ's at his coming. 24 Then cometh the end, when he shall have delivered up the kingdom to God, even the Father; when he shall have put down all rule and all authority and power. 25 For he must reign, till he hath put all enemies under his feet. 26 The last enemy that shall be destroyed is death. 27 For he hath put all things under his feet. But when he saith all things are put under him, it is manifest that he is excepted, which did put all things under him. 28 And when all things shall be subdued unto him, then shall the Son also himself be subject unto him that put all things under him, that God may be all in all* (I Corinthians 15:23-28).

Isaiah shows us that hell is from beneath, and is ready to receive the beast, and bring him down to hell at the Lord's coming: *Hell from beneath is moved for thee to meet thee at thy coming: it stirreth up the dead for thee, even all the chief ones of the earth; it hath raised up from their thrones all the kings of the nations. 15 Yet thou shalt be brought down to hell, to the sides of the pit. 16 They that see thee shall narrowly look upon thee, and consider thee, saying, Is this the man that made the earth to tremble, that did shake kingdoms; 17 That made the world as a wilderness, and destroyed the cities thereof; that opened not the house of his prisoners?* (Isaiah 14:9,15-17).

There are not many years left before the Lord is going to return. When He comes, the Stone that was cut out of the mountain will destroy the kingdoms of this world. Nebuchadnezzar's great image pictures the four empires, Babylon, Medo-Persia, the Greek Empire under Alexander the Great, Rome, and the revived Roman Empire. The Lord will smite this great image when He comes and destroy all kingdoms of this world. Many will be cast into hell, until the great white throne judgment. This will fulfill Daniel 2:31-35. The Father has already given His Son all power in heaven and earth. His kingdom will never pass away. The beast and the false prophet will be cast into the lake of fire, and the devil will be bound for one thousand years. The kingdom of Israel will last for only one thousand years, but the kingdom of the Lord will have no end, because it will stand forever: *Thou, O king, sawest, and behold a great image. This great image, whose brightness was excellent, stood before thee; and the form thereof was terrible. 32 This image's head was of fine gold, his breast and his arms of silver, his belly and his thighs of brass, 33 His legs of iron, his feet part of iron and part of clay. 34 Thou sawest till that a stone was cut out without hands, which smote the image upon his feet that were of iron and clay, and brake them to pieces. 35 Then was the iron, the clay, the brass, the silver, and the gold, broken to pieces together, and became like the chaff of the summer threshingfloors; and the wind carried them away, that no place was found for them: and the stone that smote the image became a great mountain, and filled the whole earth. 44 And in the days of these kings shall the God of heaven set up a kingdom, which shall never be destroyed: and the kingdom shall not be left to other people, but it shall break in pieces and consume all these kingdoms, and it shall stand for ever. 45 Forasmuch as thou sawest that the stone was cut out of the mountain without hands, and that it brake in pieces the iron, the brass, the clay, the silver, and the gold; the great God hath made known to the king what shall come to pass hereafter: and the dream is certain, and the interpretation thereof sure* (Daniel 2:31-35, 44-45).

Those people who delay salvation must realize that when the Lord comes, He will destroy all the Gentile world powers and every false religion by His wrath through the seven last vials and the battle of Armageddon. There will be many who were called to salvation, but refused it. They think they will have time to get right with God. The Lord said many shall be called, but few will be chosen. Some will not be chosen because they will not be ready for the Lord's coming, the same as the five foolish virgins who had no oil in their lamps. Every person who worshiped the beast will face the torments of hell forever. We must make a choice of which place we want to go—heaven or hell.

THE DEATH
SENTENCE

I believe the Word of God has pronounced the death sentence to the pretribulation theory. Scripture is given to support everything that I have written. All readers will be able to decide for themselves whether I wrote error or the truth. God's people have been deceived long enough by a pretribulation rapture theory built on a theology of interpretation, and not on fact. Dispensationalists claim that I Thessalonians 4:13-18 is the pretribulation rapture of the Church, without giving one word of proof. The Bible does not teach there are two comings of Christ, one for the rapture of the saints, and the other when Jesus comes back to earth with His saints. Jesus is going to come one time, as the Scriptures verify. God will then send His wrath upon a sinful, unbelieving world.

I also believe this book will aid Israel in seeing that God has plans to graft them back into the Body of Christ, and that He has not appointed them to wrath without giving the promise of salvation in the latter rain (Hos. 6:3, Rom. 11:15-23, James 5:7). God always sends a messenger before judgment. God will not let His people enter into the tribulation period without warning. A remnant will be saved and will be in the rapture. Those who reject the warning given in God's Word will be in darkness, and will not be prepared to face the time of testing that will come upon all the world. Let God's people pay heed to the warning in I Thessalonians 5:1-8.

It's time evangelists, pastors, and teachers come back to the truth concerning the Lord's coming and teach the Church truth once again. Without the knowledge of the Son of God that is in the Gospels, they will be carried about with every wind of doctrine to deceive them. Refer to Ephesians 4:11-14.

In conclusion, I say once again that pretribulation rapture teaching is only a theory and not fact. J. Dwight Pentecost labels it a theory in the index of his book *Things to Come* with this heading, "The Pretribulation Rapture Theory." Webster says a theory is a "doctrine or scheme of things resting merely on speculation." I believe the theory of a pretribulation rapture is as hard to prove as evolution. Those who believe in the pretribulation rapture cannot prove that the Gospels are only for the Jew, therefore it is a theory. I have given proof by the Word that the Church was started in the Gospels and the disciples were its first called-out members. I have shown how the Gospels are for the Church, and not for the Jew only.

If you ask pretribulationists, "Does the rapture take place in Revelation 4:1?" they are compelled to say yes, or else the pretribulation theory falls apart. This book has given proof that the time element of the Lord's coming takes place at the seventh trumpet in Revelation 11:15 and I Corinthians 15:52, which is after the apostasy and the man of sin is revealed (II Thess. 2:1-5). Posttribulation rapture is a fact; pretribulation rapture of the Church is a theory. Therefore, I pronounce the death sentence to pretribulation rapture theory because it has no foundation or fact.

I Rest
My Case

It grieves me very deeply when I hear the Church teaching a doctrine that I know is untrue. I believe the facts in this book will put the Church back on course. The Lord is coming for His Church. The time will be when He promised, after the tribulation period but before God's wrath. The Church has a great responsibility to correct these serious errors which have been made. For many, pride will be their worst enemy in admitting their error. I pray there are enough of God's people who see the error and correct a doctrine that has done much damage to the Church for over 170 years concerning the Lord's coming. I realize how hard it is to change people's minds from error to truth, but it's time to prepare God's people for what lies ahead, and for the coming of the Lord. I have complete confidence that this book is correct concerning the time element of the coming of the Lord. I rely on what Jesus said in the Gospels about His coming, and what Paul said in II Thessalonians 2—that before the saints will be gathered unto the Lord, the apostasy will come first and the man of sin be revealed. Paul asked the Church not to let anyone deceive them concerning the Lord's coming. Jesus told us out of His own mouth in Matthew 24 that the time would be immediately after the tribulation, and then we would see the sign of His coming. Do not deceive yourself, but remember what Jesus said in the Gospels about when He would come again, and what Paul told the Thessalonian church in II Thessalonians 2:1-5. They both are talking about the same coming of the Lord. I rest my case.

The pretribulation rapture is only a theory, not fact.

Bibliography of Works Cited

MacPherson, Dave. *The Incredible cover-up.* Medford, Oregon: Omega publications, 1975. pp. 28, 64-71, 83.

The Popular and Critical Bible Encyclopaedia and Scriptural Dictionary. Chicago: The Howard-Severance Co., 1912. Vol. II, p. 1025.

Sanford. *Cyclopedia of Religious Knowledge.* Hartford, Conn: Charles L. Webster & Co., 1890. pp. 449, 507.

Schaff, Philip. *The Schaff-Herzog Encyclopaedia,* vol. 3. New York: Funk & Wagnalls, 1883. pp. 1888, 1889.

Lange's Commentary, Schaff. *Corinthians,* New York: Charles Scribner & Co., 1889. p. 346.

Schaff, Philip. *History of the Christian Church,* vol. I. , p. 70. Grand Rapids: William B. Eerdmans Publishing Co., 1994.

Hastings, James. *Dictionary of The Bible.* New York: Charles Scribner's Sons., 1944. p. 123.

Ryrie, Charles Caldwell. *The Ryrie Study Bible.* Chicago: The Moody Bible Institute,1978. p. 1505.

Arthur Katterjohn. *The Tribulation People.* Carol Stream, Ill: Creation House, 1975. p. 26.

Hyles, Jack. *The Church.* Hammond, Indiana: Hyles-Anderson Publishers, p. 93.

Scofield, C.I., D. D. *The Scofield Study Bible.* New York: Oxford University Press, pp. vi, 5, 996.

Bromiley, G.W. *Zwingli and Bullinger.* Philadelphia: The Westminister Press, pp. 215-217.

Ladd, George Eldon. *The Blessed Hope.* Grand Rapids: William B. Eerdmans Publishing Co., 1956. p. 44.

Benware, Paul N. *Understanding End Times Prophecy.* Chicago: Moody Press, 1995. pp. 179-180, 197-198.

VanKampen, Robert. *The Sign.* Wheaton, Ill.: Crossway Books, 1992. p. 449.

Matthew Henry's Commentary. Fleming H. Revell Co., vol. 5, p 42, vol. 6, pp. 450, 455, 928.

Harding, William H. *The Life of George Muller.* Westwood, New Jersey: Barbour and Company, Inc., p. 331.

Muller, George. *Heroes of the Faith.* Westwood, New Jersey: Barbour and Company, Inc., 1995. pp. 314-315.

Wilkerson, Dave. *America's Last Call.* Lindale, Texas: Wilkerson Trust Publications, 1998. pp. 122-123.

Uplook Magazine. Grand Rapids, MI (July-August 1999): pp .17-19

Darby, J.N. *The collected writings of J. N. Darby.* Doctrinal No 3, volume 10. Paulton (Somerset) and London: Purnell and Sons, LTD. pp. 257, 267.

Darby, J.N. *Synopsis of the Books of the Bible,* vol. 5. Addison, Illinois: Bible Truth Publishers.

Ryrie, Charles C. *Dispensationalism Today.* Chicago: The Moody Bible Institute, 1965. pp. 65-85.

Jeffrey, Grant R. *Apocalypse.* Toronto, Ontario: Frontier Research Publications, 1992, pp. 87-88.

Pentecost, J. Dwight. *Things to Come.* Dunham Publishing Co., 1958. pp. 121-122.

Gregg, Steve. *Revelation: Four Views.* Nashville, Tennessee: Thomas Nelson, Inc., 1997.

Ryrie, Charles Caldwell. *The Ryrie Study Bible.* Chicago: The Moody Bible Institute, 1976. p. 1505.

Larkin, Clarence. *Dispensational Truth.* Philadelphia: Rev. Clarence Larkin Est., 1918. p. 5.

Your comments on
Errors of Pretribulation Rapture Theory

I believe I have exposed the errors of pretribulation rapture theory and related doctrines adequately. I believe every work should be judged by God's people who are students of the Word. I would appreciate hearing any personal comments from you.

E-mail: pastorshoults@aol.com

Pastor Felton Shoults
P.O. Box 8005
Flint, MI 48501

Errors of Pretribulation Rapture Theory
Order Form

Postal orders: Victory Publications
P.O. Box 8005
Flint, MI 48501

E-mail orders: PastorShoults@aol.com

Please send *Errors of Pretribulation Rapture Theory* to:

Name: _____

Address: _____

City: _____ State: _____

Zip: _____

Telephone: (_____) _____

Book Price: $16.99

Shipping: $3.00 for the first book and $1.00 for each additional book to
cover shipping and handling within US, Canada, and Mexico.
International orders add $6.00 for the first book and $2.00 for
each additional book.

Or order from:
ACW Press
85334 Lorane Hwy
Eugene, OR 97405

(800) 931-BOOK

or contact your local bookstore